INTERNAL EMPIRE

VICTOR BULMER-THOMAS

Internal Empire

The Rise and Fall of English Imperialism

HURST & COMPANY, LONDON

First published in the United Kingdom in 2023 by
C. Hurst & Co. (Publishers) Ltd.,
New Wing, Somerset House, Strand, London, WC2R 1LA
© Victor Bulmer-Thomas, 2023
All rights reserved.

Distributed in the United States, Canada and Latin America by
Oxford University Press, 198 Madison Avenue, New York, NY 10016,
United States of America.

The right of Victor Bulmer-Thomas to be identified as the author
of this publication is asserted by him in accordance with the Copyright,
Designs and Patents Act, 1988.

A Cataloguing-in-Publication data record for this book
is available from the British Library.

ISBN: 9781787389342

www.hurstpublishers.com

Every effort has been made to trace copyright-holders and to obtain their permission
for the use of copyrighted material. The publisher apologises for any errors or omissions
and would be grateful if notified of any corrections that should be incorporated in future
reprints or editions of this book.

Printed and bound in Great Britain by Bell and Bain Ltd, Glasgow

CONTENTS

Introduction	1
1. Birth of the Four Nations	13
2. Four Nations, Four States	37
3. The Rise of English Imperialism	67
4. Four Nations, One State	99
5. The British Empire	129
6. The Commonwealth	161
7. Europe	191
8. Brexit	223
9. The Unmaking of the UK	255
10. English Questions	289
Notes	321
Bibliography	353
Index	369

If I were to choose a single word to describe my art practice it would be the word 'question'. If I were to choose a single word to describe my underlying drive it would be 'freedom'. To be free we must be able to question the ways our own history defines us.

Gordon Bennett (1955–2014),
Australian artist of Aboriginal and Anglo-Celtic descent

Map 1: The contemporary Hiberno-British Isles

Map 2: The contemporary ceremonial counties of England

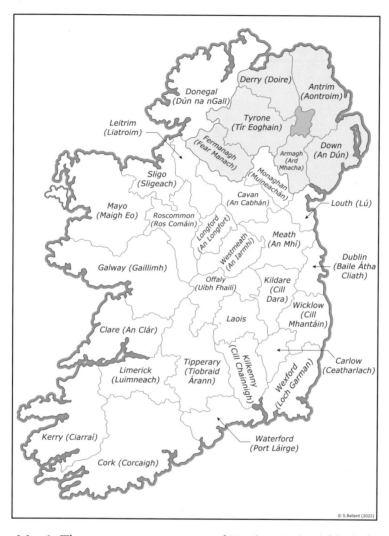

Map 3: The contemporary counties of Northern Ireland (shaded) and Ireland

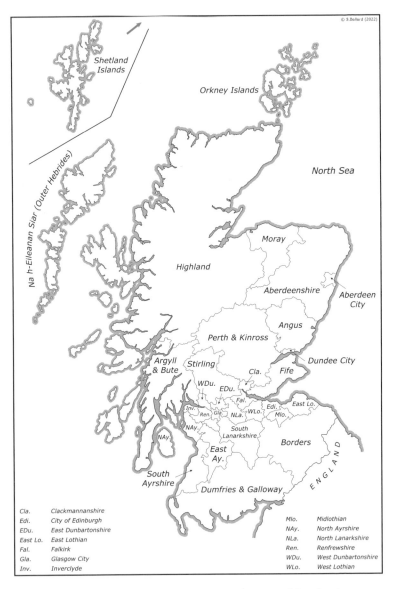

Map 4: The contemporary council areas of Scotland

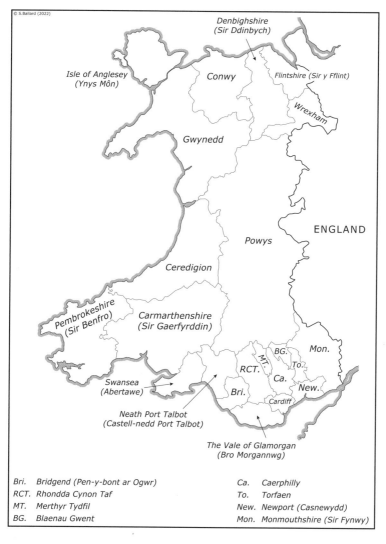

Map 5: The contemporary principal areas of Wales

INTRODUCTION

'Let us therefore brace ourselves to our duties, and so bear ourselves that, if the British Empire and its Commonwealth last for a thousand years, men will still say, "This was their finest hour."'

In what was perhaps his finest speech, Winston Churchill delivered these stirring words on 18 June 1940 (incidentally on the 125th anniversary of the Battle of Waterloo), to inspire his country and its imperial allies ahead of the anticipated Battle of Britain against Germany. Yet Churchill's estimate of the length of time the British Empire might survive was hopelessly flawed. Seven years later, in 1947, India, Pakistan and Ceylon (today's Sri Lanka) had won their independence, to be followed by Burma (Myanmar) in 1948. The imperial retreat had begun, culminating in the lowering of the British flag in Hong Kong just under fifty years later.[1]

Churchill did at least recognise that the British Empire was going to be of a finite duration. It had begun in 1707, when England (speaking also for Wales) and Scotland had formed a political union under which all previous overseas possessions, such as those in North America and the Caribbean, became British. The empire therefore lasted roughly 250 years, during which time a strong sense of Britishness had been created among the three nations making up Great Britain—England, Scotland and Wales—together with much weaker attachment to a British identity in Ireland.

Hostility to Britishness was in fact so strong in much of Ireland that a war had been fought leading to the establishment of an Irish Free State in 1922 (with only six counties in the north, of the island's thirty-two, remaining under British control). That is why it is misleading to refer, as so many do, to Ireland and Great Britain as the 'British Isles'. Not only is it geographically incorrect, but it is also very wrong in political and historical terms. In this book, therefore, these two large islands—together with their smaller insular possessions—will be known as the 'Hiberno-British Isles' (or 'the Isles' for short) to avoid confusion.[2]

The British Empire may have had a finite life, but it did not emerge out of nothing. Before 1707, there were both Scottish and English Empires, although the former had ended ignominiously in the collapse of Scotland's last overseas colony at Darién (in modern Panama). The English Empire, on the other hand, had flourished and had been functioning for over 400 years before the union with Scotland.[3] It had begun with the completion of the conquest of Wales in 1284, followed by the full colonisation of Ireland starting with the Tudors, and the founding of England's earliest overseas settlements under Queen Elizabeth I. England, it is true, had been beaten by Scotland in that country's Wars of Independence at the start of the fourteenth century, but she had still taken the Isle of Man from her northern rival and had never abandoned her claims to hegemony over the whole of Britain.

The English Empire, therefore, had a beginning, but has it ended? The external possessions, of course, were subsumed into the British Empire and have almost all gone, but the internal or insular possessions were absorbed into a greater England—a

INTRODUCTION

United Kingdom of Great Britain and Ireland in name, but an English empire (with a small 'e') in practice. Wales was formally incorporated into the Kingdom of England in 1535, Scotland became a junior partner in 1707 and Ireland was absorbed in 1801. In each case, the English parliament at Westminster simply expanded to accommodate MPs from elsewhere, but England's hegemony went unchallenged. And after the southern part of Ireland became the Irish Free State, England's dominant position within a shrunken UK became even more entrenched.[4]

Many people in England find it difficult to accept that they live in an empire, even if it is not an official Empire. Where are the colonies, they ask? Where are the governors and the other regalia of imperial power?[5] Yet it is not difficult to recognise England in the definition offered by a leading scholar of empire:

> Empire is a form of political organization in which the social elements that rule in the dominant state [England] create a network of allied elites in regions abroad [the other nations] who accept subordination ... in return for the security of their position in their own administrative unit .... They intertwine their economic resources with the dominant power, and they accept and even celebrate a set of values and tastes that privilege or defer to the culture of the metropole.[6]

Since at least the eighteenth century, the 'culture of the metropole' has included a firm belief in English exceptionalism, and the anglicised parts of the other three nations were happy to accept the role allotted to them. That is why, 150 years ago, Walter Bagehot had no trouble calling his monumental study on UK constitutional arrangements *The English Constitution*. Similarly, Michael Heseltine, a former Conservative Party Cabinet minister, could say in a radio interview in 1996 that 'many Scots have representation in the English Cabinet'. The idea of English hegemony had become so deep-rooted that Andrew Bonar Law,

INTERNAL EMPIRE

of Scottish and Irish descent, was even happy to be called 'Prime Minister of England' during his brief tenure in the 1920s.[7]

The English empire has not therefore ended, but it now faces its gravest challenge—one that has been building for several decades. The demise of the British Empire brought with it a decline in the sense of Britishness among the inhabitants of the four nations, including in England. For many years, UK governments thought they could arrest this decline through the promotion of a Commonwealth led by Britain, but that failed as the Commonwealth of Nations lost its sense of Britishness when newly independent countries understandably emphasised their own identities. And when the UK joined the European Communities (EC) on 1 January 1973, in doing so ending the system of imperial preference in foreign trade, the Commonwealth ceased to have much meaning for the bulk of British citizens.[8]

The EC, which became the European Union on 1 November 1993, was at first warmly embraced by UK citizens, who voted overwhelmingly to stay in a referendum in 1975. Some people began to acquire a European identity to sit alongside their Britishness, and there was even a hope that membership of the EC/EU would eventually replicate the role previously played by Empire and Commonwealth in successfully holding together the four nations of the UK. Yet it was not to be. The enthusiasm for Europe, so manifest in 1975, eventually turned sour in England, with the root of the problem being the clash between English exceptionalism and the 'ever closer union' promoted by the EU. England turned away after adopting a euroscepticism unmatched in the rest of Europe.

Even before then, the decline of Britishness in the three smaller nations was throwing up a new challenge in the form of demand for devolutions. This was an old problem in a new guise, since the Home Rule debate in nineteenth-century Ireland (and to a lesser extent in Scotland and Wales) had revealed the desire for

INTRODUCTION

decentralisation of power away from England. Indeed, Northern Ireland had been allowed to operate its own parliament since 1921. However, what was different this time was the combination of calls for devolution with a demand by some sections of the electorate in Scotland and Wales for independence. And in Northern Ireland, the demand by nationalists for unification with Éire (the Republic of Ireland) in the south became stronger.

After refusing at first to recognise the scale of the problem, politicians from England and anglicised ones from elsewhere showed some skill in handling these threats to the English empire. Scotland and Wales were offered a path to devolution with their own national assemblies, a path that was eventually taken in 1999. By then, the Belfast Agreement (known widely as the Good Friday Agreement) had outlined the circumstances under which reunification of the island of Ireland could proceed peacefully and democratically. And when this new approach was put to the most severe test in 2014, with a referendum on Scottish independence, it appeared to have passed the examination when a majority of Scots voted to stay in the UK.

The Scottish electorate had been persuaded that voting this way was the surest path to staying in the EU. Two years later this assumption was completely undermined. The vote to leave the EU, driven above all by the euroscepticism of voters in England, was a victory for English imperialism. English exceptionalism, the other side of the imperialist coin, had triumphed and it did not matter what voters in other parts of the UK wanted.[9] The UK government would now pursue on behalf of England a hard exit from the EU, irrespective of the interests of Northern Ireland, Scotland and Wales.

'Brexit' (the decision to leave the EU) may have met the aspirations of the majority of English voters, but it is accelerating the unravelling of the UK and, in the process, undermining the English empire. In Northern Ireland, where economic ties with the south have advanced notably since Brexit, momentum is building for a 'border poll' on reunification. Nationalists in Scotland are demanding a second vote on independence—a demand that can be resisted by the UK government, but only at the risk of increasing support for independence. Meanwhile, in Wales, even if independence is still only a remote possibility, calls for increased autonomy are growing steadily and will become more strident if Scotland votes to leave the UK.

Yet English voters seem largely unconcerned about the prospect of Irish reunification, Scottish independence and greater Welsh autonomy—in striking contrast, for example, to the attitude towards Catalonia among other citizens in Spain. Perhaps this will change, but it does not seem likely. Indeed, the electorate in England seems to welcome the chance to reassert its independence as a nation-state without 'responsibility' for the other nations in the UK, even if this means the end of the English empire. England is now about to embark on a journey for which very few people—whether politicians or ordinary voters—are prepared. And while apocalyptic warnings will be sounded as awareness increases, there are also opportunities to be grasped; opportunities that include breaking the stranglehold of established parties on the English political scene.

This is the main purpose of this book: to show that the breakup of the UK, while perhaps not inevitable, has deep-rooted causes and is not primarily due to short-term factors driven by the limited vision of English politicians. Other authors and commentators have noted the centrifugal tendencies at work, but most have failed to place them in the correct historical context. History matters, and the solutions adopted by the English political class to hold the UK together no longer work. Understanding this is crucial if the constituent parts that reemerge after the end of the UK are to live in harmony with each other. And nowhere is this truer than in England, which must come to terms with its own

INTRODUCTION

hegemonic past and confront its own demons honestly, while reordering its affairs to take advantage of the new realities.[10]

The prospect of a fragmented UK is leading to a reexamination of the history not just of England, but of the other three nations as well. Indeed, the very fact that they are all recognised as 'nations' is itself a big advance. It was not so long ago, for example, that one leading commentator on UK affairs could claim that 'Welsh nationalism is a paltry operation, not least because of the incomprehension with which many in Wales regard the concept of a Welsh nation.'[11] And many people dismissed the idea of Northern Ireland as a nation on the grounds that the population either wanted to be Irish or British.

Few would argue along these lines now. The Oxford English Dictionary (OED) definition of a nation ('a large aggregate of communities and individuals united by factors such as common descent, language, culture, history, or occupation of the same territory, so as to form a distinct people') clearly fits the cases of England, Scotland and Wales very well. Even Northern Ireland, where an increasing number of people now give 'Northern Irish' as their primary identifier rather than 'Irish' or 'British', is starting to look like a nation, although some might argue that it is still a work in progress. In any case, it is legitimate to speak of the UK now as 'four nations'.

The UK may, therefore, be returning to a situation not dissimilar to that before the conquest of Wales, when there were not just four nations, but four nation-states in the Isles. This book begins by exploring how England, Ireland, Scotland and Wales first became nations, and later (after the Romans' departure from England and Wales) nation-states—a process that took some 600 years to complete. Creating states out of these nations was hard and some historians baulk at the notion of a 'nation-state' so long ago. Yet the OED definition—'an independent political state formed from a people who share a common national identity (historically, culturally or ethnically)'—perfectly fits the kingdoms forged by leaders in the four nations roughly a thousand years ago. These polities then engaged in diplomatic and cultural relations with one another as well as other foreign powers.

The OED definition of a nation-state includes an ethnic dimension. The inhabitants of the Isles are more used to describing other peoples in ethnic terms (known as 'othering' in common parlance), but the term is clearly relevant to themselves, too, provided it is recognised that there are at least four ethnicities in the Isles and not just one. Indeed, any people that can be described as a 'nation' will normally be an ethnic group, something which is certainly applicable to England, Scotland and Wales. It also describes the people in the Irish Republic, although reducing Northern Ireland to one ethnicity is clearly a stretch. In any case, it is better than 'race'—a term which has no scientific basis and which is only used in this book when the context demands it.

These different nations and ethnicities then give rise to the concept of a '-ness'—as in Englishness, (Northern) Irishness, Scottishness and Welshness. Fifty years ago, hardly anyone thought in these terms, especially in the case of 'Englishness', but that is no longer the case. Indeed, the title of a major study of the UK after Brexit is 'Englishness: The Political Force Transforming Britain'.[12] Understanding these forces, and the identities that underpin them, is now crucial in analysing the journey that each of the four nations has embarked upon and in helping us to understand where each is heading.

The four territories that came to constitute the United Kingdom had a complicated route on their way to becoming nation-states, but none more so than England and Scotland. (Ireland and Wales, although not without their own complexities, each had a more straightforward path to becoming a nation, and later evolving from a nation to a nation-state.) This will be

INTRODUCTION

dealt with in more detail in Chapter 1, but—in order to avoid confusion later—it is worth drawing the reader's attention here to some of the more noteworthy moments in the early history of England and Scotland in particular.

The English derive their name from the Angles, one of many Germanic tribes that came from the continent of Europe as Roman rule ended in Britain more than 1,600 years ago. Together with the Frisians, Jutes, Saxons and others, they overcame resistance from the native population to establish a nation that also included many indigenous Britons, as well as later arrivals such as the Vikings—settlers in the Isles from the Norse kingdoms of Scandinavia. Collectively, they became known as the 'Anglo-Saxons', thereby ignoring the contribution not only of other Germanic tribes but also native Britons and later immigrants. Yet the term 'Anglo-Saxon' has become so entrenched that it seems hopeless to try and replace it with something more accurate. It is therefore used where strictly necessary, but not otherwise.

At the Battle of Brunanburh in 937, Æthelstan, who had begun his reign as King of Mercia and Wessex (the two most powerful Anglo-Saxon kingdoms), defeated a coalition of his enemies throughout the Isles and secured control of the powerful Kingdom of Northumbria, having already—temporarily at least—pushed the Vikings out of York. As a result of these victories, Æthelstan is often heralded today as the first King of England, and indeed was acclaimed as such after his conquest of York in 927. Yet this is misleading. His hold on the north was very tenuous, Danish power in the east had not been eclipsed, other parts of what would become England were still independent kingdoms outside of Anglo-Saxon rule, and there was no common language or system of law.

He was, however, the undisputed King of the Anglo-Saxons at the time of his death, and thus this book will use that title to refer to Æthelstan and his successors, until the final Anglo-Saxon conquest of Northumbria during the reign of his brother Eadred in 954. This event marks the beginning of a recognisable Kingdom of England, hence my decision to give the Anglo-Saxon kings the title 'King of England' only after this date—ignoring their earlier self-stylings.

Today's Scots confusingly derive their name from those Irish who started to migrate from Ireland to the west of modern Scotland some 1,700 years ago, where they formed the Kingdom of Dál Riata. These Irish—eventually called 'Scots', after *Scoti*, the Roman name for all Irish—came into conflict with an established Kingdom of the Picts further north. It was not until c. 842 that the two kingdoms merged into a single entity under Kenneth mac Alpin, which would become known as the Kingdom of Alba. The people of Alba in turn became known as Gaelic, as a result of the common Celtic inheritance of the Scots and the Picts; their language was part of the family of Celtic languages known as Goidelic (hence Gaelic).

Alba was a powerful kingdom, but it did not by any stretch of the imagination occupy all of modern Scotland, and so the rulers of Alba cannot be described as kings of Scotland. It took the mac Alpin dynasty nearly 200 years before they had enlarged their kingdom to include most of the territories that today are part of Scotland, and even then there were large swathes still under the control of the Vikings who bordered the Kingdom of Alba to the north and west.

On his death in 1034, Malcolm II was mourned as 'King of Scotland' and that seems a fair description of the territory over which he ruled—especially after his defeat of the English at the Battle of Carham in 1018, which established a boundary between the two nation-states very similar to the one that would be formally agreed by treaty in the thirteenth century. Thus, the Kingdom of Scotland emerged not long after the Kingdom

INTRODUCTION

of England, and at almost the same time as the Kingdoms of Ireland and Wales (see Chapter 1).

In a book such as this, covering more than a thousand years of history, it is impossible to avoid frequent use of dates. Some of these refer to events in the Isles before the widespread adoption of Christianity. Instead of AD (Anno Domini) and BC (Before Christ), therefore, I use CE (Common Era) and BCE (Before the Common Era). The dates are the same, but religious neutrality seems more appropriate under the circumstances. Similarly, I try to use names in currency at the time of the event rather than those adopted subsequently, although it is not always possible to be consistent.

In writing this book, I owe a great debt to many people—too many to mention all by name. However, I would particularly like to thank David Carpenter, Ruth Currie, John Darwin, James Manor, Anand Menon, Sean Newman, Huw Pryce and Richard Whitman for comments on earlier drafts of the manuscript. Needless to say, all remaining errors are mine.

On an autobiographical note, I was born in England to a Welsh father who had some Irish ancestors and an English mother with Viking, French and German origins. My wife was born in Belize and her family history includes Scottish ancestry. Our second child was born in Scotland and my first academic post was in Glasgow, where I started a few years after carrying out short-term manual jobs in different parts of the UK. It is a not uncommon story, but it has helped me to understand the 'four nations' approach to the history of the Isles that has become increasingly popular in recent years. I hope this work will be seen in that context.

1

BIRTH OF THE FOUR NATIONS

Imagine a leisurely traveller to the Hiberno-British Isles some thousand years ago, coming from the papacy in Rome, from Scandinavia or from one of the many kingdoms in continental Europe that had emerged after the breakup of Charlemagne's Holy Roman Empire. Our visitor might have started in Ireland in 1002 to witness the coronation of Brian Boru as High King. Carefully avoiding the small islands controlled by the Vikings, they could then have sailed in 1034 to Scotland to observe the funeral of Malcolm II, before riding south in 1042 to take part in the investiture of Edward the Confessor as King of England. Finally, if not too exhausted by old age, they could have travelled westward on horseback to see Gruffydd ap Llywelyn consolidate his position as the first King of Wales after 1055.

In the space of some fifty years, such a traveller could have observed first-hand four separate territories. These kingdoms' subjects might have shared a common religion (Christianity), albeit with different interpretations, and a common language (Latin) for some official documents and as a means of communication among the elites. Yet in all other respects, they had become separate nations with distinct ethnicities speaking different languages, observing different laws and practising different customs. A sense of Englishness, Irishness, Scottishness and Welshness was becoming more pronounced among the peoples of these four nations.

The four nations were also turning into states, although the process was still not complete in any of them a thousand years ago. Similar to confederations today, these states—or proto-states as many might prefer to call them—sometimes struggled to speak with a single voice or to act as an organised political community, and yet the four kings listed above all achieved it in different ways. For they were the ones who either oversaw the birth of a nation-state (Ireland and Wales) or helped to nurture one that had already been born (England and Scotland).

Ireland

Celtic culture started to spread westward from its home in central Europe in the last millennium BCE. Within a few centuries, the first Celts—traders rather than invaders—had reached Ireland along with the Celtic language. The transition from the Bronze to the Iron Age in Ireland had been underway before the Celts and Celtic influence arrived, but Celtic technological know-how provided a further stimulus to what was already happening.[1]

The fusion of Celtic and pre-Celtic cultures on the island was a long process, but not—as far as we can tell—especially bloody; and at least it was not disturbed by Roman invasion (as happened in many other Celtic strongholds). By 500 CE, a Celtic language (Irish) had long since taken hold, a system of law was in place and Christianity had recently spread across the land to create an Irish culture. And, of course, the territory of Ireland (called Ériu by the Irish and Hibernia by the Romans) had a natural boundary defined by the sea, even if migration inward and outward was common.

BIRTH OF THE FOUR NATIONS

When the Celtic language in Ireland replaced the pre-Celtic tongues can never be known for certain. Its spread over the island, however, was most likely a peaceful affair, as there is no evidence of an aggressive invasion by a Celtic army. In any case, the linguistic conquest was a very complete process—as is attested by the lack of any pre-Celtic words in the oldest surviving Celtic texts from the fourth and fifth centuries CE.[2]

Irish law is very ancient and had taken shape across the island even before the arrival of Christianity. These early laws, later known as Brehon laws (after the Irish word for a judge or jurist), covered most aspects of daily life, as well as the relationships—duties and responsibilities—between all the groups constituting the social hierarchy. In the absence of a central authority, however, there were bound to be some inconsistencies across the island in the way laws were administered or interpreted.

This changed with the arrival of Christianity. Whether it was first preached by St. Patrick or more probably had reached Ireland before him, there is no doubt that it was his efforts that had brought Christianity to the furthest reaches of the island by the end of the fifth century CE.[3] And with the establishment by St. Patrick of the bishopric at Armagh, Ireland created its first institution (the Church) whose reach extended right across the land. The replacement of both Celtic and pre-Celtic pagan religions by Christianity was swift, made possible by a single language and by energetic evangelists such as St. Patrick himself.

Language, law and religion provided the basic ingredients for an Irish nation in Ireland, but this nation was not yet a state, even after the spread of Christianity. Instead, Ireland was ruled by a multitude of kings whose authority was limited in each case to a small part of the island, known in Irish as a *túath*. These were numerous, leading to frequent clashes as rival kings sought to extend their kingdoms. Inevitably, a process of consolidation took place, and some kings were certainly more equal than

15

INTERNAL EMPIRE

others. Indeed, most kings were subordinate to the dominant five representing the provinces of Connacht, Leinster, Meith, Munster and Ulster.

Inside Meith lies the hill of Tara, and by the third century CE the 'high kings' of Ireland came here to have their status confirmed. One of the high kings was Niall Noígíallach, who died in the middle of the fifth century after having founded the Uí Néill dynasty—many of whose members would become high kings themselves.[4] Yet the high king, despite the name, was not a supreme ruler in any political sense. It was more a ceremonial rule that conferred status without power.

The right of the high king to speak for all of Ireland was very limited, and attempts to raise tribute from the other kings were always resisted. Ireland in the first centuries after St. Patrick can at best be described as a confederation (and a very loose one at that), since there was no external enemy to force greater cohesion among the kingships. This was especially so after the late-fourth-century withdrawal of Roman forces from what would become England and Wales, since the ever-present threat of a foreign invasion had now ended.

By the middle of the first millennium CE, therefore, Ireland was culturally united but politically divided, and there was little incentive to change this other than the ambition of individual kings to acquire more territory and tribute. Political unification was in any case made more difficult by the absence of primogeniture, meaning that the succession in each kingdom was always likely to be disputed. Even among the foremost dynasty, the Uí Néill, there were endless disputes over succession, which undermined all attempts at creating a kingship over the whole of the island.

It was the arrival of the Vikings at the end of the eighth century that finally challenged the status quo. Not only did the Viking invaders—Norse people from Scandinavia—carve out for

BIRTH OF THE FOUR NATIONS

themselves significant coastal enclaves to conduct trade, but they also precipitated a need for greater unification among the native kingdoms as a matter of basic survival. And as the kings succeeded in overcoming their differences to gain the upper hand against the invaders, they were able to share in the prosperity brought to Ireland by Norse trade, including in slaves, through the Viking ports at Cork, Dublin, Limerick, Waterford and elsewhere.

The first to take advantage of this new situation was Máel Sechnaill mac Máele Ruanaid, a scion of the Uí Néill dynasty and King of Tara. In the middle of the ninth century, some fifty years after the first Viking invasions, he was the first to have any realistic claim to be King of Ireland. He did this through a mixture of muscular diplomacy and warfare, negotiating successfully to become King of Ulster, taking hostages from Munster and even allying on occasions with some of the Vikings. Yet, although he died peacefully in 862, he could not overcome all opposition and failed even to unite all the branches of his own dynasty.

It would be another century before anyone could truly lay claim to the title of King of Ireland. This was Brian Boru, the youngest son of Cennétig mac Lorcáin, the leader of the Dál Cais clan and King of Tuadmumu (a *túath* of Munster). As such, Cennétig had been one of perhaps 150 kings in Ireland in his day, and not a very important one at that. However, he had been the first leader of his clan to launch military attacks outside his small kingdom and, by his death in 951, he had become a significant force in Munster (if not yet beyond).

After Cennétig's death, the cause of military expansion was taken up by his son Mathgamain, one of Brian Boru's elder brothers. Mathgamain was much more successful than his father and had become king of all Munster by 964. He would also launch campaigns against the Vikings in their western strongholds and in 967, aided by his young brother, he defeated them at the Battle of Sucoilt before burning and sacking their fortress at

17

INTERNAL EMPIRE

Limerick. The Dál Cais were now a force to be reckoned with across Ireland, and the Uí Néill dynasty, not to mention the Vikings in their remaining towns, was obliged to take note.

Mathgamain died in 976 and there was no dispute regarding the succession. Brian Boru's military exploits ensured a smooth transition and he quickly consolidated his hold over Munster. Within a few years, he had turned his attention to territorial expansion, with his focus at first on Leinster to the east and Connacht to the northwest. This brought him into conflict with the King of Tara and the Uí Néill more generally. As the forces on both sides were roughly equally matched, it would be many years before a victor could be declared. By the end of the millennium, however, Brian was in control of Leinster and therefore de facto ruler of the whole of the south of Ireland. He had even defeated the Viking king of Dublin, Sigtrygg Silkbeard, at the Battle of Glenmama in 999, although he later allowed Silkbeard to return in a subordinate capacity.[5]

It would be another decade before Brian could legitimately claim to have gained control of the north. This was made possible both by military conquests, but also by an alliance with the monastery at Armagh that ensured the support of the Church throughout the island. It was at this point that the Book of Armagh, a famous Latin-language manuscript, referred to Brian as 'Imperator Scotorum' (Emperor of the Scots, the Roman word for the Irish). This was in recognition of his success in imposing his rule over the whole of the island—unlike the 'Ardrí' (High King), whose territorial control was much more limited.

At the start of the 1000s, therefore, Ireland under Brian Boru could be considered a nation-state, despite the lingering presence of the Vikings. Yet, inevitably, Brian's process of territorial and political consolidation had left him with many enemies, and there was still the problem of the Viking settlements—especially at Dublin, where Sigtrygg Silkbeard had once again become king

BIRTH OF THE FOUR NATIONS

and had made common cause with other Norse groups based in Scandinavia. Many of Brian's enemies, including the Vikings, now forged a tactical alliance, leading to the Battle of Clontarf in 1014.[6]

Despite being perhaps the most important battle in Irish history (in which Brian was killed), it is still not clear whether Clontarf was primarily an attempt by the Irish under Brian to oust Ireland's Vikings and their allies in Scandinavia, or whether it was more like a civil war among the Irish, between Brian's forces and those of his opponents.[7] The truth is that it was probably both, so that the triumph of Brian's forces represented a victory for Irish unification and reinforced the concept of territorial control under a single ruler.

Brian Boru's Ireland was no microstate. The population has been estimated at more than 600,000[8]—about half the size of England's—and its economy, while primarily based on livestock, farming and hunting for domestic consumption, was intimately linked to both Britain and continental Europe through the Viking ports. Irish coin hoards dating to this period indicate an important export trade to England, including in slaves, leading to the importation of *specie* (gold and silver coins). Indeed, trade through the Viking enclaves was a major reason why Brian's predecessors and successors were sometimes reluctant to eradicate totally the Viking presence.

Wales

Celtic language and culture reached the island of Britain about the same time as Ireland. By the time of the Roman invasion in 43 CE, it was possible—at least for the elites—to traverse almost the whole length of the island and communicate with others using one of the family of Celtic languages. This did not mean that Britain was united in other respects and, as in Ireland, there were many tribes formed into small kingdoms. Even before the arrival of the Romans, however, the process of consolidation had begun, with some kingdoms becoming much more powerful than others.

Although its eastern boundary is not one defined by nature (unlike the western, southern and northern ones), what we now call Wales was in fact inhabited by four specific tribes before the invasion of the Romans, and the territories of these tribes did not extend much outside modern Wales. These tribes were the Ordovices in the northwest, the Deceangli in the northeast, the Demetae in the southwest and the Silures in the southeast. We cannot, of course, speak of a proto-Welsh nation at this stage, and yet it is surely no accident that the distinctive geography of Wales—with its mountains, valleys and long coastline—had to a large extent defined tribal boundaries.

Tribal rivalries had to be discarded as soon as the Romans invaded. The territory escaped the first assault, but the artificial frontier created by the invaders (running from the Humber estuary in the northeast to the Severn estuary in the southwest of Britain) then formed a barrier that the four tribes could easily penetrate to attack their common enemy. The tribes were quick to do so, and the Romans then spent twenty years subduing resistance, building forts and establishing the first towns in what would later become Wales. By the end of the first century CE, the rulers of the tribes had been crushed and the priests—Druids in the main—put to the sword.

Roman rule in Britain was withering long before the last soldiers left. By the end of the fourth century, Irish settlers had established themselves in the southwest corner of modern Wales, as well as on the island of Anglesey. The Germanic tribes, however, which would play such a large part in the formation of England, did not reach so far west. As soon as Rome left Britain to its own devices in 410, the Britons of what we now call Wales

BIRTH OF THE FOUR NATIONS

were able to establish kingdoms—albeit with different territorial boundaries from the four pre-Roman tribes—and to make common cause with others against the new (Germanic) invaders.

The inhabitants of these new kingdoms, speaking a common language, would soon follow the same religion thanks to the evangelism of St. David. Born around 500, he played the same role in spreading Christianity in Wales as St. Patrick had done in Ireland a century before. Although both saints are reputed to have been born close to each other, they could not have had more different upbringings, as David was the scion of a royal family. Christianity was probably better known in the future Wales before David than it had been in Ireland before Patrick, but the same resistance had to be overcome. David was declared Archbishop of Wales at the Synod of Brevi in southwestern Wales in 550, thereby becoming de facto leader of a Welsh Church and its intermediary with the Pope in Rome.

According to legend, King Arthur led the Britons against the Germanic invaders and, around 500, won a famous victory at Mons Badonicus (likely in Somerset, but its exact location is unknown).[9] Whatever the truth of this, Arthur would have been fighting for all Britons and not just those of Wales.[10] And while Arthur may have won the battle, he did not win the war. The Germanic advance continued into the southwest and northwest of what would become England, confining the Britons more and more to their strongholds west of the Rivers Severn and Dee. When Offa, King of Mercia, then constructed his famous dyke at the end of the eighth century, he defined the eastern boundary of the Welsh kingdoms, thereby unwittingly establishing the contours of modern Wales.

The building of Offa's Dyke accelerated the process of nation-building in Wales—the name *Cymry* (Welsh) being widely used by this time for the inhabitants, and *Cymru* (Wales) for the country.[11] For the most ambitious and far-sighted rulers,

INTERNAL EMPIRE

overcoming the rivalries between the kingdoms established after the Romans' departure would soon become the highest priority. They all now faced a common threat (the Germanic invaders settled east of the dyke), and unity was considered essential if Wales was to survive.

Rhodri Mawr (Rhodri the Great) was the first to leave his mark, expanding from his northern base in Gwynedd to Powys in the east and Ceredigion in the south. On his death in 878 he had a reasonable claim to have made himself King of Wales, a claim supported by some of the Welsh Annals; but his kingdom did not include all of the south, and the absence of primogeniture in Wales led to his kingdom disintegrating soon after he died.

This fragmentation was reversed by Rhodri's grandson Hywel Dda (Hywel the Good). He had inherited a small kingdom from his father and, by 920, had joined it with others to form the substantial kingdom of Deheubarth in the southwest. From here, using international diplomacy, marriage ties and military force, he was able to bring almost the whole of Wales under his control. By his death in 948, he had revised and codified the laws of Wales—so much so that they were known thereafter as Cyfraith Hywel (Laws of Hywel). Wales now had a defined kingdom under a single ruler, a common language, and an enforceable legal system—the basic ingredients of a nation-state.

Hywel's kingdom, like Rhodri's before him, did not survive his death. In the next fifty years, parts of Wales were subject to ferocious attacks both from Germanic kings to the east and Viking raids out of Ireland to the west. Yet, as well as these centrifugal forces, there were also centripetal ones at play. The collective memory of a united Wales was never lost. Kingdoms could be joined through marriage and the geography of the country mitigated against permanent settlement by outsiders. By the end of the tenth century, a grandson of Hywel Dda

BIRTH OF THE FOUR NATIONS

(Maredudd ap Owain) had succeeded in reconstructing much of his grandfather's kingdom.

Maredudd's realm did not include the southeast corner—a region known as Morgannwg (today anglicised as Glamorgan). Incorporating this part of Wales into the kingdom was a task performed by Maredudd's own grandson, Gruffydd ap Llywelyn. By 1039, he was king of both Gwynedd and Powys, thereby controlling the north of Wales, and later added Deheubarth to his domains to control most of the south. When he captured Morgannwg around 1055, he was recognised inside and outside the country as the undisputed King of Wales—leader of a nation-state by any standards.

As the king of an independent state, Gruffydd had to deal with rulers on the other side of Wales' land border. Gruffydd's calculations at first proved successful and he enjoyed such good relations with Ælfgar, Earl of Mercia, that he was able to reach an agreement in 1062 with the King of England, Edward the Confessor, regarding the relationship between their respective kingdoms. However, Ælfgar's death in the same year deprived Gruffydd of an important ally—one with whom he had jointly organised raids into Wessex—and Gruffydd's court was then subject to a surprise attack by Harold Godwinson, Earl of Wessex, who had a good claim to the English throne. Gruffydd fled to Snowdonia, where he was hunted down and killed.[12]

Harold Godwinson became King of England in 1066 on the death of Edward the Confessor.[13] Had he not been killed at the Battle of Hastings later that year, he might have tried to add Wales to his kingdom through conquest. His death in battle spared Wales this fate and the Welsh nation survived, even if Gruffydd's kingdom fragmented into a confederation. Wales was no longer united, but even the loosest of confederations among the Welsh kings allowed for a degree of national autonomy in the face of an increasingly powerful neighbour, and therefore

INTERNAL EMPIRE

the development of a civil society based on Welsh culture. As explained by John Davies:

> When the literature of the English was suffering eclipse [post-1066], that of the Welsh was entering one of its most flourishing periods, and when English was being exiled from court and council [in England], Welsh was developing increasing suppleness as a medium of law and government.[14]

Scotland

While the Romans successfully conquered England in the mid-first century CE, they never conquered all of modern Scotland, due to a combination of geography, tribal resistance and imperial overreach. They gave us a glimpse, however, of pre-Roman Scotland—a land occupied, according to Ptolemy, by nearly twenty tribes.[15] The Romans eventually gave the name *picti* (painted people) to all those in the highlands. The term survived despite the fact that none of the northern tribes to whom it applied would have recognised it. The Picts, a Pictish culture and Pictland would go on to play a central role in the story of Scotland, along with the Irish there, the Vikings, the Britons, the Germanic peoples and, after their conquest of England in 1066, the Normans.

The archaeological record (there is no written one) suggests that Scotland's northern tribes may have been subject to less Celtic influence than the southern ones.[16] In any case, regardless of the degree of Celtic influence and language, they were certainly less affected by Roman invasions, since their lands, like the domains of tribes on the offshore islands, were never occupied. This was very different from what happened to the mainland southern tribes, who either saw their lands occupied by the Romans or had to live in very close proximity to them. This geographical distinction meant that the task of nation-building in Scotland

24

BIRTH OF THE FOUR NATIONS

was always going to be hard, and perhaps even harder than in Ireland or Wales. And even when the mainland was unified, it would take many more years before the western and northern islands were finally absorbed into what became the nation-state of Scotland.

The frontier established by the Romans soon after their invasion of Britain in 43 CE excluded all of modern Scotland. As this unfortified line was frequently breached by the tribes, a military advance northwards was soon launched by the Roman general Agricola. Resistance brought many of the tribes together, but the Romans were still able to win a major victory at the highland Battle of Mons Graupius around 83 CE. However, they did not press home their advantage; Agricola was recalled and a frontier was established from the Firth of Forth in the east to the Firth of Clyde in the west. South of the frontier, tribes in the mainland south, such as the Votadini, remained under Roman occupation.

For nearly 200 years, the Romans vacillated between this border and another further south, from modern Newcastle to Carlisle, where they built Hadrian's Wall.[17] Emperor Hadrian began construction of the wall that bears his name in 122 CE, but it was not until early in the third century that the Romans finally settled on Hadrian's Wall as the definitive frontier, which is where it remained until their abandonment of Britain some two centuries later. The lowland tribes were therefore sometimes under Roman occupation and sometimes outside it, but always subject to heavy influence from Rome—unlike the other tribes in Scotland.

By the time the Romans left, the Pictish tribes north of the Clyde–Forth line had already formed into two kingdoms. Yet the Picts were not alone in this. Irish migrants from County Antrim had established a presence on the western coast in the fourth century, and soon created the kingdom of Dál Riata,

INTERNAL EMPIRE

which included many islands; these people would be known as the Scots.[18] Meanwhile, a kingdom of Britons, called Strathclyde, had been established in the southwest of modern Scotland, with a Germanic kingdom called Northumbria soon taking shape on the other side of the country, south of the Forth.

The Pictish kings did not leave a written record, so we are forced to rely on others to learn of their history—especially the Venerable Bede. The English monk's principal work, written shortly before his death in 735, was mainly concerned with the people of England; but he wrote that by the sixth century the Picts could be separated into a 'northern' and 'southern' branch, and that Christianity had reached them by different routes. Bede credited St. Ninian with the conversion of the southern Picts, perhaps in the fifth century, and St. Columba (an Irish priest) with the conversion of the northern Picts a century later. It is safe to assume that almost all the Picts had been converted to Christianity by 600.

The fact that the Picts now shared a common religion no doubt helped in the formation of a single kingdom in the seventh and eighth centuries. Even if this kingdom, with its headquarters at Fortriu in the highlands, may have been a fairly loose amalgam of tribes, it was sufficiently cohesive for its army to win a decisive victory against the Northumbrians in 685. The Battle of Nechtansmere (or Dún Nechtain) in the heart of Pictland is widely seen as a key moment in the making of Scotland, as it not only pushed back an invader but also helped to consolidate the cohesiveness of the Pictish kingdom itself.[19]

Pictland's most immediate neighbour, however, was the Kingdom of Dál Riata. The first Irish migrants had arrived in modern Scotland before the Romans left Britain, but it was not until the end of the fifth century that a kingdom could be said to have taken shape. Even then it had several centres of power. Yet the presence of so many Irish-speakers was no doubt

BIRTH OF THE FOUR NATIONS

a consideration for Columba when he was exiled from Ireland and chose Iona in Dál Riata as the site for a monastery in 563. Although a spiritual leader, Columba—himself of royal blood—also had secular influences and played a key role in establishing Áedán mac Gabráin as King of Dál Riata around 574. Áedán then engaged his kingdom in almost perpetual conflict with his neighbours.

Dál Riata's wars with kings of Pictland, Northumbria and Strathclyde did not end well for Áedán and the pattern was repeated by his successors. Domnall Brecc, Áedán's grandson, was killed in battle in 642 by a Strathclyde army. When, a century later, Óengus, King of the Picts, gained a major victory over Dál Riata in 741, it seemed as if the Scots' kingdom would disappear. And yet it survived for another century, in large part because the Scots and Picts were increasingly becoming one people—joined together by Celtic language, a shared interpretation of Christianity and intermarriage.[20]

Domnall Brecc's death was a testament to the importance of the Kingdom of Strathclyde in the seventh century. This kingdom of Britons had probably evolved from the Damnonii—one of the tribes mentioned in Ptolemy's atlas. At its greatest extent, the kingdom stretched from Cumbria up to the southern highlands, with its capital at Dumbarton rock. This was a substantial domain, but its borders abutted those of many other kingdoms, making it vulnerable to attack. Despite these attacks and many defeats in battle, the kingdom survived—blocking the expansion southwards of any Pictish kingdoms further north.

Equally problematic for the consolidation of a single kingdom across the whole of modern Scotland was the Kingdom of Northumbria. It had been formed in the mid-seventh century from two Germanic kingdoms (Bernicia and Deira) and may have been given its new name by the Venerable Bede. Northumbria at its height extended from the Humber in the south to beyond the

27

Firth of Forth in the north. It overreached itself, however, and the border with the Picts was temporarily settled at the Battle of Nechtansmere in 685. From then onwards the Kingdom of Northumbria was primarily engaged in military struggles on its southern flank, but it still represented a formidable obstacle to southward expansion of any northern kingdom.

The stalemate between these four kingdoms—Fortriu (Picts), Dál Riata (Scots), Strathclyde (Britons) and Northumbria (Germanic tribes)—was finally broken in the ninth century. It had begun in 811, when Domnall, son of the Pictish king Constantine, became King of Dál Riata. This was the first time one family had ruled both kingdoms and demonstrated the degree to which the Picts and the Scots were beginning to merge into one people, with a language known as Gaelic. After Constantine's death in 820, his nephew Eóganán succeeded in becoming ruler of both kingdoms and a Pictish takeover of Dál Riata seemed the most probable outcome.

The fusion of both kingdoms was then interrupted by a new threat—this time from the Vikings. Unlike what had happened at first in Ireland, the invaders did not restrict themselves to raiding and establishing enclaves on the coast. In 839, Eóganán was killed trying to drive back the invaders and his Pictish kingdom was thrown into disarray. The union of the two realms now appeared to be a hopeless cause. Yet within a few years—perhaps as early as 842—an obscure leader of Dál Riata called Kenneth mac Alpin had brought the two kingdoms together under a single Gaelic ruler.

Although he did not know it, Kenneth had become the first King of Alba—the name that would be given to his united kingdom some years later. This was a singular achievement and marked an important milestone in the making of Scotland. From now on, there would be no more separation of Picts and Scots. However, the mac Alpin dynasty faced many obstacles that

BIRTH OF THE FOUR NATIONS

needed to be overcome before Alba could claim to have become the nation-state of Scotland. It would take nearly two centuries to achieve this.

The last king of the mac Alpin dynasty would be Malcolm II, whose long reign ended in 1034. Justifiably heralded on his death as King of Scotland, Malcolm contributed to the expansion of the boundaries of his kingdom south of the Clyde–Forth line. Strathclyde was now part of Scotland, although this owed as much to the defeats inflicted on its ruling Britons, by both the Vikings and the Germanic tribes, as it did to the military prowess of the mac Alpin dynasty. Indeed, the key moment in the subjugation of Strathclyde had arguably come with the 'gift' of the kingdom to Malcolm I by Edmund, King of Wessex, after his army had conquered it in 943.

Edmund enjoyed good relations with Malcolm I, but his motivation for this gift was far from altruistic. A Viking invasion in 865, and the subsequent conquest of York by Danes, had left the Kingdom of Northumbria prey to yet more rival ambitions.[21] By the time Edmund conquered Strathclyde eighty years later, the Danes had been ousted from York, but the Vikings of Dublin threatened to take their place until Æthelstan, King of Mercia and Wessex, secured it for himself. A grand alliance was then created between Alba, Strathclyde and Dublin to reverse Æthelstan's northern conquests, but his victory at the Battle of Brunanburh in 937 temporarily halted the claims on Northumbria by both Vikings and Alba. In return for Strathclyde, therefore, Edmund expected the King of Alba to allow his own subjects a free hand as they attempted to reassert their control over the rest of the northern region.

The 'understanding' between Edmund and Malcolm I did not last long. The invasion by a new claimant to the throne of York, Eric 'Bloodaxe' Haraldsson from Norway, effectively undermined all previous agreements. Malcolm I invaded Northumbria as far south as the Tees in 949, but in 954 Northumbria was annexed by the Anglo-Saxons, becoming part of the new Kingdom of England. It now remained for England and Alba to define the border between them.

By 973, Edgar, King of England, had conceded to Alba control of Lothian (the area south of the Forth); then, around 1018, the victory of Malcolm II at the Battle of Carham established a southern frontier for the new Kingdom of Scotland along the line of the River Tweed. Two centuries later, the line from the Solway to the Tweed would be confirmed by treaty as the boundary between Scotland and England. With their territorial gains in Strathclyde and the northern part of Northumbria, the mac Alpin dynasty could therefore claim with some justification to have enlarged substantially the borders of their kingdom and to have created modern Scotland. Malcolm II had every reason to feel confident in the future of the nation-state over which he had presided for nearly thirty years.

England

What is today England consisted of many tribes before the Roman invasion in 43 CE, each with its own territory and ruler. Yet the process of territorial consolidation was already well advanced and had perhaps been accelerated by the threat posed nearly a century earlier by Julius Caesar, on his two visits to Britain. Indeed, the Roman conquest was itself based on the excuse of tribal territorial expansion: Emperor Claudius found the justification he needed to invade when minor tribes facing conquest by their neighbours appealed to Rome for help.

The kingdom most affected by the arrival of Roman troops was that of the Catuvellauni. Their leader Caratacus and his brother Togodumnus fought a guerrilla campaign against superior forces, but they were eventually defeated. At first, the Roman victory

BIRTH OF THE FOUR NATIONS

was welcomed by some of the tribes that had been conquered by the Catuvellauni, but the methods of suppression used by the new invaders soon created tensions. All rebellions were crushed ruthlessly, and imperial rule completely destroyed the political systems that had operated before the Romans' arrival. Their abandonment of Britain at the beginning of the fifth century CE therefore created something of a vacuum that had to be filled quickly.

Imperial Rome had left behind an aristocracy of Britons. They were thoroughly Romanised, but lacked the resources to rule. As a result, the Britons in post-Roman Britain were unable to resist the numerous incursions into their lands from elsewhere. These included not just the Picts, emboldened by the withdrawal of Roman troops from the north of Britain in the last quarter of the fourth century CE, but also the Irish. And when the Roman Empire abandoned the defence of the Rhine at the beginning of the fifth century CE, this accelerated the decline of the Saxon Confederation north of that river—leading in turn to increased raids on Britain by the Germanic tribes.

The most (in)famous ruler among the Britons to confront these threats was Vortigern. The name probably means 'great leader', but he does seem to have been an historical figure and a similar name (Gurthrigern) was recorded nearly a century after his death by Gildas, a monk born in the Kingdom of Strathclyde.[22] Vortigern, it appears, was a ruler of Britons (Gildas improbably says 'the' ruler) a generation after the final departure of the Romans— and the first to appeal to Germanic leaders for assistance in the fight against the Picts and the Scots. Details of the deal struck c. 450, according to legend, between Vortigern on the one side and the Germanic brothers Hengist and Horsa on the other (if the latter existed at all) will never be known for sure; but it provided the Germanic tribes with their first territorial gains in Britain and, in due course, gave them the Kingdom of Kent.

INTERNAL EMPIRE

This was the first of seven kingdoms to be created in modern England by the Germanic tribes, following waves of migration by Angles, Frisians, Jutes, Saxons and others. Collectively known centuries later only as 'Anglo-Saxons', thus unfortunately ignoring the role played by the rest, these Germanic invaders first established their presence on the eastern side of England and then pushed inland. Their advance, it seems, was made possible not just by military prowess, but also through the adoption by many Britons of the newcomers' culture. And just as the Britons adapted the language of the Germanic tribes to create what we call Old English, so the pagan invaders slowly came to accept Christianity as the new religion, through the evangelical work of St. Augustine and others.[23]

The Germanic invaders did not have it all their own way. Their probable defeat by an army of Britons at the Battle of Mons Badonicus (c. 500) set back their territorial advance. However, they had more success at the Battle of Dyrham in 577, when Germanic forces from Wessex captured Bath, Cirencester and Gloucester, effectively cutting off the Britons in Dumnonia (modern Cornwall and Devon) from the remaining kingdoms of Britons in Wales and Strathclyde. Germanic power would now be concentrated in the three kingdoms of Mercia (midlands), Northumbria (north) and Wessex (south), with Kent, Sussex, Essex and East Anglia playing a less important role.

When the Viking raids started at the end of the eighth century, it was Mercia under King Offa that was the most important of the seven kingdoms. Indeed, Offa's son and heir Ecgferth was consecrated by the Pope himself.[24] Yet Ecgferth could not hold the kingdom together after his father's death, and power started to shift to Wessex—Mercia's great rival in southern England. And soon after the first full-scale Viking invasion in 865, led by Danes and resulting in the conquest of all Northumbria in 876 and Mercia the following year, Wessex was the only Germanic

BIRTH OF THE FOUR NATIONS

kingdom in any position to provide resistance. Yet opposition proved futile; in 871, when Alfred became King of the West Saxons on the death of his father, he had to bribe the Danes in order to preserve his kingdom.[25]

It was only a brief peace, as the Danes under their leader Guthrum returned to attack Wessex a few years later. This time, however, the Saxons were better prepared and Alfred won an important victory at the Battle of Edington in 878. The subsequent treaty, known as the Treaty of Alfred and Guthrum, established the boundaries of Danelaw—the eastern territories ruled by the Vikings and in which the laws of the Danes would hold sway, from Northumbria to East Anglia and Essex.

The treaty also safeguarded the Kingdom of Wessex and allowed Alfred to introduce the institutional, military and legal reforms for which he became famous, and which earned him centuries later the title Alfred the Great. Yet he was not King of England, a country which still did not exist, and died only as King of Wessex and its dependencies (such as western Mercia). Much of modern England at the time was still under the control of Viking rulers, whose presence was starting to have an impact on language, law and social customs, while Britons still ruled kingdoms in the southwest and the northwest.

Arguably, therefore, England was more divided—institutionally, politically and linguistically—than Ireland, Scotland or Wales at this time. In the tenth century, however, at least some of these divisions would be overcome. When Alfred died in 899, he left Wessex with a system of military administration, including the famous *burh* (a fortified town), that made the kingdom almost impregnable. This allowed his son, Edward the Elder, to launch campaigns to bring parts of Viking England under the control of its southern neighbour, Wessex. In this he was helped by his sister Æthelflæd, who had become Queen of (western) Mercia on the death of her husband

33

INTERNAL EMPIRE

in 911, and whose firm grip on the territory allowed her brother to attack the Vikings elsewhere.

This he did with some success, but he died in 924 without conquering Northumbria—let alone unifying England. It was his son, Æthelstan, who came closer to achieving this goal—particularly after his victory at the Battle of Brunanburh in 937. As discussed in the Introduction, this triumph did not really make Æthelstan King of England, but did consolidate his claim to be King of the Anglo-Saxons. This gave his successors (he himself had no children) some authority in their efforts to create an English nation-state under a single ruler. The final Anglo-Saxon conquest of Northumbria took place in 954, but this time it was accompanied by other measures that were more likely to secure a long-term peace. An East Anglian of Viking descent, Oskytel, was made Archbishop of York, for example. As noted by one historian, 'The kingdom [of England] had now one king to rule it and one royal family to provide him [house of Wessex]. It had two archbishops [York and Canterbury], both appointed by that king.'[26]

Just as important was the blurring of the lines now taking place between Anglo-Saxon and Viking England. The reconquest of the Viking strongholds had not led to any reconciliation between the two peoples, even after Æthelstan had completed the process. Yet by the end of the tenth century, a single people was starting to emerge, based on a common language with deep roots in both Old English and Old Norse, a shared legal system and, of course, intermarriage. With their country at peace for much of the time with Ireland, Alba and Wales, Anglo-Saxon rulers might now have legitimately thought of themselves as kings of England in perpetuity.

Yet this ignored developments in continental Europe, where a Danelaw had been formed in Normandy after 911, and where a new Norse kingdom based in Denmark and Norway was soon to

34

BIRTH OF THE FOUR NATIONS

take shape under Sweyn Forkbeard.[27] In light of this, the order given in 1002 by King Æthelred (a direct descendant of Alfred the Great and known to history as 'the Unready') to massacre all Danes in his kingdom was an extremely unwise decision.[28] Sweyn, who had already started raiding England, now planned a full-scale invasion that brought him the kingship in 1013. His son, Cnut, would then be crowned King of England in 1017 after all resistance had been overcome.

Cnut, who went on to marry Æthelred's widow (a Norman princess called Emma), initially treated England as little more than a Danish colony. However, he became more accommodating towards the Anglo-Saxon elites the longer he ruled. Since Emma had children both by Æthelred and Cnut, an agreement was easily reached regarding the succession after Cnut, who died in 1035. Cnut and Emma's son Harthacnut would inherit the Kingdom of England, but if he then died without issue, his place would be taken by his half-brother Edward (Emma's son by Æthelred). When King Harthacnut indeed died childless in 1042, Edward (later known as the Confessor) was able to restore the house of Wessex to the throne. England was once again independent, with the outlines of a nation-state clearly visible.

2

FOUR NATIONS, FOUR STATES

England became a Norman colony in 1066 and would remain so for some 150 years. It also fragmented as a nation as a result of the divisions created by colonisation. England regained its independence, however, following the capture of Normandy by France at the beginning of the thirteenth century, by which time nation-building was once again well underway. From that time onwards English rulers, although continuing to dream for decades—even centuries—about building an empire in France, would now face a new reality in which England was the centre of their universe. English state-building could now proceed apace.

By the time England ceased to be a Norman colony in the early 1200s, Scotland (or Alba) had already been operating as an independent country with a unified kingdom for centuries. Wales had done so as well for some of the time, although there had been breaks in continuity and—unlike in Scotland—Wales was not always unified. With England's independence restored, there followed nearly a century during which the three independent countries of England, Scotland and Wales operated side by side within the British Isles. This equilibrium, sometimes amicable

37

INTERNAL EMPIRE

and sometimes uneasy, only ended when Wales was finally conquered by England at the end of the century.

Ireland was in a different situation. Part of it had been occupied by the Normans, but it had avoided full-scale colonisation. By the time England was reborn as an independent state, Ireland had enjoyed nearly 200 years of independence, either as a united kingdom or as a confederation of separate rulers with a High King. Its leaders maintained state-to-state relations not just with kings in Britain, but also with rulers in other parts of Europe. Ireland's ability to conduct such relations was much diminished after the Norman invasion in 1169, but a number of Irish kingdoms survived intact.

In due course England itself would become an imperial power, colonising two of its neighbours (Ireland and Wales) and seeking dominance over the third (Scotland). However, before that happened, England operated alongside other independent kingdoms in the Isles. What is of interest in this chapter, therefore, are the state-to-state relations of the four nations—with each other and the outside world—before the rise of English imperialism.

England

When Edward the Confessor became King of England in 1042, the politics of the English crown had become deeply intertwined with the Viking stronghold in Normandy. Edward (like his Anglo-Saxon father Æthelred) had spent his years of exile in the Duchy of Normandy, while his Norman mother Emma had later married Cnut, Danish King of England, who himself had close family ties to the Viking nobles in Normandy. The Normans believed this gave them a claim, however tenuous, to the English throne. When Edward died without issue in 1066, the crown passed to Harold Godwinson, Earl of Wessex.

38

FOUR NATIONS, FOUR STATES

The scene was set for the Norman invasion and the Battle of Hastings.

Harold's defeat at the hands of William, Duke of Normandy, would finally end the grip of the house of Wessex on the English throne. Yet the Norman conquest of England was neither quick nor simple. Anglo-Saxon resistance in the south may have been crushed fairly quickly—despite the heroic efforts of Hereward the Wake in the east and Eadric the Wild in the west—but gaining control of the north was a lengthy process. A well-organised rebellion in 1069, aided by the forces of King Sweyn of Denmark, nearly defeated the Norman army. It took a virtual war of genocide by the Normans (euphemistically described as the 'harrying of the north') to crush the opposition, and yet resistance still did not end. Only in the first half of the twelfth century did Northumbria, Yorkshire, Durham and Cumbria finally come under undisputed Norman control.

As a result of the conquest, England became a colony—its lands to be distributed among a new Norman elite. While Ireland, Scotland and Wales were slowly establishing the conditions for consolidated nation-states, England's constitutional status would regress after 1066. England may have been the largest and most populated part of the Hiberno-British Isles, but it was not at first the most important part of the Norman Empire. That was the Duchy itself, to which English interests would now be subordinate.[1]

The Norman kings of England, almost invariably dukes of Normandy and rulers of other territories as well, had no reason to treat their new conquest as anything other than a colony—its political economy subject to broader imperial ambitions. And the relabelling of Norman kings as Plantagenet or Angevin from Henry II onwards could not disguise this.[2] These were still essentially Norman rulers, whose first language was French not English, who never married English wives,[3] who had their principal interests

39

in continental Europe and who spent most of their time outside England. Indeed, the shift of name to Plantagenet was made in recognition of the vast lands in France acquired by Henry II through descent and marriage, so that England became even less of a central focus in this expanded (Angevin) empire.

Despite this, or perhaps because of this, some things happened under Norman rule that would help reestablish a nation-state subsequently. The Normans may have taken most of the land from the English, but they did not migrate to England in large numbers (perhaps no more than 8,000 were beneficiaries of land grants), and most of those that came were male. A new English society therefore began to take shape among the elites, based not only on marriage, but also on the division of responsibilities among the heirs of the Norman nobility, with some taking responsibility for English estates and others for French ones. And beneath the elites—among the freemen, serfs and slaves—life continued much as before.

As a result of these new social arrangements, Norman contempt for the English started to diminish. Early Norman attitudes were well captured by Orderic Vitalis, a monk with a Norman father and English mother, when describing England during William the Conqueror's six-month absence in Normandy in 1067: 'The English were groaning under a Norman yoke, and suffering oppressions from the proud lord who ignored the king's injunctions. The petty lords who were guarding the castles oppressed all the native inhabitants of high and low degree, and heaped shameful burdens on them.'[4]

These attitudes did soften over time. However, it would be a long process; and it would be many years before the English language regained respectability. Indeed, it was not until the beginning of the thirteenth century that kings of England dropped 'French and English' when addressing their subjects and instead referred to them only as 'English'.[5]

FOUR NATIONS, FOUR STATES

At the same time, the Norman kings' absence from England for most of their reign required a strengthening of the institutions of government within England itself, so that the colony could function effectively without the presence of its titular ruler. This required a centralised administration with strong tax-raising powers and a judicial system capable of enforcing the law. It was these changes that improved the fortunes of the English economy, especially in foreign trade, and led to a big increase in population in the two centuries after the Norman conquest.[6]

While England was slowly recovering its sense of nationhood, major developments were happening in France. It was the weakness of the Frankish state, not yet called France, that had forced Charles the Simple to grant the Vikings their foothold in Normandy in 911. Although dukes of Normandy would pay homage to the Frankish kings, their presence was always going to cause problems. Some 300 years later, a French state finally came into existence with the power and authority to establish control over the Duchy.

The first step was the coup led by Hugh Capet that brought the Capetian dynasty to the throne at the end of the tenth century; the next was the assumption of power in 1180 by Philippe II, who styled himself King of France a decade later. The French state over which he ruled had grown considerably from the days of Charles the Simple, but was still very much smaller than modern France. That, however, was about to change, as the state's boundaries expanded—an expansion that would later earn him the epithet Philippe Auguste.

Normandy was a principal target. The French had nibbled away at its borders and in the Treaty of Le Goulet in 1200 had secured the agreement of the King of England, who was also the Duke of Normandy, for a new boundary. Philippe Auguste, however, had little intention of respecting the treaty and by 1204 most of Normandy, as well as other Norman lands in France,

41

INTERNAL EMPIRE

were under his control. The English king did, however, manage to keep the Channel Islands and they remain a crown possession to this day.[7]

King John, the monarch under whom the loss of Normandy occurred, was forced to flee back to England after suffering defeat. This was no doubt a humiliating experience, but he was convinced that his territorial losses could be reversed. Yet, after joining forces with the Holy Roman Emperor and other continental rulers, he suffered an even more humiliating defeat against Philippe at the Battle of Bouvines in 1214.

This was one of the decisive battles in French history, but it had major implications for England as well. By the Treaty of Chinon in 1214, King John was forced to concede Anjou, Poitou and the Duchy of Brittany. This ended the Angevin Empire, although John was able to hold onto lands in the distant southwest of modern France. In addition, he had to pay £60,000 in reparations to France.[8] This fiscal burden was one of the factors behind the revolt against him by the English barons, who extracted a number of concessions from the king under the first version of *Magna Carta* in 1215.

Neither side respected the charter; not until 1225 was there a definitive version, properly observed by both sides. The fighting continued and the barons even invited Prince Louis, the son of Philippe Auguste, to lead them. Louis was actually in England with French troops when John died in 1216 and might have succeeded to the English throne himself. However, the rebels were divided and Louis was bought off the following year by the Treaty of Lambeth (also known as the Treaty of Kingston). He received a large payment and renounced his claim to the English throne.

John's successors would not now be rulers of a Norman Empire including an English colony, but kings of an independent English nation-state with some continental territory. By the beginning

42

FOUR NATIONS, FOUR STATES

of the thirteenth century, therefore, England, Scotland and Wales had similar status. Rulers of Scotland and Wales may have been expected to pay homage to kings of England, but this was never taken too seriously and, in any case, did not restrict their freedom of action any more than the fealty that had been sworn to kings of France by dukes of Normandy. As for Ireland, where a lordship had been created by the Normans after 1170, there were still kings there with whom English monarchs had to negotiate.

This was the diplomatic and political reality facing Henry III, still only a child at his coronation in 1216. England and its neighbours within the Isles should now have been the focus of most of his attention. The French capture of Normandy, Anjou and Poitou had ensured that almost no English nobles held land in France, leaving Henry's barons—a growing force since the first signing of *Magna Carta*—to concentrate on their English interests and to compete for power with the king. Yet there was one flaw in this argument. The Treaty of Lambeth had left King Henry in control of Gascony (Aquitaine) in southwest France. Thus, unlike the nobles, the English king still had continental interests.

Given the history of the defunct Norman Empire and its close association with territories in France, it was inevitable—if foolish—that Henry would at some point try to use Gascony as the base to recover some of the French lands lost by his father. After the cancellation of expeditions in 1223, 1226, 1227 and 1229, one was finally launched in 1230. It was a complete failure—as was a later one in 1242. Indeed, so dismal was the king's performance that one poet remarked: 'Good sauce, clear wine, white bread, chambers and tapestries, and the like, to drink, to consult with quibblers, to ride like a dean on docile mounts, the king loves better all that than to put on a coat of mail.'[9]

Under these circumstances, Henry might have despaired of holding onto Gascony. Yet the Treaty of Paris, signed with Louis

43

INTERNAL EMPIRE

IX of France in 1259, established that the King of England, after renouncing all other territorial claims on the French mainland, could retain that one territory as a vassal of the King of France. Although this condition would lead to conflict in the next century, it brought peace between England and France for many years, and finally forced Henry to focus almost exclusively on English affairs.

This he needed to do urgently, as his foreign wars had cost him heavily—not only in terms of the exchequer, but also through loss of baronial support. Although the barons' demands had been largely satisfied by the 1225 version of *Magna Carta* and the subsequent parliaments called by Henry, the barons objected to his preference for French-speaking foreigners in his closest circle—especially during the early years of his reign. This was a clash not just about the distribution of power among the elites, but also about English identity and the very nature of English nationhood.

It would take Henry almost all the years of his long reign to reach an accommodation with England's nobles and their allies. During this time he fought civil wars, faced imprisonment, gave more powers to parliament and eventually crushed the dangerous ambitions of Simon de Montfort—a Frenchman who had first been elevated by Henry to the earldom of Leicester and had then been offered the regency of France by the French nobles.

At the time of Henry's death in 1272, the nature of the English nation-state was at its least ambiguous since the Norman conquest in 1066. Its overseas possessions were much diminished, and its geographical limits within the British Isles (if not in Ireland) now seemed clear. As a result, English nationalism was no longer so confused or confusing. Kings may still have aspired to playing geopolitics on the European stage, but for the vast majority of the population, including most nobles, England was their only home and English their only language. And religion—so often a

44

FOUR NATIONS, FOUR STATES

divisive factor in later history—was still a unifying force, except for the small Jewish population that had suffered deeply at the hands of de Montfort.

Ireland

Ireland was famous in Europe from the time of St. Patrick for its monastic schools, high levels of scholarship and literary output. According to one authority: 'It is no exaggeration to say that the revolution in Hiberno-Latin grammatical studies [in the seventh century] paved the way for the remarkable contribution which Irish scholars were to make to the culture of Europe in the age of Charlemagne and after.'[10] Thus, long before the political unification of the country under Brian Boru, Ireland had been able to project itself on the European stage by virtue of its religious and literary achievements.

Although some Irish rulers had contacts with European kingdoms before Brian Boru, it was Brian—the acknowledged leader of a confederation of Irish kingdoms, with himself as High King—who first established state-to-state relations. At the Battle of Glenmama in 999, he defeated Sigtrygg Silkbeard, the Viking King of Dublin; following this victory, Brian was finally in a position to place Ireland securely among the leading states in Europe. In doing so, he used all the traditional methods of statecraft—including marriage alliances.

This strategy began with his own marriage to Gormfhlaith, Sigtrygg's mother. An alliance with this powerful family, leaving Silkbeard in charge at Dublin in an initially subordinate role, was an indicator of Brian Boru's new priorities—unlike his previous two marriages, which had been with Irish princesses. And when it came to his daughters, Brian was equally shrewd. One was married to Sigtrygg himself, thus deepening even further the bonds between Ireland and the Viking king.

45

INTERNAL EMPIRE

Pragmatic statecraft demanded a choice of a foreign spouse—one living outside Ireland—for another of his daughters. Brian could have chosen a member of England's ruling family. However, Æthelred the Unready presided over a weak kingdom that was about to be conquered (again) by the Danes.[11] At the same time Wales was unable to offer a suitable match, as the country was not yet united under Gruffydd ap Llywelyn. Instead, Brian's daughter was married to a Gaelic prince, who would ascend the throne of Alba a few years later as Malcolm II. Not only did this show the relative importance of Alba/Scotland among the three nations of Britain, but it also gave Ireland an important ally in case of a foreign attack.

Brian's long reign ended with his death at the Battle of Clontarf in 1014. Subsequently, much of what had happened in his lifetime was obscured both by the Irish legends that developed around his name and by the English myths designed to tarnish his reputation, in order to justify colonisation. Yet some things are clear. His patronage of the Church, especially the monastery at Armagh, restored the Irish schools' reputation in continental Europe and brought a flow of scholars from there to Ireland. He also ensured that Irish students could study abroad in those same countries.

The death of so many of his descendants at Clontarf robbed Ireland of the political unity achieved under Brian Boru. Yet this did not mean that the island reverted to a 'tribal state'—the denigrating phrase that English writers deployed not so long ago. Instead, ambition had been raised by Brian's achievements, so that all the leading kings in Ireland aspired to greater powers. This required larger military forces, and that, in turn, meant more efficient administration and tax collection.

Ireland, with its rival rulers after Brian, now became a popular destination for princes and kings from England and Wales seeking military support for their various campaigns. The Dublin fleet

FOUR NATIONS, FOUR STATES

sailed up the River Severn to support Gruffydd ap Llywelyn in 1049. After the Battle of Hastings, the sons of King Harold fled to Leinster, whose king (Diarmait) then sent his fleet to the coasts of Devon in an ultimately unsuccessful attempt to restore the house of Wessex to the English throne.

This Irish attempt to place Harold's family back in power in England might have caused problems with William the Conqueror. However, things would soon go in the opposite direction. Diarmait died in 1072 and within two years Toirdelbach, the grandson of Brian Boru, had become High King of Ireland, after crushing all resistance in the south and establishing alliances with the northern kings. The relationship between England and Ireland was now one almost of equals and the ruler of each country had a strong incentive to avoid invasion by the other.

The incentive may have been strongest for William in view of the numerous threats to the crown during his reign, from Danish invaders and rebellious nobles. In any case, Toirdelbach refrained from meddling in Welsh affairs (unlike previous Irish kings) as the Normans encroached into Wales and did not support any of the rebellions against William. In return, commerce thrived, with the eastern Irish ports of Dublin and Waterford enjoying a booming trade with the western English ports of Chester and Bristol.[12]

One area that might have caused friction was ecclesiastical, as Archbishops of Canterbury since the time of Bede had claimed the right to appoint Irish bishops—a claim that had been largely ignored. When Lanfranc was appointed Archbishop by William the Conqueror in 1070, he was keen to reassert this right while at the same time promoting church reform in Ireland. A series of letters between Toirdelbach and Lanfranc, however, defused the situation and even led to a correspondence between the High King of Ireland and Pope Gregory VII.

47

INTERNAL EMPIRE

Lanfranc duly consecrated the bishop at Dublin chosen by the Irish, and Toirdelbach secured the blessing of the papacy for his campaign to be recognised as king of all Ireland (he was addressed by the Archbishop as '*magnifico Hiberniae regi Terdelbach*'). The relationship between Irish kings and the Pope continued to flourish to the point where, in 1152 at the Synod of Kells, approval was given by the papal envoy for the consecration of archbishops in four metropolitan sees, with Armagh confirmed in its primacy.

Toirdelbach died in 1086 and was succeeded by his son Muirchertach as High King of Ireland after the usual conflict over the succession had been settled. Toirdelbach had already placed his son in charge of Dublin, a position that would serve him well after he became king. Dubliners participated in the First Crusade in 1095 and Muirchertach made an alliance with the King of Norway, Magnus Barelegs, through the marriage of their children—ending the Norwegian's ambitions to recapture Viking possessions in Ireland.

Muirchertach formed a close bond with Edgar, King of Scotland, who gave him the gift of an exotic animal (believed to be a camel). He also played a key role in the ambitions of favoured Welsh rulers to enlarge their kingdoms. However, his diplomatic instincts deserted him temporarily in the first years of the 1100s, when he sided with the Norman rebels seeking to overthrow Henry I in England. This incident threatened Anglo-Irish relations, but was soon resolved, as is made clear by a letter from Muirchertach (probably written in 1105) to Anselm, the Archbishop of Canterbury, thanking him for his prayers 'on my behalf, a sinner, and also because you have intervened [with Henry I] on behalf of my [rebel] son-in-law'.[13]

Muirchertach died in 1119, but even before then power had shifted from Brian Boru's house, the Ua Briain, to the rulers of Connacht. The Ua Conchobair (O'Connors) would provide the

FOUR NATIONS, FOUR STATES

last high kings of Ireland before the arrival of the Normans, and they came very close to providing the island with a stable kingdom based on a single hereditary ruling family. Indeed, the first—Toirdelbach Ua Conchobair—concentrated the years of his long rule on large infrastructure projects including roads, bridges, canals and fortifications. His navy was also formidable; he put 190 ships into one campaign in 1127.

On his death in 1156, his son Ruaidrí (Rory) struggled at first to achieve the pan-Irish dominance of his father. However, his great rival Muirchertach mac Lochlainn died in 1166, leaving Ruaidrí free to turn his attention to another rival: Diarmait Mac Murchada (Dermot Mac Murrough), the King of Leinster, in whose territories lay the port of Dublin. Diarmait was swiftly isolated and, abandoned by his allies, went into exile. Ruaidrí was now High King of Ireland and had every reason to anticipate a long reign.

What he could not have anticipated is what happened next. The year before his expulsion from Ireland, Diarmait had earned the goodwill of Henry II through the loan of the Dublin fleet—a fairly normal occurrence— for an unsuccessful campaign in Wales by the English king. It seemed natural, therefore, to ask Henry to return the favour. Since King Henry was (as usual) outside England in his French lands, Diarmait visited him in Aquitaine.

Henry had allegedly inherited a claim to Ireland through a papal document issued by Pope Adrian IV in 1155, known by the first Latin word of its text. *Laudabiliter* stated that Henry II had the right to claim Ireland in order to effect Church reform. Whatever the authenticity of the document, it is almost certain that Henry's response to Diarmait had nothing to do with *Laudabiliter* and everything to do with the normal calculations of medieval monarchs addressing geopolitical issues. Consequently, he authorised Diarmait to seek military support among the Norman nobles in England to retake his Irish lands.

INTERNAL EMPIRE

This he did with some success, but the knights who accompanied him to Leinster did not leave after restoring Diarmait to his kingdom. Instead, they proceeded to install their own rule on the eastern coast, including the ports of Dublin and Waterford. After Diarmait's death in 1171, they no longer had to share power with their Irish ally. This was not just a threat to Ruaidrí, but to Henry II as well. He came that year to the parts of Ireland controlled by his nobles in order to try and curb their ambitions—while claiming the lands they had conquered for his own. The result was the Treaty of Windsor, signed by the Kings of England and Ireland in 1175. Its short and simple text assured Ruaidrí control of those parts of Ireland not seized by the Norman knights, while recognising Henry's ownership of the Norman lands, either outright or through vassalage. It also obliged Irish kings to pay tribute and accept the overlordship of England.

It was a blow to Irish ambitions, but not necessarily a mortal one. Had it been respected by the Norman side, it would have left Ireland as a quasi-independent nation-state—albeit much diminished in size. However, far from being respected, the Norman knights simply ignored it and continued to expand their lands in Ireland. Henry's son John was appointed Lord of Ireland in 1177, and Ireland would become stuck in a limbo between full colonisation and complete independence.

It would later be claimed that Irish statehood had been eclipsed and Ireland had become an English colony. However, the truth was much more complicated, and a version of Irish autonomy would survive for another three centuries. In this long struggle, the Irish had some advantages. Perhaps the greatest was the competing pressures faced by English kings through civil war in England and costly campaigns elsewhere—especially against France during the Hundred Years' War (1337–1453). As a result, the territories in Ireland controlled directly by the crown steadily shrank until they were limited to a small area around

FOUR NATIONS, FOUR STATES

Dublin known as the Pale, in which sat the King of England's Irish parliament.

That still left the lands occupied by English descendants of the Norman knights. These territories were never fully recovered, but English occupation created resentment, and Irish kings could still win occasional military victories. The main problem was which royal family among the Irish would lead the struggle. In 1258 a consensus emerged around the primacy of Brian Ua Néill, and the Irish were able to win a number of military victories against the occupiers (notably at the Battle of Callann in 1261)— but by then Brian himself had been killed and his head was sent to London.[14]

These victories never threatened to end the English occupation completely, but a new opportunity opened in 1315, when another member of the Uí Néill dynasty and his Irish vassals invited Edward Bruce for assistance against the occupiers. Edward, whose brother Robert was already King of Scotland, agreed on condition that he be declared King of Ireland.[15] The speed with which this offer was accepted suggests that the Irish leaders involved were not entirely sincere, but it was never put to the test. Edward Bruce's campaign against the English was spectacularly successful for three years, but he was killed in battle in 1318 before he could claim the Irish throne.

The occupied territories therefore survived, but their inhabitants were becoming less and less English. Indeed, in their *Remonstrance* to Pope John XXII during the brief rule of Edward Bruce, the Irish leaders had complained: 'The English inhabiting our land, who call themselves of the middle nation, are so different from the English of England and from other nations that with the greatest proprietary they may be called a nation not of middle medium but of utter perfidy.'[16]

This, of course, was not the same as 'going native', as the English were still occupiers.[17] However, English kings became

51

INTERNAL EMPIRE

so concerned at the behaviour of their Anglo-Irish subjects that Edward III's Irish parliament passed in 1367 the Statutes of Kilkenny. This outlawed (among other practices) intermarriage, fostering of Irish children and use of Irish names and dress, while requiring the colonists to learn English.

The Statutes of Kilkenny failed to achieve their stated purpose, but the colonists still remained estranged from the rest of the population. This made it impossible to secure the reunification of the island. Ireland had avoided being absorbed fully into the expanding English Empire, but had failed to overcome divisions among the rulers of those parts of Ireland not under occupation. It had, however, operated as a nation-state for nearly two centuries before the Norman invasion and that experience would help to define the struggle against English, and subsequently British, imperialism many years later.

Wales

As King of both Gwynedd and Powys from 1039, Gruffydd ap Llywelyn had already learnt the art of international diplomacy even before he became the undisputed King of Wales in 1055. He had successfully formed alliances with rulers in Ireland and Norway not only to preserve a hold on his ancestral kingdom (Gwynedd), but also with the aim of becoming king of all Wales. The preservation of his Welsh kingdom, however, required not just the neutralisation of any military threats, but—above all—a careful reading of the politics of England.

In choosing Ælfgar of Mercia as his ally, even marrying his daughter, Gruffydd at first appeared to have made a wise calculation. The alliance brought a handsome dividend in terms of plunder and also a peace treaty with the King of England, Edward the Confessor, following a personal meeting on the banks of the River Severn. If Gruffydd had to accept Edward as

FOUR NATIONS, FOUR STATES

his nominal overlord, it seemed a small price to pay for secure boundaries with a powerful neighbour.

The death of Ælfgar in 1062 deprived Gruffydd of his chief ally in England and left him vulnerable to the ambitions of Harold Godwinson, at this time Earl of Hereford in western England. After a military onslaught by Harold, Gruffydd lost not only his kingdom but also his life. To add insult to injury, Harold then married his widow Ealdgyth. Gruffydd's northern kingdoms of Gwynedd and Powys became client states of England, while Deheubarth in the south reverted to the family of its former rulers. It was a lesson in how to deal with England that no future king or prince in Wales could afford to forget.

In 1066 William the Conqueror defeated the English. As the new King of England (crowned William I), he dealt with Ireland and Scotland as separate states—just as his Anglo-Saxon predecessors had done. The same happened with Wales, despite the absence of a single ruler. However, the relationship between England and Wales was complicated by William's grant of lands to Norman lords on the border between the two countries.

In this area, known as the March, Norman lords were almost sovereign. They paid no taxation, wrote their own rules and felt unconstrained by either English or Welsh kings—only in the case of outright rebellion did the King of England move against them. Inevitably, they encroached on Welsh lands, leading to the expression *Marchia Wallia* (territory in Wales occupied by the Marcher lords).

Marchia Wallia was extensive, if fluctuating, in size. Yet it never occupied the whole of Wales. The remainder was known as *Pura Wallia*, which was ruled directly by Welsh kings (or occasionally a single king) for more than 200 years after the Norman conquest, giving Wales and its rulers an experience of independence as a nation-state that would never be forgotten.

INTERNAL EMPIRE

The survival of *Pura Wallia* in the face of aggression by Marcher lords and English kings was not due to military superiority, although the Welsh were famous for their fighting ability.[18] It was more to do with a combination of mountainous geography, local knowledge, and divisions amongst their opponents. For the Marcher lords were never united, fighting amongst themselves and even taking opposing sides in disputes among the Welsh rulers.

The first to confront the new Norman threat was Rhys ap Tewdwr, who had secured the southern throne of Deheubarth some fifteen years after the death of Gruffydd ap Llywelyn. By then the Marcher lords had advanced into the southeast corner of Wales, but Rhys ap Tewdwr's hold on his kingdom was made secure by his victory at the Battle of Mynydd Carn in 1081, when he defeated not just a Welsh rival but also Norman mercenaries. In that same year, after his victory, he welcomed William I to his kingdom. Although we may dismiss the claims of some chroniclers that William was only interested in a pilgrimage to the home of St. David, it was clear that the Conqueror needed stability on the English border. The two rulers reached an understanding, under which Rhys ap Tewdwr would be left in peace in return for an annual payment of £40 to the Norman ruler.[19]

The agreement at first ensured good relations between the rulers of south Wales and England. However, the Marcher lords no longer felt constrained after the death of William in 1087. They continued their advance westwards and, in 1093, killed Rhys ap Tewdwr at Brecon. *Marchia Wallia* would now extend into Deheubarth—but, in the following year, Marcher lords themselves were decisively defeated in the north. Gwynedd, its Norman castles destroyed, would be a secure part of *Pura Wallia* for nearly two more centuries.[20]

Gwynedd now produced most of the preeminent Welsh rulers. The first of note was Owain ap Gruffydd, who preferred

54

FOUR NATIONS, FOUR STATES

to be known as Owain Gwynedd in honour of his ancestral kingdom. Even before his father's death in 1137, he had taken part in two campaigns against the Normans in Ceredigion. Once ruling Gwynedd, he proceeded to expand his kingdom eastward, defeating both Welsh and Norman forces. Inevitably, he began to be seen by the King of England, Henry II, as a potential threat.

Henry launched three campaigns against Owain, but none succeeded in driving him from his throne. The first two, in 1157 and 1163, ended with Owain paying homage to the English king while keeping most of his lands. The third campaign in 1165 was such a disaster for Henry II that Owain was able to declare himself no longer merely *Walliarum rex* (King of the Welsh) but now *princeps Wallensium* (Prince of Wales). As both King and Prince of Wales he would issue many charters in his royal name, most of which were designed to benefit the Welsh monasteries.

So confident had Owain become in his dealings with England that he was able to thwart the ambitions of the Archbishop of Canterbury to name the Bishop of Bangor.[21] He also began a correspondence with the King of France, Louis VII, and his Chancellor, Hugh de Champfleury.[22] And when Louis and Henry met for peace talks in 1168, Owain was almost certainly one of the envoys of Scotland and Wales who 'promised aid to the French king and offered him hostages' in exchange for a military alliance against England.[23]

In his campaigns against Henry II, Owain Gwynedd was aided by his nephew Rhys ap Gruffydd. Known after his death as the Lord Rhys, he had driven the Marcher lords out of Deheubarth to regain the kingdom for his family. This brought him into conflict with Henry, with whom he was almost constantly at war for nearly fifteen years. Indeed, at one point Rhys was taken as a prisoner to Woodstock in England, where he was obliged to submit to Henry II (although he was able to keep his kingdom).

55

INTERNAL EMPIRE

Yet, as soon as the Normans secured their first foothold in Ireland, Rhys' relationship with Henry changed. The King of England, needing to bring his knights in Ireland to heel, could not afford to have the King of South Wales as an enemy. The two men met at Pembroke in 1171 before Henry's departure for Ireland and again on his return. On both occasions, Rhys was confirmed in possession of his Welsh lands and given royal authority to deal with any disputes involving English subjects in these territories.[24] For nearly twenty years—until Henry's death in 1189—they were allies.

The close relationship between Rhys and Henry was between two kings rather than two kingdoms. It did not, therefore, survive Henry's death. However, Henry's successor Richard I was abroad for so much of his ten-year reign that the Lord Rhys was relatively untroubled by English ambitions. When Rhys himself died in 1197, however, a competition for supremacy in Wales was already underway between Gwenwynwyn of Powys and Llywelyn ap Iorwerth of Gwynedd. Inevitably, this created an opportunity for English intrigue, which John—on becoming King of England in 1199—was only too happy to provide.

King John, perhaps fearful of the power of the Kingdom of Gwynedd, at first lent his support to Gwenwynwyn and, in the first year of his reign, made a grant 'confirming his lands and castles in north Wales, south Wales and Powys, and all rights acquired or to be acquired from [his] enemies.'[25] However, within a few years John had switched sides and gave his daughter Joan to Llywelyn ap Iorwerth in marriage.[26]

When King John imprisoned Gwenwynwyn in 1208, Llywelyn's position as the dominant force in Welsh politics was further enhanced. John again switched sides, invaded Wales in 1211 and occupied a large part of Gwynedd. Yet this was a game that two could play. Llywelyn ap Iorwerth, with the blessing of Pope Innocent III and in alliance with the King of France, joined

FOUR NATIONS, FOUR STATES

forces with other Welsh rulers, recovered all his lands, and played an important role with the English barons in forcing John to sign *Magna Carta* in 1215.[27]

Llywelyn was now in a strong position to put an independent Welsh state on a stronger footing. John had died in 1216, but his son (Henry III) was still a child. Henry could not even safely occupy the English throne until a French invasion had been ended by treaty in 1217.[28] The two kings then met the following year to sign the Treaty of Worcester in the presence of a papal delegate, who was given responsibility for overseeing the implementation of the terms.

Superficially the treaty favoured English interests, with a commitment by Llywelyn to give back to the King of England various castles and lordships and to return to the Marcher lords all lands taken from them in southern Wales.[29] However, the royal properties were immediately regranted to Llywelyn until Henry should come of age, and the Welsh ruler proceeded over the next fifteen years to play off the Marcher lords against each other through warfare, diplomacy and even marriage alliances. This left Llywelyn in control of almost all Wales. At the Peace of Middle in 1234, Llywelyn achieved a truce with Henry III for two years—a truce that was then renewed every year until the Welsh ruler's death in 1240.

Llywelyn's victories over the Marcher lords were impressive, but statecraft demanded more than territorial acquisition. In particular, he needed to secure the succession through a more orderly transfer of power than had previously occurred in Wales. That required differentiating between legitimate and illegitimate offspring, while moving towards primogeniture. It also required close cooperation with the King of England—and with a papacy that had long been scandalised by the rights given in Wales to 'natural-born' children.

Llywelyn the Great, as he would soon be known to history, once again showed his mastery of statecraft. In 1220 Henry III

57

INTERNAL EMPIRE

accepted Dafydd, the eldest son of Llywelyn by marriage, as the heir to the kingdom of Gwynedd.[30] In 1222 the Pope gave his blessing, and in 1226 so did the minor Welsh rulers in the south. Dafydd swore homage to Henry in 1229, but the succession in 1240 was anything but orderly, due to English duplicity. Henry invaded Gwynedd in 1241 and took Dafydd's half-brother to England as a prisoner. Although Dafydd recaptured most of Gwynedd, he was unable to reassert his authority over the rest of Wales—as his father had done—before his death in 1246.

The restoration of Welsh territorial integrity was a task left to Llywelyn ap Gruffydd, Dafydd's nephew and grandson of Llywelyn the Great. He had inherited a weak hand, being forced to sign the Treaty of Woodstock with Henry III in 1246. This recognised his right to the kingship of (western) Gwynedd, but little else. However, from this modest beginning he would go on to assert his authority over almost the whole of Wales.

In doing so he was able to take advantage of resentment against English rule in eastern Gwynedd, as well as national divisions and indecisions during the long reign of Henry III. Indeed, Llywelyn recognised that disunity in England was crucial— because, without it, the English 'would blot us out from the face of the earth, and crush us irreparably, like a clay pitcher'.[31] Pushing eastward from his base in western Gwynedd from 1255 onwards, and playing off one Marcher lord against another, he had reunited his grandfather's principality within a decade.

His reward was the Treaty of Montgomery, signed with Henry III in 1267 and witnessed by the future Pope Adrian V. The title of Prince of Wales was recognised for Llywelyn and his heirs as well as the homage and fealty of all minor Welsh rulers.[32] The treaty, despite the onerous requirement to pay £20,000 in instalments to the King of England, was a triumph for Wales in many ways. And, although Llywelyn had to acknowledge more formally than before that he was the tenant-in-chief of the King

FOUR NATIONS, FOUR STATES

of England, he clearly did not feel unduly constrained—as he made clear in a letter a few years later.[33]

Scotland

Statecraft by Scottish kings always required a detailed understanding of the relationship with England. For many years it also demanded careful handling of relations with Norse rulers in Norway and Denmark. While relations with Norway were fraught with difficulties (because of Norwegian occupation of offshore islands and the northern mainland), an alliance with Denmark was seen as the best route to maintaining control of Lothian and gaining control over Northumbria. For, without both these regions, it would have been difficult for an independent Scottish state to hold sway over Cumbria and the Kingdom of Strathclyde.

The invasion of England by the Danish king Sweyn and the subsequent rule of his son Cnut were therefore welcomed by Scotland's rulers. Malcolm II was already on good terms with Sweyn before the invasion, and the Scottish victory over the Northumbrians at the Battle of Carham on the River Tweed owed a great deal to prior Danish acceptance of Scottish goals.[34] This battle in 1018 left Scotland in control of Lothian and gave it a legitimate claim to part of Northumbria.

Malcolm II paid a price for Danish collusion, but it was not a heavy one. After Cnut's visit to Rome in 1027 to witness the accession of the new Holy Roman Emperor, he received the submission of the King of Scotland. Yet submission of one king to another was nothing new in the medieval world, nor did it imply much—if any—diminution of sovereignty. It was more about the acceptance of a subordinate position in an alliance made for political or territorial advantage.

The transactional nature of submission had already been illustrated on numerous occasions in Scotland's relations with

59

INTERNAL EMPIRE

England. After Edward the Elder, the son of Alfred the Great, had extended his rule over part of Danelaw, he had received the voluntary submission of the King of Alba (as well as rulers of Northumbria, Cumbria and Wales). Yet this had been no more than a mutual defence pact, and the same had been true a few years later in 927, when Edward's son Æthelstan, King of the Anglo-Saxons, received the submission of Constantine II of Alba. This was part of an Anglo-Scottish Treaty (arguably the first ever) and it had allowed the Scottish a free hand in Lothian. However, Constantine II evidently had not felt unduly constrained, as he broke the treaty a few years later. This had provoked an English invasion, with Constantine obliged to give his son as a hostage. This hostage-taking was a much more serious matter than submission, as it implied vassalage. Even then, however, a new treaty had been signed in 945, not only largely restoring the status quo ante, but also giving Cumbria to Alba (see Chapter 1).

The relationship between Alba and England had then continued on similar lines for more than a century. However, the seizure of the Scottish throne by MacBeth (of Shakespearean fame) in 1040 ruptured the alliance. The son of the ousted king sought asylum in England during the reign of Edward the Confessor and was considered a vassal. His recovery of the throne as Malcolm III in 1058 was only possible with the support of the English, leaving him dangerously exposed.

Malcolm's dependence on Anglo-Saxon goodwill was put to the test by the Norman conquest of England. Many nobles fled to Scotland, where they were welcomed, and Malcolm even married an English princess (Margaret). The stage was set for violent conflict with William the Conqueror, but this was settled when the two kings met in 1072 in Scotland and signed the Treaty of Abernethy. Now free of any obligations of vassalage, Malcolm Canmore (the Great)—as he would later be called—

FOUR NATIONS, FOUR STATES

paid homage to William. However, the question of Scottish claims to the northern counties of England was left unresolved.

The border dispute would now be one of the two defining issues in relations between Scotland and England for the next 150 years (the other being responsibility for ecclesiastical appointments). Scotland's cause ebbed and flowed, although the survival of the kingdom was hardly ever in doubt, while each side took advantage of any weakness in the other. Opportunism was the order of the day.

Such a strategy could easily backfire. When, for example, England descended into a civil war (known as the Anarchy) after the death of Henry I in 1135, King David I of Scotland (grandson of Malcolm Canmore) scented an opportunity to push the border south to the Humber. However, his army was defeated at the Battle of the Standard in 1138 by Stephen (despite the latter's struggle with Matilda for the English throne). Scottish territorial ambitions then had to be temporarily curtailed.

David may have lost the battle, but he won the peace. In this he was helped by the close ties that had developed between the Norman and mac Malcolm dynasties after the death of Malcolm III. David I had allowed Henry I to marry his sister Edith, while Henry had returned the favour by giving David the hand of the heiress of Huntingdon—'one of the richest matrimonial prizes of the Anglo-Saxon world'.[35] These Scoto-Norman ties had not ended with Henry's death; in the peace treaty, David was able to hold on to Cumbria, while his son was allowed to keep Northumbria in return for homage to the English king.

David's army at the Standard had consisted of 'Normans, Germans, English, Northumbrians and Cumbrians, men of Teviotdale and Lothian, Galwegians and Scots.'[36] This polyglot force showed the complexity of the Kingdom of Scotland following its expansion out of a Pictish heartland. Malcolm III, despite his rivalry with Norman rulers, had not hesitated to

61

invite Norman and English knights to settle in the lowlands with their followers—a policy strongly supported by his English wife Margaret. His son David had continued this practice, leading to an important Anglo-Norman—soon to be Scoto-Norman—constituency in the Kingdom of Scotland.

The warm relationship between England and Scotland did not survive for long. Henry II, who ruled England after the Anarchy, took back Cumbria and Northumbria in 1157 from the adolescent King Malcolm IV, grandson of David. When Malcolm died in 1165 at the tender age of 23, his brother William succeeded to the throne with a determination to recover the lost lands. As he reigned for nearly fifty years, only dying in 1214, he had plenty of time to do it—but fortune would not favour him.

William I, or William the Lion as he is usually called, considered the loss of Cumbria and Northumbria to be a humiliation. Taking advantage of a rebellion against Henry II by one of his sons in 1173, William invaded Northumbria while his brother David campaigned further south. This first attempt ended in disaster when William was captured and forced to sign the Treaty of Falaise in Normandy. William had to swear fealty for the whole kingdom of Scotland; the Scottish clergy were to submit to the English church; and five key castles were to be handed over to Henry's representatives. The treaty even allowed Henry to choose William's bride!

The English were not in a position to enforce all the clauses of the treaty, but it still took skilful diplomacy by William the Lion to undo its impact. First, he secured a papal bull in 1188, ruling that the Church in Scotland was subject only to Rome and not Canterbury or York. Secondly, in the following year after Henry II had died, he was able to terminate the treaty itself through a payment to the new King of England, Richard I, who needed money for the Third Crusade. The termination left the border between the two kingdoms unresolved, but this

FOUR NATIONS, FOUR STATES

was addressed by the Treaty of York in 1237, which confirmed English dominion over Cumbria and Northumbria, and stabilised the border—which remains largely unchanged today.[37] It was signed by Henry III of England and Alexander II of Scotland (the son of William the Lion), who reigned for thirty-five years until his death in 1249.

Alexander II's only son (also called Alexander) now succeeded to the throne, but he was still a child. Despite this, Alexander III was married at the age of ten to Henry III's daughter at York, and amicable relations between Scotland and England continued for the remainder of both kings' reigns.[38] This left Alexander III free to pursue other ambitions. The most pressing was deemed to be the annexation of the western islands and the provinces in the far north. These territories, including the Isle of Man, had been under the control of Norway for centuries; Norwegian control had been formalised by treaty in 1098, leaving Scotland dangerously exposed.

Alexander at first tried diplomacy, sending a delegation to King Haakon IV in 1261. When that failed, force was used, leading to a retaliatory expedition by the Norwegian king. Although the fighting was inconclusive, Haakon died in 1263 in Orkney (a Norwegian stronghold) on his return to Norway. His son, Magnus VI, was more amenable, and a peace treaty was agreed in 1266 after intense negotiations. The Treaty of Perth brought all the western islands and the northern provinces under Scottish control.[39] Like the Treaty of York thirty years earlier, it was a significant diplomatic achievement.

Although relations between Scotland and England were generally amicable during the long reigns of Alexander II and III, nothing could be taken for granted. England was always ready to take advantage of any Scottish weakness, and the memory of the humiliating Treaty of Falaise in 1174 still lingered. Henry III had tried to secure homage for the Kingdom of Scotland from

INTERNAL EMPIRE

Alexander III at the child's marriage to his daughter, but the issue had been kicked into the long grass (according to the *St. Albans Chronicle*, Alexander replied that he had come to marry and not 'to answer about so difficult a question').

The question of which country was best placed for Scotland to provide a counterweight to England was easy to answer. Only France, England's mortal enemy, could play that role. Indeed, one scholar has argued:[40]

> Ever since 1173 [after William the Lion was captured by the English] it had been normal, one might almost say routine, practice for a French king at war with England to call upon Scottish support, and for a Scots king at odds with England to look for help with France.

It is no surprise, therefore, to find a letter written by the English author John of Salisbury soon after the Treaty of Falaise, referring to a proposed alliance between William the Lion and Louis VII of France.

No formal treaty was reached while William was alive, and the marked improvement in Anglo-Scottish relations under Alexander II and III made such a treaty less necessary. However, the relationship between the two states deteriorated rapidly after the death of Alexander III (see Chapter 3), and it was not long before a French alliance was struck. This was the Treaty of Paris, signed in 1295 and ratified the next year— the first of many Franco-Scottish treaties, which marked the birth of the *Auld Alliance*.

The treaty was a mutual defence pact committing each side to come to the aid of the other in the event of war with England.[41] It was renewed by the Treaty of Corbeil in 1326, and the *Auld Alliance* was signed by every Scottish and French monarch (with the exception of Louis XI) from 1295 to the mid-sixteenth century. Its importance to Scotland cannot be underestimated,

FOUR NATIONS, FOUR STATES

and may still be relevant in the years to come, but it was also celebrated in France, as was made clear by a fifteenth-century French poet:

The *Auld Alliance* is not written on parchment in ink,
But engraved on the living flesh of man's skin in blood.[42]

3

THE RISE OF ENGLISH IMPERIALISM

The equilibrium established in the thirteenth century between England and the rest of the Hiberno-British Isles did not survive. It was not inherently unstable. However, even before the Norman conquest England had claimed to be *primus inter pares* and this was bound to cause problems in the long run. As the biggest of the four nations in terms of population, whilst enjoying strong trading links with continental Europe, it had the largest economy—and therefore potentially the most powerful military; and ecclesiastical privilege, established with the blessing of the papacy, had given Canterbury and York a claim over the nomination and consecration of bishops elsewhere.

All these claims to English primacy could be and, indeed, were disputed by leaders of the other three nation-states. Yet there was another factor after 1066, and that was the legacy of Norman imperialism. The Normans were addicted to conquest—not just in the Isles, but also in other parts of Europe and even the Middle East. Empire was in their blood, and they passed it on to the nobility ruling England alongside the Norman monarchs descended from William the Conqueror.[1]

67

INTERNAL EMPIRE

The Norman inheritance brought with it a poisonous legacy of prejudice in England towards the 'other'—in this case the Irish, Scots and Welsh. Writing c. 1130, Henry of Huntingdon had said, 'Britain, the noblest of islands, is now called England', thereby beginning a linguistic (and imperialist) tradition that exists to this day. Even more extraordinary was the appropriation of Arthur to the English cause, despite the fact that—as a Briton—he had been the Anglo-Saxons' mortal enemy. In the words of Rees Davies, this was 'the appropriation of the tales of a world-conquering hero, whose exploits were too wonderful to be reserved for the defeated Britons.'[2]

English imperialism in the Isles began with the conquest of Wales towards the end of the thirteenth century (the partial conquest of Ireland c. 1170 is best seen as a Norman project). This was followed by a long struggle to try and add Scotland to the English Empire. Attention then turned to the continent, with kings of England calling themselves kings of France from 1340 onwards—a practice that did not stop until 1801. By then Ireland had been an English colony for hundreds of years, as the English completed in the sixteenth and seventeenth centuries the colonial project begun by the Normans.

Wales

In their military campaigns in France, the English justified their actions through ancient claims, inheritance and treaty rights. However, they always considered their opponents to be equal in status. In the case of their fellow inhabitants of the Isles, it was different. The non-English inhabitants—including the nobility—were frequently referred to as 'savage', 'barbaric' and 'uncivilised'. Although the ferocity of the language had been toned down somewhat by the thirteenth century,[3] the damage had been done. And Wales would feel the full effect.

THE RISE OF ENGLISH IMPERIALISM

No one was more scathing of the Welsh than Gerald of Wales, whose father was Norman. Although born in Wales to a Welsh mother of royal blood, he soon left to complete his education elsewhere. Yet he was considered by the English as an authority on his native land and his two short books on Wales were very influential. Thus, when he wrote in harsh terms about his fellow countrymen (as he also did about the Irish) it had a damaging effect:[4]

> These people [the Welsh] are no less light in mind than in body and are by no means to be relied upon. They are easily urged to undertake any action, and are as easily checked from prosecuting it—a people quick in action, but more stubborn in a bad than in a good cause and constant only in acts of inconstancy. They pay no respect to oaths, faith or truth.

This literary bombardment prepared the ground for colonial aggression, in which English settlers would be distinguished from Welsh subjects.[5] And, unlike the conquest of Ireland, it would be a swift affair when it was eventually launched.

Henry III had acquired the area in Wales between the Rivers Conwy and Dee by the Treaty of Woodstock in 1247. He had then given it to his son, the future Edward I, who faced such strong Welsh opposition that Llywelyn ap Gruffydd was able to recapture it a decade later. This area, known as Perfeddwlad to the Welsh and the Four Cantrefs to the English, was then confirmed as part of Llywelyn's kingdom by the 1267 Treaty of Montgomery, which recognised Llywelyn and his descendants as Prince of Wales (see Chapter 2). Henry III abided by the treaty for the rest of his reign.

It might have been assumed that Edward, on becoming king in 1272, would do the same, and at first he did. However, Llywelyn married Eleanor, the exiled daughter of Simon de Montfort, by proxy in 1275. This was a risky move for relations with

INTERNAL EMPIRE

England, in view of de Montfort's fatal rebellion against Edward's father only a decade earlier. Simon may have been killed, but the memory of treason lived on. On her voyage to Wales from France, therefore, Edward hired pirates to capture Eleanor and demanded an explanation from the Prince of Wales—soon to be declared a rebel—for this perceived slight.

None was forthcoming, and by now Llywelyn was seriously in arrears on the debt promised to the King of England by the Treaty of Montgomery. Although new terms could easily have been agreed, Edward I used the unpaid debt as an excuse to invade in 1277, employing overwhelming military strength. At the Treaty of Aberconwy in the same year, Llywelyn was forced to accept humiliating terms, including the transfer of Perfeddwlad to his brother Dafydd as tenant-in-chief to the English crown, and loss of homage from most of the other Welsh rulers. His marriage to Eleanor then went ahead (in England) in the presence of Edward himself.

This was not yet an English colonisation of Wales, as previous kings of England had tried to achieve much the same without, in the long run, succeeding. However, this time there would be a different outcome. Rebellion by the Welsh soon ensued, driven in part by Edward's attempt to impose English law on those parts of Wales he now controlled. Although the uprising was initiated by his brother Dafydd, Llywelyn did not oppose it—Edward now had the excuse he needed to launch a colonial war.

The military campaign started in 1282 and was, by Welsh standards, unprecedented in scale. In addition to English troops, Edward's army consisted of knights and crossbowmen from Gascony as well as castle-builders from Savoy. There were also Welsh soldiers from those parts of Wales whose rulers were hostile to Llywelyn, as well as troops from the Marcher lordships that were nominally under royal control. Finally, Edward financed the campaign with the help of Italian banks.[6]

THE RISE OF ENGLISH IMPERIALISM

It would be easy to assume that such a large military force was guaranteed success. However, the English army did not have it all its own way and suffered, at first, a series of defeats. It was only when Llywelyn made the strategic error of leaving the safety of his heartland in north Wales that English fortunes changed. Llywelyn was ambushed in December 1282 and killed. He would now be known, for obvious reasons, as Llywelyn the Last. Although Dafydd assumed the title of Prince of Wales and continued the struggle, he himself was captured in June of the following year. The conquest of Wales was now complete, and Dafydd was executed in 1284.

A ring of steel, or more accurately of stone, would now be constructed across Wales to ensure that England's mainland colony was fully subjugated. Edward had already built two castles after the war of 1277. He would now build many more, giving responsibility for the work to Master James of St. George from Savoy. To ensure supplies in the face of future rebellions against English colonial rule, the fortresses were placed by the sea, and 'planned in conjunction with new towns which formed supporting English enclaves'.[7]

Almost all the Welsh rulers were deprived of their lands. The only exceptions were those who had thrown in their lot with Edward before the final conquest. Some of the confiscated land was then distributed to English nobles, but Edward kept most of it for himself. This was to be not just an imperial exercise, but a very personal one, and that required a colonial system of administration, in which local Welsh officials were answerable to provincial governors—who in turn owed loyalty to the king.

The key document in the transformation of Wales into an English colony was the Statute of Wales. Signed at Rhuddlan in 1284, it was a king's charter, as it would never be approved by the English parliament (it remained on the statute book until 1887, when it was finally repealed). Its opening paragraph revealed

71

INTERNAL EMPIRE

everything both about the absolutist nature of Edward I's rule and the scale of ambition in this colonial project:

> Edward, by the grace of God King of England, Lord of Ireland, and Duke of Aquitaine, to all his Subjects of his Land of Snowdon, and of other his Lands in Wales, Greeting in the Lord. The Divine Providence, which is unerring in its own Government, among other gifts of its Dispensation, wherewith it hath vouchsafed to distinguish Us and our Realm of England, hath now of its favour, *wholly and entirely transferred under our proper dominion, the Land of Wales with its Inhabitants,* heretofore subject unto us, in Feudal Right, all obstacles whatsoever ceasing. (Author's emphasis.)

The Statute of Wales then imposed on Wales the same administrative structure as in England, with counties, shires and sheriffs.[8] The laws of England were applied in criminal cases, with Welsh law—despite being protected by *Magna Carta*—now limited to civil cases only. Many of the counties were then surveyed to give the English king an accurate account of his colonial holdings. All that was left was to bring the Marcher lords to heel. This task, begun by Edward I, was advanced by his grandson Edward III, when a law was passed in 1354 requiring the Lords of the Marches of Wales to be 'attendant and annexed to the Crown of England and not to the Principality of Wales.' This reduced the semi-autonomous space occupied by the March hitherto.[9]

The Statute of Wales, together with the new towns near the coastal castles, opened Wales to English settlement. Settler colonialism in the south of Wales had been going on since the Norman conquest of England, and Henry I had even encouraged immigration by Flemish families in the lands he controlled. However, Edward's conquest opened the door for a new wave of immigrants, who this time would be overwhelmingly

THE RISE OF ENGLISH IMPERIALISM

English. And, as always, the settlers expected and received special treatment within Wales. By statute it was eventually decreed that no Welshman could purchase lands in England, nor in the 'English towns of Wales'; no Englishman could be convicted by Welshmen; and no Welshman was to be armed, 'nor bear defencible armour to Merchant Towns, Churches or Congregations'.[10]

The most draconian restrictions on the Welsh were introduced in response to rebellion. Yet it was the restrictions themselves that often provoked rebellion in the first place. We may perhaps dismiss the revolt of Rhys ap Maredudd in 1287, as this was primarily a dispute between nobles. However, the uprisings throughout Wales in 1294–5 were due in large part to the system of levies imposed by the new colonial authorities a few years before. Having, in 1290, expelled the Jews (a major source of lending to the king), Edward approached parliament for funds to finance his recent military campaign in Gascony.[11] Having initially intended to raise the money from England alone, he changed his mind in 1291 and sent a request 'to the earls, barons, knights, free men and whole commonality of Wales'.

The rebellions of 1316–17 probably owed a great deal to the economic hardship that affected much of northern Europe at that time, leading to a drop in population everywhere. Although we have no hard data, depopulation may in fact have started in Wales even earlier, as a result of the large numbers of young men taken by Edward I for his military campaigns elsewhere. However, the Black Death pandemic, which reached Wales in 1349, was the main factor behind a fall in population—from around 300,000 at the time of the Edwardian conquest in the 1280s to 200,000 by the end of the 1300s. And yet, despite such a demographic disaster, this was in fact the moment when the most spectacular Welsh rebellion against English colonial rule was launched.

73

INTERNAL EMPIRE

The revolt, also known as the Last War of Independence, had a most improbable origin. Owain ap Gruffydd (later known as Owain Glyndŵr) was an Anglo-Welsh landowner who had fallen into a dispute with one of his English neighbours. He had also benefited greatly from the patronage in Wales of Richard II. When Richard was deposed in 1399, Owain launched a revolt backed by a small number of followers and one Welsh bishop. This was hardly a promising beginning for a national revolt, yet it succeeded brilliantly, as resentment in Wales against English rule was now widespread.

The military campaign went from strength to strength, in no small part as a result of the help given by the Tewdwr family in Anglesey, which had—like Owain himself—benefited greatly from the patronage of Richard II. By 1405 Owain Glyndŵr had declared himself Prince of Wales; called a Welsh parliament; and outlined his plans for a church separate from England, the establishment of two universities and a return to Welsh law for both civil and criminal cases. In addition, he had negotiated a formal treaty between Wales and France for mutual defence.

This would be the high point. Starting in 1406, the English military strategy changed under the direction of Henry IV's son (the future Henry V). Owain Glyndŵr was never defeated, but his kingdom had crumbled by 1412. France did not provide the support that had been promised and defections in Owain's own ranks became a major problem. He was forced to lead the life of a fugitive, but he was never betrayed, captured or killed. Indeed, the date and circumstances of his death (perhaps in 1416) remain shrouded in mystery.[12]

The colony of Wales would now be subject to a form of collective punishment by England. No Welshman could be made 'Justice, Chamberlain, Chancellor, Treasurer, Sheriff, Steward, Constable of Castle, Receiver, Escheatour, Coroner nor Chief Foresters nor other officer, nor Keeper of the Records, nor

74

THE RISE OF ENGLISH IMPERIALISM

Lieutenant in any of the said offices in no part of Wales, nor of the Council of any English Lord.' Nor could any Englishman married to a Welsh woman of the 'amity and alliance' of Owain hold office. And, to rub salt in the wound, any goods re-exported to England from Wales without paying English customs duties would be seized without compensation.

Despite these draconian measures, a Welsh nation survived. This was due above all to the durability of the Welsh language, which continued to be the medium of communication for the vast majority. It was also helped by the survival of Welsh law for the trial of civil cases. And, of course, by the end of the fifteenth century a member of the house of Tewdwr—now calling himself Tudor—had seized the English throne, putting a scion of the Anglo-Welsh nobility on the throne of England (Henry VII) and giving the nation of Wales the chance to have its voice heard at court.

Ireland

The colonisation of Wales had been swift and affected the whole country immediately. The colonisation of Ireland, by contrast, was slow and piecemeal. It had begun a century after William I's conquest of England, as a result of Norman opportunism in response to treachery by an Irish leader; but the Treaty of Windsor in 1175 only secured direct royal control over a relatively small part of Ireland. Even this area shrank in the next 350 years, as the English royal presence in Ireland found itself largely confined to the Pale in and around Dublin. Kings of England, it would seem, had other priorities than the full colonisation of Ireland.

What did expand in Ireland was the territory controlled by the Norman, soon to be English, lords. Under the Treaty of Windsor, these nobles were supposed to recognise the overlordship of the King of England for their territories in Leinster, Munster and

INTERNAL EMPIRE

elsewhere. However, the lack of attention by almost all English kings in their role as Lord of Ireland (after King John, only Richard II bothered to visit) meant that the English lords had a relatively free hand to pursue their own agendas, and could ignore most of the directives emanating from royal officials and the colonial Irish parliament in Dublin.

Gradually, an Anglo-Irish (known as 'Old English') society developed among the lands controlled by these nobles; but it was not an English colony in the usual sense, as it was not subject to much—if any—royal control. Nor was it particularly successful. The Black Death in the mid-fourteenth century took the same dreadful toll on the Irish population as on the rest of Europe, but when wages subsequently climbed in England due to the inevitable labour shortage, there was a flow of migration *from* Ireland—the exact opposite of what a successful colonisation scheme required. This depleted the fiscal resources available both to the English king as Lord of Ireland and to the Anglo-Irish nobles.

Only those with vast estates were now willing to take official positions, since the rewards were so small. One such family were the Kildares, whose earldom in Ireland had been created in 1316. They became the king's representative from 1470, holding the office of Lord Deputy, despite the fiscal impecunity of the crown at the time. Indeed, royal receipts in Ireland at the end of the fifteenth century could only be levied in the Pale, Waterford and Wexford. They averaged £1,000 per year, whereas in the time of Edward I they had reached £6,000.[13]

Kings of England may have claimed the Lordship of Ireland, but the island was quite different from colonial Wales after the Edwardian conquest. Instead, it was a society in which Irish chiefs, Anglo-Irish lords and royal officials competed for land, power and very limited resources, with frontiers that constantly shifted. Robin Frame put it well when he wrote:

76

THE RISE OF ENGLISH IMPERIALISM

Once we give a proper prominence to Anglo-Ireland's frontier character and fragmentation, the history of the Lordship looks different. It is no longer sufficient to see as its main theme the Dublin government's failure to defend it against the Irish reconquest of its more lightly settled parts. Colonial Ireland was a collection of pockets of land separated by natural features and areas of Irish supremacy. Without substantial additional immigration and a sustained royal presence—both of which were inconceivable in the later middle ages—it could only be maintained through a wide dispersal of power.[14]

All this started to change after the ascent to the English throne of the first Tudor king, the Anglo-Welsh Henry VII. Gerald FitzGerald, the eighth Earl of Kildare, had supported a rebellion against Henry in 1487—only two years after the latter's victory at the Battle of Bosworth Field. Although the earl was later pardoned, England's laissez-faire approach to colonial affairs in Ireland was about to end. A trusted English noble, Sir Edmund Poynings, was appointed Lord Deputy of Ireland, and its legislative body was made subject to the English parliament in 1495. Specifically, under Poynings' Law, an Irish parliament:

> Could not be convened without prior licence from the English monarch and council. In order to obtain such a licence, an Irish chief governor and council had first to certify into England, under the great seal of Ireland, the causes and considerations for calling parliament, along with all bills to be enacted in that parliament. If the causes and considerations were deemed valid, some or all of the bills, along with the monarch's licence for holding parliament, would be transmitted back to Ireland under the great seal of England.[15]

And, just to reinforce the colonial nature of Poynings' Law, the same Irish parliament in Dublin ruled that existing English statutes applied to Ireland, while later it was made explicit that

INTERNAL EMPIRE

the English monarch and council had the power to amend or reject any bills sent from Ireland.

Poynings returned to England in 1496, his work seemingly complete. Yet it soon became apparent that little had changed in the Lordship of Ireland—and nothing at all in 'free' Ireland. The Kildare family, despite their lack of loyalty to the Tudor crown, were still allowed to operate in the parts they controlled in the usual way and the Lordship of Ireland remained a drain on the English exchequer. Henry VII did consider a full-scale invasion in 1507 to colonise the whole island, but died two years later before this could be carried out.

His son, Henry VIII, was at first equally unenthusiastic about colonial exploits in Ireland. However, his break with the papacy over his marital affairs in 1533 completely changed the status quo: England's legal justification for invading Ireland had originally been provided by papal authorisation, and there was no certainty that the Anglo-Irish community, yet alone the Irish themselves, would transfer their loyalty to the new state religion. Henry therefore moved swiftly and recalled Gerald FitzGerald, the ninth Earl of Kildare, to London. FitzGerald's son, known to history as Silken Thomas, launched a rebellion in 1534 after declaring Henry to be a heretic. The rebellion was defeated and Kildare authority in Ireland finally destroyed.

English forces now moved into the vacuum and established the crown's direct rule in the Lordship. However, they also tried to push English authority into lands still held by Irish chiefs—a sure sign that the whole island of Ireland was about to become England's colony. And, to make sure there was no misunderstanding, in 1542 the Irish parliament ended the Lordship and declared Henry to be King of Ireland—a move also intended to signal that England's colonisation of Ireland was no longer dependent on papal goodwill.

The driving force behind Henry's Irish policy was Sir Anthony St. Leger. Appointed Lord Deputy of Ireland in 1540, having

THE RISE OF ENGLISH IMPERIALISM

already carried out a commission of inquiry into conditions on the island, he developed a policy that came nearly 400 years later to be known as 'surrender and regrant.'[16] The purpose of the policy, which had already been tried with some success in the 1530s, was to secure the peaceful subjection of the Irish chiefs (and the more recalcitrant Anglo-Irish nobles) to the English crown. In return for surrendering their clan territory, the chiefs would be restored to ownership and receive aristocratic titles— on condition that they renounce the authority of the Pope and accept the English monarch as Supreme Head of the Church of Ireland; accept English law (including primogeniture); speak and dress as English subjects; and pay rent for the 'regranted' lands.

'Surrender and regrant' was a highly sophisticated system of official bribery. At a stroke, the policy extended English colonialism to the whole island of Ireland without the need for a military campaign, while at the same time providing a flow of revenue to the exchequer, reducing the risk of papal intervention and creating a much-enlarged constituency of English subjects. Not surprisingly, it proved attractive to many Irish chiefs and to Anglo-Irish leaders, who now found themselves in either the Irish or the English House of Lords with grand titles. The arrangement even survived the transition from the Protestant Edward VI (son of Henry VIII) to his Catholic sister Mary I.

Despite its sophistication, 'surrender and regrant' had within it the seeds of its own destruction. Many Irish chiefs and some Anglo-Irish nobles were content to observe the formalities without changing customary behaviour within their territories. Others were not prepared to renounce the Catholic Church and the authority of the Pope. Last, but not least, English laws of inheritance were so different from Irish ones that disputes soon arose over the transfer of lands on the death of the previous owner. In a few cases, these erupted into rebellions against the crown, such as in Munster—revolts that could quickly acquire a

INTERNAL EMPIRE

religious character after the Pope's excommunication of Protestant Queen Elizabeth I, who succeeded Mary in 1558.

Faced with this dangerous situation, English policy towards Ireland changed in favour of settler colonialism. The principal architect of this new policy was the poet Edmund Spenser, whose *View of the State of Ireland* used the language of bigotry to argue for a different approach:[17]

> So were these people [the Irish] at first well handled, and wisely brought to acknowledge allegiance to the Kings of England ... but, being straight left unto themselves and their own inordinate life and manners, they eftsoones forgot what before they were taught, and so soone as they were out of sight, by themselves shook of their bridles, and beganne to colte anew, more licentiously than before.

Spenser's proposal of settler colonialism, already tried in a small way in Leinster by Edward VI and Mary I, would now be adopted aggressively in Munster after a second rebellion (1579–83) had been brutally crushed. Large-scale plantations (including one awarded to Spenser himself) were designed to attract English settlers and recreate English pastoral conditions. The largest estate was given to a favourite of Queen Elizabeth, Sir Walter Raleigh, and yet the policy in the end failed. It could not attract sufficient Protestant settlers from England, leaving much of the labour in Munster to be provided by the Irish and Anglo-Irish—most of whom were still Catholic.

The next target of settler colonialism was Ulster. This was a much more ambitious project that intended to saturate the province with Protestant migrants and segregate them from the native Irish—through expulsion if necessary. It required huge amounts of land to make it feasible. Expropriation of existing landholders without compensation was normally only possible in the case of treason through rebellion, so progress was at first

THE RISE OF ENGLISH IMPERIALISM

slow. However, it was sufficiently fast to alienate Hugh O'Neill, Earl of Tyrone, who had acted as Elizabeth's proxy in Ulster for many years. In the 1590s, with support from Catholic Spain, he launched a rebellion that acquired overtones of a struggle for national independence. In the end, however, he was defeated; and in 1607 he left Ireland with other Irish chiefs in what became known as the Flight of the Earls.

The end of the rebellion provided England with the land it needed in Ulster, now divided into nine counties on the English model. Yet progress in attracting settlers was still slow until an agreement was reached in 1610 with the guilds of London. The city of Londonderry would now be established on top of the old monastic settlement at Derry and the English government could proceed rapidly with its project of settler colonialism. This time, however, Ulster oversaw increasing migration not just from England. Ulster also experienced rapid migration from Scotland, many of the incomers being Presbyterians whose King (James VI) had become James I of England in 1603.[18]

By 1640 there were an estimated 40,000 settlers in Ulster.[19] At this point, however, Ireland was about to be caught up in the English Civil War and the corresponding turmoil in Scotland. An Irish Confederacy was hastily assembled, not so much to fight for national independence, but more to defend Catholicism from what was (correctly) seen as religious discrimination by its opponents. Atrocities were committed, especially in Ulster, where their memory has been kept alive by the Protestant community to this day. Yet the revenge exacted against the Confederacy and its Irish Catholic supporters was far more ferocious than the atrocities themselves.

The instrument of revenge was Oliver Cromwell, the victor in the English Civil War and ruler of England from 1649.[20] Cromwell's barbaric campaign in Ireland starting in that year is well known—especially the massacre at Drogheda.[21] Yet Cromwell

INTERNAL EMPIRE

was driven not merely by hatred of Catholicism, but above all by the desire to complete the English colonisation of Ireland. An Act of Settlement was therefore passed in 1652 that expropriated most of the land still held by Catholics, reducing it to some 10 per cent of the total by the time Cromwell died in 1658. The main beneficiaries were a class of landholders, perhaps no more than 5,000 families, that created the Protestant Ascendancy in Ireland.

Ireland now belonged to England. Resistance had been crushed and much of the land distributed to loyal Protestant settlers. The population may have remained predominantly Catholic, but the Irish language was decreasing in importance and the island was becoming an attractive destination for England's expanding population. In the light of realpolitik, Spain's hopes faded of forging an alliance with native Irish and/or Anglo-Irish leaders to drive the 'new' English out of Ireland and restore Catholicism in Britain. In any case, Spain now had other priorities—especially after the restoration of Charles II as King of England in 1660.

Yet there would soon be another twist in the long saga of Anglo-Irish relations. Charles I's son, the future James II, had deep Catholic sympathies. Although his daughter by his first marriage (Mary) had been raised as a Protestant and married into the anti-Catholic House of Orange in the Netherlands, James had married again and this time his wife was Catholic. When the couple produced a son and heir, the stage was set for an English coup, in which James was driven from the throne of England by a Dutch invasion in 1688. Mary and her husband, William of Orange, became joint monarchs in his place.[22]

James, of course, had been crowned King of Ireland—not just England—and so confrontation loomed. Landing in Ireland in 1689, he quickly gathered a multinational force to his cause, while also enjoying at first the overwhelming support of Irish Catholics. His defeat at the Battle of the Boyne, and later Aughrim, led to the Treaty of Limerick in 1691, which—to the

THE RISE OF ENGLISH IMPERIALISM

surprise of many—suggested the victors favoured reconciliation and religious tolerance. Article I stated:

> The Roman Catholics of this kingdom shall enjoy such privileges in the exercise of their religion as are consistent with the laws of Ireland, or as they did enjoy in the reign of king Charles the second: and their majesties [William and Mary], as soon as their affairs will permit them to summon a parliament in this kingdom, will endeavour to procure the said Roman Catholics such farther security in that particular, as may preserve them from any disturbance upon the account of their said religion.

These were far-sighted words, but there were too many ambiguities in the treaty, and these were ruthlessly exploited by the anti-Catholic decision-makers on the island of Ireland. Within a few years, Irish Catholics were subject through the penal code to a degree of legalised discrimination more extreme than anything that had gone before.

Irish resistance to English colonisation had been effectively broken by the end of the reign of Queen Elizabeth I— the rebellions in the seventeenth century were not wars of independence. A unified Irish state had been undermined even earlier, starting with the Treaty of Windsor. Yet an Irish nation somehow survived these disasters and, despite the withering of the native language, nationalism gained in strength after the Treaty of Limerick, driven by a burning sense of injustice and a strong memory of history. Like Wales, therefore, Ireland had avoided the fate of many other kingdoms in Europe, where nationalism had been eclipsed after colonisation.

Scotland

During the long reign of Henry III of England (1216–72), Alexander II and Alexander III of Scotland had managed to put

INTERNAL EMPIRE

Anglo-Scottish relations on an equitable and amicable basis, and this looked set to continue under Edward I after Henry died. Alexander III had even married one of Henry's daughters, so that Edward was his brother-in-law. Although the royal couple's children all died before Alexander's own death in 1286, there was at least an infant grandchild—Margaret—who was the offspring of one of Alexander's daughters and Eric II of Norway.

There was therefore no reason for Scotland to fear the worst as the child Margaret, the 'Maid of Norway', set sail for her native land in 1290. By then Scottish affairs had been for four years in the hands of the Guardians, six members of the Scottish elite who had signed the Treaty of Birgham with England, which stipulated—among other things—that the Maid should in due course marry Edward I's son. This proposed union was typical of medieval statecraft and (after Edward's death) would have left England and Scotland with the same royal couple in power, but ruling over separate kingdoms. In particular, the treaty specified that Scotland was to remain 'separate and divided from England according to its rightful boundaries.'

Tragically, Margaret died in Orkney (still in Norwegian hands) on her way to Scotland. This created a succession crisis, as there was no longer a direct heir in Scotland. Instead, there were thirteen male candidates known as the Competitors, each of whom had varying degrees of claim to the throne. However, only four of these had a serious chance and, in the end, the choice came down to just two: John Balliol and Robert de Brus.

The Guardians struggled with the choice of Balliol or de Brus, and asked Edward I to adjudicate. This in itself was not necessarily controversial, as succession crises were common in medieval Europe and it was standard practice to ask a leading foreign personality—sometimes the Pope, sometimes a monarch—to intervene. However, the choice of Edward was disastrous—especially in view of England's colonisation of Wales

84

THE RISE OF ENGLISH IMPERIALISM

just a few years before. Edward insisted that the Competitors recognise his overlordship before undertaking the request and gave them only three weeks to accept. A panel of 104 arbiters was then set up—forty each for de Brus and Balliol, plus twenty-four from the arbiters' English council.

The ruling Guardians, unlike the Competitors, had previously refused to accept Edward's claim to overlordship, arguing that it applied only to the English lands held by Scottish kings. But de Brus and Balliol had little choice.[23] When the arbiters chose John Balliol in late 1292, the English king was then in a position to impose his own terms. King John of Scotland was immediately forced to pay homage in England and acknowledge Edward as the sovereign lord of the realm of Scotland. Other humiliations quickly followed.

Balliol was allowed to continue with the title of King of Scotland, but the Scottish nobility had now sensed the dangers from English imperialism. A parliament held in July 1295 put the real power back in the hands of a new Guardianship, leading to the alliance with France under the Treaty of Paris in the same year (see Chapter 2). Conflict with England was now inevitable, and started in 1296. The Scottish army, which had last fought a war in 1263 against Norway, was no match for England's battle-hardened troops; within a few months, Scotland had become in effect a colony of England. It would in due course be declared a Lordship—like Ireland and Wales. John Balliol was ritually stripped of his royal trappings—and so his regal status—at Montrose Castle. As a result of this insult, normally reserved for traitors, John Balliol would later be known by the Scots as Toom Tabard (Empty Jacket). He left Scotland permanently.[24]

The Scots were now obliged to fight an anti-colonial war against England or lose their independence. They had much more success than Ireland or Wales, although the final outcome was by no means clear for many decades. The episodes and characters

85

INTERNAL EMPIRE

from this long contest—called the Wars of Independence—
are well known to contemporary readers thanks to paintings,
books, poems and films, although historical accuracy has usually
been sacrificed in the process of creating Scottish heroes. Yet
there *was* something epic about the contest, which helped to
consolidate the nation-state of Scotland and gave the country a
compelling national myth—something without which no nation
can properly function.

The victory of William Wallace at the Battle of Stirling Bridge
in 1297, and his subsequent sole Guardianship of Scotland the
following year, paved the way—despite numerous setbacks—for
Robert Bruce (grandson of Robert de Brus) to become King
of Scotland in 1306. Forced into exile almost immediately, he
gradually recovered the military initiative, and his defeat of
Edward II's army at Bannockburn in 1314 was a major victory.
(Edward even lost his court poet, who was forced to compose
victory verses for the Scots.)[25] Yet this was not sufficiently
decisive to end the colonial war, and the Scots were soon under
pressure from the papacy to reach a truce with England. Indeed,
so determined was Pope John XXII to end the conflict between
two Christian states that he excommunicated King Robert and
three of his nobles.

It was at this moment that Scotland's leaders produced one
of the most remarkable documents of the medieval period.
Sent to the Pope in 1320 to persuade him to change his
mind, the Declaration of Arbroath was not just a statement of
independence but also a constitutional document setting out the
limits of kingship:

> From these countless evils [committed by England] we have been
> set free ... by our most tireless prince, King and lord, the lord
> Robert ... Yet if he should give up what he has begun, seeking to
> make us or our kingdom subject to the King of England or the
> English, we should exert ourselves at once to drive him out as

THE RISE OF ENGLISH IMPERIALISM

our enemy and a subverter of his own right and ours, and make some other man who was well able to defend us our King; for, as long as a hundred of us remain alive, never will we on any conditions be subjected to the lordship of the English.

These powerful words had the desired effect on the papacy. A truce was agreed with England in 1323 and, five years later, following the coronation of Edward III, an Anglo-Scottish treaty was ratified by both sides, providing for the marriage of David (Robert's son) and Joan (Edward's sister). This was supposed to end hostilities forever between the two kingdoms, but there was a catch:

> The said kings, their heirs and successors, shall be good friends and loyal allies, and the one shall aid the other in suitable manner as good allies: *saving on the part of the king of Scotland the alliance made between him and the king of France.* But if it happen that the said king of Scotland ... by reason of the said alliance or for any cause whatever make war upon the said king of England ... that the said king of England may make war on the foresaid king of Scotland. (Author's emphasis.)

Given the renewal of the *Auld Alliance* between France and Scotland only two years before these words were written (see Chapter 2), the prospect of permanent peace between England and Scotland was therefore remote. This was especially true after Robert I died in 1329, leaving his 5-year-old son to inherit the throne as David II.

The English strategy initially was to enable a pliant king to secure the throne of Scotland, thus avoiding the formal charge of breaking the treaty. The chosen candidate was Edward Balliol, son of John Balliol, who did indeed secure the Scottish throne in 1332 and promptly not only swore homage to the King of England, but also gave permission for England to annex southern Scotland 'in all time coming.'[26] The following

87

year, Edward III threw off all pretence at neutrality and Balliol was allowed to rule Scotland north of the Forth as a puppet king, while Lothian in the south was subjected to total war by the English army.

Balliol's rule as a proxy for Edward III was unsustainable, not least because it was opposed by France. His forces were defeated by Scottish patriots at the Battle of Culblean in 1335. This prompted English invasions in support of their client, leading to retaliatory raids into England by Scottish forces. At the Battle of Neville's Cross in 1346, David was captured and held prisoner. Balliol made another attempt to recover the throne, but—as an English puppet—lacked sufficient support among the Scots. This, together with the demographic disaster of the Black Death and English embroilment in war with France, led to a gradual reappraisal by Edward III of England's interests.

The result was the Treaty of Berwick, signed in 1357, under which David—now in his 30s but still childless—agreed to name Edward his successor as King of Scotland, and to pay a huge ransom for his own release, over a period of ten years. The Scottish parliament agreed in principle to the ransom (although only two instalments were actually paid), but rejected outright the English king's claim to the throne. Thus, when David died in 1371, to be replaced by his nephew as Robert II (the first king from the House of Stewart), English imperial ambitions towards Scotland were left unfulfilled.

The root of these ambitions was an English claim to suzerainty over Scotland based on mythology. It was Geoffrey of Monmouth, a Welsh cleric with a gift for tall tales, who had sketched out the foundation myth of Britain in his *Historia Regum Britanniae*, written c. 1136. The Trojan Brutus, it was said, had established the kingdom of Britain and, on his death, given England to his oldest son, while Scotland and Wales were ruled by younger offspring. This gave England, according to later

THE RISE OF ENGLISH IMPERIALISM

English writers, a special status, 'confirmed' by the numerous occasions on which Scottish kings had done homage to their English counterparts.

However absurd this story may sound to modern ears, it was taken very seriously in medieval England. Edward I had been the first English king formally to exploit this myth, and its associated claim to overlordship, to justify invading Scotland. Robert I and his son David II had then responded through military campaigns to safeguard Scottish independence. The House of Stewart, whose eight kings and one queen ruled Scotland until the union of the two crowns in 1603, would have to confront the same English threats. Henry IV, for example, demanded homage of Robert III (the son of Robert II) in 1401, while Henry VIII claimed as late as 1542 that no king 'hath more iuste title, more evident title, more certayn title, to any realme ... than we have to Scotland.'[27]

During the centuries of Stewart rule, the English would try military force, muscular diplomacy, marriage and kidnapping to back up their claims. Yet, if the tactics differed, the strategy was always the same: to place Scotland in a subordinate position in its relationship with England, and thus consolidate English imperialism in Britain and Ireland. And, until the sixteenth century, the instability of Scottish politics, coupled with demographic stagnation and economic weakness, gave England reason to think that its methods would succeed.

The English came close on a number of occasions in the fourteenth and fifteenth centuries, but their own difficulties—especially the Hundred Years' War with France (1337–1453) and the civil Wars of the Roses (1455–87)—thwarted their efforts. It was not, therefore, until the reign of the Tudors that a more strategic approach to Scottish affairs could be taken. Henry VII duly arranged for his daughter Margaret to marry James IV of Scotland as part of the Treaty of Perpetual Peace in 1502.

INTERNAL EMPIRE

In response to the concerns of members of the English Privy Council that this could mean a Scot inheriting the throne of England, Henry replied: 'What then? Should anything of the kind happen (and God avert the omen), I foresee that our realm would suffer no harm, since England would not be absorbed by Scotland, but rather Scotland by England, being the noblest head of the entire island.'[28]

In the end, it was not Margaret and James but Margaret's brother, Henry VIII, who inherited the English throne. And it was Henry's break with the papacy in 1533 that gave greater impetus to England's imperial ambitions towards Scotland. This was because the House of Stewart had remained loyal to Catholicism despite the growth of Protestantism among the Scottish population; England could ill afford to have a rival Catholic kingdom, in alliance with France, on its borders.

Henry had waged war on Scotland early in his reign and won a victory at Flodden Field in which James IV of Scotland had been killed. However, this had been part of an intra-European power struggle, in which Scotland had come to the aid of its French ally while Henry was on the continent fighting for the Pope. It was therefore not of great consequence in terms of relations between Scotland and England. It was the next battle, in 1542, that was much more significant, as Henry VIII saw an opportunity to achieve through a marriage alliance what his father had tried to do in 1502.

This battle (Solway Moss) led to the defeat of Scotland, whose King James V would die within a few weeks—leaving behind an infant daughter, Mary, who was only 6 days old. The prospect that the child would become Queen of Scotland inspired Henry in 1543 to propose to the Scottish regent the Treaties of Greenwich, under which Mary would marry Henry's own son and heir apparent, the future Edward VI. Article 4 of the second treaty specified: 'Within a month after she completes her tenth

THE RISE OF ENGLISH IMPERIALISM

year she shall be delivered to commissioners of England at the bounds of Berwick, provided that before her departure from Scotland the contract has been duly made by proxy.'

The Scottish parliament, faced with the prospect of their future monarch growing up as a Protestant in the Tudor court, taught by English teachers, naturally rejected the treaty and quickly crowned Mary as Queen of Scotland. Henry VIII now had to resort to more muscular tactics known euphemistically as the 'Rough Wooing'. In truth, this was little more than imperial bullying on an industrial scale, which included the last pitched battle between England and Scotland. Yet the victory of England at the Battle of Pinkie in 1547 did not achieve its purpose, as Queen Mary—still a child—was soon sent to France, where she married the dauphin a few years later.

Mary Stuart (the spelling of the surname would now change from Stewart) would be widowed in 1560, and her infant child by her next husband, a Scot, would become James VI of Scotland after she was forced to abdicate in 1567. Her tragic death at the hands of her cousin, Queen Elizabeth I of England, is well known and seemed to mark a nadir in relations between the two kingdoms. And yet James, raised as a Protestant in Scotland, would become King James I of England on the death of Elizabeth in 1603. The two crowns were now united in one person, but Henry VII's prophecy would largely be fulfilled. James would spend almost his entire reign in England, returning only once to Scotland, despite his promise to return every three years.

James had hoped to establish a political union of the two kingdoms, but faced overwhelming resistance in England. His son, Charles I, favoured religious reform, which ran into such opposition in Scotland that a National Covenant was signed in 1638 to resist change.[29] The conflict soon turned violent and the Covenanters seized power in Scotland. When the English Civil War erupted in 1642, the Covenanters threw in their lot with the

INTERNAL EMPIRE

English parliamentarians. However, by 1645, Scottish influence in England was in serious decline. When Charles was executed in January 1649, the Scottish parliament chose to recognise his son as King of Scotland, England and Ireland. He was crowned at Scotland's Scone Abbey in 1651 as Charles II, paving the way for an English invasion.

Oliver Cromwell's successful military expedition against Scotland then turned it into a colony of England. Scotland was incorporated into 'the free state and Commonwealth of England'. Although it was described as a union, formalised in the English parliament's *Tender of Union* declaration, it was no such thing. The union of the crowns had therefore ended in disaster for Scotland, with only thirty seats reserved in the Westminster parliament (and half of those taken by English army officers)— although it did briefly enjoy free trade with England before the restoration of Charles II to the English throne in 1660. The imperialist campaign starting with Edward I at the end of the thirteenth century had now brought about the long-desired subordination of Scotland by England.

Gascony

Despite the loss of Normandy and other continental possessions in 1204, English rulers still dreamt of capturing territory in France—this time with England as the imperial power. England had become a Norman colony after 1066 and, while the relationship had become less 'colonial' in the following century, it must have been a considerable shock after 1204 to find the 'mother' country under the control of a rival power. England would now compete with France for centuries to build an empire, not only on the continent but also in the rest of the world. It was, and is, an imperial rivalry that has still not been forgotten by either side.

THE RISE OF ENGLISH IMPERIALISM

Where was England to start? The Anglo-French Treaty of Paris, ratified in 1259, confirmed the loss of Normandy, Anjou and Poitou, leaving England with a much-diminished status. However, England was not entirely driven out of the continent, as there was one possession that England was allowed to keep. This was Aquitaine, excluding Poitou and other parts of the province ceded to France under the treaty, which obliged the English king (then Henry III) to do homage to the French king (Louis IX) for the territory he retained.

Henry's grandfather, Henry II, had married Eleanor of Aquitaine—the former wife of the King of France— in 1152, and had acquired the vast principality of Aquitaine as a result. Although Duke of Normandy from 1150, Henry II did not become King of England until 1154. Thus, Aquitaine was a personal fiefdom by virtue of his marriage to Eleanor, and not an English colony.[30] That changed after 1204, when King John—son of Henry II, father of Henry III—found himself stripped of his other territories in France, yet left in possession of the most remote part of Aquitaine north of the Pyrenees. This land, Gascony, was virtually autonomous, as neither Spain nor France—yet alone England—had had any real control over it since the breakup of Charlemagne's empire in the ninth century.

To retain Gascony after 1204, in the face of continuing French hostility, had required the appointment of English officials to the top positions, as well as expenditure on the territory's defence. To offset the cost, Gascony was then subject to a considerable tax burden, while some estates were awarded to English nobles from whom additional funds could be obtained. Those resources, in turn, would be used not just to fund military campaigns in Gascony, but also to fund English wars in the Isles. Gascony therefore had become an overseas colony of England, albeit without many English settlers: a dependent territory subject to the priorities of the English state.[31]

INTERNAL EMPIRE

Since it included Bordeaux, with its profitable wine trade, Gascony was a prized possession, and the royal descendants of Henry II expended considerable efforts to retain it in the face of opposition from France and occasional revolts by the Gascons. Henry III, for example, appointed Simon de Montfort as Gascony's lieutenant in 1248 and it took him four years to end what was in effect an anti-colonial rebellion. De Montfort's military campaign succeeded, but at a terrible cost due to the violent methods used; he had to be recalled to defend his actions.

Confirmation in the 1259 Treaty of Paris that Gascony would remain an English colony, provided that homage was paid to the French king, brought a temporary measure of security— although the definition of 'Gascony' would now include some parts of Aquitaine whose nobles were hostile to English governance, due to their traditional allegiance to France. English colonial rule now embodied two strands that would become familiar in future in other parts of the world: subjugation of the native rulers, and competition with rival imperial powers for control of the same territory.

The problems of colonial rule in Gascony after the Treaty of Paris were eased at first by the phenomenal growth of the wine trade centred on Bordeaux. This boom extended to shipbuilding in Bayonne and related activities in other towns. A constituency therefore started to develop among some Gascons that favoured English rule, easing administration of the colony. Economic growth and trade then brought increased tax revenues, making England more determined than ever to hang on to this overseas possession—despite the fact that 'Gascony' was steadily shrinking in size, as France succeeded in chipping away at those parts that had traditionally been loyal to the French kings.

As the prosperity of Gascony increased, French opposition to English rule hardened, while English resentment at the need to pay homage for Gascony became more intense—especially as

THE RISE OF ENGLISH IMPERIALISM

Gascons had the right of appeal to the King of France in the case of disputes with English officials. Tensions between England and France steadily mounted and were made more acute by a claim to the French throne put forward by Edward III, on the death (without children) of Charles IV in 1328. Edward's claim was rejected by the French nobles, but the memory lingered, and the new French king (Philip VI) announced in May 1337 that Gascony would be taken back under French rule—by force if necessary. Edward III had no intention of allowing the colony to be given up without a fight, and hostilities commenced.

This was the start of the long conflict with France that came to be known as the Hundred Years' War. Imperial rule in Gascony therefore dragged England into a conflict that it was bound to lose in the long run. The wealth and military strength of France, coupled with the logistical advantage conferred by geography, were always going to make it impossible for England to retain a permanent presence on the continent.

Despite this, the Hundred Years' War started badly for France. Within a few years the kingdom's population had declined by perhaps 50 per cent as a result of the Black Death—an even sharper fall than in England. Military conflicts, especially under the stewardship of Edward III's son (the Black Prince), favoured England; in the Treaty of Brétigny of 1360, the King of France not only acknowledged Gascony as an English possession outright, but also transferred to England some previously English-held territories, such as Poitou.

The new possessions would soon be lost, but once again England retained Gascony. Its population might have shrunk dramatically (it was estimated at 150,000 in 1414, compared with about 600,000 a century before),[32] but it was still considered an imperial possession worth defending. And England was about to enjoy its greatest successes in the Hundred Years' War, raising the real prospect of winning other continental possessions at the

INTERNAL EMPIRE

expense of the French state, even if the kingship of France itself proved to be elusive.[33]

These ambitions ended in 1453 with English defeat at the Battle of Castillon in Gascony, terminating the Hundred Years' War and leaving England in possession only of the Pale of Calais (finally lost to France in 1558). Gascony ceased to be an English colony, although cultural ties survived for many years. The trade ties between England and Bordeaux also continued, but this time the taxes on wine and other exports went to the French state.

Gascony had been an imperial adventure undertaken by England alone, although some Welsh troops had been involved after Wales had become an English colony in 1284, and Anglo-Irish soldiers took part in some campaigns. Not only was it almost exclusively an English endeavour, but in many battles during the Hundred Years' War Scots had fought on the French side, so that victories for England were defeats for Scotland and vice versa. Thus, the Hundred Years' War today is seen in a very different light north versus south of the Anglo-Scottish border.

The loss of Gascony might have signalled the end of England's overseas empire, confining her colonial ambitions to the Hiberno-British Isles. However, that proved not to be the case, as other imperial opportunities were about to open up. This was a result of the voyages of Christopher Columbus to the Americas. Although Henry VII had turned down a request from Bartholomew Columbus (brother of Christopher) to fund a transatlantic voyage to the Indies, he was quick to make amends. In 1496, by letters patent, he granted to John Cabot (an Italian-like Columbus):

> that [he and his family] may conquer, occupy and possess whatsoever such towns, castles, cities and islands by them thus discovered that they may be able to conquer, occupy and possess, as our vassals and governors lieutenants and deputies

THE RISE OF ENGLISH IMPERIALISM

therein, *acquiring for us the dominion, title and jurisdiction of the same towns, castles, cities, islands and mainlands discovered.* (Author's emphasis.)[34]

Cabot was required by the letters patent to operate out of Bristol, and the city was given a monopoly on future colonial trade in the same way that Lisbon and Seville were given commercial privileges by Portugal and Spain respectively. He 'discovered' Newfoundland in 1497, and other mariners operating on behalf of England would explore different parts of the Americas. In 1532, as a result of Henry VIII's Ecclesiastical Appeals Act ruling out appeal to the papacy, it was declared that 'this realm of England is an Empire', thus emphasising the imperial nature of the English state and the extent to which it now differed from the other three nations in the Isles.

It was not until the reign of Queen Elizabeth I that settler colonies were first attempted, in Newfoundland, Virginia and present-day North Carolina. By this time, 'England' had become 'England and Wales' (see next chapter), so that colonisation was no longer an exclusively English project. Yet the foundations of empire had been firmly laid down by England long before the union with Wales. A class had been formed of English imperial administrators, whose ancestors were familiar with service in Gascony, Ireland, Scotland and Wales, while a colonial mindset had become deeply embedded in the English psyche. Indeed, that was certainly how it was seen by the Benedictines of Dunfermline when they wrote in 1442: 'The tyranny, cruelty and usurpation of the English are notorious to all the world as manifestly appears in their usurpation against France, Scotland, Wales, Ireland and neighbouring lands.'[35]

4

FOUR NATIONS, ONE STATE

Between 1535 and 1801, England merged with the rest of the Isles into what would eventually become the United Kingdom of Great Britain and Ireland (the original UK). The process of passing acts of union between England and the other three nations started with Wales in 1535 and 1542, moved on to Scotland in 1707—when 'Great Britain' came into existence for the first time—and finally ended in 1801 with Ireland and the creation of the UK. There was now only one state, with its own flag, parliament and armed forces.

A similar process of enlarged state-building happened in many parts of continental Europe. In some cases, notably France and Italy, the process not only brought an end to the underlying states, but also eclipsed the nations such as Burgundy (in France) and Genoa (in Italy) that had been brought under one roof. In other cases, such as Germany and Spain, state-building did not eliminate all of the nations that came together. On the contrary, some of these—such as Bavaria in Germany and Catalonia in Spain—preserved a strong sense of nationhood.

INTERNAL EMPIRE

The UK followed the second path, so that state-building left four nations, with none of them eclipsed after the acts of union. However, within this single state, one nation, England, was dominant—and, by virtue of that dominance, effectively acquired the right to act on behalf of the other three nations in foreign affairs and usually in domestic ones as well. This was the internal or insular empire, separate from the external or overseas British Empire that flourished after the union with Scotland. English imperialism towards the rest of the UK did not, therefore, end with the union of the four nations, although it took a different form.

This English imperialism was largely hidden from view, as most of the inhabitants of the smaller nations accepted without complaint their unequal relationship with England. Not until the Irish rebellion in the first quarter of the twentieth century would English imperialism come under serious attack. This widespread acceptance of the internal English empire was down to the fact that the external British Empire provided rich compensation for many, while the most ambitious in the other three nations could aspire to top positions in England, as no formal barriers existed to prevent them from doing so. English imperialism therefore went largely unchallenged, as long as the majority of the population in Ireland, Scotland and Wales accepted the status quo.

Wales

The first nation to be affected by acts of union was Wales. The break between England and the papacy at the start of the 1530s risked the hostility of Catholic states, raising the possibility that the long coastline of Wales might be used to mount an invasion by France or Spain. At the same time, the loyalty of the largely autonomous Marcher lords could not be assured. Wales, including the March, was therefore absorbed into England by an

FOUR NATIONS, ONE STATE

act of the English parliament in 1535[1]—a parliament in which there were still no Welsh members.

It was not called an act of union, as the preamble claimed that Wales had 'always' been part of England. Instead, it was called 'An Act for Laws and Justice to be Administered in Wales in like Form as it is in this [English] Realm.' The act then began (with the author's partial modernisation of the English words):

> Albeit the dominion, principality and country of Wales justly and righteously is, and ever have been, incorporated, annexed, united and subject to and under the imperial crown of this realm ... yet notwithstanding, because that in the same country, principality and dominion divers rights, usages, laws and customs be far different from the laws and customs of this realm, and also because the people of the same dominion have and do daily use a speech nothing like nor consonant to the natural mother tongue used within this realm, some rude and ignorant people have made distinction and diversity between the king's subjects of this realm and his subjects ... of Wales ... His Highness therefore ... minding and intending to reduce them to the perfect order, notice and knowledge of his laws of this his realm, and utterly to extirpate ... the sinister usages and customs differing from the same ... hath ... ordained, exacted and established that *his said country or dominion of Wales shall be ... and continue for ever from henceforth incorporated, united and annexed to and with this his realm of England.* (Author's emphasis.)

This preamble, written by Thomas Cromwell (Henry VIII's principal secretary at the time), made it clear how Wales had, through its own language, laws and customs, succeeded in remaining a nation during the 250 years of colonial rule since the Statute of Wales in 1284; but it also revealed the extent to which this was now seen as a threat to English interests. The rest of the act explained how, in return for the abolition of all trade barriers and the end of legal discrimination between subjects of England

and Wales,[2] the core characteristics of Welsh nationalism were to be eroded—if not eliminated.

There would be no change of name for the expanded state, which remained 'England', with the same flag. The act of union (for that is effectively what it was) then laid down the administrative structure for all of Wales and the March, using the same county system as in England. Justices of the peace were to be appointed in each county to administer the law. This would now be exclusively English law (including primogeniture) and the English language would be the only one officially allowed in the courts. The Church of England would become the established state Church for all Wales. Finally, no monoglot Welsh-speakers would be permitted to hold public office, which meant that the twenty-six members selected to attend parliament in London (as well as those administering justice) had to speak English.

The main beneficiary of Tudor policy towards the Welsh was the minority English-speaking landed gentry of Wales—many of whom, like Henry VIII himself, were Anglo-Welsh.[3] In addition, the dissolution of the monasteries allowed some of them to acquire cheaply the freehold to lands they had been previously renting. The Welsh gentry provided all of the justices of the peace and members of parliament. Unsurprisingly, those members of the gentry who did not yet speak English were now quick to learn the language.

The 1535 act of union was soon followed by another in 1542. This law, entitled 'An Act for Certain Ordinances in the King's Majesty's Dominion and Principality of Wales', tidied up the administrative boundaries of the thirteen Welsh counties. Twelve of these were then made subject to a new Welsh institution, the Court of Great Sessions, which was to meet twice a year to administer English law (the remaining county, Monmouthshire, became subservient to the courts in England, while remaining

FOUR NATIONS, ONE STATE

part of Wales). The act also gave statutory recognition to the Council of Wales, an administrative body that had previously operated only under royal prerogative. An additional member of parliament was added to give the principality twenty-seven seats in the House of Commons, which had 376 seats in total. With the number of Welsh estimated at some 275,000 at the time, compared with 3.75 million for England, this gave Wales roughly the same share of parliamentary seats as the Welsh share of the combined population.

If the intention of the two acts of union had been to force Wales into a greater England, ending Wales' history as a separate nation, this is the moment at which it might have succeeded. The English-speaking landed gentry, who benefited greatly from the ending of all formal discrimination against people born in Wales, would not have objected, and the bulk of the population (at least 90 per cent) was in no position to object. Strongly anglophile, and in many cases related by blood to the English, the Welsh gentry formed an elite increasingly distant from the Welsh-speaking masses over whom they ruled. Welsh nationalism therefore lacked an effective voice and would at first struggle to be heard.

To make matters worse, from the point of view of Welsh nationhood, the Council of Wales was abolished in 1689 and the Court of Great Sessions in 1830. This ended two distinctive features of Wales that had marked it out as different from England. Furthermore, the Welsh language was not only forbidden in the judicial system, but also frowned upon at school, where the punitive 'Welsh not' became an invidious symbol of English imperialism.[4] The nineteenth century saw the introduction of compulsory education, which was in English, and migration of English-speakers to provide the labour for Wales' expanding mining industry. Finally, the notorious *Reports of the Commissioners of Inquiry into the State of Education in Wales*

INTERNAL EMPIRE

(1847), widely known in Wales as *The Treachery of the Blue Books*, added fuel to the fire by denigrating not only the use of the Welsh language, but Welsh morals as a whole.

And yet Wales as a nation not only survived, but also prospered in the centuries after the acts of union, with the sense of nationhood never in doubt despite the pressures on the Welsh language. When football and rugby started to be played throughout the UK in the late nineteenth century, it was considered appropriate for Wales (like Ireland and Scotland) to be represented by its own national team, rather than being absorbed into an English one.

Why did this happen? Although Welsh law ceased to exist after the acts of union, the use of the Welsh language continued in the courts through interpreters, as so many people had no other means of communication. The acts of union had finalised the borders between the counties, but they had also settled forever the border between England and Wales—turning it into much more than a 'line in the sand'. And, for the first 100 years after the acts of union, the Welsh members of parliament tended to act as a caucus to defend the nation's interests—until the rise of party politics in England forced them to take sides.

Perhaps the most important reason for the survival of Wales as a nation, however, was religion. The English authorities were determined to impose their language on Wales for secular purposes, but they had no objection to the use of Welsh in ecclesiastical contexts. Indeed, it was a necessity, if the Welsh masses were to accept the need for the new religion adopted by Henry VIII (dubbed later as 'Catholicism without the Pope'). The first book ever printed in Welsh, *Yny lhyvyr hwnn* ('In this book'), was published in 1546, and it contained such things as the Lord's Prayer and the Ten Commandments. Then, in 1551, the main texts of the common prayer book were also published in Welsh (*Kynniver Llith a Ban*).

104

FOUR NATIONS, ONE STATE

The publication of *Kynniver Llith a Ban* helped Wales to avoid the rebellion that had taken place in Cornwall in 1549, after the English version of the prayer book had been forced on the Cornish-speaking people of southwest England. The rebellion, it is true, was also motivated by the strongly Catholic views still held in that part of the country. That was less of an issue in Wales, where a myth started to circulate suggesting that 'the Celtic Church was a Protestant Church whose purity had been defiled by the Romish practices imposed upon it in the centuries following Augustine's arrival at Canterbury.'[5] This myth was given added authority in the introduction to the Welsh version of the New Testament printed in 1567. A Welsh version of the whole Bible was then published in 1588.

Wales, therefore, made the transition from Catholicism to Protestantism without much of the traumas that occurred in Ireland, Scotland or even parts of England, while the use of Welsh in ecclesiastical settings helped to keep the sense of a nation alive. Yet a rejection of Roman Catholicism by the vast majority of the population did not automatically translate into support for the new religion represented by the Church of England—and this was even more true of the Puritanism espoused by Oliver Cromwell during the Commonwealth of England.

To counter this, the English parliament in 1650 passed an 'Act for the Better Promotion of the Gospel in Wales'. This gave Wales, according to the great Welsh theologian Robert Tudur Jones, a measure of 'religious home rule', and the results were so impressive that Cromwell declared that God had planted in Wales 'a seed ... hardly to be paralleled since the primitive times.'[6] Indeed, the Nonconformist tradition in Wales, already evident before the 1650 act, was now strengthened and flourished, with the growth of all kinds of dissenters such as Baptists, Presbyterians and Quakers.

The established Church of England, refusing to accept a division of the institution within the two nations, was known

INTERNAL EMPIRE

in the principality as the Church 'in' Wales. As Nonconformism became more and more important, especially with the rapid growth of Methodism founded by John Wesley in the eighteenth century, tensions grew between the state Church in Wales, and the mass of the population belonging to the Nonconformist chapels. Matters became so heated that parliament introduced a bill to disestablish the Church of England in Wales just before the First World War. David Lloyd George, Chancellor of the Exchequer in 1913, spoke for many in Wales when he said, during the debate in the House of Commons:

> Wales became Methodist and Puritan 150 years ago. England moved on, but which way? In the direction of being ritualistic and High Church. So we [the Welsh] have always been at cross purposes and we have always had to accept as the national religion something which has been fashioned to meet the view of our neighbours. Can anyone be surprised at what has happened? It has been a failure. This is not the story of thirty or forty years. It is not the story of a hundred years. It is the story of hundreds of years of spiritual neglect, of spiritual degradation, from which generation after generation of Welshmen have suffered. What do they suffer for? They suffered purely and simply because of an Establishment which was imposed upon them.[7]

The Church in Wales was finally disestablished in 1920. The long struggle to achieve it showed the extent to which religious Nonconformism and the Welsh language, despite its declining use, had helped to define Wales as a nation even after the acts of union in the reign of Henry VIII. At the same time, the opposition to disestablishment—not just in the Church of England, but in the House of Lords—illustrated the strength of the forces in favour of 'greater England' and the suppression of Welsh nationalism. The nation of Wales may have survived unification with England, but this had by no means been a foregone conclusion.

FOUR NATIONS, ONE STATE

Scotland

The restoration of the monarchy in 1660 ended Scotland's decade under English occupation. The restored monarch, Charles II, had already been crowned King of Scotland after the execution of his father in London in 1649, but he was now proclaimed king again in Edinburgh in May 1660. The union of the two crowns was then reestablished, with the coronation of Charles as King of England. He would also claim to be King of Ireland and, somewhat fancifully, King of France.

The Scottish parliament, judiciary and privy council were all restored after 1660, while Scotland—now a separate state—no longer enjoyed unrestricted free trade with England and its colonies. Scotland was once again independent, but the contradictions in the 'two crowns' model were worse than before. Charles II, who never visited Scotland during his long reign, was even more captive to English lobbies than his father and grandfather. And, as English interests expanded abroad—both on the continent of Europe and through an embryonic overseas empire—Scotland increasingly found itself caught up in the geopolitics of imperial England without any influence over the policies themselves.

Charles largely ignored Scotland, leaving its affairs for most of his reign (he died in 1685) in the hands of John Maitland, the first Duke of Lauderdale. Yet Charles remained passionate about one aspect of Scottish affairs, and that was the restoration of bishops, which was duly introduced in 1661. Conflict with Presbyterian Scotland was, therefore, inevitable and became even more intense during the short reign of his brother (James VII of Scotland and James II of England); but when James fled England at the end of 1688, Scotland found itself without a king. Although the Scottish parliament would eventually reconcile itself to England's choice (the dual monarchy of William and Mary), once again Scotland

INTERNAL EMPIRE

found itself dragged into the intrigues of English politics with no control over the outcome. The Scottish estates did, however, abolish bishops in 1689 with the support of William and Mary, while passing in the same year the Claim of Right Act: a Scottish version of the Bill of Rights passed a few months earlier by the English parliament.[8]

Mary, a Stuart by birth, died in 1694, and her husband (William II of Scotland and William III of England) eight years later. Although the crowns of both Scotland and England passed to Mary's sister Anne, it was clear even before William's death that this next monarch would have no children to succeed her. The English parliament therefore passed in 1701 the Act of Settlement, which announced that the next ruler of England would be from the House of Hanover; but it made no effort to consult Scotland, despite the fact that the Scottish parliament in 1689 had asserted its right to decide what should happen in future.

William, seeing the unworkability of the 'two crowns' model, had put forward various suggestions for deepening the union, but had been rebuffed by the English parliament. Nor was Scotland much more enthusiastic in view of the sharp differences between the two states in both domestic and international affairs. The problems associated with the union of two crowns were reaching boiling point, therefore, when his sister-in-law Queen Anne—who told her first English parliament, 'I know my heart to be entirely English'—ascended the throne of both countries in 1702 and immediately dragged Scotland into an English war against France.[9] Scotland and England looked set for a long and unhappy marriage under a shared monarch, with neither side able or willing to break the stalemate. And yet it was eventually broken—and this came about, at least on Scotland's side, more as a result of economics than religion or geopolitics.[10]

108

FOUR NATIONS, ONE STATE

The end of unrestricted free trade after the restoration affected not just Anglo-Scottish commerce, but also Scotland's trade with the English overseas territories. These colonies had been expanding rapidly in number during the seventeenth century, and had also grown as a result of the marriage of Charles II to Catherine of Braganza from Portugal. Her dowry had included various territories, such as Tangiers in North Africa and the Seven Islands of Bombay, as well as trading privileges in the Portuguese colonies of Brazil and the East Indies. And while the English colonies in North America were slowly becoming economically viable, those in the Caribbean were booming after the switch from tobacco to sugar exports. This threatened to enlarge even further the economic gap between Scotland and England.

English trade policy was governed by mercantilism. This discriminated against imports from outside the English Empire and had been a major factor in the Anglo-Dutch Wars of the seventeenth century. Scotland had no problem with the policy, which was widely adopted in Europe at the time, but needed colonies of its own in order to implement it. The first colony, established in Newfoundland in 1629 and called Nova Scotia, had ended in 1632 as a result of Charles I's desire not to offend France. Fifty years later, the Scottish privy council had then approved the establishment of plantations in the Americas; one was set up in New Jersey in 1683 and another in South Carolina in 1684. However, both struggled, and the one in South Carolina was destroyed by the Spanish in 1686.

By this time the English had given trading monopolies to two overseas enterprises: the East India Company and the Royal Africa Company. Both had prospered, with the latter trading in slaves as well as goods. The time had therefore come for a more concerted Scottish effort, and in 1695 an act was passed for a Company of Scotland Trading to Africa and the Indies (English modernised). The driving force behind it was a London-based

INTERNAL EMPIRE

Scot, William Paterson, who had helped establish the Bank of England. As a result of his connections in both England and Scotland, he proposed to raise £600,000 from the two countries in equal measure to establish a colony (New Caledonia) in Darién on the Isthmus of Panama, where the settlement would act as an entrepôt between Europe and Asia.

The East India Company saw this as a threat to its interests, gained the support of the king and killed off English participation. The plans were revised, this time without English participation, and £400,000 was subscribed by Scottish shareholders on their own. This was a huge sum of money, amounting to perhaps half of all liquid capital in the country, but the Darién scheme was a complete disaster, with shareholders—a not insignificant part of the population—losing everything. The collapse of the company also coincided with a run of bad harvests in Scotland, which killed off at least 5 per cent of the population (which totalled just over 1 million at the time). The Scottish economy was therefore very fragile and in desperate need of assistance.

Despite this, resistance to political union with England was still strong, and when it was raised by King William, just before his death in 1702, it was summarily rejected. Indeed, memories of English duplicity over Darién and resentment at becoming embroiled in England's overseas wars were still so strong when Anne embarked on war in 1702 that the Scottish parliament passed an 'Act anent Peace and War' the following year, to prevent Scotland ever again being dragged into an English fight. In 1704, parliament went further, passing by a large majority an Act of Security which gave Scotland the right to choose a different monarch, 'unless ... there be such conditions of government settled as may secure the Honour and Sovereignty of this Crown and Kingdom; the Freedom, Frequency and Power of Parliament; Religion; *and Liberty and Trade of the Nation from English or any Foreign Influence*'. (Author's emphasis.)

FOUR NATIONS, ONE STATE

The implication was that Scotland would only accept the Hanoverian succession after the death of Queen Anne if granted free trade with England. On the other hand, if Scotland were to choose a different monarch, this could have led to a revival of the *Auld Alliance* with France—a grim prospect for England. Yet, far from reacting in a conciliatory manner in order to avert this possibility, the English parliament passed the Alien Act in 1705, stating that:

> From and after the 25 day of December 1705, no Person or Persons being a Native or Natives of the Kingdom of Scotland ... shall be capable to inherit any Lands ... within this Kingdom of England ... or to enjoy any Benefit or Advantage of a natural-born Subject of England; But every such Person shall be from henceforth adjudged and taken as an Alien born out of the allegiance of the Queen of England, *until such time as the Succession to the Crown of Scotland be declared and settled by an Act of Parliament in Scotland.* (Author's emphasis.)

These crude attempts at blackmail by both sides were hardly the most propitious background to negotiations on a political union. And yet, in 1706, perhaps in recognition of the dangers of continued tit-for-tat hostile diplomacy, both parliaments agreed to establish a commission to explore the possibility. This in itself was no guarantee of success, but the prospects improved dramatically when the Duke of Hamilton—no doubt suitably rewarded[11]—suddenly put forward a proposal to the Scottish parliament that all the commissioners (not just the English ones) should be chosen by Queen Anne. As the queen was a strong supporter of political union, it could safely be assumed that the commissioners would reflect her views.

Hamilton's proposal squeaked through parliament by the narrowest of majorities and the commissioners set to work. Articles of union were then drafted (there were twenty-five),

INTERNAL EMPIRE

and presented to the Scottish parliament in October 1706. It took ten weeks and considerable 'inducements' before the articles were finally approved, after which they moved to the English parliament, where approval was given quickly.[12] England and Scotland were now united as 'Great-Britain' (the hyphen would later be dropped).

The Acts of Union had something for everybody, which—together with the bribes—had made their passage through the two parliaments possible. Article II had given England what it wanted, through Scottish agreement to the Hanoverian succession. Article IV, on the other hand, had given Scotland what it needed, through English agreement to free trade: 'That all the Subjects of the united Kingdom of Great-Britain shall, from and after the Union, have full Freedom and Intercourse of Trade and Navigation, to and from any Port or Place within the said united Kingdom, and the Dominions and Plantations thereunto belonging ...'

Scotland also secured compensation for the Darién disaster through an ingenious device called 'The Equivalent', under which England paid nearly £400,000 to shareholders in the Company of Scotland. This was never going to win 'hearts and minds' among those opposed to union, but it went a long way to assuage the pain, even if it took many years for the shareholders to receive their money. And since the articles of union had very little to say on the domestic affairs of either nation, there was little risk of friction from the different institutions of religion, law and education in England and Scotland.

The union was the ultimate marriage of convenience. Both nations secured the primacy of Protestantism and discrimination against Catholicism.[13] England secured the succession, an improvement in its security, and a seemingly inexhaustible supply of manpower from the highland clans for its expanding army and navy. Scotland acquired unfettered and immediate

112

FOUR NATIONS, ONE STATE

access to the huge English market (that of Wales was much smaller), and eventually the colonies, as well as compensation for the shareholders in the Company of Scotland. Yet there was little popular enthusiasm for Great Britain. Daniel Defoe, who had spied in Scotland for the English government before penning his masterpiece *Robinson Crusoe,* was surely right when he wrote that 'a firmer union of policy with less union of affection has hardly been known in the whole world.'[14]

The Scottish parliament was immediately abolished, and Scotland was allocated forty-five seats in an expanded House of Commons where England had 489 members and Wales twenty-four.[15] Scotland's share of the seats (8 per cent) was about half its share of the population, as Scots numbered some 1.1 million, while the total for England and Wales came to 5.1 million. This was a considerable underrepresentation (Wales had done better in 1535) and, to make matters worse, the Scottish privy council was then abolished in 1708, while the post of Secretary of State for Scotland disappeared a generation later.

They may have been called Acts of Union, but Scotland—like Wales before it—had effectively been absorbed by England. For some Scots, this was an acceptable price to pay for the economic advantages and job opportunities political incorporation brought; but for many—perhaps a majority—it was too high a price.[16] Resistance in Scotland to union with England was widespread, with petitions in many towns, riots in some (especially Glasgow) and a growing sense among Scotland's representatives in the British parliament that union was not working as expected. Indeed, a motion to dissolve the union in the House of Lords in 1713 only failed by four votes.

England was unmoved, but it was nearly forty years before union brought the anticipated gains in security. The reason was the support in Scotland for James VII's son (known by his enemies as 'the Old Pretender') and the alliance he was able to

INTERNAL EMPIRE

strike with France. Indeed, Louis XIV had planned an invasion in support of James VIII (as he would have become) as early as 1708, but it had been abandoned at the last minute as a result of storms. More serious was the uprising in 1715 by Jacobites (supporters of James), which was widely expected to succeed by many people in both Scotland and England. The last Jacobite uprising, which took place in 1745–6 in support of James' son Charles (known as 'the Young Pretender'), ended in crushing defeat at the Battle of Culloden. This put paid once and for all to the risk of a foreign invasion of England in support of a separate monarch for Scotland.

Scotland may have lost its independence through union with England in 1707, but it did not cease to be a nation. Nationalist roots ran deep, despite all the divisions between and among highland clans, lowland farmers, townspeople and nobles. History, and the ancient rivalry with England, played an important part in this, as did the survival of separate religious, educational and legal institutions. Furthermore, governments in England—the security threat having diminished—tended at first to ignore Scotland, and left the Scots to manage their own affairs as long as their actions did not impinge on their southern neighbour. As a marriage, the union of Scotland and England began life as a somewhat sullen affair.[17]

Ireland

The Irish parliament in Dublin was summoned to meet in 1692—the year after the Treaty of Limerick was passed. The parliament, and its successors, rapidly introduced the Penal Laws, ensuring that the treaty's provisions for Catholic freedoms were effectively rendered null and void. The government in England, although it had the power to do so, did nothing to block the adoption of the penal codes against Irish Catholics

FOUR NATIONS, ONE STATE

(the vast majority of the population), as it was busy enforcing its own version at home.

And yet, despite this meeting of minds on discrimination against Catholics, relations had become fractious within a few years. Although Poynings' Law had been relaxed in 1694 to allow a measure of autonomy to the Irish parliament in fiscal affairs, there was nothing that Dublin could do to prevent the House of Commons in London from passing laws that hurt the Irish economy. With an English ban on the import of wool from Ireland in 1698, among other hostile commercial measures, the Irish parliament found itself forced to consider seriously the issue of an incorporating union that would have removed such discrimination.

Union had been considered before, notably during the Commonwealth of England (1649–60). In these years, when the Irish parliament was in abeyance, a number of Irish members had sat in the English parliament, and a bill for the union of England and Ireland had even been drafted in 1659. However, the issue had dropped off the agenda after the restoration, until the end of the century, at which point the colonial restrictions imposed on Ireland, coupled with the beginnings of negotiations for a union of England and Scotland, brought the issue to the forefront of Irish parliamentary interest once again. A widely read pamphlet, almost certainly authored by the Irish parliamentarian Henry Maxwell, spoke of the benefits of union by stressing the commercial advantages:

> For ... the trade and communication of those kingdoms being as free and easy as between any two parts of the same country, it will naturally and necessarily follow that the business and trade of Ireland will be diverted from foreign nations, and chiefly confined to England. So that England will not only regain that part of the Irish trade which it has lost, and is likely to do more and more, but will likewise put itself into a more full and

115

INTERNAL EMPIRE

absolute possession of Irish trade than ever it had, or can have, under any other circumstances than those of the union.[18]

The result of all these efforts was an official 'representation' from the Irish parliament to Queen Anne in 1703, calling for an end to commercial discrimination and either for greater autonomy of the Irish parliament with more regular meetings or for 'a more firm and strict Union with your Majesty's subjects of *England*, which will be to the advantage of that Kingdom' (emphasis original). Months passed, however, before the queen could be bothered to reply—and when she did it was in the most dismissive terms:

> Her Majesty having considered of the representation made by the House of Commons in Ireland, has commanded this answer to be returned. That the first part of it seems to relate to matters past in parliament; and the other part, consisting of things general, her Majesty can give no particular answer at present, but will take them into her consideration.[19]

England, it seemed, had no interest in changing the colonial condition of Ireland—especially as the representation had made clear that the Irish parliament supported the Hanoverian succession, would continue to provide finance for the English army, and was only too happy to discriminate against Catholics (as well as Presbyterians). This was very different from what had happened with post-restoration Scotland, an independent state, whose parliament had been prepared to threaten England before a political union was agreed.

The Irish parliament would make two more attempts in the next six years to promote union, but both failed. Then, in 1720, the new British parliament passed the Declaratory Act, reaffirming that it had the power to make law for Ireland and stating that the British House of Lords was the final court of appeal in matters of Irish law. That confirmed the colonial status of Ireland, after which support for union in Ireland diminished

FOUR NATIONS, ONE STATE

rapidly—so much so that a Dublin paper's inaccurate reference to an imminent union prompted large protests on College Green in 1759, with the mob forcing a number of members of the Irish parliament to swear 'a solemn obligation never to consent to a union.'[20]

Why this lack of interest? The Irish parliament, which represented the Protestant, Church of Ireland minority in the colony, had clearly decided that a measure of legislative autonomy within the British Empire was the best method to preserve the interests of the Protestant Ascendancy, as well as privileges for its members. That was also the view of the British government, unless security issues—as had happened with Wales and Scotland—reared their head. As long as there was no danger of invasion from outside or rebellion from inside, the status quo served British interests well. The Irish parliament raised the taxes needed by the Irish army, while Irish people—Catholic as well as Protestant—were willing recruits to the imperial cause.

Yet security issues did intervene, and a change in Britain's attitude to its Irish colony was first triggered by the consequences of the Declaration of Independence in 1776, made by the thirteen colonies in North America (the future United States). The victory of the rebels made clear to the British government that the status quo in Ireland was no longer viable. Either the colony had to be offered greater freedom, with the risk that this would lead eventually to independence, or it had to be absorbed by Great Britain in a legislative union.

By the end of the US War of Independence in 1783, an Irish Protestant militia had come into existence that no British government could afford to ignore. In theory dedicated to defending Ireland from invasion by Catholic France or Spain, The Volunteers had demonstrated their support for the Protestant Ascendancy in Dublin as early as 1779.[21] The British government therefore opted in 1782 for the easier option of greater freedom

117

INTERNAL EMPIRE

for the colony through a new constitution, which repealed previous restrictive legislation and gave the Irish parliament more autonomy.

There were, however, limits to this freedom; when, ten years later, the British government raised the issue of admitting Catholics to the political process (Presbyterians had already been admitted in 1780), the Irish parliament's hostility towards union in the previous half-century started to change. If such a process of Catholic integration were to go forward, the Protestant monopoly in the Irish parliament would no longer be assured; therefore a union—in the view of some parliamentarians—might be a better option, even if it meant the end of a separate assembly in Ireland.

The idea of a legislative union was now linked inextricably to Catholic emancipation. As the British Prime Minister William Pitt explained to the Lord Lieutenant of Ireland, the abolition of the Irish parliament and an enlargement of the British would give Catholics political rights without conceding any power: 'The admission of Catholics to a share of the suffrage could not then be dangerous—the protestant interest in point of power, property and church establishment would be secure because the decided majority of the supreme legislature would necessarily be protestant.'[22]

This cynical proposal assumed that Irish Catholics would be content to go along with parliamentary union, on the grounds that the harshest aspects of discrimination would then come to an end. However, the assumption proved to be wide of the mark—especially after the French Revolution in 1789 led many to challenge old beliefs. When Theobald Wolfe Tone published a pamphlet in 1791 called 'Argument on Behalf of the Catholics in Ireland', it struck a chord not only with many Irish Catholics (some of whom had already formed their own militia called the Defenders) but also with a number of Presbyterians in Ulster. These dissenters had their own grievances against the Protestant

118

FOUR NATIONS, ONE STATE

Ascendancy, which had led to many migrating to North America in previous decades, and they were attracted by Tone's appeal to 'Irishmen of all denominations'.[23]

The result was the formation in October 1791 of the Society of United Irishmen. Ostensibly dedicated to parliamentary reform and an end to discrimination against both Catholics and Presbyterians, it was in truth an organisation dedicated to a revolutionary struggle for national independence. Therefore, when Great Britain and France went to war in 1793, Tone—now at the head of a banned organisation—threw in his lot with the French, who provided a naval force for an invasion at the end of 1796. Only bad weather prevented a successful landing and Ireland remained a British colony. A subsequent rebellion was then launched by the United Irishmen in 1798, but it was ruthlessly crushed. Tone himself was captured and sentenced to death, but cut his own throat before the sentence could be carried out.

The United Irishmen were not the only casualty of the rebellion's failure. The alliance between (some) Catholics and (some) Presbyterians also ended, as long-held suspicions and hatreds reemerged during the uprisings of the 1790s. By the end of the decade, the Orange Boys—an offshoot of the violently anti-Catholic Peep o'Day Boys—had merged with other militants to form the Orange Order, while the Volunteers increased recruitment among disaffected Protestant youth. The Defenders and other Catholic organisations were severely weakened, and were now left with little alternative other than the prospect of a legislative union, to be followed—it was assumed—by emancipation.

The British government, having abandoned any hope that the Irish parliament could impose order on the unruly colony, now saw union as the only way forward. It was considered politically expedient to strip the bill of any reference to Catholic

119

INTERNAL EMPIRE

emancipation, on the assumption that this could be tackled more easily by a single parliament in Westminster at a later date. Yet the first vote proposing union failed in January 1799, since a majority of Irish parliamentarians—all members of the Protestant Ascendancy—were reluctant to close down a legislature that had served their interests well for so many centuries.

The British government was now obliged to provide the necessary 'inducements', above all in the form of patronage, and the bill passed the Irish parliament in May 1800. It was swiftly followed by a similar bill in the British parliament. At the end of his hopes for an Ireland of equal status with England, the great Irish orator and parliamentarian Henry Grattan exclaimed in the debate on the union bill: 'I see her [Ireland] in a swoon but she is not dead. Though in her tomb she lies helpless and motionless, still there is on her lips a spirit of life and on her cheek a glow of beauty ... While a plank of the vessel sticks together I will not leave her.'[24]

On 1 January 1801, the United Kingdom of Great Britain and Ireland came into existence, and the single parliament met for the first time three weeks later. And yet for the English, despite a new UK flag and other symbols of union, this was not very different from what had gone before. Ireland, like Scotland and Wales before it, had simply been absorbed into existing English institutions. England remained the dominant nation within the UK—just as it had been dominant in Great Britain after the absorption of Scotland in 1707, while England had not even troubled to change the name of the expanded state after the annexation of Wales in 1535.

Ireland was allocated by the Acts of Union 100 members in the House of Commons, which amounted to 17.9 per cent of the new total.[25] However, its share of the Isles' combined population was closer to 30 per cent, as the 1801 census had counted 8.87 million in England and Wales, while Scotland had 1.6 million

120

FOUR NATIONS, ONE STATE

and Ireland between 4 and 5 million.[26] This underrepresentation was a bitter pill to swallow, but at least for the Catholic majority in Ireland there was now the promise of emancipation. This turned out to be hollow, however, as King George III informed Prime Minister Pitt, after the passage of the Acts of Union, that he could never agree to it.

Ireland survived as a nation. Its history, culture, language and majority religion made sure of that. Nor would there be any attempt to conjure up a new name for the Irish subjects of the expanded state. However, Catholics soon reacted to union with a sense of betrayal, making reconciliation difficult if not impossible, while the Presbyterian minority still experienced discrimination under Article 5 of the Acts of Union:

> That the Churches of England and Ireland ... be united into one Protestant Episcopal Church, to be called, the United Church of England and Ireland; and that the Doctrine, Worship, Discipline, and Government of the said United Church shall remain in full force for ever, as the same are now by Law established for the Church of England; *and that the Continuance and Preservation of the said United Church, as the established Church of England and Ireland, shall be deemed and taken to be an essential and fundamental Part of the Union.*' (Author's emphasis.)

Union, therefore, appealed in Ireland only to a small part of the population. That was similar to what had happened initially in Scotland and Wales, but support for union had grown subsequently in these two nations through marriage ties, social mobility, commercial prosperity and expansion of the British Empire. Whether the appeal of union might broaden in Ireland could not be taken for granted, in view of the hostility it faced from such a large part of the population in 1800. The United Kingdom of Great Britain and Ireland therefore faced an uphill struggle from the beginning.

INTERNAL EMPIRE

England, Great Britain and the UK

A new state may have been formally initiated in 1801, but it still contained four nations—the same ones that had existed for centuries. At the start of the nineteenth century, a sense of nationhood was still alive amongst the Welsh, strong amongst the Scots and arguably even stronger amongst the Irish. Nor had England ceased to be a nation after annexing Wales and absorbing Scotland and Ireland. Not only was a sense of nationhood deeply embedded among the English, but the other three nations reinforced that sense by frequently referring to 'England' rather than 'Great Britain'—let alone the 'United Kingdom of Great Britain and Ireland'. Wolfe Tone, for example, whose famous pamphlet was published in 1791, when Great Britain had been in existence for eighty-four years under a single monarch, wrote: 'The misfortune of Ireland is, that we have no National Government, in which we differ from *England*, and from all Europe. In *England* the King is resident, and his presence begets infinite advantages; the Government is *English*, with *English* views and interests only.' (Author's emphasis.)

Despite her dominant position among the four nations, England was not a state. That was Great Britain from 1707 and the UK from 1801. Could the state itself become a nation? It had happened in France, but only by suppressing the sense of nationhood among the separate provinces. That was a much trickier proposition in the Isles. 'England' could coexist with the label 'Great Britain' or 'UK', but that was because in the eyes of most English there was little difference between the two—a prejudice reinforced by the regularity with which others (especially foreigners) made the same mistake. Meanwhile, for the people of Ireland, Scotland and Wales, the label 'GB' or 'UK' meant something very different.

Statehood, therefore, did not automatically turn the United Kingdom into a nation. That, it was assumed at first, would

122

FOUR NATIONS, ONE STATE

require a dual strategy by England and its anglophile allies in the other nations: on the one hand, suppressing—or trying to suppress—Irish, Scottish and Welsh nationalisms in favour of a British identity, while on the other encouraging a sense of English and British nationalism to flourish side by side. Whether this strategy could have worked is hard to judge, as the advance of external imperialism in the end created a British Empire with which very many citizens of the four nations could identify, without the need to lose their own sense of nationhood within the Isles (see next chapter).

At the same time, the unincorporated parts of the Isles needed to be included into this expanded ideal of nationhood. The Isle of Man, with its distinctive Manx language with many Viking words, had finally come under English rule in the fourteenth century, after a long struggle between England and Scotland— but it did not become part of either Great Britain in 1707 or the UK in 1801. Instead, it became a self-governing crown dependency, with its population increasingly defining itself as British. The Manx language, still spoken as a first language by some 30 per cent of the population in 1874, was used by only 1 per cent fifty years later.

In the Channel Islands, the only part of Normandy held by the English crown after 1204, a similar solution was eventually found. Neither the Bailiwick of Jersey nor that of Guernsey (with its dependencies) became part of Great Britain or the UK. Instead, they remained crown dependencies, with the islanders, despite their proximity to France, gradually losing their French identity and using English as their first language.[27]

The replacement of the Manx language had started with the introduction of English-language schools in the seventeenth century and had proceeded without the need for additional coercive measures. Other inhabitants of the Isles not speaking English were less fortunate. In Scotland there was a serious

123

INTERNAL EMPIRE

attempt to suppress not only the use of Gaelic, but also 'Scottis' (the language of the lowlands that closely resembled English). No less an authority than the Scottish moral philosopher David Hume produced a list of 'Scotticisms' that Scots were discouraged from using. Annexed to his volume of *Political Discourses* published in 1752, they were reprinted in *The Scots Magazine* in 1760 with a note from the editor stating that 'they may be useful to such of our countrymen as would avoid Scotticisms in writing or speaking.'

Gaelic, the language of the rebellious highlanders, did indeed decline dramatically, although this was as much to do with prejudice against it on the part of lowland Scots as of the English. The Statutes of Iona, passed in 1609 during the union of the two crowns, marked the beginning of the official assault on Gaelic, with clan chiefs required to send their eldest male child to school in the lowlands to learn English.[28] Seven years later, the Scottish privy council's School Establishment Act mandated the establishment of an English-language school in every parish of Scotland, so that 'the Irish [sic] language, which is one of the chief and principal causes of the continuance of barbarity and incivility among the inhabitants of the Isles and Highlands, may be abolished and removed.' After the Acts of Union in 1707, the Society in Scotland for Promoting Christian Knowledge went one step further by banning the use of Gaelic not only in the schoolroom, but in the schoolyard as well.

Welsh had faced a similar onslaught for a much longer period, but had survived because of its association with the Nonconformist chapels. Its endurance was a serious affront to educational commissioners, who did not hold back in expressing their contempt for the language in their 1847 *Enquiry into the State of Education in Wales*, labelling it 'a vast drawback to Wales and a manifold barrier to the moral progress and commercial prosperity of the people.'[29] And yet, despite this official hostility,

124

FOUR NATIONS, ONE STATE

Welsh was still spoken as a matter of choice by 70 per cent of the population as late as the 1880s.[30]

The example of Welsh showed the limitations of a strategy of suppression in building support for an expanded state—whether Great Britain or the UK. What was needed, it became increasingly clear, were values that all nations could share—thus allowing for flexible nationalities. The need for this had not been apparent in 1535, when Wales was annexed, since the inhabitants of the principality were simply expected to become English or Anglo-Welsh. If they did so, as did the gentry from the start, the rewards could be enormous. If they chose not to, they could be ignored or—if necessary—punished. However, such an approach could not be used with Scotland, as Scots were never going to become English, and 'Anglo-Scottish' had very limited appeal.

The need for a new approach was recognised early on by the Earl of Cromartie, who wrote in the same year as the union itself, 'May wee be Britons and down goe the old ignominious names of Scotland and England'.[31] This, of course, was easier said than done. However, in an effort to bring the earl's dream to fruition, a serious attempt was made to rebrand Scotland as 'North Britain'. Two Scottish regiments changed their name to include 'North British' in their title in place of 'Scots', so that the Royal Scots Greys became the Royal North British Dragoons in 1707, while the Royal Scots Fusiliers became the Royal North British Fusiliers in 1713.

The change of name required that England accept the soubriquet 'South Britain'. James I (James VI of Scotland) had even attempted this when introducing a flag to symbolise the union of the two crowns, but it was doomed to failure. The inhabitants of the south were slowly acquiring a second identity (British as well as English) and did not therefore object to being identified as 'Britons' in the jingoistic poem *Rule Britannia*, penned in 1740 by a Scot living in England.[32] However, they

INTERNAL EMPIRE

were never going to replace one with the other. It was therefore unrealistic to expect the Scots to do so. Gradually, therefore, the name 'North Britain' died out, although the North British Railway only dropped it in 1923.

The attempt to replace 'Scotland' with 'North Britain' was therefore a failure. However, the Scots—like the English—slowly acquired a second, British identity after the Acts of Union in 1707. Meanwhile the inhabitants of Wales—who, for nearly two centuries since union in 1535, had been struggling to find a way to be both Welsh and English—were now faced with the easier option of being both Welsh and British.

The adoption of an additional British identity was made easier for the peoples of all three nations by the Arthurian myth developed so successfully by Geoffrey of Monmouth. However, there were more prosaic reasons as well. One, stressed by Linda Colley, emphasised the shared Protestant experience in the face of constant hostility and regular wars with Catholic France in the century following the 1707 union.[33] Another was the development of the armed forces of Great Britain, which almost by definition could not be organised and put into battle on anything less than a British level.

There was also the duopoly exercised in the British parliament in the same period by the two dominant political parties (Whigs and Tories). The members from Scotland and Wales had little choice other than identifying with one of these two parties, which therefore became increasingly 'British' rather than 'English' in the process.[34] Much prejudice, however, had to be overcome. It was 1761 before John Stuart, third Earl of Bute, became the first British Prime Minister from Scotland, and during his two years in office he had to endure an extraordinary level of abuse from the English media.[35] Meanwhile, Wales had to wait another 150 years for its first (and—so far—only) Prime Minister.[36]

126

FOUR NATIONS, ONE STATE

Great Britain therefore inched its way slowly to becoming a British nation, in which the subjects could adopt dual nationalities if they wanted. For ambitious Scots and Welsh, there was in truth no choice, since to reject the label 'British' was the surest way to block their own social and professional progress. The English, however, faced no such obstacle and many preferred to stick with a single identity rather than adopting a British one as well. Yet no sooner had these customs and habits started to form than the name of the state changed once again in 1801, in order to incorporate Ireland into a 'United Kingdom'.

How were the Irish to respond? A minority, the Anglo-Irish of Protestant faith, were happy to identify as British. However, for some Protestants and almost all Catholics the label made no sense at all. Yet they were expected to join a British Army and swear loyalty to a British monarch. And while Catholics had been granted the vote in 1793, no Catholic could take their seat in the House of Commons until 1829, so that the UK parliament remained a foreign institution for most Irish in the first three decades after its creation.

Yet the entry of Irish Catholics into the Commons offered only short-term relief from the crisis of identity experienced by so many inhabitants of Ireland. Resentment of non-members against the mandatory tithe to the established Church of Ireland steadily mounted until 1869, when the Irish Church Act ended the practice by disestablishing the Church of Ireland itself. The Irish voice, Protestant and Catholic, could now come to the fore. Its members in the House of Commons deserted the Liberal Party (successor to the Whigs) and defected in large numbers to a new Home Rule Party, winning nearly sixty seats at the first attempt in 1874.

Home rule did not necessarily mean the end of the UK and certainly members of the first home rule parties in Ireland did not expect that to happen. Yet support for the idea showed how

127

INTERNAL EMPIRE

difficult it was to create institutions with which citizens of both Great Britain and Ireland could identify. It had, after all, been hard enough at first to persuade the inhabitants of Scotland and Wales, let alone England, to identify as British. However, help was at hand—for state-led imperialism had been slowly but surely providing opportunities for professional and entrepreneurial advancement with which both British and Irish could identify. It might have been officially called a British Empire, but it distributed its largesse to all inhabitants of the Isles.

5

THE BRITISH EMPIRE

The United Kingdom of Great Britain and Ireland (the first UK) may have brought the English, Irish, Scots and Welsh under one roof. However, given the rivalries and hatreds accumulated over centuries between England and the other three nations, this expanded state could never on its own have created a strong sense of Britishness. England and institutions largely controlled by the English, including parliament, were too dominant to have inspired loyalty from a majority of the subjects of the other nations. The internal empire built by England may have been a fact of life for inhabitants of Ireland, Scotland and Wales, but this did not necessarily make it a source of affection.

A strong case has been made, notably by Linda Colley, that a sense of Britishness was forged in the eighteenth century through a shared Protestantism, anti-Catholicism and almost perpetual war with (Catholic) France.[1] There is some truth in this, although the divisions among Protestants were bitter and intense, while the majority of the population of Ireland remained staunchly Catholic. Yet, as Colley herself recognised, overriding all these factors was the glue provided by the external (overseas)

INTERNAL EMPIRE

empire. English at first, this would become in due course a British Empire to which all subjects—even the Catholic Irish—could adhere with pride.

Not all did, as became dramatically apparent in and after the 1916 Easter Uprising against British rule in Dublin, but for the vast majority of subjects in all three nations of Great Britain (as well as for many in Ireland), the British Empire was the bond that held them together and created a sense of Britishness that had previously been lacking.

And the explanation was simple. England may have controlled the internal empire, but it could not dominate the external one. It was too vast and required the input of all four nations. English elites might continue to refer to 'England' when they should have said 'Great Britain' or the 'United Kingdom of Great Britain and Ireland', but they hardly ever referred to the empire as anything other than 'British'. Thus, an arch-racist and white supremacist such as Cecil Rhodes, with his fanatical belief that the Englishman was the greatest species in the world, had no trouble in proclaiming at the age of 24, 'the object of which I intend to devote my life is the defence and extension of the British Empire.'

For a long time, the British Empire was phenomenally successful in holding together the four nations. It offered the prospect of a better life for those who chose to migrate, as so many did; it created opportunities for trade far in excess of what the internal empire could provide; and the super-profits made possible by the slave trade, slavery and labour coercion in the colonies created fortunes for the politically ambitious that allowed for a degree of social mobility that had never existed before. Empire seeped into every pore of British society and was reflected in the architecture of all city centres. It also created an 'other', in the form of non-white colonial people, that not only reinforced a sense of Britishness, but also laid the foundations for a deep and lasting racism that has still not been eradicated.

130

THE BRITISH EMPIRE

What the British Empire did not do was eliminate the internal empire and English imperialism. The hegemonic position of England inside Great Britain and later the United Kingdom was unchanged. Indeed, this hegemony was—if anything—reinforced by the relative strength of the English economy and demographic expansion under British imperialism. State institutions remained dominated by English representatives while residual bodies representing the interests of the other three nations were in many cases eliminated. The elision of 'England' with 'Great Britain' or 'the United Kingdom' by the English remained as great as ever, while most foreigners assumed the labels were interchangeable.

England

When the Acts of Union with Wales were passed in the reign of Henry VIII, there was no overseas English empire.[2] Elizabeth I tried to change this, but the efforts of Englishmen to establish colonies during her rule were not notably successful. Only under the first Stuart kings of England (James I and Charles I) were overseas colonies established that would survive. These were the islands in the Caribbean such as Antigua, Barbados and St. Kitts (shared with France), to which Jamaica was added in 1655 during the Protectorate of Oliver Cromwell; the colonies in North America, such as Virginia and Massachusetts; and small outposts in Newfoundland. The later Stuart kings of England (Charles II and James II) would add further colonies to this list in the Caribbean and North America, with tiny footholds in Asia.

These settlements, despite the union of the two crowns, were not in theory accessible to the Scots. Nor were the Irish welcome, with direct trade banned between the colonies and Ireland at the end of the seventeenth century. This was supposed to be a Protestant English overseas empire—albeit one in which

131

INTERNAL EMPIRE

Welsh subjects were tolerated. However, from the very beginning England found it difficult to block access completely to other migrants. The shortage of labour was too acute, and screening the colonists proved all but impossible. Maryland in North America, for example, was founded by a Roman Catholic who had difficulty recruiting other than Catholics, who came from all over the Hiberno-British Isles and even continental Europe.

The colonies of this English overseas empire would become the foundation stones in the eighteenth century of the British Empire. At the core of the English overseas imperial system was the charter—a document issued by the crown to individuals to establish settlement colonies, or to companies to form trading businesses. The charters to individuals were used by the Stuart kings to reward favoured aristocrats, and the terms of the charter were sufficiently vague to allow a great deal of flexible interpretation by the holders. They could be changed by royal decree, and frequently were, but the details were always left to the holder(s). And since all the settler colonies were plagued by a shortage of labour, this meant that, in practice, attempts to restrict colonists to the Protestant English were doomed to failure. These early English charters therefore paved the way for a truly British culture to take root in the colonies.

The charters for companies were different, but equally important. As the English crown sought to expand its overseas empire at the expense of the continental European empires (especially Denmark, France, Holland, Portugal and Spain), companies were formed with royal authority to trade in disputed areas. Protected against charges of piracy by their royal charters, these companies—especially the East India Company, established in 1600—were allowed to use force to protect their interests. And, although the original plan was not for the companies to establish settler colonies, inevitably that is what happened as they developed the military infrastructure

132

THE BRITISH EMPIRE

to protect trade routes, ward off foreign imperial powers and suppress local resistance.

One of the most important of the English charter companies was the Royal Africa Company (RAC), established by Charles II as soon as he secured the throne of England in 1660. Nominally dedicated to the extraction of gold from West Africa, its real purpose was soon revealed to be the sale of cheap manufactured goods in exchange for slaves. Although England had entered the slave trade under Queen Elizabeth I, when Sir John Hawkins had made a fortune from the sale of slaves to the Americas in 1562, it was not until the Stuart kings and Cromwell's Protectorate that African slaves were being transported in sufficiently large numbers to 'solve' the labour shortage in the settler colonies of North America and the Caribbean.

The RAC now took England's participation in the slave trade and Atlantic slavery to a whole new level. It is estimated that this company and its successors, controlled by English merchants and led by the Duke of York (the future James II of England), would be responsible for the transfer of more slaves from Africa to the Americas than any other company.[3] And, although the RAC surrendered its charter in 1672, it was replaced by a new company whose English credentials were emphasised by the change of name to the Royal Africa Company of England. This successor company fell temporarily out of favour following the flight of James II from England in 1688, but one of its directors—Edward Colston of Bristol—soon secured royal approval once again, by transferring a large part of his shares to William III (who, with his wife Mary Stuart, had replaced James II in the so-called Glorious Revolution).

The company lost its monopoly on the African trade in 1697, when the English parliament passed the Trade with Africa Act. It still competed successfully with the newcomers, helped by its incumbency advantages, but after 1707 it was no longer

INTERNAL EMPIRE

an English company. The Act of Union with Scotland turned all such English firms into British ones, while the external English Empire was now the British Empire. This transition was remarkably smooth, with little or no resistance to the change of name on the part of the English. Rabble-rousers might object, and frequently did, to the 'privileges' enjoyed by Scots and others in England, but they did not raise any objections to the notion that the overseas empire was now a British one.

Surprising as this might seem to us today, it appeared quite natural to contemporaries. The union with Scotland had taken place in the middle of the War of the Spanish Succession, in which England had sided against France to block a Bourbon (related to the French king) from assuming the Spanish crown. In almost the last act of its overseas empire, England had captured Gibraltar in 1704; it briefly became an English colony before becoming a British one. After 1707, however, all such territorial conquests would be British, and the Treaty of Utrecht in 1713[4] handed Great Britain on a plate a series of territories designed to ameliorate the British pain of being unable to prevent France from placing a Bourbon on the throne of Spain.

These new territories included not only Gibraltar, but also Menorca in the Balearic Islands, former French possessions in Newfoundland, and the French part of St. Kitts in the Caribbean. However, the concession most desired by Great Britain was the *asiento*—the monopoly assigned by Spain since the sixteenth century to another country, to supply slaves to Spanish America. Queen Anne's government had in fact proposed this to Spain as early as 1707, but it was not until March 1713 that it was finally agreed. The South Sea Company, established by the British government in 1711 for the purposes of managing public debt, was given a monopoly to handle the contract. The Company now had the right to transport 4,800 slaves each year to Spanish colonies in the Americas, as well as the right to engage in a limited

134

THE BRITISH EMPIRE

trade in goods, which of course generated endless possibilities for contraband.

The South Sea Company was dominated by Englishmen, among the most powerful and influential in England, who were already fully engaged in the slave trade with Britain's colonies in the Americas. Spain would end the *asiento* after thirty years, as agreed in the treaty, but by then England was so deeply involved in transatlantic slavery and the slave trade that it remained the key player throughout the eighteenth century. Its Atlantic-facing ports, especially Bristol and Liverpool, were transformed by the trade, and received finance from London to fuel their expansion. In turn, the profits from the slave trade and slave plantations in the British Empire made their way back to England—fuelling the industrial revolution, transforming infrastructure and accelerating economic growth as well as demographic expansion. Although the empire might have been English in origin, the nation's subjects had every reason to accept a British label for their expanding overseas enterprise.[5]

Territorial acquisitions now continued apace. Wars with continental European powers, especially France, brought new colonies, and the British Empire spread to Asia—especially the Indian subcontinent—where control was exercised by the East India Company rather than the British government. The most spectacular gains were made at the end of the Seven Years' War (1756–63), when the Treaty of Paris confirmed British control of what would become Canada, undermined almost completely the French presence in North America, demolished the threat to British interests in India and added new colonies in the Caribbean. The Seven Years' War, together with all those since the War of the Spanish Succession at the start of the century, also consolidated Great Britain's naval supremacy over its European rivals and gave the empire a competitive edge in international commerce. This was then reinforced by the 'discovery' in the

INTERNAL EMPIRE

1700s of Australia and New Zealand, which were subsequently added to the British Empire.

In the thirteen colonies that would become the United States of America, Great Britain had been aided greatly during the Seven Years' War by the troops raised locally. These were drawn from the migrants who had left England, Ireland, Scotland and Wales. The largest number were English, but they were not a majority and represented a far smaller proportion of the settlers than their share of the population of the Isles. This pattern continued and, in the fifteen years after 1760, 55,000 Protestant Irish, 40,000 Scots and 30,000 English emigrated to North America.[6] As a result, the English, now heavily outnumbered, considered themselves British; the military officers among them—such as George Washington—identified as British officers. Indeed, they continued to see themselves as British right up to the War of Independence, which began in 1775.

In 1783, under another Treaty of Paris, Great Britain was forced to recognise the independence of the thirteen colonies. It looked to some English politicians as if the defeat marked the end of the British Empire. Yet the opposite happened. The other colonies stayed loyal; many of the settlers in the United States moved to Canada, the Bahamas and other Caribbean islands in order to remain subjects of the British Empire rather than throw in their lot with the 'Americans'; and—within a few years—trade between Great Britain and the US had not only recovered its pre-war level but exceeded it.[7] The British Empire, with its British settler populations, showed remarkable staying power in the postwar years, suggesting that the concept of 'Britishness' was now firmly and deeply rooted.

And the territorial gains continued. The Congress of Vienna in 1814–15, at the end of the Napoleonic Wars, brought a swathe of new colonies into the British Empire, including Ceylon, Mauritius, Malta, Heligoland, the Cape of Good Hope, Trinidad

THE BRITISH EMPIRE

and the former Dutch territories of Berbice, Demerara and Essequibo (soon to be united as British Guiana). The new United Kingdom also acquired a series of protectorates, especially the Ionian Islands in the Mediterranean, while its dominant position in international trade and naval power started to give it an additional 'informal' empire in various parts of the world where sovereignty nominally resided in independent states, despite their lack of independence in practice. And although the UK abolished the slave trade in 1807, British—or more realistically English—pragmatism trumped principle in allowing the slave trade to Trinidad and British Guiana to continue, in order to overcome the perceived labour shortage in the new colonies.[8]

Slavery itself was abolished in 1834 in those parts of the British Empire under direct rule,[9] to be replaced by a system of indentured labour in colonies suffering from an acute lack of labour.[10] With the UK's shift to free trade in the 1840s and an end to preferential treatment of colonial exports, many West Indian possessions entered a long period of crisis, while the colonies with large numbers of British settlers became more assertive. Since British imperialism had been based on trade restrictions designed to favour the 'mother' country, free trade ran the risk of undermining the whole imperial project. Indeed, even an arch-imperialist such as Benjamin Disraeli felt compelled to write to the Foreign Secretary in 1852, 'These wretched colonies will all be independent too in a few years and are a millstone round our necks.'[11]

This anti-imperialist wobble among English elites did not last long, and never took hold among the masses. India became subject to direct rule in 1858, following the crushing of Indian resistance in the first War of Independence the previous year, and Queen Victoria was declared Empress of India. By the 1870s, imperial fervour had returned with a vengeance, and the 'scramble' for Africa in the following decade took it to new heights. Great

INTERNAL EMPIRE

swathes of the continent were annexed to the British Empire, in some cases using the old charter model of the Stuart kings. In 1897, England was subjected to an orgy of imperialism as part of the celebrations for the queen's Diamond Jubilee.

Empire had created a strong sense of Britishness both at home and abroad and, among the settler communities in the colonies, the English were by and large content to identify as British.[12] However, at home the English never lost their sense of Englishness, with its associated undertones of superiority towards the rest of the UK. Reinforced by pride in empire, the industrial revolution and naval supremacy, Englishness gained in strength towards the end of the nineteenth century.[13] Needless to say, when the time came to create a national football team in 1872, it would be one representing England—not Great Britain or the United Kingdom—that was established and internationally recognised.

While other countries, including the US, created anti-imperialist organisations to counter overseas expansion by the state, nothing similar happened in England. The radical and socialist movements were notoriously silent on dismantling empire (Engels was particularly unhelpful and Marx little better), so that by the end of the nineteenth century anti-imperialism in England was confined to a handful of brave individuals, mainly intellectuals.[14] Furthermore, English voters (unlike their counterparts in Scotland and Wales) were strongly opposed even to home rule in Ireland—such was their commitment to British Empire.[15] The empire had indeed created a sense of Britishness across the Isles, but it had also—in a much more subtle way—reinforced Englishness among the inhabitants of England.

Wales

The annexation of Wales by England as a result of the Laws in Wales Acts of 1535 and 1542 left no space at first for a new

THE BRITISH EMPIRE

identity among the Welsh. The expanded state was still 'England', with its 'English' parliament and 'English' army and navy, while the Welsh were clearly not English and were therefore left in a sort of identity limbo. And, of course, the English remained 'English' despite the expanded nature of their state. Yet there were Welshmen who both welcomed annexation and saw it as a means of creating a new British identity that would—if not supersede—at least sit comfortably alongside their Welshness. Although confined largely to the Welsh and Anglo-Welsh gentry, comprising no more than 10 per cent of the population, this was an important and influential group.

Among them was Humphrey Llwyd, whose *Cronica Walliae* was written in 1559 and published in 1584. It was the first history of Wales written in English and included the legendary story of Prince Madoc, a son of Owain Gwynedd (see Chapter 2), which had circulated in Welsh for at least a century and recalled the daring voyage of the Welsh prince at the end of the twelfth century:

> And at this tyme [c.1170] another of Owen Gwynedhs sonnes, named Madocke, lefte the lande in contention betwixt his bretherne, and prepared certaine shippes, with men and munition, and sought adventures by the seas. And sayled west levinge the cost of Irelande [so far] north that he came to a lande unknownen, where he saw many strange things. And this lande most needes bee some parte of that lande the which the Hispaniardes affirm them selves to be the first finders ... For by reason and order of cosmographie this lande to which Madoc came to, most needs bee some part of Nova Hispania, or Florida. And so hit was by Britons longe afore discovered before eyther Colonus or Americus lead any Hispaniardes thyther.[16]

The Madoc legend was of immense appeal to the Welsh elite— so much so that several of them were instrumental in ensuring

139

INTERNAL EMPIRE

that the work was indeed published and made available to an English-speaking audience. The legend not only undermined the Spanish claim to the Americas, but also established a British, not English, identity for overseas colonies. The logic of this was then pursued vigorously by John Dee, another man of Welsh descent, at the court of Queen Elizabeth, where he was a leading advisor and had been asked as early as 1570 to produce a report on the state of the realm's political, economic and social affairs.[17] Seven years later, he proposed in his influential *General and Rare Memorials pertayning to the Perfect Arte of Navigation* the establishment of a 'British Empire'. Although it is sometimes claimed that Humphrey Llwyd had first coined the phrase, there is no doubt that John Dee had more influence, due to his proximity to Queen Elizabeth.[18]

The name 'British Empire' did not become official until the union with Scotland in 1707, but it was in common use long before that—and some of the credit for this must go to those members of the Welsh gentry who saw in it a means of resolving the problem of identity thrust upon them after annexation in 1535. Thus, a Welsh privateer such as Henry Morgan—considered a mere pirate by Spain for his sacking of various Spanish ports in the Americas—had no trouble presenting himself as one of the architects of a 'British' empire, and using his new identity (and wealth) to leverage himself into the Lieutenant-Governorship of Jamaica and a knighthood in 1674. He would go on to acquire several sugar plantations in Jamaica and may have been the island's largest slaveowner before being recalled to England.

Morgan did not participate in the triangular trade (he was wealthy enough without it), but other members of the Welsh elite were not so coy. The Jeffreys family from Brecknockshire was especially active.[19] John Jeffreys (c. 1614–88) had been an assistant of the RAC and imported large numbers of African slaves into Virginia. His nephew Jeffrey and his younger brother

140

THE BRITISH EMPIRE

John, another assistant of the RAC, went further and advanced the money for the RAC to charter the *Hannibal*, for participation in the triangular trade. Fortunately for modern readers, and unfortunately for the Jeffreys family, the captain of the *Hannibal* kept an incredibly detailed log of all three parts of the triangle.[20] In addition to the exceptional cruelty towards the African slaves, we learn in intricate detail about the kind of goods sold to West African chiefs in exchange for slaves, the products needed by the slave-traders to clothe the slaves and control them during the middle passage, and the commodities bought in the Caribbean for the final leg.

These products and commodities were what started to bring the mass of the Welsh population, still largely monoglot Welsh-speakers, into the web of the transatlantic economy and the embryonic British Empire.[21] Chief among these products were the copper and brass items that were essential for slave-traders on the west coast of Africa as they sought to barter for slaves. And if, at the beginning of the seventeenth century, the source of these manufactured goods was mainly continental Europe, by the end it had become Wales, through a series of unanticipated events. First, the enormous copper mine at Falun in Sweden collapsed in 1687. Secondly, the tin-miners of Cornwall were going deeper underground and discovering rich deposits of copper ore. Thirdly, south Wales had the abundant coal deposits that could smelt Cornish ore into useable copper products. And, finally, zinc from Wales or elsewhere could be added to copper to make highly desirable brass manufactures for use in the triangular trade.

The Swansea–Neath area of south Wales was therefore drawn into the transatlantic economy through the trade in slaves, but it did not stop there. The rapidly expanding sugar industry in the British Caribbean islands, based on slavery, demanded a huge array of copper and brass products; much of it was supplied by south Wales. If the capital came from a mixture of Welsh and English

141

INTERNAL EMPIRE

entrepreneurs, the labour was supplied almost entirely by a Welsh proletariat drawn from the hinterland. These workers were among the first of the Welsh masses to be drawn into the commercial networks of the British Empire, and they acquired in the process a British identity to complement their Welsh one. When copper ore started to be mined at Parys Mountain in Anglesey in the second half of the eighteenth century, workers in the north of Wales were also brought into the British imperial web.

The coal in south Wales soon found further uses in the British Empire and, combined with other minerals (especially iron ore), led the region to be dubbed 'Imperial South Wales'. The key was the coke-smelting technology used in blast furnaces, which spread to south Wales in the 1750s and led to massive investments in ironworks over the next decades. The most important was the one at Cyfarthfa in Merthyr Tydfil, which was owned by Anthony Bacon—a man who had already made his fortune in imperial trade, including in slaves. With his partners, Bacon pioneered a method of refining pig iron that made the works at Cyfarthfa a global leader in technology.

Bacon was quick to see where the main market for the output of his ironworks would be: the imperial British navy. A cannon foundry was established that cast the cannon as a solid piece of metal and then bored out the barrel. The British Board of Ordnance ordered no fewer than 561 artillery pieces from the factory in 1778 during the US War of Independence.[22] By 1800 the Cyfarthfa iron foundry, now owned by Richard Crawshay, was the world's largest. It was the British Empire that sustained the factory and all the families who lived there, giving them a British identity to complement their Welsh one. The same was true of the other ironworks that had sprung up in the northeast of the country around Wrexham.

The miners were not the only Welsh workers to be drawn into the empire's commercial networks. The slaves themselves

142

THE BRITISH EMPIRE

had needs—especially the need to be clothed—and rural Wales would turn out to be the source of much of the cloth required. Welsh woollen textiles had been sold via Shrewsbury to England and elsewhere for centuries, but slavery in the British colonies of the Americas created new markets. 'Welsh cottons' (they were actually made of wool) and 'Welsh plains' became the staple article of dress for the slaves. The raw textiles were produced on the farms of rural Wales before being finished elsewhere, so that great swathes of the Welsh population were drawn into the networks of the British Empire. There was even a demand for Welsh textiles in the barter trade for slaves on the coast of West Africa.

The British Empire therefore came to Wales and gave a British identity to the Welsh. The people of Wales did not emigrate to the colonies in vast numbers, and their share of the settler population was less than their share of the UK population. Yet some did leave, and left their mark on the countries where they settled. In the thirteen colonies, 'Welsh Neck' on the upper Pee Dee River in South Carolina was named in honour of the Baptists who settled there in the first half of the eighteenth century, while Bryn Mawr ('big hill') in Pennsylvania, settled at the same time by Quakers, gave its name to the US women's college that is famous today. Welsh-speaking settler colonies were also established in the informal British empire, especially Argentina, while hundreds of Welsh places had their names inscribed in the colonies during the imperial years.[23]

One place where the qualitative impact of emigration from Wales was much greater than its quantitative one was in the Indian subcontinent, where the East India Company in particular attracted Welsh administrators, diplomats and soldiers. The best known is probably Sir William Jones, who founded the Asiatic Society of Bengal in 1784, and whose linguistic brilliance is widely recognised today.[24] However, several Welsh migrants to

INTERNAL EMPIRE

India and other parts of Asia used their East India connections to make fortunes that would come back to the economy of Wales—none more so than Sir Harford Jones.[25] Although a British diplomat by profession, he made a fortune trading in a wide range of commodities, which he subsequently reinvested in his home nation after his retirement.

The really serious money, however, was not made by Welsh entrepreneurs in India, but on slave plantations in the Caribbean, with the fortunes put back into Wales. No family illustrates this better than the Pennants, with Gifford Pennant settling in Jamaica shortly after its seizure from Spain in 1655.[26] A significant land- and slaveowner by the time of his death, the estates passed through the male line until they reached his grandson John, who no longer bothered to live in Jamaica, having become an absentee owner. His son, Richard, acquired through marriage a half share in the Penrhyn estate in Snowdonia, then used his Jamaican wealth to purchase the rest. The estate would now be used to extract slate to fuel the building boom in Great Britain.

Richard Pennant, later Lord Penrhyn of Louth, would become the richest man in Wales with investments in his native country that far outstripped those in Jamaica. His slate mines spawned a vast network of infrastructure projects that were needed to bring the slate to market and, of course, there was an ostentatious castle for the family to display its wealth. Yet he remained conscious of the role that slavery in the British Empire had played in building the family fortune and defended the slave trade vigorously in parliament, claiming in 1789 that 'if they [should pass] the vote of abolition they actually [would strike] at seventy millions of property, they [would ruin] the colonies, and by destroying an essential nursery of seamen, [give] up the dominion of the sea at a single glance.'[27]

By the middle of the nineteenth century there was no part of Wales that had not been touched by the British Empire. The

144

THE BRITISH EMPIRE

Welsh had become British, despite the fact that—even now—so many only spoke Welsh. Other factors contributed to a sense of Britishness, as Gwyn Williams made clear so brilliantly in a series of books,[28] but participation in the imperial project was the most important. Indeed, so powerful was the sense of Britishness brought by the empire that many intellectuals worried about the loss of a Welsh identity among the population at large. That did not happen, as Chapter 4 has made clear, but the pull of the British Empire was very powerful—and the Welsh were enthusiastic supporters.

Scotland

Scotland's attempts to forge an empire of its own had ended in failure in Darién, while penetrating the English one involved numerous obstacles even after the union of the two crowns. Since full access to the English colonies was a large part of the motivation for union with England, it is no surprise that Scots would become enthusiastic participants in the British Empire. The Jacobite rebellions imposed some restrictions at first, especially on those from the highlands and islands, but from the second half of the eighteenth century Scots were disproportionately represented in every sphere of imperial life, and would remain so right to the end. Indeed, one of the largest exhibitions ever held to celebrate the British Empire was hosted by Glasgow in 1938.

As in the case of Wales, empire offered many in Scotland a solution to English dominance in the Isles: the creation through empire of a British identity that did not overwhelmingly favour the English, and a way around discrimination faced at home. With the Church of England denied a monopoly overseas, for example, Scottish Presbyterians faced no institutional obstacles in the colonies, and church ministers were prominently represented in colonial society. Meanwhile, those denied access to land in

145

INTERNAL EMPIRE

Scotland could seek it in the British Empire, under conditions that could never have been replicated in their own country.

The Scottish roles in imperial administration and military affairs have long been known. More recently major Scottish participation in slavery, and to a lesser extent the slave trade, has come to light.[29] And the roles of Scottish merchants, planters, manufacturers and traders are central to understanding the economic history of virtually all colonies in the British Empire, a legacy that has left behind dozens of place names that survived decolonisation. In the process, Scots acquired a British identity through empire both at home and abroad that complemented their long-established Scottishness, rather than subsuming it.

Scottish merchants had tried to enter the English slave trade before 1707, but without much success. The Act of Union, however, removed the legal obstacles to transporting slaves to the now British colonies, but there was still the risk that parliament would restore the monopoly previously enjoyed by the RAC. Between 1709 and 1711, no fewer than eight petitions from six Scottish cities were despatched to oppose this, suggesting that the ports in question (Glasgow, Edinburgh, Aberdeen, Dundee, Inverness and Montrose) were seriously interested in participating in the slave trade.[30]

The monopoly was not restored, but direct Scottish participation in the trade in slaves turned out in the end to be relatively minor. This was not due to squeamishness on the part of the merchants, but more likely was a consequence of the dominant role in the trade already taken by Bristol, Liverpool and London. Instead, Scottish participation took a more indirect form, with Scots active as masters and surgeons on slave ships sailing from English ports and as merchants in the ports themselves. Indeed, it has been estimated that one in ten of London's slave-traders were Scots at the height of the trade.[31]

THE BRITISH EMPIRE

Much more important for Scotland than the slave trade, as a route into the British Empire, was slavery itself. Even before the Act of Union, Scottish merchants had been active—albeit 'under the radar'—in England's North American colonies, as agents for slave-grown tobacco-planters in the Chesapeake Bay area. These merchants not only purchased the tobacco, but also provided the finance to allow the planters to buy slaves. And the tobacco so acquired was usually then smuggled into Scotland for domestic consumption, or reexported to continental Europe. After 1707 these activities in British North America, no longer illegal, expanded rapidly; some Scots even became owners of slave-grown tobacco plantations themselves, while employing their countrymen as factors, overseers, surgeons, accountants and so on.

Yet it was not tobacco but another commodity that led to the deepest link between Scotland and slavery in the British Empire. That commodity was slave-grown sugar, in which English colonies in the Caribbean had started to specialise in the second half of the seventeenth century, as a result of the spectacular profits that could be made. Scottish merchants had been quietly purchasing sugar from the English colonies even before the Act of Union, but after 1707 there was nothing to stop Scots from participating openly and legally in all aspects of the sugar industry, and they took full advantage.

The most important Caribbean colony for Great Britain was Jamaica, to which Scots were particularly attracted, so much so that one observer could write in 1774, '[the colony was] greatly indebted to North Britain [Scotland], as very nearly one third of the inhabitants are either natives of that country or descendants from those who were.'[32] Much the same could be said of other Caribbean islands, especially those ceded to Great Britain by France in the eighteenth century, where Scots figured prominently and disproportionately in those buying land from the crown.[33]

147

INTERNAL EMPIRE

As happened in Wales, slavery provided a big stimulus to industrialisation in Scotland. The Scottish clothing industry was a particular beneficiary, with cheap linen clothing from the eastern lowlands being purchased by plantation-owners for the slaves, while salted herring from the western highlands became a staple of their diet. On the notorious Bance Island off the west coast of Africa, used by slave-traders as a holding station for slaves before the middle passage to the Caribbean, it was a Scot (Richard Oswald) who insisted the African caddies on his golf course be dressed in tartan loincloths; and at least one Scottish planter in Jamaica purchased tartans from the same supplier in Bannockburn for the use of his slaves.[34] When the planters started to export sea island cotton, it became a vital raw material for the new textile mills of the western lowlands.

The city that benefited most from this first wave of Scottish industrialisation was Glasgow. This was due to the grip that the city had established over slave-grown tobacco imports from the British colonies in North America. By the 1760s, Glasgow—with its two outports of Greenock and Port Glasgow—accounted for 98 per cent of Scottish imports of tobacco, while controlling about 40 per cent of total British tobacco imports. The links between Glaswegian merchants and tobacco plantation-owners then provided the city with an incentive to diversify: 'Tobacco houses set up many of their own centres of production by investing heavily in tanneries, bottleworks, linen manufactures, sugar-refining, breweries, ironworks, collieries, printworks and many other economic activities in Glasgow and the hinterland of the city.'[35]

These links with plantations in North America also included credit, making Glasgow one of the key centres for international finance until the flows of finance and tobacco imports were interrupted by the US War of Independence, which started in 1775. Yet Glasgow soon recovered, with sugar merchant houses

THE BRITISH EMPIRE

now coming to the fore. Their representatives dominated the politics of the city and established the Glasgow West India Association in 1807 to fight against slave emancipation, alongside the *Glasgow Courier*. These interests would be a formidable barrier for the Scottish abolition movement, which was gaining momentum at the same time and drawing inspiration from the more progressive writers among the Scottish Enlightenment.

By the beginning of the nineteenth century, there were few parts of the Scottish economy that had not been affected by unrestricted access to the British Empire. The population of Scotland (1.2 million in 1755) may have grown to 1.6 million by 1801, but this was dwarfed by the numbers of people in the colonies of the Americas being served by Scottish exports. In 1770, for example, on the eve of the US War of Independence, there were 2.7 million in the British mainland colonies and nearly a million in the British Caribbean. This latter market became so important that 65 per cent of Scottish home-produced goods for export were destined for the West Indies as late as 1813.[36]

It was textiles, especially linens, that explained this high figure. This was an industry, as in Wales, that affected families throughout Scotland. An estimated 40,000 weavers were directly involved in the 1780s, and some 170,000 women are reckoned to have found their principal source of income in spinning linen yarn. Adding in those employed in finishing trades, a total of perhaps 230,000 found employment through an industry with direct links to the colonies, giving them every reason to adopt a British identity. As John Naismith commented in 1790, 'The linen manufacture has been the most universal source of wealth and happiness introduced into Scotland. To how many thousands has it afforded bread for these forty years past?'[37]

There would be other spin-offs from the linen industry, especially the jute industry based in Dundee with its sacks, packaging and ropes. This industry, however, was intimately

149

connected with the Asian part of the British Empire, where newly acquired colonial possessions would provide the impetus for the next stage of Scottish industrialisation in the nineteenth and early twentieth centuries, based on iron, steel, shipbuilding and engineering. So large were the fortunes made by Scottish industrialists and financiers that the export of capital to the British Empire—not just goods and services—became a crucial part of Scottish economic success. Indeed, nearly half of the increase in Scottish capital between 1885 and 1910 came from overseas investments.[38] Small wonder, therefore, that Scots became such enthusiastic cheerleaders for Great Britain and the overseas empire in its expansionary phase.

It was not just capital that left Scotland for the empire. Emigration, especially to the settler colonies, was hugely important. This was partly 'push', given the clearances in the highlands, and partly 'pull', given what the colonies could offer. Not all went to the British Empire, many preferring to emigrate to the United States after it gained its independence, but the impact of Scottish emigration on the colonies was enormous in quantitative terms. The 1901 census, for example, revealed that Scotland—with 10 per cent of the UK population—accounted for 15 per cent of the British-born in Australia, 20 per cent in South Africa, 21 per cent in Canada and 23 per cent in New Zealand.[39] As for the qualitative impact, Scottish missionaries, merchants, military officers and administrators played an outsize role in almost all the colonies, not just the settler ones. Indeed, in 1937 the Governors-General of Australia, Canada, India and South Africa were all Scots.

The role of Scots in building the British Empire inspired a spate of books on the theme of a Scottish empire, the first of which was published by Andrew Gibb in 1937.[40] Gibb was a huge admirer of the role that Scotland had played in imperial construction and expansion, paying particular attention to the

THE BRITISH EMPIRE

Scottish governors all over Africa, Australia and Canada, and he saw no contradiction between being Scottish and British. Yet he had no illusions about the role that Scotland played in this imperial exercise, and he concluded:

> The existence of the Empire has been the most important factor in deciding the relationship of Scotland and England in the last three centuries. The relationship of the two countries was embittered and the future in great part determined by the jealousy of the English in the Darien affair. It might be possible to permit the Scot to share in an English Empire, as a subordinate ... but that he should pretend to an empire of his own was inadmissible and intolerable. And so it came about that a share in the trade of the nascent English Empire was offered to the Scottish commissioners for the union of the parliaments ... *But let there be no mistake about this partnership. The will, the direction, the philosophy of the Empire have been all but wholly England's. In this Scotland has loyally and even blindly acquiesced under the leadership of the ruling classes, who wedded themselves enthusiastically to the imperial idea.* (Author's emphasis.)[41]

Ireland

Ireland, with its own parliament, had become a kingdom in 1542—just before the English Empire went offshore. However, this could not disguise the fact that Ireland was at the time an English colony, would become a British one in 1707, and would remain so until 1801. Furthermore, the King/Queen of Ireland was always none other than the King/Queen of England or Great Britain, while the Irish parliament had little autonomy as a result of Poynings' Law dating from 1494. This meant that Ireland, unlike Scotland and Wales, began its participation in the empire as a colony, subject to all kinds of restrictions in foreign trade, imperial appointments, religious affairs and the distribution of public offices. It was not until the nineteenth century, therefore, that all Irish subjects and citizens could participate fully in the imperial project. This was bound to have an impact on the spread of a sense of Britishness among the population at large.[42]

Faced with discrimination at home and loss of access to land, in the seventeenth century many Irish—invariably Catholics—chose to migrate to English colonies in the Americas as indentured labourers (others were forced to do so as a result of convictions for various offences). However, some prosperous Irish merchant families—mainly Protestant—also established themselves in the Caribbean, where they funded the tobacco trade on the English islands before the switch to slave-grown sugar.[43] Thus, there was a strong Irish presence in the empire even before it became a British one in 1707—although it would be fanciful to imagine that many of these migrants felt much imperial pride, as most of them had been driven across the Atlantic by a combination of dire economic circumstances and discrimination at home.

As indentured European labour was replaced by African slave labour in the colonies, Irish workers and their descendants moved to different parts of the empire. A particular favourite was the island of Montserrat, where—as early as the middle of the seventeenth century—the majority of the white population were Irish Catholics.[44] Following the mass expulsion from Ireland after Cromwell's conquest, the numbers of Irish on Montserrat increased further and, as a proportion of the white population, reached 70 per cent by the close of the century.[45] At this time, with sugar now as the main export, the labour force consisted almost entirely of African slaves, so that the Irish—Protestant and Catholic—simply replicated the social and economic role played by the British in other Caribbean islands. And yet there was an important difference: their loyalty to the British crown was considered suspect, following the support given by some

152

THE BRITISH EMPIRE

of the Irish settlers to French forces in various occupations of the island.[46]

Slavery and the slave trade had played a big part in linking the Scottish and Welsh economies to the empire and creating a sense of Britishness in the process. There would be echoes of this in Ireland, but the island's colonial status until union in 1801 changed the impact significantly. Ireland had exported live cattle to England until the English parliament prohibited the trade by passing the Cattle Acts in 1665 and 1667. Farmers, especially in Munster, found a solution in the export of salted provisions to the Caribbean (beef, pork and butter), but not all of this went to the British islands. Those exports marked for France invariably ended up in the French, not British, Caribbean, where salted beef was a staple of the slave diet. And, in large part because of the increase in the slave population of Saint-Domingue (modern Haiti), exports jumped from 30,000 barrels a year at the start of the eighteenth century to 100,000 some fifty years later.[47]

Exports of salted provisions may have made Munster farmers prosperous in the 1700s, but did not necessarily create a sense of Britishness. On the contrary, Munster continued to export its young men in large numbers to enter into French military service until at least the 1730s, following a tradition after the Treaty of Limerick in 1691, when 12,000 had fled the province to join the French army.[48] For this part of Ireland, association with the British Empire was much more transactional or even non-existent. For example, following the passage by the English parliament of the Wool Act of 1699, which banned the export of Irish woollens, a textile industry developed around Cork that found its main (and illegal) market in the Portuguese colony of Brazil.[49]

By the 1760s, the export of salted provisions accounted for the largest share of direct Irish exports to the British colonies in the Americas. The only serious competitor was linen exports, which

153

INTERNAL EMPIRE

had grown rapidly after 1705, when restrictions were removed on Irish sales of the product to the colonies and the trade became legal.[50] Although the vast bulk of exports went first to England (a consequence of the 'bounty' system operated by the British Exchequer), they were then reexported to the Americas, where they clothed the slaves and were known simply as 'Irish'.

This was a clear link between Ireland, slavery and the British Empire, and it might have been expected to create a sense of Britishness among those involved. However, the epicentre of the linen industry was Ulster, where Presbyterian settlers and their descendants had their own quarrels with the British government, over various forms of discrimination against dissenters in Ireland. Many in fact chose to emigrate from the middle of the eighteenth century onwards, with British North America a particular favourite. When the War of Independence broke out in 1775, a large number of these 'Scots-Irish' were to be found fighting for the rebels, rather than the British. Those loyal to the crown soon departed when the war ended, but the first federal census of the United States in 1790 showed that between 14 and 17 per cent of the white population were of Irish origin—a very high figure by any standards and an indication that 'Britishness' did not have much appeal among this group.

Catholics had faced no formal discrimination if they were willing to work as indentured labourers in the English/British colonies (the shortage of labour throughout the empire made this inevitable). They would even be recruited en masse for the British armed forces after the Seven Years' War, despite legal restrictions. Before 1801, however, the more prestigious colonial positions, including nearly all the officer class, were reserved for the Anglo-Irish. This group—Church of Ireland by religion and part of the dominant Protestant Ascendancy— saw themselves as quintessentially British, and for some of them their Irishness was simply a matter of place of birth.

THE BRITISH EMPIRE

Among their number were many of the most famous names in imperial history, including Arthur Wellesley (later first Duke of Wellington), who was born in Dublin and first commissioned into the British Army in 1787.

Yet English bigotry and prejudice could still cause problems for some members of this privileged elite. One example was the Anglo-Irish colonel Edward Marcus Despard, who became the first Superintendent of the British Settlement in the Bay of Honduras in 1786, after a stellar military career fighting alongside Horatio Nelson in the Caribbean. Recalled to London after a stream of complaints by slave-owning British settlers, he was acquitted on all charges. However, the British government halved his salary, refused to pay his expenses and at first denied him a pension. As a result, he ended up in a debtors' gaol. On release, he was then accused of treason, on the basis of false claims that he had plotted with Irish revolutionaries to overthrow the British state. Despite Nelson's pleas, he was hung, drawn and quartered—the last person in the Isles to suffer this fate—just two years after Ireland ceased to be a British colony.[51]

War with France had started in 1793, and the Irish rebellion a few years later; there was the constant fear that France would invade Ireland. The clamour from Catholics and Presbyterians against the formal and informal discrimination they faced grew ever stronger, while the restrictions on Ireland's commerce looked increasingly anachronistic. Prime Minister William Pitt (the Younger) had therefore concluded that the best solution to the Irish 'problem' was a legislative union between Great Britain and Ireland. Since Ireland was nominally a kingdom, this was also a proposal to merge two separate realms. Unlike previous arguments for unification, however, this one put British imperialism at its heart. It was, said Pitt, a union that would increase 'the general power of Empire ... to a very great extent by a consolidation of the strength of the two kingdoms.'[52]

155

INTERNAL EMPIRE

As we know, Pitt's arguments carried the day, and the Act of Union came into force in 1801. However, as the previous quote implied, Pitt had imagined a new state with new institutions, including a 'General Imperial Legislature'. Sylvester Douglas, a Scot and former Chief Secretary for Ireland, was even more explicit arguing that 'Ireland, by an Union, no more becomes a *province* in any offensive sense of the word, than Great Britain: they both became provinces, or component parts of one whole and integrated Empire.' The imperial theme was also taken up by a Scot: Henry Dundas, Secretary at War and notorious for delaying the abolition of the slave trade, who argued that after union 'the voice of Irishmen ... would be heard, not only in Europe, but in Asia, Africa and America.'

This did not happen; instead, Ireland was simply absorbed into the existing institutions of the British state, with no constitutional change in discriminatory laws against Catholics (that against Presbyterians had largely ended by this time). However, anti-Catholic discrimination did in practice diminish after union and ended almost completely soon after 1829. From that point onwards, and in many cases before, all Irish were in theory free to participate in the imperial project at every level, even if it was a 'British' and not a 'Hiberno-British' Empire. Many did so, including Catholics and Presbyterians, and Irish of all denominations were commonly found among imperial military officials and colonial administrators.

The empire therefore offered a convenient avenue for those in Ireland seeking new opportunities, and (after union) it often added a British identity to their existing Irish one. However, some Irish rejected the British Empire, in exactly the same way previous generations had opposed English/British overlordship of the island's affairs; and their numbers were greatly increased by the crass and insensitive response of the British government to the onset of the Irish famine in 1845–6. Even if emigration was

156

THE BRITISH EMPIRE

not an official policy, it did not look that way to the millions who left Ireland in the wake of the disaster, lowering the population from 8.2 million in 1841 to 6.5 million ten years later. The population would continue to fall, dropping to 4.7 million by 1891, as Ireland failed to reap the benefits of imperial expansion to the same extent as Great Britain.

The British Empire was, therefore, much more controversial in Ireland than in England, Scotland or Wales. It may have reinforced 'Britishness' among those willing to wear the label after union, but it failed to bridge national divisions. When, for example, Queen Victoria's Diamond Jubilee was celebrated with huge pomp throughout Great Britain in 1897, Irish anti-imperialists marched through Dublin carrying an empty coffin representing the death of the empire; when the protesters were blocked by the police, the coffin was then unceremoniously dumped in the River Liffey.[53] More seriously, during the Boer War in South Africa (1899–1902), Irish fought on different sides, with some joining the British Army in the imperialist cause while others saw in the Boers' fight against British rule an echo of their own struggle against the British Empire.

The founders of the home rule movement in Ireland in the 1870s thought they could bridge the divisions in Irish society with their call for an Irish parliament for local affairs. Ireland would have remained in both the UK and the British Empire under this plan, but with devolved powers to address local grievances. The movement's rise was spectacular, winning fifty-nine seats in the 1874 general election, and increasing this to eighty-six under the leadership of Charles Parnell (a Protestant landowner) in 1885. William Gladstone, Prime Minister for the third time, now had little choice, and embraced home rule the following year. However, the first bill was defeated in the House of Commons, a second in the House of Lords and a third one, although successful, was suspended following the outbreak of the First World War in 1914.

INTERNAL EMPIRE

The prospect of home rule, leading to an Irish parliament dominated by Catholics, was a source of concern to many Protestants, despite the non-sectarian nature of Parnell's Irish Parliamentary Party. These concerns were particularly acute in Ulster, with its long-established British connections and anti-Catholic traditions. Unionists, as they would now be called, were not afraid to use violence in support of their political aims, and paramilitary organisations began to emerge. Inevitably, the hardening of sectarianism in Ulster was matched by an increase in radicalism among Irish nationalists. This led to the launch of Sinn Féin in 1905, with its members demanding a break from the UK and the British Empire altogether, rather than home rule.

Difficult as it would prove for Irish republicans to sever the link with the UK, it would be even more difficult for them to leave the empire. The Easter Uprising in 1916 may have been easily suppressed by the British authorities, but in the 1918 general election Sinn Féin swept the board at the expense of 'home rulers'. The British government indicated its willingness to grant devolution, and even passed legislation in 1920 for two parliaments (one in the north and the other in the south of Ireland). However, this came nowhere near meeting the aspirations of the new generation of Irish nationalists led by Sinn Féin, who had launched a war against the British state in 1919 under the command of an 'Irish Republican Army'.

At the conclusion of hostilities, in the Anglo-Irish Treaty of 1921, the Irish negotiators secured their own independent country (the Irish Free State), separate from the UK—the minimum that was now acceptable for nationalists. However, they also had to accept the partition of Ireland with a diminished Ulster of six, not nine, counties—to ensure a large Protestant majority—remaining in what would now be the United Kingdom of Great Britain and *Northern* Ireland. This was a bitter pill to swallow,

THE BRITISH EMPIRE

but perhaps even more bitter was the British insistence that the rest of Ireland remain a member of the empire. Arguably, it was this second concession that was the most painful. The survival of the empire, it would seem, was more important to the British state than the territorial integrity of the UK itself.

6

THE COMMONWEALTH

Empire provided a strong British identity for most citizens of the UK—especially after the partition of Ireland in 1922, when those who most rejected the label of 'British' became part of the Irish Free State. The First World War had also shown the importance of Britishness in recruiting a volunteer army—at least for the first two years, until combat losses made conscription inevitable—and even the incompetence shown at times during the conflict by military and political leaders did not significantly dent support for a war effort that was always described as 'British'.

When the Great War started in 1914, the British Empire had been in existence for more than 200 years. A sense of Britishness in the Isles had not only taken hold, but had also become stronger with the passage of time. This was intimately related to imperial expansion, which continued without a break at the end of the war as a result of the Treaty of Versailles in 1919 and the establishment of the League of Nations in 1920. This paved the way for the grant to the UK of various 'mandates'—the word used by the new League of Nations in preference to 'colonies'.

INTERNAL EMPIRE

The most important British mandates were Palestine and Mesopotamia, both carved out of the defeated Ottoman Empire.

For imperial subjects in the colonies, Britishness was more complicated. Anxious to avoid what had happened in the thirteen colonies, when rebellion against Great Britain had led to an independent United States, British governments in their more strategic moments recognised that the relationship to the metropolitan state in the colonies—at least those with a large white settler population—needed to evolve. In this way, it was hoped, colonial subjects would stay loyal, while UK citizens would continue to take pride in being British.

It took a long time, but the text of the Anglo-Irish Treaty of 1921 outlined a new official imperial concept. This was a British Commonwealth of Nations, to sit alongside (and inside) the British Empire, with participating countries no longer described as colonies, but as self-governing dominions. Dominion status, it was at first assumed, would be limited to those countries where white British settlers formed a majority—but eventually British governments of all stripes hoped that dominion status might be adopted by other colonies as well.

Yet, if the British Commonwealth of Nations would become the institution designed to preserve a sense of Britishness among colonial subjects, what about the citizens of the UK itself, whose loyalty was primarily to a British *Empire*? That dilemma was only resolved when the empire itself collapsed after the end of the Second World War. The British Commonwealth of Nations would then become known just as the Commonwealth of Nations, albeit with the British Head of State as its most senior figure, and the hope was that this new body—British in all but name—would now command the loyalty not just of citizens of former colonies, but also of UK citizens themselves.

THE COMMONWEALTH

Dominions

The aftermath of the US War of Independence had left the remaining British colonies in North America in a vulnerable situation. If it were not for the arrival of thousands of English-speaking loyalists from the US, French-speakers would have been in a majority among the white settlers in Canada. Yet these same French settlers, who had been encouraged by France to rebel against British rule during the war, could not be expected willingly to accept a subordinate status now that they were a minority.

The threat of rebellion by French settlers in Canada meant that a solution had to be found quickly. An ingenious ruling by William Pitt the Younger, the British Prime Minister, defused the situation. The Constitutional Act of 1791 divided the Province of Quebec in two—Upper Canada, with its majority of English-speakers; and Lower Canada, with a majority of French-speakers—with each part given its own representative assembly. The maritime provinces, which were majority-anglophone— Nova Scotia, New Brunswick and Newfoundland—were left unaffected.

The creation of the two new assemblies defused a potentially dangerous situation for the British Empire. All the provinces, including Lower Canada, stayed loyal during the war between the UK and US that started in 1812. However, the 1791 Constitutional Act did not rescind the veto power of the resident British colonial governors. This would prove as irksome to English-speakers in Upper Canada as to French-speakers in Lower Canada, and rebellions broke out in both provinces in 1837. They were easily suppressed, but the British government still felt sufficiently worried to establish an inquiry, led by Lord Durham.

The Durham Report, published in 1839, made a number of recommendations, including the merger of Upper and Lower

163

INTERNAL EMPIRE

Canada into a new Province of Canada. This was relatively uncontroversial for the British government and was adopted the following year, although it was by no means uncontroversial for the francophone population. This was because the report had enraged French-speakers and French writers all over the world by describing French Canadians as 'a people with no literature and no history', leading to a deluge of critical comment.[1] Durham, however, had no reservations and wrote:

> I entertain no doubts as to the national character which must be given to Lower Canada; it must be that of the British Empire; that of the majority of the population of British America; that of the great race which must, in the lapse of no long period of time, be predominant over the whole North American Continent ... it must henceforth be the first and steady purpose of the British Government to establish an English population, with English laws and language, in this Province, and to trust its government to none but a decidedly English Legislature.[2]

This recommendation chimed with the Colonial Office, and British emigration to Canada was strongly encouraged. Much more radical for British authorities, however, was the proposal that all the provincial assemblies in Canada be given 'responsible government', meaning that the crown's power of veto could only be exercised rarely if at all.[3] This was too much for the British government of the day, but in 1848 it was quietly adopted without any fanfare following a vote of no confidence in the executive by the provincial assembly of Nova Scotia. Instead of exercising his veto, the Lieutenant Governor of the province (the queen's representative) sent for the leader of the opposition and asked him to form a new government. Governors of the other Canadian provinces then had no choice but to accept responsible government as normal practice and did so in the next two years.

164

THE COMMONWEALTH

The significance of this was not immediately apparent, but would become so a decade later. By this time, the British government had been implementing for some years a strict policy of free trade that it was assumed would operate across the empire. When, therefore, the government of the Province of Canada passed a budget in 1859 that included import duties, this led to a potential constitutional crisis. The provincial government stood firm, and the Finance Minister stated a case that would come to represent an important milestone on the path from British Empire to British Commonwealth:

> Self-government would be utterly annihilated if the views of the Imperial Government were to be preferred to those of the people of Canada. It is therefore the duty of the present Government distinctly to affirm the right of the Canadian legislature to adjust the taxation of the people in the way they deem best, even if it should unfortunately happen to meet the disapproval of the Imperial Ministry. Her Majesty cannot be allowed to disavow such acts, unless her advisers are prepared to assume the administration of the affairs of the Colony irrespective of the views of the inhabitants.[4]

The British government chose not to challenge this argument. As a result, the Canadian provinces now enjoyed a degree of self-government that was very different from what had gone before. In effect, they were being decolonised while remaining British—and the next step was to dismantle the barriers between the provinces themselves. This was achieved through the British North America Act of 1867, which created a confederation of all the provinces except Newfoundland.[5] The name of the new country was to be the Dominion of Canada, with the British monarch always acting as Head of State. (A proposal to call it the Kingdom of Canada was allegedly rejected on the grounds that it might offend US republican sensitivities.)

165

INTERNAL EMPIRE

This was the first time within the British Empire that a colony had become a dominion, and it marked the beginning of a new concept of Britishness for imperial subjects. It is probably fair to say that the vast majority of UK citizens and subjects within the home Isles were not aware at first of any great change, but it did represent a significant difference for those living in Canada. Instead of having to choose between staying as a colony or becoming an independent state, they could remain British while enjoying a high degree of autonomy. And that autonomy would steadily increase—so much so that, by the end of the First World War, Canada had effectively become an independent state, without the need formally to declare independence, and while remaining part of the British Empire.[6]

The Dominion of Canada's autonomy transformed the country, albeit at the expense of the indigenous peoples, who suffered grievously from territorial expansion and ethnic cleansing; dominion status also led to a period of prosperity rivalled only by that in the US. The population, whether they spoke English, French or an indigenous language, slowly began to become Canadian, but they—or at least the English-speakers—did not cease to be British. The first premier of the Dominion of Canada, John Macdonald, famously declared in his last election address, 'A British subject I was born—a British subject I will die.' It was a common sentiment. And, for the inhabitants of the UK, Canada's dominion status meant that there was no reason to question the basis of their own Britishness. The British Empire was still flourishing, even as the colonial system on which it depended was evolving in a different direction.

The Canadian experiment with responsible government was deemed to have worked sufficiently well for British governments to extend it to other possessions where white British settlers formed a majority: the six Australian colonies, Newfoundland and New Zealand. The same happened to the two South African

166

THE COMMONWEALTH

colonies (the Cape Colony and Natal), where British settlers predominated among the white population and where non-white peoples had almost no political rights. (The Transvaal and the Orange Free State, with their white settler Afrikaans-speaking populations, were effectively outside British control until the end of the Boer War in 1902.)

In these colonies, as in Canada, dominion status followed the adoption of responsible government. The Australian colonies, having formed a federation, became a dominion in 1900. Newfoundland and New Zealand did the same in 1907.[7] The four South African colonies formed a political union and became a dominion in 1910. The UK, it seemed, had found an evolutionary formula for those colonies where the white British population was in a majority among those exercising political rights. All the dominions were then given increasing autonomy, including in defence and foreign policy, while remaining part of the British Empire, with a shared monarch.

Self-government was used by all the dominions to reinforce their British character. Emigration from the UK soared, especially in the first decade of the twentieth century, when 63 per cent of those leaving Great Britain left for different parts of the empire—mainly Australia and Canada.[8] The dominions then used their control over domestic affairs to restrict non-white immigration. A 'white Australia' policy was adopted by the new federation, while Asian migration was restricted into Canada and New Zealand. Voting rights for native populations were severely curtailed, especially in the Union of South Africa, where the Afrikaner political parties became increasingly important after the Boer War. The bonds between white British settlers and their relatives in the UK then reinforced a shared British, and heavily racist, identity.

The dominions played a key role in helping the UK emerge victorious from the First World War, for which they had voluntarily provided large numbers of troops. This contribution could not

167

go unrecognised and, even before the war had ended, the British government had hosted an Imperial War Conference, whose Resolution IX had recognised the importance of the dominions 'as autonomous nations of an Imperial Commonwealth', as well as agreeing that the dominions should have 'an adequate voice in foreign policy and in foreign relations, and should provide effective arrangements for continuous consultation in all important matters of common Imperial concern, and for such necessary concerted action, founded on consultation, as the several governments may determine.'[9]

But what would happen to those colonies in which the white population was in a tiny minority? Such possessions, after all, had also provided vast numbers of volunteers for the war effort, even if they had had no choice about declaring war, and none more so than India.

Dominion status for India was raised by some in Great Britain as well as by a faction of the Indian independence movement, but it was opposed by the existing dominions and the government in London. As a result, India had to be content with warm words at the 1917 Imperial War Conference and a promise, at some unspecified future date, of 'a share in the framing of the foreign policy of the Commonwealth.' Other colonies were not even mentioned.[10]

The dominions would now be a very small and select club. However, there would be one important—if reluctant—addition in the immediate aftermath of the First World War. In the negotiations leading up to the Anglo-Irish Treaty of 1921, the British government had insisted that the Irish Free State remain in the empire. All attempts by the Irish delegation to avoid this fate failed, and the British delegation also insisted that Ireland accept dominion status. This was then written into Article 1 of the treaty: 'Ireland shall have the same constitutional status in the Community of Nations known as the British Empire as

THE COMMONWEALTH

the Dominion of Canada, the Commonwealth of Australia, the Dominion of New Zealand, and the Union of South Africa...'

As a concession to Irish nationalism, however, the oath sworn by parliamentarians would *not* be to the British Empire. Instead, Article 4 of the treaty stated that Members of the Parliament of the Irish Free State would declare:

> I ... do solemnly swear true faith and allegiance to the Constitution of the Irish Free State as by law established and that I will be faithful to H.M. King George V, his heirs and successors by law, in virtue of the common citizenship of Ireland with Great Britain and her adherence to and membership of the group of nations forming the British Commonwealth of Nations.

This was the first time the phrase 'British Commonwealth of Nations' was ever used in an official document and, to emphasise the point, it was repeated in the first article of the constitution of the Irish Free State. Ireland may have been partitioned and forced to stay in the British Empire, but it had obliged the UK government to make explicit the difference between empire and Commonwealth, while providing a possible roadmap for the remaining colonies to follow. Thus, when the empire retreated after the Second World War, the Commonwealth was there to take up the slack and preserve a sense of Britishness among the citizens of the UK.

The British Commonwealth of Nations

At the Treaty of Versailles, Woodrow Wilson, President of the United States, had insisted on the right to self-determination by those nations that were not states. Yet, in much of the world outside Europe, the opposite happened. In particular, the British Empire expanded significantly after the First World War as a result of the League of Nations mandates awarded to the UK and

INTERNAL EMPIRE

the dominions. Large areas of the Middle East, southern Africa and the Pacific, denied a right to self-determination, were now under British or dominion control, having previously belonged to the German or Ottoman Empires.

At the same time as the British Empire was expanding, the UK itself was about to shrink—for the first time in 120 years. This was because of events in Ireland. The Government of Ireland Act in 1920 had paved the way for two Irish parliaments (one in the north and one in the south), consisting in each case of a House of Commons and a Senate.[11] However, the Anglo-Irish Treaty of 1921 established an Irish Free State that, in principle, extended across the whole of Ireland. To reconcile these two conflicting positions, Article 12 of the treaty gave the northern parliament an opt-out:

> If ... an address is presented to His Majesty by both Houses of the Parliament of Northern Ireland to that effect [opting out of the Free State], the powers of the Parliament and the Government of the Irish Free State shall no longer extend to Northern Ireland, and the provisions of the Government of Ireland Act ... shall so far as they relate to Northern Ireland continue to be of full force and effect...

Needless to say, both the Senate and the House of Commons in Northern Ireland took full advantage of Article 12, and the Irish Free State was launched in December 1922 shorn of six counties in Ulster. However, the UK was also diminished in size, with the loss of the Irish Free State, and was reborn as the United Kingdom of Great Britain and Northern Ireland. Thus the island, or at least part of it, had shown that it was possible to secede from the union—just as the US had demonstrated it was possible to leave the British Empire 150 years before.

The creation of the Irish Free State was bound to have implications for the rest of the UK in the long run. However,

170

THE COMMONWEALTH

these implications were muted by the success of British negotiators in keeping the free state within the British Empire as a dominion. This success would prove to be temporary (see below), but in the first few years of the Irish Free State, the controversies surrounding the Anglo-Irish Treaty were largely confined to Ireland itself, where a short and vicious civil war was fought between those who supported and those who opposed the treaty (the supporters were victorious).

British voters had other concerns, and there were now many more of them. In 1918, the Representation of the People Act had extended the vote unconditionally to all men over 21, and to all women over 30 who met minimum property qualifications. (The requirements for men and women were finally aligned in 1928.) Over 8 million women gained the vote for the first time and so did over 5 million men, indicating the narrowness of the franchise that had operated until then. How would the expansion of the electorate affect the issue of Britishness?

The first test of the new system was the 1918 general election, held on 14 December. However, this was fought with all of Ireland still in the UK, and was most noteworthy for the extraordinary success of Sinn Féin, which won the third largest number of seats in the UK House of Commons, seventy-three of the 105 Irish constituencies.[12] The next test was the 1922 election, marked by the rise of a Labour Party representing the British working class—which was even able, after the election in 1923, to form a short-lived minority government. This was a significant moment in the evolution of British party politics, and a direct consequence of the extension of the franchise, but the Labour Party had no quarrel either with self-governing dominions or indeed with the concept of empire itself. Britishness and the British Empire were not going to be challenged by the triumph of a workers' party that drew its support from across all of Great Britain.

171

INTERNAL EMPIRE

Postwar British governments of all stripes therefore shared a consensus on the need to preserve the British Empire. On the one hand, there was a willingness to formalise self-government among the 'white' dominions—including South Africa, despite the fact that whites were clearly a minority there—provided that these dominions preserved the trappings of the British Empire in their formal proceedings. This strategy even included Ireland, where British governments bent over backwards to pretend the country was still part of the British Commonwealth of Nations long after it had effectively left. At the same time, there was a determination to prevaricate on dominion status for other British possessions, especially India, in order to delay the moment when Great Britain would cease to be a major imperial power.

For most of the British public, whose Britishness derived in large part from empire, there was no reason at first to change attitudes or shift identities. In any case, recession after the First World War, the slump caused by the return to the gold standard and a general strike in 1926 were reasons enough to focus on domestic issues. The secession of the Irish Free State from the UK may have proved inspirational for independence movements in the overseas colonies, especially India, but attempts to replicate the Irish success within the UK itself had only limited appeal.

In 1925, Welsh nationalists formed Plaid Genedlaethol Cymru (National Party of Wales), a merger of two nationalist bodies created the previous year. Plaid Cymru, as it soon became known, then contested one seat in the 1929 general election, but gained only 609 votes. Welsh voters, who were leaving the Liberal Party in droves despite its leadership by David Lloyd George (the only Welshman to have been Prime Minister), preferred—it would seem—the imperial continuity offered by the Labour Party over the rupture hinted at by Plaid Cymru.

It was much the same in Scotland. The National Party of Scotland was formed in 1928 as a merger of three bodies

THE COMMONWEALTH

supporting independence. It contested two seats in the 1929 general elections and secured a total of only 3,313 votes. It then amalgamated in 1934 with the Scottish Party to form the Scottish National Party (SNP). Although the SNP contested eight seats in the following year's general election, none of its candidates had any success. Furthermore, the SNP was split on the issue of whether devolution or independence was the best path to pursue.

As for Irish nationalists in Northern Ireland, who represented at least a third of the six counties at the time of partition, their cause seemed hopeless. Condemned to live under the sectarian rule of the Ulster Unionist Party for the next fifty years, their electoral options in the Westminster parliament were thwarted by internecine fighting among the nationalist parties. Northern Ireland was, to all intents and purposes, a one-party state, and the representation of nationalists in Stormont (the Belfast parliament) was distorted not only by bitter disagreements within the nationalist movement itself, but also by gerrymandering, vote-rigging and outright intimidation by unionist opponents. The identity of Northern Ireland as British therefore looked unassailable in the interwar years.

With Britishness secure in what remained of the UK, governments were able to concentrate on imperial reforms designed to ensure that the colonies themselves retained a British identity. In the case of the dominions, which included after 1922 the Irish Free State, this meant giving greater diplomatic and legal substance to their de facto independence. This was demonstrated very clearly at the 1926 Imperial Conference, after which a report was published by a committee chaired by Arthur Balfour.[13] What became known as the Balfour Declaration (not to be confused with the earlier Balfour Declaration on Palestine) stated:

> [The dominions] are autonomous Communities within the British Empire, equal in status, in no way subordinate one

173

INTERNAL EMPIRE

to another in any aspect of their domestic or external affairs, though united by a common allegiance to the Crown, and freely associated as members of the British Commonwealth of Nations.[14]

Giving five dominions (six if Newfoundland is included) such a high degree of freedom could only result in a unified British foreign policy, if there was a similar outlook among the states concerned. It was, however, naively assumed by policymakers across the spectrum that the fundamental Britishness of the dominions would provide the necessary support for whatever 'common cause' the empire might adopt. This view was not challenged in the UK and, in 1931, the British parliament passed the Statute of Westminster, giving legal force to the Balfour Declaration.

One 'common cause' had been on the agenda for decades, and its time would come soon after the passing of the Statute of Westminster. This was imperial preference in commerce, a practice adopted by all other empires, but which had been abandoned by Great Britain in the 1840s in favour of free trade. The issue, however, had resurfaced at the beginning of the twentieth century, when Joseph Chamberlain had formed the Tariff Reform League to demand reciprocal preferences among the colonies and dominions of the British Empire, but the Liberal Party—in power from 1906—was strongly committed to free trade and able to resist.[15]

The decline in support for the Liberals in the 1920s was followed by the Great Depression, starting at the end of the decade. The United States raised its tariffs unilaterally in 1930 and the dominions demanded a response from Great Britain. An imperial economic conference was held in Ottawa in 1932, attended by the UK, all the dominions, India and—for the first time—Southern Rhodesia.[16] Stanley Baldwin, representing the UK, captured the mood:

THE COMMONWEALTH

> There is not one country represented here that is not suffering from depression and disappointment—not one that does not look to Ottawa to give fresh stimulus and hope ... I trust that we will end the Conference with definite arrangements made for our mutual advantage. But the real importance of Ottawa lies in the fact that it marks the point where two roads diverge, the one leading to the development of purely national interests, the other to closer Imperial unity, and to the recognition of advantages in mutual cooperation in trade.[17]

The 'definite arrangements' demanded by Baldwin soon materialised, and imperial preference now became standard practice in all parts of the British Empire. For the first time, the British Commonwealth of Nations had more than warm words to hold it together, relying instead on mutual preferential tariffs between the Commonwealth member-nations, leading to a rapid rise in intra-imperial trade—albeit at the expense of trade with the rest of the world. Both UK citizens and imperial subjects now shared common interests that gave the Commonwealth practical meaning and reinforced Britishness among the four nations.

Yet there was one dominion within the British Commonwealth of Nations that was prepared to risk losing material benefits of mutual interest, and that was Ireland. One of the first acts of Éamon de Valera's government, after winning the 1932 Irish elections, was to remove the oath that members of parliament were required to take before they could take their seats.[18] Since this was in direct breach of the 1921 Anglo-Irish Treaty, it provoked a furious response from the British government. Yet de Valera could not have been clearer in his own answer:

> [T]he government of the Irish Free State feel obliged to make clear beyond any possibility of doubt the attitude of the Irish people towards the British Commonwealth. The Irish people have never sought membership of the Commonwealth. Their

INTERNAL EMPIRE

association with Great Britain and the Commonwealth has never on their side been a voluntary association.[19]

De Valera then ramped up the pressure by unilaterally abrogating various other features of the Anglo-Irish Treaty and systematically removing the symbols of Commonwealth membership.[20] He used the abdication of Edward VIII in 1936 as an excuse to introduce a new constitution that declared Ireland to be 'a sovereign, independent, democratic State'. He refused to attend the Imperial Conference in 1937. Last, but not least, Ireland remained neutral throughout the Second World War, with de Valera declaring that 'from the moment that the war began there was for us only one policy possible—neutrality. Our circumstances, our history, the incompleteness of our national territory from the partition of our country made any other policy impractical.'[21]

Despite these assertions of independence, British governments insisted on treating Ireland as if it were still a dominion within the British Commonwealth of Nations.[22] The official explanation was that the 1937 constitution had not defined Ireland as a republic, leaving the British monarch free to play a small if undefined role in Irish constitutional affairs. Yet, in truth, the British Commonwealth of Nations had come to play such an important role in the life of UK citizens that it was unthinkable to contemplate a reduction in its size. It was not for nothing that Prime Minister Winston Churchill, in his famous June 1940 speech during the Second World War, referred to the territorial space from which wartime sacrifices would be required as the 'British Commonwealth and Empire'.

The Commonwealth of Nations

The national government formed by Churchill in the Second World War contained many politicians who had always been

THE COMMONWEALTH

sceptical about self-government for those colonies without a dominant group of white settlers.[23] Furthermore, not all of these were Conservatives or Liberals. Clement Attlee himself, the Leader of the Labour Party and Prime Minister from 1945, was among those who had written before the war about the lack of 'readiness' for dominion status in the majority of British possessions, and he was not alone among Labour politicians.[24]

The war, however, changed everything. Great Britain's desperate call for volunteers, answered by almost every part of the British Empire, could not pass without a response. This was especially true of India, whose contribution was immense, despite the refusal of the Indian National Congress to back the war effort unless the UK granted independence. By 1942 Stafford Cripps, a Labour politician sent to New Delhi by Churchill, had therefore promised in a draft declaration an Indian Union 'which shall constitute a Dominion, associated with the United Kingdom and the other Dominions by a common allegiance to the Crown, but equal to them in every respect, in no way subordinate in any aspect of its domestic or external affairs.'[25]

The Cripps mission was a failure, as Congress was unpersuaded by British promises of independence, but the genie was out of the bottle. At the end of the Second World War, it was clear that the UK—now under a Labour government—had dropped its opposition to minority-white colonies becoming dominions. 'Empire' increasingly came to be replaced by 'Commonwealth' in describing the territories that would continue their association with Great Britain, and the British public were encouraged to change their allegiance accordingly. The House of Lords even formalised this new approach in 1947, when it was stated by a government minister that 'the word "Commonwealth" alone can properly be given the wider meaning of all territories within the Empire, including the Dominions.'[26]

177

INTERNAL EMPIRE

It is doubtful how much of this change in nomenclature was absorbed by British voters at the time. The economic and financial difficulties facing the UK were immense, and the country had just survived one of the harshest winters on record without adequate housing or heating. Yet the change would be permanent and eventually UK citizens had little choice but to accept that a large part of their British identity now came through the Commonwealth rather than through the Empire. It was a demonstration of how flexible British constitutional arrangements could be.

Where the British government showed no flexibility, however, was on the requirement that former colonies must become a dominion and not a republic in order to be a self-governing member of the Commonwealth. This, of course, preserved the role and function of the British monarch in postcolonial affairs and gave Great Britain formal leadership of the Commonwealth. Yet, for many in the nationalist movements of the colonies, it diluted the meaning of independence. Furthermore, dominion status had been a running sore in the relationship between Ireland and the UK ever since the creation of the Irish Free State.

Following partition in 1947, therefore, both India and Pakistan had to become dominions as a condition for decolonisation within the Commonwealth. The same happened to Ceylon (today Sri Lanka). This left the British monarch as Head of State, causing grave disquiet among many of those who had fought for independence. Yet to have rejected dominion status in pursuit of independence would have put at risk all the privileges of Commonwealth membership. And while many of these 'privileges' might have seemed minor or even redundant, they did include imperial preference in trade, and that gave former colonies a strong incentive to accept British conditions. To have lost access to the British market at the start of independence would have been a costly and painful process—

THE COMMONWEALTH

not to mention the opposition it would have generated from powerful business groups.

Despite this, there were two countries that—albeit for different reasons—chose to sever their links with the Commonwealth at this time. The first was Ireland, which had signalled its disinterest in participation on many occasions since the Anglo-Irish Treaty (if not before), but which had not yet managed to convince any British government that it was serious. Although de Valera had lost the 1948 general election, his successor wasted no time in introducing a Republic of Ireland Bill that the former Taoiseach (Prime Minister) was only too happy to support. From now on, there was no scope for ambiguity on behalf of the British government, and it was finally accepted by the UK and all the dominions that the new Republic of Ireland would no longer be part of the Commonwealth, starting from 18 April 1949.[27]

The second country was Burma (now Myanmar), which had been occupied by the Japanese during the Second World War. Anti-British feeling in the prewar independence movement had been so strong that a part of it, operating according to the principle 'my enemy's enemy is my friend', had collaborated with the occupying forces. Faced, therefore, with a choice of independence as a dominion within the Commonwealth or as a republic outside, the nationalist leadership chose the latter. It was the 'Britishness' of dominion status and of the Commonwealth that led to this decision.

Burma's secession was a blow to UK ambitions to replace all parts of the British Empire with a British-led Commonwealth, to which the British people would themselves transfer their loyalty. Yet it was not a mortal blow, as Ceylon, India and Pakistan had set a precedent for postcolonial dominion status. Much more worrying, therefore, was the announcement by India in 1948 that it wished to become a republic. It was British inflexibility on the issue of monarchy that had made it impossible for Burma to join

INTERNAL EMPIRE

the Commonwealth; but, at the same time, India was such an important former colony that it would make a mockery of the Commonwealth if it were thrown out.

Fortunately for Great Britain, India had also indicated that it wished in principle to stay in the Commonwealth. Since it would not budge on the issue of becoming a republic, it was just a question of coming up with a formula that allowed the UK not to lose face. This was provided by Canada at the 1949 meeting of Commonwealth prime ministers. Known as the London Declaration, the following was agreed:

> The Government of India have informed the other Governments of the Commonwealth of the intention of the Indian people that under the new constitution which is about to be adopted India shall become a sovereign independent republic. The Government of India have, however, declared and affirmed India's desire to continue her full membership of the Commonwealth of Nations and her acceptance of the King as the symbol of the free association of its independent member nations and as such the Head of the Commonwealth.

Thanks to the London Declaration, the British government had been given a way of almost seamlessly transiting from the British Empire to a postcolonial arrangement in which a Commonwealth of Nations would be the central institution. However, it would be at first a confusing journey. In answer to a question in the House of Commons on the use of 'Commonwealth' in preference to 'British Empire', Prime Minister Attlee replied in May 1949:

> All constitutional developments in the Commonwealth, British Commonwealth, or the British Empire—I use the three terms deliberately—have been the subject of consultation between his Majesty's Governments, and there has been no agreement to adopt or to exclude the use of any one of these terms, nor any decision on the part of His Majesty's Government to do so.[28]

180

THE COMMONWEALTH

Within a few years, however, it was clear not only that 'Commonwealth of Nations' had become the preferred name, but also that 'dominion' was no longer needed, as so many colonies chose on independence to become republics.[29] Indeed, the post of Secretary of State for Dominion Affairs had been abolished in 1947 to be replaced by Secretary of State for Commonwealth Relations. The post of Secretary of State for the Colonies was then abolished in 1966, leaving only a Secretary of State for Commonwealth Affairs.[30] Empire Day, celebrated since 1902, was replaced somewhat awkwardly by British Commonwealth Day in 1958, which was then changed more appropriately to Commonwealth Day in 1966.

Gradually the British public adjusted to the changes. The academic world was among the first, with London University establishing an Institute of Commonwealth Studies in 1949, its outreach programmes helping to explain what was going on. The British Empire Games, which started in 1930 (with separate teams for England, Scotland, Wales and the island of Ireland), added 'Commonwealth' to their name in 1954 and then dropped 'Empire' from 1970. The Imperial War Graves Commission, responsible for maintaining the cemeteries of those who died in the two world wars, became the Commonwealth War Graves Commission in 1960. The Imperial Institute, founded in London in the 1880s, changed its name to Commonwealth Institute in 1958, before moving in 1962 to an iconic building where it received a stream of visitors from schools across the country. The Universities Bureau of the British Empire, founded in London in 1913, became the Association of Commonwealth Universities in 1964.[31] 'Empire' and 'British' were gradually being expunged from the myriad institutions established during the previous 250 years.

The British public could not fail to notice the change, especially with the process of decolonisation gathering pace after

INTERNAL EMPIRE

India became a republic within the Commonwealth in 1950. The Gold Coast in West Africa became independent in 1957, adopting its former name of Ghana before entering the Commonwealth, and was joined by many other African countries over the next two decades. Jamaica was the first in the Caribbean to become independent (1962), followed by many of its neighbours—all of whom joined the Commonwealth. Tonga (1970) was the first in the Pacific, by which time most of the remaining Asian colonies had also left the British Empire and joined the Commonwealth.

Postwar British governments had hoped to simplify the process of decolonisation through the creation of federations, but they had failed. The West Indies Federation, established in 1958, was unable to bridge the rivalries among member countries and ended after Jamaica voted by plebiscite to leave in 1961. The Central African Federation—which had been established in large part to prevent white settlers in Southern Rhodesia (future Zimbabwe) imposing the same apartheid system as adopted by the National Party in South Africa after its election victory in 1948—broke up when Northern Rhodesia and Nyasaland chose to become independent in 1964, as Zambia and Malawi respectively.[32] As federations collapsed, the numbers joining the Commonwealth accelerated and had reached 56 at the end of 2022.[33]

Holding together this disparate group of countries needed more than warm words, a common language and a shared imperial history. The extra ingredient was imperial preference, which gave special treatment not only to exports from Commonwealth countries to the UK, but also exports from the UK to Commonwealth countries. Indeed, in 1961 no less than 43 per cent of British exports of goods went to what was known as the 'Commonwealth preference system'.[34] Since such a large part of the British economy consisted of exports, a significant number of workers and their families depended directly on the survival of these special arrangements within the Commonwealth.

THE COMMONWEALTH

In the absence of contemporary public surveys, we can never be sure to what extent the Commonwealth of Nations, headed by the British monarch, replaced the empire as the foundation of Britishness among the citizens of the four nations of the UK. Yet there was no doubt as to the salience of the issue among many of the politicians who claimed to represent these same citizens. Addressing the Labour Party Conference in 1962 on the issue of Britain's possible membership of the European Economic Community (EEC), the party's leader, Hugh Gaitskell, focused heavily on the damage this might do to the Commonwealth and therefore to the UK itself:

> We must be clear about this: it does mean ... the end of Britain as an independent European state. I make no apology for repeating it. It means the end of a thousand years of history. You may say 'let it end' but, my goodness, it is a decision that needs a little care and thought. And it does mean the end of the Commonwealth. How can one seriously suppose that if the mother country, the centre of the Commonwealth, is a province of Europe (which is what federation means) it could continue to exist as the mother country of a series of independent nations? It is sheer nonsense.[35]

Gaitskell's arguments were designed to help the Labour Party win an election that was no more than two years away. His words were expected to resonate with voters in the four nations, for whom the Commonwealth—a substitute for Empire—had become an expression of their Britishness. Yet his remarks also revealed the English imperialism hidden beneath the veneer of British politics, since the 'state' whose 'thousand years of history' was threatened with extinction, which was designated as the 'centre' of the Commonwealth and which was said to be the 'mother country' of the Commonwealth, was in Gaitskell's eyes none other than England.

183

INTERNAL EMPIRE

The Commonwealth in Crisis

Hugh Gaitskell died before the victory of the Labour Party in the 1964 general elections, but his successor was equally committed to the Commonwealth. The Wilson government oversaw the establishment in London of the Commonwealth Secretariat in 1965 and the Commonwealth Foundation in 1966, while the Commonwealth Prime Ministers' Conferences were replaced by the more formal Commonwealth Heads of Government Meetings, starting in Singapore in 1971.[36] As the word 'Commonwealth' increased in circulation, it came to replace the more cumbersome 'Commonwealth of Nations'. With Queen Elizabeth as its head,[37] the body would go on to issue a series of declarations that kept it in the public eye. It seemed on the surface like an organisation in rude health.

Yet all was not well in the eyes of the British public.[38] There was still huge affection for the countries of the 'old' Commonwealth, with their white settler populations and multiple references to 'kith and kin'. Many households in the UK had family links to these countries, and British emigration was even encouraged—the 'ten pound pom' becoming a term of affection for those who migrated to Australia and New Zealand on assisted schemes. However, this affection was not automatically transferred to the states of the 'new' Commonwealth, with their majority non-white populations—and it became increasingly eroded in the case of one of the old Commonwealth states as well.

The big problem, especially for those on the left, was South Africa. The rise of the National Party (representing Afrikaners) had been largely ignored in the UK before the Second World War, but its electoral victory in 1948 came at a time when parts of British society were becoming more aware of the racism endemic in the empire and, indeed, in the UK itself. The policy of apartheid by the new South African government became

THE COMMONWEALTH

more extreme every year, and made a mockery of the fine words uttered by British political leaders about the Commonwealth's promotion of multiracial societies. Even if the leaders of the old white dominions refused to denounce the evils of apartheid, the same was not true of the new Commonwealth members. India, in particular, was very vocal—in part because of the large Indian population in South Africa, which was itself the subject of legal discrimination.[39]

The National Party was committed not just to apartheid, but also to South Africa becoming a republic. Following a referendum in 1960, the government announced it would no longer have the British monarch as Head of State and was therefore applying to rejoin the Commonwealth as a republic.[40] Some members of the old Commonwealth (including Great Britain) would have accepted this, but the new members were strongly opposed, and South Africa therefore withdrew its application. South Africa would now continue the practice of apartheid outside the Commonwealth for three more decades, but the policy of appeasement by British governments did not end for many years. It created deep disquiet in many parts of UK society.

If the failure of the Commonwealth to respond to the rise of apartheid led to a disillusionment with the organisation on the left of British society, the free movement of people among member-states produced a sometimes violent reaction against non-white immigrants to the UK, and opposition to the Commonwealth on the political right. Such immigration from different parts of the British Empire had been going on for decades, if not centuries. There had even been occasional ugly riots, such as in Liverpool and other ports in 1919, but migration had not become an electoral issue—except in the case of Irish immigration to a few big cities. All this now changed after the Second World War.

The postwar British economy, after an initial period of high unemployment, suffered from severe labour market shortages in

INTERNAL EMPIRE

key sectors, and these were filled in large part by encouraging the immigration of non-white workers from countries that would soon join the Commonwealth or were already members. This welcome by British governments was not matched by the local population, and 'race' riots occurred in a number of cities. The Conservative administration of Prime Minister Harold Macmillan therefore responded in 1962 by introducing the Commonwealth Immigrants Act, which targeted in particular non-white immigration from new Commonwealth countries.

Far from ending discontent with the Commonwealth on the right of British society, however, this simply fomented it. Enoch Powell, a Conservative MP, was quick to seize the opportunity. Two years before his infamous 'rivers of blood' speech, he made a connection in 1966 between hostility to non-white immigration and what he later called the 'sham' of the Commonwealth:

> One [current issue] is Commonwealth immigration. True, in some parts of the country, such as that from which I come, this has been a visible menace now for a decade; but over most of Britain it is only in the last few years that people's eyes have been opened to what has really been happening. Largely because of the legal fiction of Commonwealth citizenship and our determination to maintain it, we clung year after year to the assertion that our nearest European neighbours were aliens, to be strictly excluded from Britain, but that the myriad inhabitants of independent countries in Asia, Africa and the New World were British, indistinguishable from native-born inhabitants of these islands, and that no limitation could be placed on their inherent right to enter and leave this realm at will. For fear, so it was said, of 'offending the Commonwealth', we persisted in this course until we had entailed upon ourselves a fearful and wholly unnecessary problem...[41]

Powell's speech, and others like it, was not yet a mortal blow against the Commonwealth, but it undermined the foundations

186

THE COMMONWEALTH

of an institution that was supposed to sustain Britishness in the wake of imperial decline. Indeed, for many of its architects, the Commonwealth was expected to be British Empire 2.0, an empire-lite body that would bind the four nations to each other and keep the former colonies close to the 'mother' country. And although Powell would be marginalised within the opposition Conservative Party, his hostility to non-white immigration, and by implication the Commonwealth, found an echo in the Labour government's own Commonwealth Immigrants Act of 1968. More and more people therefore began to question the point of the Commonwealth, other than to provide preferential trade terms for its members.

Imperial preference had survived the transition from empire to Commonwealth, but it was inconsistent with joining the European Economic Community, which was defined by a common external tariff. The Treaty of Rome in 1957 had created a common market among six countries (Belgium, France, Italy, Luxembourg, Netherlands and West Germany), and it was British reluctance to abandon imperial preference that appeared to be an insuperable obstacle to the UK's participation.[42] The British government had responded to the creation of the EEC with a European Free Trade Association, which was consistent with Commonwealth trade preferences, as it did not require member states to adopt a common tariff.

These arrangements had been passionately defended in 1962 by Hugh Gaitskell when outlining the Labour Party's opposition to the first British application for EEC membership (an application that was eventually vetoed by France). Yet the trends in British trade were conspiring in favour of a change. The dominions (including India) had taken nearly 40 per cent of British goods exports in 1950, but by 1970 the share had fallen to 20 per cent, despite the preferential treatment that many British goods received in those markets.[43] Meanwhile, British exports to

INTERNAL EMPIRE

the EEC were increasing, but were subject to a tariff by member-states that did not apply between those states themselves.

By 1972, at the third time of asking, the UK's application succeeded, and on 1 January 1973 Great Britain became—along with Denmark and Ireland—a member of the European Communities (EC). Commonwealth preference now had to end, and so did the economic rationale for the Commonwealth itself. The institution was left to justify itself through a commitment 'to promote prosperity, democracy and peace, amplify the voices of small states, and protect the environment'.[44] The institution survived and new members joined, but it ceased to play the unifying role that had previously been played first by the British Empire and later by the interwar British Commonwealth of Nations. Indeed, within a few years of the UK joining the EC, the Commonwealth had become completely irrelevant to any understanding of Britishness within the Isles themselves.

Imperial retreat, followed so soon by the eclipse of the Commonwealth, created a vacuum in the definition of what it meant to be British. Many hoped it would be filled by integration with Europe, but that would take time even on the most optimistic assumptions. In any case, the gap was starting to be occupied—even before Britain joined the EC—by the rise of nationalism in the three 'subaltern' nations, Scotland, Wales and Northern Ireland. This would in turn provoke a reexamination of nationalism in the hegemonic fourth nation, England.

Wales was the first to catch the attention of policymakers in England. The Labour government formed in 1964, mindful of the rise of Welsh nationalism, had committed to creating a Welsh Office with a Secretary of State for Wales. The initiative appeared to have succeeded when Plaid Cymru failed in the 1966 general elections to win many votes. Three months later, however, its leader Gwynfor Evans won a byelection in Carmarthen, and Plaid Cymru entered the UK parliament for the first time. Over

THE COMMONWEALTH

the next two years, it came very close to winning two additional seats in byelections, in the Labour strongholds of Rhondda West and Caerphilly.

Scotland was not far behind. Under the leadership of Arthur Donaldson, the Scottish National Party had performed well in byelections since 1961, albeit without actually winning a seat. This changed in 1967 when Winnie Ewing won the Hamilton byelection and the SNP took its first seat at Westminster.[45] The SNP also performed well in local elections across Scotland in that year, suggesting that its appeal was broad-based, and not just a protest vote against unpopular policies from London. The question of how to respond to the rise of nationalism in Scotland was now firmly on the political agenda, and in 1968 the Leader of the Opposition even promised that the Conservative Party would establish a Scottish Assembly if elected.[46]

The Labour Party, given its large number of MPs who came from Scotland and Wales, could not ignore these developments. Prime Minister Harold Wilson therefore established a Royal Commission on the Constitution in 1969 with powers to consider all changes, including the breakup of the UK into separate sovereign states. The Kilbrandon Report, as it was known, was finally published in 1973.[47] It rejected independence for each of the nations, as well as federalism for the UK as a whole— but it did support the establishment of devolved assemblies in Scotland and Wales.[48] Although it would take some years for this to happen, it was now abundantly clear that neither empire nor Commonwealth were sufficient to hold the countries of the UK together on their own.

The commission's terms of reference had included Northern Ireland, but the Kilbrandon Report had nothing to say on this topic.[49] Given the rapid developments in Northern Ireland in the period before the publication of its recommendations, this was perhaps just as well. In 1969, the same year as the Commission

INTERNAL EMPIRE

had been formed, the 'Troubles' erupted in Northern Ireland; the IRA split into 'officials' and 'provisionals', with the latter committed to armed struggle against the British state in pursuit of Irish reunification. The following year, Sinn Féin itself split, paving the way for one of the factions to become the political wing of the Provisional IRA, and gaining electoral support among the nationalist community in all elections involving Northern Ireland voters.

The British government could not ignore the rise of nationalism in Northern Ireland any more than it could do so in Scotland or Wales. The Northern Ireland parliament, the legislative instrument of unionist domination since 1921, was therefore suspended in 1972 and replaced by the new Northern Ireland Assembly, after the passage in 1973 of the Northern Ireland Constitution Act. The new parliament allowed nationalist parties to compete on much more even terms with their unionist rivals, and in 1982 Sinn Féin joined the nationalist Social and Democratic Labour Party (SDLP) in the assembly after winning five seats. (Unlike what has always happened in the Westminster parliament, Sinn Féin took up these seats.)

By the early 1970s, the fissures in the unity of the UK were all too apparent. Although England itself was still immune to these centrifugal forces, the call for regional parliaments having fallen on deaf ears, it was clear that political developments in Scotland, Wales and Northern Ireland were potentially a threat to the union. The integrationist pull of the British Empire was now at an end, and the Commonwealth had not proved an adequate replacement. The UK, however, was now embarking on a new integrationist experiment by joining the European Communities. Only time would tell if Europe would replace the British Empire and the Commonwealth as the glue holding the UK together.

7

EUROPE

Political leaders in the UK had spurned the opportunity to participate in European integration in the decade after the project first started in 1950. This began to change in the 1960s, and yet public support for joining any kind of European trade agreement was still low. The opposition came partly from a political right that feared loss of sovereignty, and partly from a political left that saw the European Economic Community (EEC), finally launched in 1958, as an anti-labour capitalist club. Both, however, saw participation as a threat to the continuation of a Commonwealth led by the UK. Membership was therefore seen as undermining British identity, defined for so long by overseas possessions outside Europe.

Overcoming this opposition was a major problem, and it took many years before the two main political parties—Conservative and Labour—were persuaded. (Even then, there were large minorities in both parties that resisted.) After membership of the European club was finally agreed upon in 1972, opposition was sufficiently strong to persuade the Labour government in 1974 of the need for a 'confirmatory' referendum. This

INTERNAL EMPIRE

was duly held in 1975 and, to the surprise of many, led to an overwhelming vote in favour of staying in the 'common market'.[1] It seemed as if the pull of empire and Commonwealth was now much diminished with the public in all four nations expressing the view that there was little alternative other than a closer relationship with Europe.

Support for European membership among the British public was confirmed in numerous surveys after the 1975 referendum, and participation brought tangible benefits for the British economy: jobs, trade, regional aid and investment, to name only a few. Furthermore, the benefits were felt not only by England, but by the three other nations as well. As a result, a part of the UK population came to feel that Europe contributed to their sense of identity, even if it could not fully replace empire in their understanding of Britishness. During the years when European integration was expanding, both through widening (addition of more member-states) and deepening (further reduction of barriers to trade and investment between member-states), this sense of a European British identity continued, despite the tumultuous splits it caused within Conservative government in the decade before the Labour Party's victory in 1997.

It was only towards the end of the Labour government's period in office (1997–2010) that public opinion started to move against membership of the European Union (as it was called after 1993), and this shift was concentrated in England. Until then, those groups in favour of leaving had found little support among the English public, but everything changed after a big increase in migration to the UK once a number of Eastern European countries had acceded to the EU. Suddenly, opponents of the UK's continued European membership had a cause with which many members of the English public identified (stopping free movement of labour from other member-states), and they ruthlessly exploited it. By the early 2000s, therefore, the attempt

EUROPE

to redefine Britishness among the English by including within it a European dimension began to look like a losing proposition—but the road to this crisis point would be long, and that fifty-year history is an important one for the story of Englishness.

From Commonwealth to Europe

At the very moment when the British government was celebrating the launch of a Commonwealth of Nations that would give continued substance to the 'Britishness' linking UK citizens together, six countries in continental Europe were embarking on their first steps towards the creation of a major integration project. The European Coal and Steel Community (ECSC), finally launched by Belgium, France, Italy, Luxembourg, the Netherlands and West Germany in 1952, created institutions that would later form the blueprint for the EEC. Above all, it provided for decisions to be taken by a supranational authority. This was a major concession by France, perhaps the most nationalist of the six countries, and one that was deemed necessary in order to prevent a return to nationalism in West Germany, now that the Second World War had ended.

The undoubted success of the ECSC led to discussions on the further widening and deepening of European integration. A conference was held in Messina in 1955, which the UK did not attend.[2] Despite this, or more realistically because of this, the six members of the ECSC were sufficiently optimistic about the results of the conference to push on with plans for a common market. The UK attended the first of these meetings, but with little enthusiasm, on the grounds that 'ever deeper' European integration would restrict its freedom of action.[3] London, it seemed, had secured its geopolitical needs through the Commonwealth of Nations on the one hand, and its so-called special relationship with the US on the other.

193

INTERNAL EMPIRE

Just how 'special' the relationship truly was became embarrassingly clear the year after the Messina conference. The US administration was provoked to anger by the Anglo-French invasion of the Suez Canal in Egypt, in collusion with Israeli special forces, to protect the interests of all three countries involved. Not only had President Eisenhower (1953–61) not been informed in advance, but the three aggressors were engaged in an act that ran counter to US interests, in Egypt in particular and during the Cold War in general. Britain was threatened by the US government with severe financial penalties, and the invaders withdrew.

France and the UK drew very different lessons from this act of imperial hubris. For France, it confirmed the wisdom of pushing ahead with European integration, so that the decline of its power on the international stage after the end of the French Empire could be offset by increasing influence in its own region—a space it did not (yet) need to share with the UK.[4] The UK, on the other hand, while also recognising that its imperial power was in serious decline, concluded that the best hope was to align much more closely with Washington, in order to avoid a similar humiliation in future and increase its leverage in the world.

That Britain at first chose this path was not surprising. The Commonwealth of Nations was still popular with the public, business broadly supported the imperial preferences that Commonwealth membership brought, and the US was held in high esteem by almost all sections of society. In addition, integration with Europe was not especially popular. In a series of surveys carried out by the United States Information Agency from 1954 onwards, support for European integration was much lower in the UK than in the other European countries sampled. Furthermore, British support as measured in these surveys declined, rather than rose, as the details of European integration became clearer.[5]

EUROPE

Only one political organisation showed any enthusiasm for European integration in the 1950s, and that was the Liberal Party. However, since the Liberals had no chance of forming a government (they won six seats in the 1955 general election), their policy preferences on Europe counted for little. By contrast, the nationalist parties in Scotland and Wales expressed a strong preference for remaining in the Commonwealth, while nationalist parties in Northern Ireland wanted reunification with the Republic of Ireland. It was to be expected, therefore, that neither the ruling Conservative Party nor its allies, the Ulster Unionist Party and the Scottish Unionist Party, felt under any pressure to change their stance on Europe when the Treaty of Rome was signed in 1957, establishing the EEC.[6] The same was true of the opposition, despite a vocal minority on the right wing of the Labour Party that favoured membership.

Harold Macmillan, who replaced Anthony Eden in 1957 after the Suez debacle, was the first UK Prime Minister to contemplate jettisoning Britain's imperial connections. Yet, as Chancellor of the Exchequer in 1956, he had still had no doubt that Britain's future lay in the Commonwealth:

> If the United Kingdom were to join such a Customs Union [the future EEC], the United Kingdom tariff would be swept aside and would be replaced by this single common tariff. That would mean that goods coming into the United Kingdom from the Commonwealth, including the Colonies, would have to pay duty at the same rate as goods coming from any other country not a Member of the Customs Union, while goods from the Customs Union would enter free. Judged only by the most limited United Kingdom interests, such an arrangement would be wholly disadvantageous.[7]

When Macmillan finally announced in 1961 that his government was formally entering into negotiations to join the EEC, he

INTERNAL EMPIRE

was not only performing a U-turn, but also taking a huge risk with his own party.[8] Indeed, he confided to his memoirs: 'It was ... asking a great deal of the Conservative Party, so long and so intimately linked with the ideal of Empire, to accept the changed situation.'[9]

On this occasion, British accession was eventually blocked by France, but Macmillan (although nervous about President de Gaulle's views) could not have known this would happen. To this day, no one is certain why Macmillan took such a calculated risk, which could have split the Conservative Party and provoked electoral disaster. Yet there is a consensus that the decision to apply for membership was broadly linked both to imperial decline and the need to cultivate better relations with the US in the aftermath of Suez, for all Cold War administrations in Washington were keen to bolster European integration as a bulwark against the Soviet Union, despite the economic risks it carried for US business itself.[10]

There is therefore no need to go as far as Henry Kissinger and others in claiming that the UK's *principal* motivation in applying to join the EEC was 'the cultivation of Great Britain's "special relationship" with the United States.'[11] While this was no doubt part of it, there was also a recognition that neither the British Empire nor the Commonwealth were going to provide the influence on the world stage that British people—elite and mass—had come to expect. This loss of influence would now need to be replaced, if only in part, by Britain playing a leading role in Europe. And this meant that Britishness would need to be redefined to incorporate a European dimension. No one, not even Macmillan, could be sure how that would work out, given Great Britain's troubled historical relationship with some of the countries on the continent.

The Labour Party abstained on the crucial 1961 parliamentary vote in favour of starting negotiations on joining the EEC

EUROPE

(alongside Denmark, Ireland and Norway), and the party's position had not changed when Labour narrowly won the 1964 elections. The Commonwealth of Nations was still seen as the best option for the country, with imperial preference providing some protection for an increasingly beleaguered manufacturing sector. As Prime Minister, Harold Wilson in any case had little room for manoeuvre, with his government enjoying only a tiny majority in parliament. However, his substantial election victory in 1966 changed the political calculations, and the Labour government began to explore the possibility of a second application.

Following informal talks with the six member-states, the formal application to start negotiations on joining the European club (again together with Denmark, Ireland and Norway) was made in May 1967. The application had the enthusiastic support of five members, but the French position remained ambiguous. However, the devaluation of the pound sterling on 18 November 1967 removed all ambiguity. President de Gaulle again vetoed the British application, arguing that the UK economy first needed to undergo a major transformation before it could join. In truth, the general would probably have vetoed the application anyway, since he saw the Commonwealth as a fundamental obstacle to British participation in a club whose rules had already been established.

De Gaulle's veto did not come as a complete surprise to the British government, but at the same time it had not been fully anticipated. Wilson had thought that changes in the British negotiating position since the first attempt would be sufficient to overcome French reservations. Following the Merger Treaty of 1967, the EEC had come under the same leadership as the ECSC and the energy agency Euratom, with the three together being known as the European Communities (EC). The UK could not apply to join the EEC without accepting fully the body of law concerning all three organisations. This time, therefore, the UK had been prepared from the beginning of negotiations to abandon

197

INTERNAL EMPIRE

its Commonwealth partners by adopting the common external tariff and Common Agricultural Policy.[12] Yet, unlike Macmillan, Wilson was not driven so much by geopolitical considerations and the need to maintain good relations with the US. On the contrary, he had kept the UK out of the Vietnam War and was prepared to live with US opprobrium as a result.

What concerned Wilson, an economist by training, was the relative underperformance of the British economy compared with the members of the EEC. This had been much less of a problem at the time of the first application, when the rapid growth of the six could be attributed to catch-up after the continental devastation of the Second World War.[13] By 1967, with the British economy yet again facing a sterling crisis, relative underperformance could no longer be ignored. Furthermore, the share of British exports going to the Commonwealth was continuing to fall, while the share going to the newly combined EC was rising rapidly—but not as fast, it was assumed, as if there were no tariffs imposed by the six on imports from the UK. For the sake of the national economy, therefore, the Labour government—with the support of the opposition Conservative Party—was prepared to sacrifice the imperial inheritance from which the British had derived such a large part of their identity.

By the time of the general election in 1970, the UK was ready to try again. This time both Labour and Conservative manifestos committed their parties to negotiations, and General de Gaulle had resigned the previous year. The Conservative Party won the elections and Edward Heath became Prime Minister. The third application to join was made in 1971 and quickly reached a successful conclusion. The British negotiating position (a relatively weak one) no longer sought special terms for the Commonwealth, as it was clear that the six members of the EC would not accept any major changes to the existing arrangements.[14]

EUROPE

The following year, the UK parliament narrowly gave its approval to the European Communities Bill (Labour, now in opposition, objected to the details of the deal and voted against, while there were still many rebels in the Conservative Party).[15] UK membership of the European Communities began on 1 January 1973—along with Denmark and Ireland, but not Norway.[16] Commonwealth countries and UK citizens alike accepted the new reality, knowing not only that there was nothing they could do to change it, but also that the meaning of Britishness was about to change. Not surprisingly, this caused a great deal of uncertainty in all four nations.

One English member of the House of Lords expressed his confusion publicly: 'As a Victorian youth I should have been brainwashed into the knowledge that I was British, and that Britain was something. Today I am vaguely aware of being a Yorkshireman, but I have not a clue what Britain is or where it is going, if it has not gone already.'[17] Meanwhile Quintin Hogg, an English member of the House of Lords with impeccable imperialist credentials, vented his fury: 'Can anyone doubt ... that we are a people that has lost its way? Can anyone doubt that the British people is in the act of destroying itself; and will surely do so if we go on as at present?'[18]

This confusion over identity and the meaning of Britishness was not limited to the English elite. In early 1971, a question on how voters would feel if Britain joined the EEC had found that only 4 per cent would be 'very pleased', while a further 24 per cent would be 'quite pleased'.[19] A few months later, just before the publication of a white paper on membership of the European Communities (EC), a mere 29 per cent of the British public approved the idea of UK membership.[20] Clearly, persuading citizens that Europe—not the empire or the Commonwealth— would now be part of their Britishness was going to be a struggle.

INTERNAL EMPIRE

The 1975 Referendum

When UK participation in the EC started, there was a Conservative government, led by a party whose parliamentary members strongly supported membership. Just over a year later, however, there would be a new minority government led by Labour, most of whose MPs had voted against the bill taking Britain into Europe. Even if this had not been a vote against the 'principle' of joining, it still presented a problem—a problem that became more acute eight months later, when a second election in one year returned a Labour government with a small majority.

The Labour Party may have won two elections in 1974, but its leader Harold Wilson was acutely aware of the opposition, inside and outside his own party, to continued membership of the EC. Many of his own cabinet were well known for their hostile views, and five of the most prominent chose to emphasise the 'threat to democracy' from staying in the EC, using words that conjured up the traditional view of what it meant to be British: 'Twenty-five years ago Britain dismantled a vast Empire in the belief that no country has the right, or wisdom, to govern another. Now we demand for ourselves what we freely conceded to the 32 members of the Commonwealth, the right to democratic self-government.'[21]

To make matters worse for the Prime Minister, there were also signs of a split on the issue between England and the other three nations. In England, a majority of seats usually went to the Conservative Party, which was solidly in favour of staying in.[22] In the other three nations, however, all nationalist parties opposed membership without exception. Furthermore, they had done well in the second 1974 election, with Plaid Cymru winning 11 per cent in Wales, the SNP winning 30 per cent in Scotland and the newly formed Social and Democratic Labour Party (SDLP) in Northern Ireland taking 22 per cent.[23]

200

EUROPE

Under these circumstances, Wilson's government felt it had no choice other than to try and renegotiate membership of the EC with the other eight members (the original six plus Denmark and Ireland), before putting a (hopefully) revised deal to voters in the four nations by means of a referendum. Even if the chances of a substantial revision were small (zero in the case of the founding treaties), it was expected that there would be sufficient concessions to overcome opposition in the UK at large, and to avoid the risk of a split between England and the other nations.

The Labour Party's position had been laid out before the first elections of the year in February, but nothing much could be done about it during its minority government. Renegotiation (described by Brussels as 'the so-called renegotiation') therefore did not begin in earnest until late 1974. It focused on four topics: the budget, agricultural policy, policy towards the developing world, and rules governing regional and industrial policies. Progress was then sufficiently rapid for the Prime Minister to be able to announce in March 1975 that the government would recommend the electorate vote in favour of continued membership in the upcoming referendum.

This did not impress the Scottish Labour Party Conference, which voted a few days later in favour of leaving the EC (by 346,000 to 280,000). On the other hand, the House of Commons vote on 9 April was strongly in favour of staying in—396 to 170, even if 145 of the votes against came from Labour MPs. All that remained was legislation to clear the path for the first-ever UK-wide referendum on 5 June 1975; the question adopted, after much discussion, was: 'The Government has announced the results of the renegotiation of the United Kingdom's terms of membership of the European Community. Do you think the United Kingdom should stay in the European Community (the Common Market)?'

INTERNAL EMPIRE

The campaign itself focused heavily on issues such as jobs, prices and taxes. However, overshadowing everything was the key, if unstated, issue of whether membership of the EC was an adequate substitute for the Commonwealth—yet alone the empire—without which Britishness might become less meaningful. If Europe was a realistic alternative, then British identity would slowly acquire a European dimension that had previously been lacking for most citizens. If it was not, then membership would leave British identity dependent on a mixture of nostalgia and inertia built up by a shared history over a relatively short period of time. For both sides in the campaign, the stakes were extremely high.

The British public were in no doubt that joining the EC meant a decline in the importance of the Commonwealth, and in 1974 two thirds of those surveyed had responded positively to a statement that 'Britain should have developed links with the Commonwealth rather than joined the Common Market'. The same proportion agreed with the proposition that 'the Commonwealth nations are better friends to Britain than the French, Germans or anybody in Western Europe will ever be'— although subsidiary questions revealed that respondents assumed 'Commonwealth' to mean 'white Commonwealth'. And in 1975, the year of the referendum itself, 90 per cent wanted the UK to keep its links with the Commonwealth—however unrealistic that had clearly become.[24]

In the light of these widely held views, the 'yes' campaign (Britain in Europe) could not ignore the issue of the Commonwealth and produced a series of somewhat disingenuous posters with headlines such as: 'In Kingston Jamaica, last week, the leaders of 33 Commonwealth countries said they wanted us to stay in the Common Market. If we leave now, who is there to turn to?' The Labour Campaign for Britain in Europe went further and claimed in one advert, 'Harold Wilson Says ... "I

EUROPE

have made it clear that on these terms as renegotiated, while we have not got all we wanted, the outcome is ... GOOD for the Commonwealth..." Say YES to Europe'.[25]

It is doubtful whether this sugar-coating of the Commonwealth pill persuaded much of the electorate that joining the common market did not mean weakening links with erstwhile partners. However, the 'leave' camp (the National Referendum Campaign) chose not to make much of it, focusing instead on issues of parliamentary sovereignty, tax-raising powers and the ability to trade freely with all countries. Since the latter itself implied an erosion of imperial preference, there was no significant constituency calling for the preservation of the Commonwealth in its traditional form. The institution that had carried Britishness onwards from empire would now be a shell—respected in name, but empty in content.

The question of identity implied by remaining in the EC was felt with particular force by the three UK nations with small populations: Scotland (5.2 million), Wales (2.7 million) and Northern Ireland (1.5 million). The Kilbrandon Report in 1973 had argued for a measure of devolution, transferring powers from Westminster to national capitals, but the European Communities Act in 1972 had transferred even more powers from Westminster to Brussels. Furthermore, while discussion of devolution within the UK had only just begun, the transfer of powers to Brussels had already taken place on 1 January 1973. Small wonder, therefore, that the three nations initially expressed considerable opposition to staying in the EC.

Before joining the common market, Scotland had been the most opposed—one poll in early 1971 registering only 14 per cent in favour. At the beginning of 1975, by which time Scotland had been a member for two years, opposition was still high—at 60 per cent, if 'don't knows' are excluded. Scots, it seemed, who had identified strongly with the British Empire for some 250

INTERNAL EMPIRE

years and with the Commonwealth for some fifty years, were not yet ready to cast aside their traditional ideas of Britishness in favour of Europe. Furthermore, EC regional policies were seen as a potential threat to a nation that was suffering more than its fair share of deindustrialisation, and which was geographically more distant than England from the main continental European markets.

Scottish views on Europe on the eve of the referendum also reflected the political changes in Scotland over the previous twenty-five years. In 1951, Labour and the Conservatives had each taken nearly 50 per cent of the vote in the general election, and each had won thirty-five of the seventy-one Scottish seats at Westminster. In October 1974, the Conservative share of the Scottish vote had fallen below 25 per cent and they had won only sixteen seats; Labour, by contrast, increased its seats to forty-one, but its share of the vote likewise fell, to 36 per cent. The SNP, in those years a somewhat conservative party,[26] was the big winner, with 30 per cent of the Scottish vote and eleven seats. Thus, the largely pro-Europe Conservative Party was losing votes to the anti-Europe SNP, and this was bound to be reflected in the polls before the referendum. The prospect of Scotland voting differently from England was therefore a very real one.

Like Scotland, Wales was also expected to support leaving the EC.[27] There were many reasons for this. The share of the vote in general elections going to Plaid Cymru, which opposed membership, had been rising, while that of the Conservative Party had been falling. However, by far the biggest share of the Welsh vote in general elections went to the Labour Party. This had fallen from 60 to 50 per cent in the quarter-century before the referendum, but it meant that the views of Labour voters would still be critical on how Wales voted as a whole.

The Labour Party was split on the issue of Europe at every level—cabinet, government, parliamentarians and members.

EUROPE

Yet the left of the party, so strong in Wales, was solidly against staying in the EC. This was not so much about national identity and the Welsh language, the issues at the heart of Plaid Cymru's opposition, as about deindustrialisation and the constraints that the European Commission might apply to regional policy and industrial subsidies. In particular, the commission had suggested that coal output in Wales should be halved by 1985—with all that this implied for jobs and incomes received by Welsh families.

The referendum in Northern Ireland took place only two years after voters had been asked if they wanted to remain in the UK. With that poll boycotted by nationalists, the result was never in doubt and had delivered a 98.9 per cent majority in favour of union. However, this was a period when Northern Ireland politics were in flux, with the formation of new parties, the separation of the Ulster Unionist Party (UUP) from the Conservative Party, and splits within the unionist movement. No one could therefore be sure exactly how this would impact on the referendum, although it was widely assumed that Northern Ireland would vote to leave the EC.

For unionists—now represented not just by the old UUP, but also by the new Democratic Unionist Party (DUP)—the EC was seen as diminishing the Britishness of Northern Ireland. On the other hand, the Vanguard Unionist Progressive Party—a splinter group from the Ulster Unionists that had been formed in 1972—was in favour of staying in, as was the small Alliance Party founded in 1970.[28] Meanwhile, the nationalists were also divided, with the SDLP (formed in 1970) in favour and Sinn Féin against. With eight parties having won seats in the new Northern Ireland Assembly in 1973, the referendum was bound to present complexities not apparent in the other three nations. However, the combined strength of the UUP, DUP and Sinn Féin was assumed to guarantee a 'no' vote in Northern Ireland.

INTERNAL EMPIRE

There was a risk, therefore, that all three smaller nations would vote against. That left England, where the Conservatives and Labour had each won about 40 per cent of the popular vote in both elections of 1974. The balance had almost all gone to the Liberal Party, whose members and supporters were strongly in favour of staying in the EC. Provided, therefore, that a majority of Conservative supporters voted 'yes', there was a good chance of England choosing to remain in Europe, even if most Labour supporters were opposed. And if England (population 47 million) voted by a significant margin to stay in, it was safe to assume that the UK would do so—given the disparity in population size between the four nations.

England's hegemony had been a structural feature of the UK ever since its creation in 1801—just as had been the case within Great Britain after the union with Scotland in 1707. Indeed, England's dominant position had been made even greater when the south of Ireland became independent in 1922 as the Irish Free State. The resolution of UK contests and disputes therefore tended to be settled by English votes—something that those in England took for granted, and those in the other three nations had to accept. This did not matter if voters in the four nations were in broad agreement; and it was not necessarily a problem even if that was not the case, as long as no single party dominated English politics.

The 1975 referendum, however, drew attention not only to the possibility of a split between England and the other nations, but also to the risk of the Conservatives—the most successful party in British history—becoming a de facto English National Party. In 1945, the Conservatives may have lost many seats, but more than 20 per cent of those it did win had been outside England.[29] By the time of the second election in 1974, this share was down to 8.7 per cent—and in 1997 it would fall to zero.[30] This growing concentration of Conservative seats in England

206

EUROPE

was therefore a feature of postwar British elections, and it was made sharper by the party's choice of quintessentially English leaders from 1965 onwards—especially Margaret Thatcher, who led the Conservatives from 1975 to 1990.

The split between the nations was averted by a brilliant 'yes' campaign run by Britain in Europe, and an incompetent 'no' one run by the National Referendum Campaign. All four nations voted to stay in the EC, with a UK figure of 67 per cent. England voted 69 per cent (very close to the UK figure), Wales 65 per cent, Scotland 58 per cent and Northern Ireland 52 per cent. Furthermore, of the sixty-eight returning areas for the referendum, all but two (Shetland and the Western Isles) voted to stay. No English area voted to stay by less than 63 per cent, and many by more than 70 per cent. English Conservative supporters, together with their temporary Liberal allies, were enough to carry the day despite considerable Labour opposition, and to determine the outcome for the UK as a whole.

It looked as if the European issue had been laid to rest as a factor in UK politics. The referendum, however, had merely opened up faultlines that remain to this day in relation to Europe—noticeably on global influence, national sovereignty, democracy and free trade, with only one subsequently added (free movement of people, which hardly figured in 1975). Yet, if the faultlines remain largely the same today as they did back then, British political parties—with the exception of the Liberals—would spend the next fifty years traversing them, and taking up a position contrary to what they had argued in 1975. Thus, the nationalist parties would become doughty defenders of European integration, while the Conservatives (increasingly indeed 'the English national party') would become its fiercest critic.

INTERNAL EMPIRE

Britain into Europe

The referendum in June 1975 confirmed support for British entry into the EC—an entry that had begun on 1 January 1973. By joining, the UK had agreed to a common external tariff (the customs union), free movement of labour (the common market) and 'ever closer union' (per the Treaty of Rome). It had accepted the supranational nature of some institutions, in particular the European Commission and the European Court of Justice. It had also agreed not just to a European parliament, but also to direct elections to the institution once a voting system had been agreed by all member states.

Before the UK joined, the original six members had agreed to set 1980 as the date for economic and monetary union (EMU). London accepted the principle during negotiations in 1972, but ahead of renegotiation in 1974 had asked for 'safeguards against any form of Economic and Monetary Union that might hamper a government's ability to tackle unemployment.'[31] By the end of the year, however, Prime Minister Harold Wilson had signed a declaration on behalf of the UK as a member-state saying that, as far as EMU was concerned, the heads of governments' 'will has not weakened and their objective has not changed' and that 'the time has come for the Nine to agree as soon as possible on an overall concept of European Union.'[32]

Wilson, like some other heads of government among the nine member states, was insincere in his commitment to establishing EMU by 1980. He even told the House of Commons on 18 March 1975 that:

> there has been a major change in the attitude of other European Governments to the practicability of achieving EMU by 1980. As a long-term objective it was restated in the Paris communiqué, but for all practical purposes it has been tacitly abandoned ... its realisation in the foreseeable future ... is as likely as the ideal

EUROPE

of general and complete disarmament which we all support and assert.[33]

This was a sadly typical British misreading of the European project, seriously underestimating the commitments that had been made. Nonetheless, Wilson had not only committed the UK to EMU, but also to a journey where the direction of travel and the final destination—if not the speed—were clear.

The first post-referendum surveys on British public opinion towards Europe gave no hint of troubles to come. The findings of Eurobarometer, which questioned voters in all member-states, suggested that UK citizens were broadly supportive of the EC and, if not the most europhile among the nine states, were certainly not the most eurosceptic—yet alone europhobic. In the Standard Eurobarometer issue for December 1975, for example, 50 per cent thought the EC was 'a good thing', compared with 31 per cent two years earlier. Furthermore, on the key question of European unification, 51 per cent were either 'very much in favour' or 'in favour on the whole' (only 11 per cent were strongly against).

These findings might be dismissed as reflecting the euphoria among voters a few months after the referendum had shown a strong preference for remaining in the EC. Yet in the British Social Attitudes Survey, which started to ask questions about Britain and Europe in the 1990s, the results were not dissimilar. In answer to a question on Britain's relationship with the EU (which replaced the EC in 1993), no less than 54 per cent said either 'leave things as are', 'stay and increase EU's powers' or 'work for a single European government'. Only 10 per cent were in favour of leaving, and this was still only 15 per cent as late as 2003.

British voters therefore appeared comfortable with the direction of travel as the UK with its partners set about deepening and widening European integration in the first few decades after the UK joined—and the results could be seen almost immediately. The share of UK goods exports going to EC countries had been around 20 per cent just before joining (similar to the share going to Commonwealth countries) but jumped to 40 per cent by the end of the 1970s, while the Commonwealth share fell to 10 per cent. By the end of the 1980s, the share going to Europe had reached nearly 60 per cent, and it stayed there for the next twenty-five years. (A trade deficit in goods was then partially balanced by a trade surplus in services, with European partners accounting for 40 per cent of British service exports by the end of the millennium.)[34]

At first, the trade figures were collected and published only for the UK as a whole. However, regional trade statistics began to appear regularly after 2000, showing how each nation compared when it came to the export of goods to European partners. By 2005, for example, no less than 62.3 per cent of Welsh exports were going to the EU—much higher than for England (53.5 per cent).[35] The number for Northern Ireland was almost the same as for Wales, while for Scotland it was 50 per cent. And while the share of exports going to Europe fell for all four nations in the 2010s, it dropped most sharply for England. Scotland, Wales and Northern Ireland now all had a higher share of goods going to the EU than England.[36]

If there was a point of friction in the UK's relationship with its European partners in the first decade after the referendum (and all member-states had their complaints), it was the British contribution to the EC budget. The rules on payments and receipts by member-states, leaving each with a net contribution, had been drawn up long before the UK joined, and these rules put the UK in an invidious position. A large part of the payments came from the tariff collected on extraregional imports (relatively large in the British case, for historical reasons), while most of the

EUROPE

receipts went to farmers (a relatively small sector for the UK). This meant that the UK's net contribution was higher than all other states except West Germany.

An attempt had been made to correct this as early as 1974, during the renegotiation of the terms of entry, but it had proved insufficient. It was therefore made a priority by Prime Minister Margaret Thatcher after the Conservative Party's election victory in 1979. A temporary solution was found in 1980, and a permanent one in 1985, after much hard bargaining by the British side. The net contribution was cut by two thirds. This particular boil in the relationship was therefore lanced, despite the fact that the other EC partners now had to pay more.

The UK was never going to be a major recipient of payments from European institutions, both because of the relatively small size of its agricultural sector and because of its relatively high GDP per head—especially after the entry of lower-income countries. However, the European Commission divided all countries into regions, and some British ones were considered 'less developed' (GDP per head less than 75 per cent of the European average) or 'in transition' (75–90 per cent of the European average). Over time, proportionately less money was spent by European institutions on agriculture, and more given to regional, structural and cohesion funds that took into account income differentials.

All of Northern Ireland and much of Scotland was considered to be 'in transition', while most of Wales was classified as 'less developed'. Thus, payments per head to these parts of the UK exceeded those to England. In the last spending round before the UK left the EU, for example, the impact of the five funds disbursed under the European structural and investment initiative was very different for the four nations. Wales received £123 per head, Northern Ireland £50, Scotland £40 and England only £24 (making the UK average £31).[37] Nor was this the end of

INTERNAL EMPIRE

the story, as each nation also received payments from European institutions for agriculture and other purposes.

The budget battle fought by the UK had been a backward-looking one, reflecting the fact that the country had been late to join the club and the rules were already set. It did nothing to comfort those who saw in Europe a chance to increase British influence on the world stage and to provide a substitute for the empire and the Commonwealth. Yet the EC was not static, and by the mid-1980s it was ready to embark on the next stage of its evolution. This was EMU, to which Harold Wilson had only agreed on the assumption that it would never happen.

Prime Minister Thatcher at first was of a very different mindset. Here was an initiative, she thought, where the UK could leave its mark. The Conservative Party's manifesto for the first direct elections to the European Parliament had supported, in principle, British participation in the 'European monetary system', which linked member-states' currencies. This was, of course, a Franco-German initiative and one that had already started without British participation, but it allowed the UK to show goodwill and to prepare for the next step.

This next step was the creation of a single European market, sweeping aside the non-tariff barriers that prevented member-state firms from enjoying economies of scale, and which gave firms the same position as those based in other member-states. This was very much a Conservative Party ideal and one which allowed the UK to take a lead. Thatcher and Lord Cockfield, a former minister in her cabinet and now a European commissioner, drove the project forward, leading to the signing by all member-states of the Single European Act in February 1986. It paved the way for the genuinely free movement of goods, services, capital and labour.

Unfortunately for Margaret Thatcher, and despite the major British input, the act did much more than that. It also

EUROPE

'expanded the areas of EU interest to include foreign policy co-operation, the environment and social policy, and increased the powers of the European Parliament, giving it a veto over any single market legislation.'[38] This was anathema to large parts of the Conservative Party, including its leader, and—despite the fact that the UK had actively supported the creation of a single market—the official British position now shifted. The deepening of European integration would no longer be seen as an arena for expanding the UK's global influence, but became a project to be delayed, through a series of tactics including opt-outs and threats of a national veto.

The dilatory tactics employed by the British government had little impact. The European exchange rate mechanism, the prelude to the launch of a single currency, was gaining ground. The UK reluctantly agreed to join in June 1989, but was able to delay entry until October 1990. However, on 16 September 1992 (known forever as 'Black Wednesday'), it was forced to leave, following a speculative attack against the pound sterling. The economic and political repercussions were immense.

Thatcher had resigned in November 1990, but her successor, John Major—despite claiming he wished to put Britain 'at the heart of Europe'—only succeeded in securing a British opt-out (along with Denmark) from the single currency. Signed in 1992, the Maastricht Treaty creating the European Union (EU) both granted this opt-out and unambiguously committed member-states without one to launch the euro at the end of the decade. Major also secured an opt-out from the 'social chapter', on the grounds that it might undermine British competitiveness.

The British approach to deepening European integration was expected to change with the victory of the Labour Party in 1997, when Tony Blair became Prime Minister. The language and tone certainly altered, but the reality was much the same. The new government ratified the Amsterdam Treaty that year, transferring

INTERNAL EMPIRE

more powers to the European Parliament, but still did not participate in the Schengen agreement, which abolished national borders for the citizens of member-states (the Conservative government had stayed out when the scheme was first launched in 1985). Blair made positive noises about the single currency, but his Chancellor of the Exchequer then imposed five tests for joining the euro that were designed to ensure that they could never be met. The decision of other member-states to press ahead with a new constitution for Europe was met with a sullen response and the promise of a referendum, although the British government's blushes were saved by opposition from some other countries. (Instead, the Treaty of Lisbon was signed in 2007; Blair deemed it did not need a plebiscite.)

The one area where the UK, under both Conservative and Labour governments, remained fully engaged was the widening (rather than deepening) of European integration. Britain had supported the entry of Greece in 1981, Portugal and Spain in 1986 and Austria, Finland and Sweden in 1995. By this time, the Berlin Wall had come down and many more countries were on the way to membership. Ten joined in 2004, mainly from Eastern Europe, and two more in 2007 (Bulgaria and Romania).[39] It looked like a rare British success, but there was a sting in the tail. After the big enlargement in 2004, the UK (along with Ireland and Sweden) waived the requirement that free movement of labour should be phased in over seven years. Workers and their families were free to move immediately, and most of those who did headed for Great Britain. In particular, they settled in England; and this—through no fault of their own—would have major implications.

The English Backlash

As we have seen, all four nations favoured staying in the EC in the 1975 referendum, with English voters expressing the greatest

214

EUROPE

support. In the following four decades, however, attitudes among the nations would start to diverge. Nationalist parties in Northern Ireland, Scotland and Wales, all of which had opposed staying in the EC in 1975, changed their position to one of support. The financial benefits of membership for the three smaller nations were considerable, and the European flag was increasingly visible on infrastructure projects. By contrast, English voters started to turn against the European project.

As the hegemonic power in the UK and the driving force behind British global expansion, England had never lost the imperial mindset acquired even before the formation of Great Britain. Joining the EC was a chance, in the eyes of many English, to provide leadership in a different space. In the words of *The Sun*, England's bestselling newspaper: 'After years of drift and failure, the Common Market offers an unrepeatable opportunity for a nation that lost an empire to gain a continent.'[40] This sense of superiority had been brilliantly captured in *A Song of Patriotic Prejudice*, written in 1956 by Michael Flanders and Donald Swann expressing contempt for people in other countries. These 'other peoples', of course, included the citizens of the three smaller nations, for whom the song reserved the greatest bigotry and prejudice.[41]

Even before it was clear that England was not going to lead in Europe, the Labour manifesto in 1983 had committed the party to withdraw the UK from the EC if elected. This might have looked like a prescient move, but the manifesto statement made clear that this was a backward-looking step reflecting a different age:

> Geography and history determine that Britain is part of Europe, and Labour wants to see Europe safe and prosperous. But the European Economic Community, which does not even include the whole of Western Europe, was never devised to suit us, and

INTERNAL EMPIRE

our experience as a member of it has made it more difficult for us to deal with our economic and industrial problems. It has sometimes weakened our ability to achieve the objectives of Labour's international policy.

Four years later in the next manifesto, the Labour Party changed its policy in favour of continued membership, and the 1983 manifesto was quietly forgotten.

The first signs of a real English backlash then appeared in 1988, with a speech in Bruges by Prime Minister Margaret Thatcher, that most English of political leaders—the previous year, she had easily won the general election almost entirely on the back of English constituencies. Now, in Bruges, Thatcher warned of the alleged dangers of a European federal state. Yet she did much more than sound a note of euroscepticism in her speech. Despite being Prime Minister of the United Kingdom of Great Britain and Northern Ireland, she gave an English interpretation of UK history that must have come as something of a shock to many voters outside England (and some inside it):

> For three hundred years, we were part of the Roman Empire ... our nation was ... 'restructured' under the Norman and Angevin rule in the eleventh and twelfth centuries. This year, we celebrate the three hundredth anniversary of the glorious revolution in which the British crown passed to Prince William of Orange and Queen Mary.[42]

She then went on to make the statement for which the speech is most famous: 'We have not successfully rolled back the frontiers of the state in Britain, only to see them re-imposed at a European level, with a European super-state exercising a new dominance from Brussels.'

This resonated well with many members of the Conservative Parliamentary Party, 95 per cent of whom represented English constituencies after the 1987 election. However, things were not

216

EUROPE

so clear-cut in Scotland (50 out of 72 seats won by Labour) and Wales (24 out of 38 seats to Labour). Voters in both nations had favoured a party backing a strong state to deliver public services and jobs in the wake of deindustrialisation. And even in Northern Ireland (12 out of 17 seats taken by unionists, the rest by nationalists) the demand was for a powerful state to provide security for all communities. Thatcher was therefore appealing to English voters, and she knew it.

Thatcher's speech made English euroscepticism respectable. Yet she had not called for an exit from the EC. A big step towards that would be taken by the Referendum Party, founded in 1994, which campaigned for a plebiscite on the question 'Do you want the UK to be part of a Federal Europe? Or do you want the UK to return to an association of sovereign nations that are part of a common trading market?' With a large war chest provided by its founder, Sir James Goldsmith, the Referendum Party then fought the 1997 general election on this single issue.[43]

The Referendum Party put up candidates in most constituencies of Great Britain (none in Northern Ireland) and secured an average of 3.1 per cent of the vote in the constituencies it contested. Detailed analysis of the results, however, shows that all seats where it won more than 4 per cent of the vote were in England, while in most Scottish and Welsh seats it secured less than 1 per cent. This was an English party that appealed to some English voters, most of whom would otherwise have voted for the Conservatives. Although the party collapsed after the death of its founder two months later, it served as a warning to English politicians of the appeal of euroscepticism among some of their constituents.

Even the Referendum Party had not explicitly campaigned for the UK to leave what was now the EU. It was therefore left to the United Kingdom Independence Party (UKIP) to make that demand. Founded a year before the Referendum Party, it made

217

INTERNAL EMPIRE

no impact until the 1999 elections for the European Parliament, where it won 7 per cent of the vote and secured three seats. Although it claimed to be a UK-wide party, as its name stated, it was essentially an English one. Of the 696,100 votes that UKIP polled, 663,800 were in England. And while its share of the vote in the 1999 election was 7.9 per cent in England, its share in Wales was only 3.1 per cent, and in Scotland a paltry 1.3 per cent (it did not even contest Northern Ireland).

Emboldened by this performance, in the 2001 general election UKIP put up 428 candidates. Once again, nearly all of its votes were secured in England (374,775 out of 390,563) with only 12,552 in Wales and a dismal 3,236 in Scotland. Yet, although performing much better than in 1997, when it had had to compete with the Referendum Party for the eurosceptic vote, UKIP still could not make an electoral breakthrough anywhere in the UK, and secured only 1.7 per cent of the vote even in England. English voters, it would seem, had not yet abandoned their attachment to the EU, even if those ties had been slowly dissolving ever since it had become clear that England was not going to be a leader in Europe. However, after the major EU enlargement of 2004, UKIP and eurosceptics in England were presented with a gift that would change everything.

The decision by the UK to waive the phased entry requirement for workers from the new EU member-states brought a big increase in those coming from Bulgaria, Poland and Romania in particular. Although the Labour government had anticipated a small increase in arrivals, the actual numbers were large (see Table 7.1). And since the only certain way to limit migration from member-states was by leaving the EU, eurosceptics found a very effective platform on which to campaign.

It was the 'uncontrolled' nature of EU immigration, rather than the numbers themselves, that played into eurosceptic hands. Even at its peak, net migration—taking into account emigration

EUROPE

Table 7.1: Population Resident in England, Including Those Born Elsewhere for Selected Countries (in Thousands)

Year	Bulgaria (joined EU in 2007)	Poland (joined EU in 2004)	Romania (joined EU in 2007)	England
2001	3	53	8	48,398
2005	15	156	17	49,946
2010	51	458	78	51,975
2015	63	713	209	54,086

Source: derived from Office of National Statistics (various years). 'Population of the UK by Country of Birth and Nationality: Individual Country Data'.

from the UK—added only about 0.5 per cent annually to the population.[44] In addition, a majority of migrants normally came from non-EU countries and were therefore subject to border controls. Furthermore, the labour market was built around an inflow of EU migrants, without whom shortages of goods and services would soon appear. Yet none of this seemed to matter to English eurosceptics, and the media were soon full of stories of public services being 'overwhelmed' by EU migrants who were 'unfairly' claiming welfare benefits.

Public opinion in England was starting to turn against EU membership. In surveys of UK voters, just 15 per cent had wanted to leave in 2003, but this had become 30 per cent by 2012—a figure strongly influenced by English voters, given their dominant demographic position within the UK.[45] Two years later, a third of English voters were defining themselves as either 'English, not British' or 'More English than British'. Another two years later, in 2016, the former group supported leaving the EU by 69 per cent.[46] Meanwhile, nearly half of all UK voters

219

INTERNAL EMPIRE

in 2015 (most of them in England) agreed that 'membership of the EU undermined Britain's distinct identity', while only 16 per cent identified as 'European'. Joining Europe in 1973, it was clear, had not succeeded in giving Britishness a European dimension, and had therefore not replaced the British Empire and the Commonwealth in the affections of English citizens.

Surveys are based on small samples, so the important question was how euroscepticism in England would translate at the ballot box. In the 2005 general election, UKIP had only modestly increased its share of the vote in England to 2.6 per cent; but the impact of higher inward migration from the EU, coupled with a resolution of UKIP's leadership crisis, then started to transform the party's fortunes.[47] Even so, it only won 3.5 per cent of the English vote in the 2010 general elections, when the Labour Party was defeated and a coalition government was formed, headed by the Conservative David Cameron with a Liberal Democrat as his deputy.[48]

Since UKIP's share of the vote was much lower than predicted by opinion polls, it seemed safe to assume that the party was struggling to make its mark in general elections as a result of the winner-takes-all voting system ('first past the post'). Yet it had taken most of its votes from the Conservative Party, and the trend looked set to continue.[49] Cameron, fearful of haemorrhaging more votes to UKIP, made a speech in January 2013 promising that, if the Conservatives should win an outright majority at the next election, he would renegotiate British membership of the EU before holding an in/out referendum. It was an almost exact replay of the promise made by Harold Wilson in 1974.

With this announcement, UKIP now had the wind in its sails; the first big test would come in elections subject to proportional representation, where the party could expect to do much better than in a 'first past the post' contest. This was the 2014 election for seats in the European Parliament. The results were astonishing

220

EUROPE

(see Table 7.2). UKIP, with 91.6 per cent of all its votes cast in England, secured more support than any other party. In particular, it won 29.2 per cent of the English vote, rising to 31.5 per cent outside of London (where the party performed relatively poorly), and it massively outpolled both the Conservative and Labour Parties in England.[50] Given the many Conservative and some Labour voters who also wanted to leave the EU, this was a stark warning ahead for Cameron's proposed referendum.

Table 7.2: Votes in Elections for European Parliament, 2014

	Conservative	Labour	UKIP	UKIP Share (%)
England	3,429,333	3,466,095	4,009,534	29.2
London	495,639	806,959	371,133	16.9
Excl. London	2,933,694	2,659,136	3,638,401	31.5
UK	3,792,549	4,020,646	4,376,635	26.6
% of votes coming from England	90.4	86.2	91.6	–
% of votes coming from outside London	77.4	66.1	83.1	–

Source: derived from Electoral Commission (2019).

The UKIP performance in 2014 could not be repeated in the 2015 UK general elections, but the party did quadruple its share of the vote in England to 14.1 per cent. This was as much as could have been expected at the time, given the voting system. By now, however, UKIP had played a central role not only in

INTERNAL EMPIRE

turning many English voters against continued membership of the EU, but also in securing the promise of a referendum that would give voters their first chance since 1975 to express a view. And the outright victory of the Conservative Party in 2015 meant that Prime Minister Cameron no longer needed a coalition. A referendum to be held in 2016 was therefore announced by the new government.

Despite more than forty years of membership in the European club, the inhabitants of England had not formed a European identity, and many were even beginning to question their own post-Imperial Britishness—preferring to emphasise their English identity instead. Not for the first time, what England decided would be the decision of the UK as a whole—irrespective of what the citizens elsewhere might want.[51] In the past, the other three nations had either been known to support what England preferred (as in 1975), or assumed to have been in favour—or else it had been safe to ignore them. This time, it would be different.

8

BREXIT

The referendum in June 1975 had delivered a huge vote in favour of staying in the European Communities across the four nations and within the largest city, London. Some forty years later, in June 2016, another referendum would deliver a small majority to leave the EU. This time, however, the decision would be split across the UK. Scotland and Northern Ireland voted by large margins in favour of staying. Wales (narrowly) and England (decisively) voted to leave. London—the UK capital and by far the largest city in England—voted for remain, as did the capitals of the other three nations.

Turning Brexit into a reality was no simple matter, as neither side in the referendum debate had properly thought through the consequences of leaving the EU. It was left to the UK parliament to implement the decision, and that meant the key choices would have to be made by the ruling Conservative Party. Dominated as it was by English MPs, the Conservative administration eventually adopted a form of Brexit that was heavily influenced by the preferences of voters in England outside the capital. The interests of the other nations were largely ignored.

INTERNAL EMPIRE

The nation whose interests were most immediately affected was Northern Ireland. Ever since the Good Friday Agreement had brought an end to the sectarian strife known as the Troubles, there had been no 'hard border' on the island of Ireland, with goods and people moving freely between the republic in the south and the UK in the north. To avoid the return of a hard border, with (likely armed) personnel on the boundary line, the Brexit agreement had included a protocol that, in effect, placed a maritime border down the Irish Sea instead, between Northern Ireland and Great Britain. This avoided the need for physical checks on the land border between the north and south of the island, but did require them on goods exports to Northern Ireland from the rest of the UK. For the first time since 1800, goods from Great Britain to Northern Ireland could be subject to customs regulations. The rationale behind this was that such goods might be 'at risk' of being 'moved on' from Northern Ireland, via the republic, to an EU member-state: since there was still no real border between north and south, and since the republic was still in the EU and therefore the single market, this would mean goods being exported from Brexit Britain to the EU without the requisite tariffs or checks.

The economic, political and constitutional implications of this Irish Sea border were likely to be serious. However, the modifications to Northern Ireland's position within the UK were only some of the consequences of Brexit. Others included an impact on the demographics of the four nations following changes to migration rules; the implications of increased trade barriers with the EU, by far the UK's largest trade partner, and the prospects for reduced barriers on trade with non-EU countries; and the impact of all these changes on long-term productivity in the UK. And, of course, all this would have to be separated from the impact of the COVID-19 pandemic, which reached the UK just as the country withdrew from the EU in 2020.

BREXIT

The 2016 Referendum

When Prime Minister David Cameron had promised an in/out referendum on EU membership in January 2013, he recognised the risks associated with this; in his own words, 'democratic consent for the EU in Britain [was] now wafer thin.'[1] To reduce the risk, he had committed a future British government to a renegotiation with the rest of the EU that would focus on five principles: competitiveness, flexibility, subsidiarity (i.e. power flowing back to member-states), democratic accountability and fairness. Only after negotiations concluded, assuming they were successful, would the referendum be held.

Cameron had chosen these principles in the expectation that other member-states might be sufficiently attracted for the renegotiation to avoid being seen as the UK, yet again, seeking special privileges for itself (as it had done with the budget rebate, the adoption of the euro and membership of the Schengen zone). Instead, he had hoped that Britain would secure a set of reforms that would not only increase support for the EU among UK citizens, but could also be 'sold' to other EU members as a package in their interests as well.

Since his government's then coalition partners, the Liberal Democrats, would never have approved a referendum, Cameron knew that what he was proposing could not be implemented unless a future election delivered an outright majority for the Conservative Party. Much to his surprise, this happened in 2015 and left the Prime Minister with no choice—as he saw it—other than to commit to a referendum. He therefore promised that one would be held before the end of 2017.

This meant that negotiations with the EU had to begin immediately. Far from being a process involving a coalition of like-minded member-states, however, it proved to be another exercise in Britain versus the rest. In this respect, it was similar

INTERNAL EMPIRE

to what had happened in 1974 in negotiations between Harold Wilson's government and the other eight members of the EC, but with an important difference: Wilson had been able to wring out a small number of concessions requiring neither treaty revisions nor votes in the European Parliament, nor future decisions from other members. The task that Cameron had set himself was much more difficult.

Furthermore, the rather abstract principles that the Prime Minister had outlined in his 2013 speech now had to be converted into substantial issues that the electorate, as well as other EU states, could easily understand. And that meant focusing above all on migration and welfare benefits—issues that resonated very strongly with voters in England in particular, and which he had not even mentioned in his original speech.

Eurosceptics dismissed the chances of success even before negotiations began, with former Conservative Chancellor of the Exchequer Nigel Lawson declaring on 1 October 2015, 'It is increasingly clear that the package of reforms the government will manage to secure from the EU ahead of our referendum on membership will be wafer thin.'[2] Yet the President of the European Council, Donald Tusk, went out of his way to secure reforms from other member-states that would meet almost all of the demands formulated in writing by Cameron.

The Prime Minister's letter to Tusk focused on four areas, one of which (immigration and welfare restrictions) was expected to be contentious.[3] Yet Cameron did not demand an end to free movement. Instead, he wrote: '[W]e have proposed that people coming to Britain from the EU must live here and contribute for four years before they qualify for in-work benefits or social housing. And ... we should end the practice of sending child benefit overseas.'[4]

This was the kind of practical demand from a member-state that the European Council had been dealing with for decades;

226

BREXIT

at the end of negotiations in February 2016, a declaration was issued by all states that took account of the 'pull' factor arising from a member-state's national in-work benefits by establishing a 'mechanism' in response to any inflow of workers that was of 'exceptional' magnitude:

> A Member State wishing to avail itself of the mechanism would notify the Commission and the Council that such an exceptional situation exists on a scale that affects essential aspects of its social security system ... On a proposal from the Commission after having examined the notification and the reasons stated therein, the Council could authorise the Member State to restrict access to non-contributory in-work benefits ... for a total period of up to four years from the commencement of employment.[5]

Cameron had effectively secured what he had demanded.[6] A date was therefore set for the referendum, 23 June 2016, and the campaign soon began. The Electoral Commission declared that Britain Stronger in Europe would be the official campaign group for 'remain', while the designated group for 'Brexit' would be Vote Leave. UKIP and its supporters were left to rally around Leave.EU. With the European Union Referendum Act in 2015 having set the question to be put to voters ('Should the United Kingdom remain a member of the European Union or leave the European Union?'), the stage was set for perhaps the greatest drama in domestic British politics since the repeal of the Corn Laws 170 years earlier.

Although two UK-wide bodies had been given official status, the actual campaign was fought out in the four nations by a range of organisations. This meant that the emphasis was different depending on which nation was being targeted. In Scotland, the Scottish Vote Leave campaign focused on the trade benefits to Scotland of ending EU membership, on the assumption (false, as it turned out) that powers over agriculture and fishery would

227

INTERNAL EMPIRE

be repatriated from the European Commission in Brussels to the Scottish Parliament at Holyrood. Immigration and welfare benefits, by contrast, were hardly mentioned at all. Meanwhile, the official Scotland Stronger in Europe campaign was effectively overshadowed by the SNP, which only a few weeks before the referendum had won nearly 50 per cent of the vote to secure another term in office—this time as a minority government—on the basis that Scotland was better off economically in the EU.

The results in Scotland were never in doubt, but nonetheless were extraordinary in the message they delivered. Among the thirty-two voting areas, not a single one was in favour of leaving. In three councils, the vote to remain was greater than 70%—the highest (nearly 75%) was in Edinburgh, the capital city. In another thirteen, it was above 60%. Only in Moray was the result remotely close, with 50.1% in favour of remain. Altogether, on a turnout of over two thirds, 62% of Scotland voted to stay in the EU.

Like Scotland, Northern Ireland had also held elections for its national assembly in the month before the referendum. The Democratic Unionist Party (DUP) had once again emerged as the largest single party and its leader, Arlene Foster, therefore remained as First Minister. The DUP had always been a eurosceptic party and made clear before the elections that it would be campaigning for Brexit, on the grounds that Cameron's deal had not changed anything in the relationship between the UK and the EU. Having just won nearly 30 per cent of the vote in the assembly election, the DUP leadership's preference for Brexit was bound to be an important factor in the referendum campaign. However, not all unionists were in favour of leaving the EU, and the nationalist parties were all in favour of staying.

The referendum result in Northern Ireland was therefore not a foregone conclusion. In the end, however, there was a significant majority in favour of remaining, including in the capital city,

BREXIT

Belfast. For counting purposes, Northern Ireland was treated as one area and, on a turnout of nearly two thirds, over 55 per cent voted to remain. The Electoral Commission, however, did publish the results broken down by Northern Ireland's eighteen constituencies for the UK parliament. Of these, eleven voted to remain—one, Foyle, with a vote of nearly 80 per cent—and nearly all were represented at Westminster by nationalist politicians. Meanwhile, all seven of the constituencies that voted to leave had unionist representatives in the House of Commons (six DUP, one UUP).

In view of the massive support given to Wales by the institutions of the EU, the Welsh electorate might have been expected to follow Scotland and Northern Ireland in voting to remain.[7] However, there were two qualifications to this assumption. First, UKIP had made substantial gains in Wales not only in the European parliamentary elections of 2014, but also in the Welsh assembly elections the month before the referendum, when it had won seats for the first time. Second, and probably related to the first, the 2011 census had shown that over 500,000 people in Wales (nearly 20 per cent) did not consider themselves to be Welsh at all. The overwhelming reason for this is likely to have been their English heritage, as 21 per cent of the Welsh population had been born in England.

This meant that a sizeable proportion of the Welsh electorate might be expected to vote in line with 'English' rather than 'Welsh' preferences. This may have proved decisive, as the vote was very close, with leave winning by a margin of 82,000 votes. In the twenty-two voting areas for Wales, just five voted to remain—but in only one constituency (Blaenau Gwent) was the vote to leave above 60 per cent, with most contests settled by a few thousand votes. Meanwhile, the capital city of Cardiff voted overwhelmingly to remain, as did most of the Welsh-speaking areas of Wales.

229

INTERNAL EMPIRE

That left England—including, of course, London. The capital city, where UKIP had always struggled, was expected to be in support of remain, and that proved to be the case. Out of thirty-three counting areas in Greater London, only five were in favour of Brexit. The London vote was 60:40 in favour of remain. All four capital cities had therefore strongly supported remain, and the combined votes from Northern Ireland, London, Scotland and Wales (NILSW) were overwhelmingly in favour of staying in the EU (see Table 8.1). Indeed, NILSW, with its eighty-eight counting areas,[8] had a mere twenty-two that supported leave, with a large differential in favour of remain (1.4 million) and a gap of 15.8 per cent between the two sides.

The final outcome, therefore, depended on England excluding London (EexL). This large constituency, with 293 counting areas spread across eight regions, was known to be the most eurosceptic part of the UK and the most supportive of UKIP. Yet the margin of victory for leave was extraordinary (see Table 8.1). More than 80 per cent of these counting areas were in favour of Brexit, rising to above 90 per cent of counting areas in three regions (North East, East Midlands and West Midlands). All eight regions voted to leave, and the result was only extremely close in one (South East). EexL delivered a differential of nearly 2.7 million between votes for leave and remain, and a gap of more than 10 per cent between the two sides. Even if London is included in the England figure, the differential was still nearly 2 million votes.

This margin in favour of leave was more than enough to compensate for NISLW's margin in favour of remain. The final result was therefore in favour of the UK leaving the EU by a 'narrow' majority of 51.9 to 48.1 per cent. Yet the result was only close when the UK was considered as one unit. When the votes are broken down by geographical area, it was not really close at all. And the area that mattered most was England, with

230

or without London. This hegemonic nation had delivered its verdict to the rest of the UK, and the other nations would have to follow.

Table 8.1: Results of the 2016 Referendum on Membership of the EU

	Counting Areas	% for leave	Vote Difference (leave minus remain)	% Difference (leave minus remain)
N. Ireland, London, Scotland, Wales (NILSW)	88	25.0	-1,402,196	-15.8
England excl. London (EexL)	293	82.6	2,671,697	10.8
East	47	89.4	431,751	13.0
East Midlands	40	95.0	442,443	17.6
North East	12	91.7	215,508	16.1
North West	40	82.5	267,905	7.3
South East	66	63.6	176,247	3.6
South West*	37	78.4	166,692	5.3
West Midlands	30	96.7	548,512	18.5
Yorkshire & Humber	21	85.7	422,639	15.4
United Kingdom	**381**	**69.3**	**1,269,501**	**3.8**

* Excluding Gibraltar.

Source: derived by author from Electoral Commission (2019)

INTERNAL EMPIRE

The Brexit vote was English imperialism in action—does anyone seriously believe that if England had voted to remain, but the other three nations had voted to leave, the UK would not still be in the EU, regardless of the size of the national votes? The electorate in England, which had overwhelmingly supported staying in the EC in 1975, had now changed its mind. This was not the first time the other three nations had been forced to dance to England's tune, nor would it be the last. Yet it was not just the EU on which English voters were turning their backs, but also a definition of Britishness that included Europe. With the empire gone and the Commonwealth fading, this would make it even harder to pinpoint what being British meant. And, as we shall see in Chapter 10, the implications of this for Englishness would slowly become apparent.

The Agreement(s)

The referendum was not legally binding, but the vote in England meant that there was soon an understanding by all parties that the result would have to be respected. David Cameron, so closely associated with the remain side, therefore resigned, and the parliamentary Conservative Party was offered a number of candidates as his successor. Most of these had supported leave in the campaign, but the Conservative MPs consistently favoured a remainer during the voting process, and she became Prime Minister in July 2016.[9] Although she had voted to remain in the EU, Theresa May was at first accepted by advocates of leave, as she promised no second referendum (her mantra was 'Brexit means Brexit') and—as Cameron's Home Secretary—had pursued hardline anti-immigration policies that had won her support among party members.

To leave the EU, the UK government had to invoke Article 50 of the Treaty on European Union (as amended by the Treaty of

232

BREXIT

Lisbon); once Article 50 was triggered, there would be a maximum of two years of negotiation (with the possibility of an extension for a further two years, if agreed by both sides). Yet Prime Minister May was at first so uncertain about what form Brexit should take that Article 50 was not triggered until the end of March 2017. This meant that an agreement on withdrawal was supposed to be reached by March 2019, but it soon became clear that—despite the long delay in invoking Article 50—there was still no consensus within the Conservative administration on the way forward.

The problem was that there were many ways to leave the EU, and the referendum result did not in itself provide any guidance. What was clear, however, from opinion polls before and after the referendum was that voters in England, the nation whose preferences had decided the outcome of the referendum, wanted above all to end unrestricted migration—the free movement of labour that Cameron had hoped to slow down through changes to welfare rules. As late as mid-2018, for example, those in England who had voted to leave still ranked immigration as the most important issue facing the country.[10]

English views on migration appeared to point the May government in one direction only. Yet, while ending unrestricted migration might have been the highest priority for the mass of English voters, that was certainly not the case for those English business elites who had supported Brexit. Indeed, this small group—with its large influence on the Conservative Party— benefited hugely from the flexible labour market and modest wage increases that unrestricted EU migration had brought. These business leaders were much more interested in lowering regulation and shifting international trade towards the fastest growing parts of the world. They had not thought they could do so effectively while remaining in the EU and so, for them, the priority once Brexit was won was not to restrict migration, but to legislate for sole UK control of trade and regulation policies.

233

INTERNAL EMPIRE

To give herself a mandate for whatever path was chosen, May had been persuaded to hold a general election in June 2017—despite the fact that the Conservative Party had won 330 seats in the previous election of 2015, with all but twelve of its MPs representing constituencies in England. In the new parliament, however, the Conservatives were reduced to 317 seats (296 in England), so that May was forced to enter into an alliance with another party in order to stay in power. The only realistic one was the DUP, with whom a 'confidence and supply' agreement was eventually reached.[11] This meant that May now had to craft an exit strategy from the EU that gave more weight to the views of unionists in Northern Ireland. The 2017 election had therefore made her task even more difficult.

May proceeded cautiously, but by December 2017 the government had agreed with EU negotiators a joint report that mapped out progress so far. Much of this left open the final outcome of negotiations, but on Northern Ireland there were very specific commitments. These were needed because of the 'soft' border between the north and the republic, which was guaranteed by the Good Friday Agreement—an agreement ratified by both the UK and the Republic of Ireland. With the UK now leaving the EU, but Ireland remaining in it, this created a conundrum in the event that the UK should leave the single market and the customs union. The joint report therefore stated:

> The United Kingdom remains committed to protecting North–South cooperation and to its guarantee of avoiding a hard border. Any future arrangements must be compatible with those overarching requirements. The United Kingdom's intention is to achieve these objectives through the overall EU–UK relationship. Should this not be possible, the United Kingdom will propose specific solutions to address the unique circumstances of the island of Ireland. *In the absence of agreed solutions, the United Kingdom will maintain full alignment with*

BREXIT

those rules of the Internal Market [UK] *and the Customs Union* [EU] *which, now or in the future, support North–South cooperation, the all-island economy and the protection of the 1998 Agreement.* (Author's emphasis.)[12]

The words outlined in italics soon became known as 'the backstop'. They committed the UK to staying in the customs union in the event of no agreement being reached between the two sides. Unlike the single market, which would have committed the UK to continue with free movement of labour, continued membership of the customs union would have met the concerns of ordinary leave voters (primarily English) for whom restricting migration from EU member-states was so important. However, it would also have committed the UK to the EU's common external tariff, regulatory framework for goods and settlement of disputes by the European Court of Justice. This was not acceptable to the Brexiteer elites (almost entirely English), for whom the top priorities were deregulation and freedom to enter into new trade agreements with the rest of the world.

The parliamentary voice of this English Brexiteer elite was to be found in the European Research Group (ERG) of the Conservative Party. This eurosceptic parliamentary bloc, founded in 1993, had been little known before the referendum, but now acquired extreme importance as a 'party within a party'. With its chairs and deputy chairs almost invariably English, the ERG should perhaps have been known as the English Research Group.[13] All of its leading figures, and all of those who came to speak for the group, represented English constituencies during May's administration. And despite May's efforts to recruit members of the ERG to her government to ward off splits within the Conservative Party, she faced a formidable uphill battle against the group—one that ultimately cost her the premiership.

INTERNAL EMPIRE

Despite this, May pressed ahead with negotiations, seeking a withdrawal agreement that would leave many of the big issues on the future UK–EU relationship unresolved, but would still allow the UK formally to exit the EU by the end of March 2019. By November 2018, a draft agreed with the EU negotiating team was ready, but its publication created a storm of protests orchestrated by the ERG. In January 2019, May's draft agreement was defeated by a margin of 230 votes (202 in favour and 432 opposed). She survived a vote of no confidence in her leadership the next day, tabled by members of her own party, but the failure to pass her deal was the heaviest parliamentary defeat ever inflicted on a British government in a 'meaningful' vote.

The Prime Minister struggled on in the face of this humiliation, inflicted by English MPs in the Conservative Party, but it was soon clear that the bill was never going to pass, despite the deadline for negotiations being extended beyond the end of March 2019. She resigned in June and another chapter in the Brexit saga opened. This time, the ERG demanded someone whose views on the withdrawal agreement chimed with their own, and their choice was unanimous. Boris Johnson, who had resigned from the May cabinet over her draft agreement, still had to face a vote by the Conservative Party membership—but, as the other candidate (Jeremy Hunt) had been in favour of remaining in the EU, the outcome was never in doubt.[14]

Johnson became Prime Minister in July 2019. Addressing the House of Commons that same month, he made clear what he saw as the way forward:

> The withdrawal agreement negotiated by my predecessor has been three times rejected by this House. Its terms are unacceptable to this Parliament and to this country. No country that values its independence, and indeed its self-respect, could agree to a treaty that signed away our economic independence

BREXIT

and self-government, as this backstop does. A time limit is not enough. If an agreement is to be reached, it must be clearly understood that the way to the deal goes by way of the abolition of the backstop.[15]

It took a further three months, but by October 2019 a new draft withdrawal agreement had been negotiated between the UK and EU that did indeed abolish the backstop—but only by drawing a maritime boundary between Great Britain and Northern Ireland that would entail checks on goods flowing between different parts of the UK. Northern Ireland would be part of the UK customs territory de jure, but de facto it would be part of the EU customs union—thus avoiding the need for a north–south barrier on the island of Ireland itself.

Unionists in Northern Ireland were predictably outraged. However, any leverage they might have exerted on the British government through the Conservative Party's 'supply and confidence' agreement with the DUP was removed when Johnson called an early election for December 2019. The Conservatives increased their seats in the House of Commons to 365 and no longer needed a coalition partner. And while the overall number of Conservative MPs increased by forty-eight, those in England increased by forty-nine: the party now even had sufficient members in English constituencies (345) to vote through any bills required, in the event that such a condition might be imposed.[16]

The act enshrining the government's withdrawal agreement sailed through parliament, with minimal scrutiny, by the new deadline of 31 January 2020. While not unwelcome to a minority of voters in the devolved nations, the form Brexit took was primarily a triumph for those English voters who had voted to leave, together with their parliamentary representatives in the House of Commons. Once the transition period ended on 31

237

December that year,[17] the UK would no longer be in the single market, and so unrestricted EU migration would end. Yet—to the satisfaction of the Brexiteer elites—the UK would also no longer be in the customs union, regardless of what happened on the island of Ireland.

The transition period for the duration of 2020 not only kept the UK in the single market, but also allowed time for both sides to negotiate a free trade agreement. Unlike other such agreements negotiated by the EU, this one would be about *increasing* trade barriers, rather than lowering them. Yet the alternative (no deal) would have meant even higher barriers, as both sides would have had to apply the tariffs in place for third countries under World Trade Organization rules. In the end, common sense prevailed, and a Trade and Cooperation Agreement was reached just before the deadline (31 December 2020). It ruled out tariffs or quotas on goods qualifying under rules of origin, but gave no special privileges for most services. In particular, according to the European Commission:

> The Trade and Cooperation Agreement does not cover any decisions relating to equivalences for financial services, the adequacy of the UK protection regime, or the assessment of the UK's sanitary and phytosanitary regime for the purpose of listing it as a third country allowed to export food products to the EU.[18]

There was one more piece of legislation that the UK needed to put in place, although this did not involve the EU. When the UK first joined the EC on 1 January 1973, it had transferred various powers to Brussels. At the time, the Westminster parliament could pass legislation to do this without consulting Scotland or Wales, as they did not have their own assemblies, while the one in Northern Ireland was suspended. These powers would now be coming back to the UK, but where would they go? The British

BREXIT

government did its own assessment and found 154 distinct policy areas where competencies overlapped between the UK parliament and the devolved assemblies.[19] This threatened the so-called Sewel convention, under which the UK parliament will 'not normally' pass laws on matters within the competence of the devolved assemblies without their legislative consent. Sorting this out was clearly going to test the constitutional arrangements between the three devolved nations and the British government.

The Johnson administration now started to use language hardly ever previously heard or needed. The 'internal market' referred to the domestic market constituted by the four nations, while the 'common framework' described the arrangements to be put in place for devolved powers that overlapped between the central and devolved parliaments. Inevitably, there were tensions. When the Internal Market Bill was published in September 2020, reserving powers for the UK government that were normally considered part of the devolved assemblies' responsibilities, it was described as a 'power grab' by both the Scottish and Welsh assemblies, while being roundly condemned by nationalists in Northern Ireland.

Shorn of its most offensive elements, the bill finally passed into law in December 2020—just before the end of the transition period.[20] Its potential impact on the relationship between the four nations would quickly be disguised to a large extent by the coronavirus pandemic, which struck the UK in March 2020. Yet the Internal Market Act, riding roughshod over the Sewel convention, highlighted the unequal relationship between the three devolved nations on one side and England on the other, acting through its proxy, the Conservative-controlled Westminster parliament. It created mistrust and hardened suspicions about English intentions. It was bound to present problems in the future, and that is exactly what happened.

239

INTERNAL EMPIRE

The Northern Ireland Protocol

When the Brexit referendum took place, the Good Friday Agreement (GFA) had been in operation for nearly twenty years. Formally the Belfast Agreement, but often named for its signing just before Easter in 1998, it addressed a whole range of sensitive issues in Northern Ireland, as well as creating new organisations to promote closer relations between the south and north of the island.[21] In the light of new governance arrangements for the north set out in the agreement, the UK administration had repealed the Government of Ireland Act 1920, while the Irish administration had committed to revising the country's constitution so that reunification of the island of Ireland could only be done on the basis of consent by all sides.[22]

The GFA was, and is, a remarkable document for the breadth of its ambitions and its contribution to peace in Northern Ireland.[23] Not surprisingly, references to the need to 'respect' the GFA and avoid a 'hard' economic border became frequent after 2016. Yet the agreement itself had made almost no mention of an economic border, and the reason for this was simple. Both Ireland and the UK had become part of the single market when it was launched on 1 January 1993, so trade in goods had already been frictionless for more than five years by the time the GFA was signed.

Frictionless trade would therefore continue as long as both states remained in the single market, so the possibility of a vote to leave in June 2016 might have been expected to generate heated debate on this issue across the UK. Yet a close examination of the leaflets circulated by the two campaigns outside Northern Ireland reveals that it was never mentioned at all.[24] And on the rare occasions when it was discussed in debate, it was widely assumed that the UK (if it voted to leave) would remain either in the single market or the customs union, so that frictionless

240

trade between the north and south of Ireland would continue regardless and the GFA would be preserved.

In Northern Ireland, of course, it was not possible to take such a cavalier approach to the possibility of Brexit, with remainers pointing out the risks to frictionless trade. However, the same sweeping assumptions about the economic border were made by any leave politician who was challenged on the question. Boris Johnson, for example, was interviewed by the BBC during a visit to Northern Ireland in February 2016.[25] He claimed that Brexit would leave arrangements on the border 'absolutely unchanged' and stated: 'there has been a free travel area between the United Kingdom and the Republic of Ireland ... getting on for 100 years ... there is no reason at all why that should cease to be the case.'

The vote to leave the EU created shockwaves, but it was not at first seen as a threat to the GFA. That only happened when Prime Minister May announced on 17 January 2017 that the UK would be leaving both the single market and the customs union. Conscious that this could pose a problem for the frictionless border, she claimed:

> We cannot forget that, as we leave, the United Kingdom will share a land border with the EU, and maintaining that Common Travel Area with the Republic of Ireland will be an important priority for the UK in the talks ahead ... So we will work to deliver a practical solution that allows the maintenance of the Common Travel Area with the Republic ... Nobody wants to return to the borders of the past, so we will make it a priority to deliver a practical solution as soon as we can.[26]

A 'Common Travel Area'—assuming it could be achieved—was not the same as frictionless trade in goods, as the EU was well aware from its relations with Switzerland. Alarm bells started to ring, including in the US, where those of Irish descent play such a large part in Congress, and usually in the executive as well. Indeed, sensitivity on this issue was heightened by the role of the Clinton administration, and Senator George Mitchell in particular, in achieving the GFA in the first place.[27] And without US support for post-Brexit arrangements on the island of Ireland, it was widely assumed that there could be no free trade agreement between the UK and the US—a key aspiration for any government leaving the European Customs Union.

May's speech, and its implications for UK–US relations, now set in motion a frantic search for solutions to avoid a hard border between north and south. At first the emphasis was placed on technology that might allow the free flow of goods, services and people across the island without physical checks. However, it soon became clear that such technology did not yet exist and might never be available. The negotiators for the European Commission therefore suggested a border down the Irish Sea, but this was dismissed out of hand by a Conservative administration at the time only able to govern thanks to the support of the unionist DUP, for whom any border between Northern Ireland and the rest of the UK was understandably anathema.

In response to a question about a maritime border, May told the House of Commons on 28 February 2018 that 'no Prime Minister could ever agree to it', as it would threaten the 'constitutional integrity' of the UK. Yet, as we have seen, her own preferred solution—the backstop—was rejected by her own party and ultimately led to her resignation. When her successor, Boris Johnson, then opted in October 2019 for the maritime border, the very option May had said no Prime Minister could ever accept, it initially looked like a case of déjà vu. However, Johnson would soon be free of his unionist partners following the Conservative landslide in the general election of December 2019. The DUP was understandably livid at the separation of Northern Ireland from the rest of the UK, but—for the time being—was now powerless to do anything about it.

242

BREXIT

The *Agreement on the withdrawal of the United Kingdom of Great Britain and Northern Ireland from the European Union and the European Atomic Energy Community*, as it is officially called, entered into law at the end of January 2020. Buried within it, but very much part of the agreement, is the 'Protocol on Ireland/Northern Ireland'. Article 4 assures the nervous British reader that 'Northern Ireland is part of the customs territory of the United Kingdom', but Article 5(1) contains the bitter pill: 'No customs duties shall be payable for a good brought into Northern Ireland from another part of the United Kingdom by direct transport ... *unless that good is at risk of subsequently being moved into the [European] Union, whether by itself or forming part of another good following processing.*' (Author's emphasis.)

Article 5 avoided the need for a hard border on the island of Ireland, since Northern Ireland would remain in the customs union, with disputes ultimately settled by the European Court of Justice. Yet, as there was no way of knowing beforehand which goods were at risk of being 'moved on', checks would be needed in principle on all goods going from Great Britain to Northern Ireland.[28] The 'constitutional integrity' of the UK therefore had indeed been undermined, and there was no way of hiding this from the DUP and its supporters. All that could be hoped for was that the European Commission would show as much flexibility as possible in applying the checks and use common sense.

This it did, but there was a limit to the number of 'grace' periods that could be applied without undermining the integrity of the EU's single market. As it became clear that the EU was serious about applying all articles in the protocol, it likewise became apparent that checkpoints had to become permanent, leading to inevitable delays and additional costs for the companies exporting goods from Great Britain to Northern Ireland. Some gave up, leading to shortages on the shelves of supermarkets,

INTERNAL EMPIRE

while others complained about the bureaucratic obstacles they now faced.

The DUP may have lost their influence in the Westminster parliament, but they were still powerful in the Northern Ireland Assembly, where they held the post of First Minister while commanding a network of sympathetic organisations throughout the nation. Meanwhile, other unionist groups were prepared to resort to violence to disrupt the checks arising from the maritime border. The long peace brought by the GFA was now at risk and, by the summer of 2021, the DUP was threatening to walk out of the power-sharing Northern Irish executive if the protocol was not subject to major changes. This was no idle threat, as the GFA made clear that the assembly could not function if either the main unionist party (the DUP) or the main nationalist party (Sinn Féin) withdrew from government.[29]

The DUP threat threw the UK government into something approaching panic. It could not abandon the protocol without tearing up the withdrawal agreement. This, however, would lead to a hard border on the island of Ireland that would not only undermine the GFA, but also alienate the US government, whose support was needed if Brexit was to have any chance of being a success. On the other hand, it could not stick to the protocol without risking a collapse of the Northern Ireland Assembly if the DUP walked out. Yet the British government was not powerless, as Article 16 of the protocol stated:

> If the application of this Protocol leads to serious economic, societal or environmental difficulties that are liable to persist, or to diversion of trade, the [European] Union or the United Kingdom may unilaterally take appropriate safeguard measures. Such safeguard measures shall be restricted with regard to their scope and duration to what is strictly necessary in order to remedy the situation.

BREXIT

The Johnson government was confident that at least some of the conditions for triggering Article 16 were in place when it published a command paper in July 2021.[30] These conditions included the information that Irish exports to Northern Ireland had risen by 40 per cent that year compared with the same period in 2020, and by more than 50 per cent when compared with the same period in 2018. This was clear evidence of trade diversion—Northern Ireland replacing imports from Great Britain with goods from the Republic of Ireland—and a sign that the protocol was leading to the incorporation of the north into the economy of the south.[31] This was warmly welcomed by nationalists, but was of huge concern for the DUP and all those worried about the 'constitutional integrity' of the UK.

Despite this, the British government did not immediately trigger Article 16, but instead embarked on negotiations with the European Commission in the hope of changing the way the protocol operated. The European negotiators showed considerable flexibility on the need for checks, but would not budge on the need for the European Court of Justice as the ultimate judicial arbiter, on the grounds that Northern Ireland was in the customs union and only the court could interpret European law in the case of trade disputes. As a result, in June 2022 the UK government introduced into parliament the Northern Ireland Protocol Bill, which—if passed—would have the effect of nullifying unilaterally the most controversial parts of the protocol itself.

The main sponsor of the bill was none other than Liz Truss, Foreign Secretary at the time and a staunch supporter of Brexit despite the fact that she had voted to stay in the EU. Thus, when Truss replaced Johnson as Prime Minister in September 2022, Johnson having resigned as a result of a series of scandals, the stage was set for a major confrontation between the UK and EU—despite the fact that both sides were strongly allied

245

both politically and militarily following the Russian invasion of Ukraine in February of that year.

Regardless of what might happen in the future, there was no doubt that the protocol had changed the delicate balance between nationalists and unionists in Northern Ireland and increased the chances of reunification with the republic. The DUP had alerted the British government to the risks, and the Johnson administration had tried to deliver a revised package that would satisfy hardline unionists. Yet the UK government had itself ratified the withdrawal agreement, including the protocol, as recently as January 2020—so its sincerity was in doubt not just among its European partners, but with the DUP as well.

The protocol carried a further threat for the DUP and its unionist supporters. Article 18 stated that 'democratic consent' would need to be given by the Northern Ireland institutions to that part of the protocol concerned with trade, four years after the end of the transition period (December 2024).[32] The UK government subsequently explained that 'consent' in this context meant a simple majority in the Northern Irish assembly, which is completely different from the cross-community support normally required for decision-making in Northern Ireland. The DUP and its allies could therefore be overruled if its opponents could muster the votes, even with no unionist buy-in.[33] After assembly elections in May 2022, when Sinn Féin performed better than the DUP, that prospect looked more likely than ever. Power was shifting in Northern Ireland, away from Britain and towards reunification—and the shift was a direct consequence of Brexit.

Implications

The logic of Brexit for its supporters was clear enough: leaving the single market would end free movement of labour, while withdrawing from the customs union would allow the UK to

BREXIT

reach free trade agreements with other regions or countries and reduce regulation. If the price for that was an immediate increase in non-tariff barriers facing UK exports to the EU, that was a price worth paying. In the long run, the UK economy—it was hoped—would perform better as a result of the new trade relationships and deregulation that Brexit would permit. And improved economic performance would then allow the UK to exercise enhanced geopolitical influence without the constraints of being in the EU. In other words, the costs of withdrawal would be felt early on, but the benefits would come later.

It would have taken many years to evaluate these costs and benefits to the UK under the best of circumstances, but the calculus was made infinitely more complicated in the short term by the pandemic that arrived just as the country formally withdrew from the EU. COVID-19, as it was called, claimed its first victim in the UK on 2 March 2020 and, within a few weeks, lockdowns were imposed. (As health is a devolved responsibility, this had to be done nation by nation.) The economies of all four nations went into a tailspin with a series of restrictions on economic activity, making it very difficult to separate out the impact of Brexit from that of the pandemic.

Difficult, but not impossible, since most of the pandemic effects were likely to resolve in the medium term, whereas the main consequences of Brexit were expected to be irreversible and to have an impact over the long term. Furthermore, neither the pandemic nor Brexit were going to change some of the structural transformations in the UK that also affected the economy. Foremost among these were demographic trends: the fertility rate (the average number of children born to a woman) had been falling for decades in all four nations, dropping in 2021 to an estimated 1.5 for mothers born in the UK and 2.0 for those born outside. This meant that fertility had for many years been under the rate required for a stable population, estimated at 2.1—in

INTERNAL EMPIRE

other words, without substantial net inward migration, the UK population would soon be in decline.

Net inward migration had in fact kept the population of all four nations of the UK growing for many years. However, Brexit and COVID-19 were about to change this. The pandemic was badly handled at first and deaths, not only those from COVID-19, rose sharply. As a result, and for the first time since 1976, UK deaths exceeded births in 2020.[34] Meanwhile, many EU migrants headed back to continental Europe at the start of the pandemic, so that net EU migration was actually negative for a few months. And the end of free movement from 1 January 2021 meant that net migration from Europe was never again going to reach the levels it had before the referendum.[35]

All this suggested that any future population growth in the UK would have to come from increased non-EU net migration. And it was certainly true that the new rules for migration, outlined in October 2020 and applied from 1 January 2021, were more flexible than they had been before Brexit.[36] Indeed, without increased net inward migration from outside the EU, the UK would soon start to suffer from the kind of ageing problems familiar in Japan, Italy and many other developed countries. In those nations, the number of dependents compared with those of working age had risen so rapidly that pension systems, and the implied fiscal burden, were becoming unsustainable. And in some cases, notably Japan, the population itself was falling at a discernible pace.

Increasing net migration from outside the EU may have made economic sense and met the concerns of the English Brexiteer elite. Yet reducing the number of migrants from all sources was still a top priority for the mass of voters in England, many years after the referendum. Squaring this circle was always going to be hard, so the UK government settled on a compromise, under which unskilled and/or low-paid migrants would be severely restricted, while the entry of skilled workers would be facilitated. If this meant shortages of workers with low skills, the government was prepared to accept it—even if that implied wage increases (leading to price inflation) and the replacement of some goods and services by imports.

This might have satisfied voters in England, but it was deeply problematic for the three devolved nations: Scotland, Wales and Northern Ireland. For as long as free movement of labour from the EU had been in operation, these nations had been able to attract migrant workers into the many temporary low-skilled jobs needed during the tourist and agricultural seasons, as well as permanent jobs in healthcare and other sectors. This would now change, since migration policy was the responsibility of the UK government, held to account by a parliament dominated by English MPs. In other words, the demographic future of Scotland, Wales and Northern Ireland was going to be determined by the priorities of English voters and their representatives in parliament, who were set on reducing low-skilled immigration.[37]

At first sight, the trade implications of Brexit looked more straightforward, but that turned out to be far from the case. The UK's difficulties in fulfilling the leave campaign's promises about a new 'global Britain', and the resulting impacts on the UK economy, have been troubling in themselves—but it is also worth going into these in depth, because of the threat this situation now poses to England's hold over the other three nations.

Having reduced the economic partnership with the EU to a free trade deal, embodied in the trade and cooperation agreement in force from 1 January 2021, what was left to be settled was the relationship with the rest of the world. While this was of less interest to the mass of leave voters, especially in England, it was of supreme importance to English Brexiteer elites. As a country now independent of the EU in almost all matters of economic policy, so the argument went, the UK could now redefine its relations with the rest of the world in order to improve its economic performance.

In 2019, the last year before the distortion to trade statistics brought by the pandemic and while the UK was still in the EU, British exports of goods and services were £691 billion, while imports were £721 billion—so, roughly in balance—with exports of goods worth slightly more than exports of services. There was—as had been the case for decades in trade with the EU—a substantial deficit in goods, largely matched by a surplus in services. Meanwhile, the share of exports of goods and services going to non-EU countries had been rising for some years and reached 57.4 per cent in 2019. The largest market for these non-EU exports was the US, followed by China; India, in third place, was some distance behind. Imports followed a similar pattern, although in 2020 China would become the most important non-EU supplier, ahead of the US.

These were the 'stylised facts' about UK foreign trade on which the country's economic welfare was so dependent. The trade and cooperation agreement with the EU, however, imposed non-tariff barriers on UK goods exports to the EU, while service exports (largely ignored in the agreement) now faced many new obstacles. Even financial services, so important to the British economy and London in particular, had been left out of the agreement. It was therefore of vital importance to gain improved access to non-EU markets, to compensate for the increased barriers to trade with the EU.

The EU negotiates trade agreements on behalf of all its members, so the UK had enjoyed a network of such deals with many countries and regions in the rest of the world (ROW) as a result of its EU membership. These included all Latin American, Caribbean and African countries, most Middle Eastern ones, and many in Asia-Pacific, including Canada and South Korea. When the UK left the EU, however, it immediately lost the trading

BREXIT

privileges associated with these agreements. Recovering them was therefore the top priority as soon as the transition period ended at the start of 2021.

The UK could not realistically go much beyond what had already been agreed—otherwise, the EU would immediately demand the same—and the main task of negotiations with all these countries and regions was 'grandfathering' the existing EU agreements so that they left the UK in roughly the same position as it had enjoyed before Brexit. The same would be true of new agreements still in negotiation between the EU (now 27 members) and other countries.

By the end of 2021, the UK had signed nearly seventy of these agreements, but the conclusion of many experts was that these would add nothing to UK trade and might even 'harm it very slightly', as they were not perfect replicas of what had gone before.[38] There have also been two new free trade agreements, with Australia and New Zealand, which had been agreed in principle and where there was no prior agreement with the EU— but the impact was expected to be minimal, in view of the low level of bilateral trade.[39]

That left three of the world's biggest economies—India, China and the US—with which the UK hoped to sign trade agreements before the EU could do so. Any one of these would indeed have been a big prize with potentially large net gains for the UK economy. Negotiations with India (by far the smallest economy of the three) did proceed rapidly, but India made it clear that any trade agreement would have to include some services, requiring the employment of Indian nationals on contracts in the UK and much increased numbers of visas for students. This made it difficult for the British government, in view of the opposition of so many leave voters to an increase in immigration, while the Indian government was reluctant to open up its economy to the kind of services that the UK wanted to sell.

251

INTERNAL EMPIRE

This did not mean a deal could not be reached, but it suggested that any final agreement would fall far short of what Brexiteers had originally hoped.

China—by virtue of its size, the extent of trade and investment flows, and the absence of frictions related to migration—was different, and the UK government at first went out of its way to support China's Belt & Road Initiative, to encourage its participation in UK infrastructure projects (including nuclear power) and to allow the Chinese telecommunications giant Huawei into British plans for a 5G network. However, this happened just as the US administration was shifting from containment of China to a policy of confrontation. As a close ally of the US, the UK found itself in an uncomfortable position, effectively forced to choose between the two superpowers. This dilemma was not removed when President Biden (2021–) replaced President Trump (2017–21), as US policy towards China became even more confrontational.

There was never any doubt that, faced with such a choice, the UK would not opt for China, even if this decision meant wiping out the chances of a trade agreement. All it could hope to do was minimise the friction, and even that was very difficult. Thus, the need for a trade agreement with the US became ever more paramount. As the UK's biggest non-EU market, for both goods and all types of service exports, the US was clearly going to be crucial for the plans of any British government after Brexit. However, this left the UK in a weak bargaining position, as it was not just the smaller economy, but also somewhat desperate.

The Trump administration looked to exploit this weakness in sectors of special interest to US companies, including pharmaceuticals and agrifoods, despite public opposition across the UK to what was proposed. However, his defeat in the presidential elections of November 2020 signalled a change in US policy, as his successor Biden soon made it clear both that a

252

BREXIT

US–UK free trade agreement was not a short-term priority, and that any progress towards it would be contingent on the British government honouring its commitments on the island of Ireland.

The trade agreements with China and the US—the ones that might have made a substantial difference, as well as compensating for the loss of trade with EU countries—were therefore blocked for the foreseeable future. As a result, the independent Office for Budget Responsibility (OBR), a highly respected institution reporting to the British government, was forced to conclude more than five years after the referendum:

> Since our first post–EU referendum ['Economic and Fiscal Outlook'] in November 2016, our forecasts have assumed that total UK imports and exports will eventually both be 15 per cent lower than had we stayed in the EU. This reduction in trade intensity drives the 4 per cent reduction in long-run potential productivity [that] we assume will eventually result from our departure from the EU.[40]

This meant that growth in non-EU trade was not expected to make up for the fall in trade with EU partners and, because the UK would now be less specialised in trade and therefore less efficient, that GDP would ultimately be lower than might have been expected if the UK had stayed in the single market. This was not what had been assumed by Brexiteers, but the authority of the OBR, using all the evidence available since the UK had left the EU, made it hard to dismiss.

A small 'scarring' (the OBR's word) to British GDP might have been considered a price worth paying for many Brexiteers. Yet the UK was no longer part of one of the world's largest economic blocs. Including the UK, the EU had represented over 15 per cent of world GDP.[41] The UK on its own would be a mere 2.2 per cent. This was still the tenth largest global economy, as confirmed by the numbers for 2021 (the first year after the end

INTERNAL EMPIRE

of the transition period).[42] However, Brexit's potential impact on productivity as indicated by the OBR, coupled with the faster growth of other large economies such as China and India, suggested that the UK's share of the world economy was set to shrink further. And, as this share shrank, the UK's ability to exercise geopolitical influence outside of the EU would diminish accordingly. English exceptionalism was supposed to inject into a post-Brexit UK some much-needed dynamism, which would transform the growth prospects not just of England, but of the other three nations as well. Yet, if the promise held out by English Brexiteer elites did not materialise, then the foundations of Britishness would crumble even further. For what would be the point of accepting English hegemony if it did not yield material benefits for the other three nations in the UK?

9

THE UNMAKING OF THE UK

The United Kingdom of Great Britain and Ireland (the original UK) had partially unravelled following the Anglo-Irish Treaty in 1921, but for the next fifty years what remained of the UK seemed so secure that it was hardly ever questioned, other than by the small number of nationalists in Scotland and Wales and the larger number in Northern Ireland. This comfortable assumption was increasingly challenged from the 1970s onwards, once the British Empire was definitely over and the Commonwealth of Nations lost its meaning. Devolution was now on the table in all the nations, including in principle England, and it remained to be seen what impact this would have on the union itself.

Northern Ireland had experienced devolution since the creation of a parliament in 1921, but for the first fifty years it was a distortion of what devolution was supposed to mean. With a rigged franchise for local elections, discrimination in the labour and housing markets, and the blind eye shown by the Westminster parliament to these practices, devolution only worked for the unionist (and Protestant) community. This corrupt arrangement ended soon after the outbreak of the Troubles in

INTERNAL EMPIRE

1968, but it was not until the Good Friday Agreement thirty years later that Northern Ireland could make real progress. That it did, and rapidly, so that by the time of the Brexit vote in 2016 Northern Ireland had become a very different place, with the old assumptions all needing to be challenged. Indeed, after the May 2022 elections for the Northern Ireland Assembly, a meaningful border poll on reunification started to look like a real possibility.

Scotland had toyed with devolution in the late nineteenth century, inspired by what was happening at that time in Ireland, but the campaign foundered. It started again in earnest with the spectacular byelection victory of the Scottish National Party (SNP) in 1967, which forced the UK government to address the question. It took some years before the Scots and the British government were jointly willing to take the leap, but by 1999 a Scottish assembly was operating at Holyrood in Edinburgh and was opened with the immortal words of Winnie Ewing: 'The Scottish Parliament, adjourned on the 25th day of March in the year 1707, is hereby reconvened.' Scottish devolution would now open up a path leading inexorably to a referendum in 2014, in which a majority voted against independence. The UK government hoped that this would settle the issue for a long time. Any hopes that the 2014 result might do this, however, were undermined two years later by the decision of voters in England to support Brexit. The arguments for and against independence would now need to be revisited, with opinion polls suggesting that a second referendum on the issue might now command majority support in Scotland.

Wales had preserved a strong sense of cultural nationalism after becoming an English colony, protected as it was by the survival of the Welsh language amongst a largely monoglot population. Welsh even survived annexation into England despite the explicit efforts of the Tudors and their successors to phase out its use. However, Welsh efforts to move beyond cultural nationalism in

THE UNMAKING OF THE UK

the nineteenth century, as the language declined in importance, proved ineffective. Even the birth of Plaid Cymru in 1925 made little impact, and when the Welsh people massively rejected a parliament in 1979, it looked as if the cause of Welsh nationalism was hopeless. And yet, from that low point, Welsh nationalism not only recovered but, in due course, became much more self-confident. A minimalist Welsh parliament was established in 1999 and accumulated greater powers over the next decades, as a result of popular support for devolution. Independence began to be discussed seriously for the first time since colonisation.

England's hegemonic position within the UK had gone unchallenged until the events that led to the creation of the Irish Free State in 1922. Yet the partition of Ireland at first strengthened English dominance of a shrunken UK, despite Northern Ireland now having its own parliament, as England was a bigger proportion of what remained. It was the developments of the late 1990s—devolution in Scotland and Wales, and the creation of a power-sharing executive in Northern Ireland under the Good Friday Agreement—that really began to test England's privileged position within the union. Brexit then exacerbated these stresses, while its aftermath revealed the lack of interest in union affairs among most English voters. England's hegemony has survived, but it is looking increasingly fragile. The unmaking of the UK is now underway.

Northern Ireland

For nationalists—i.e. those in favour of the reunification of Ireland—ties with the south were maintained in numerous ways after the 1922 partition. These included a common travel area, family ties and cultural links. The latter even included an agreement between the Irish and British Olympic committees that those selected from the north could decide for themselves

INTERNAL EMPIRE

whether to compete in the Olympics for Great Britain or the Irish Free State. However, the Catholic minority, assumed mainly to be nationalist, became second-class citizens.[1] Nor was this a small minority. Most of the UK had held a census in 1921, but it could not be carried out in either the north or the south of Ireland because of armed conflict. It was not until 1926 that the population of Northern Ireland was reported to be 1,256,561, with roughly one third declaring their religion to be Catholic.

What, then, was the nature of the society over which the new Northern Irish parliament would preside? It was not a state, despite its chief executive being called 'Prime Minister', as it had only limited powers. It was not strictly speaking a nation, as the Protestant majority considered themselves primarily British, while the Catholic minority thought of themselves as Irish. It was not a province, although it was often described as such, as it did not include the whole of the prepartition Province of Ulster; while to describe it as a region of the UK was wholly misleading. It was not a colony, although it did have a British governor, appointed in 1922. It could, however, at inception perhaps best be described as a British protectorate, with the Westminster parliament being responsible for 'excepted' and 'reserved' powers, while the devolved parliament at Stormont was responsible for everything else.[2]

Northern Ireland had held competitive elections in May 1921, before the creation of the Irish Free State, for a bicameral parliament to be based in Belfast.[3] The Ulster Unionist Party (UUP), led by James Craig, had won two thirds of the vote and gained more than 75 per cent of the seats in the Commons (forty, out of a total of fifty-two). Designed to ensure a built-in majority for Protestants loyal to a union with Great Britain ('a Protestant parliament for a Protestant people'), the lower house had clearly met the expectations of its creators. Yet Protestant hegemony

THE UNMAKING OF THE UK

went even further, as the Senate (elected by the Commons) was initially composed only of unionists.

This left the UUP in full control of most internal affairs, and the party used it to devastating effect.[4] The labour and housing markets were rigged to favour Protestants over Catholics, elections were 'arranged' to ensure Protestant majorities at every level despite the increase over time in the relative size of the Catholic population, and the paramilitary Ulster Volunteers were converted into the militarised Ulster Special Constabulary (usually known as 'B-Specials' or 'B-Men') to enforce these discriminatory practices.[5] Even the new Royal Ulster Constabulary, the police force committed by law to give one third of its posts to Catholics, became increasingly dominated by Protestants.

The Westminster parliament and the British government turned a blind eye to these abuses. The UUP members in the UK House of Commons invariably voted with the Conservative Party, so this indulgence was understandable (if wrong-headed) when the Tories were in power. Labour had no such excuse, and its failure to address the problem during the Attlee government (1945–51) could only be explained by the impeccable war record of many Ulster unionists. By the time Harold Wilson became Prime Minister in 1964, however, the behaviour of the UUP and its allies in Northern Ireland could no longer be overlooked— especially as Wilson's first government, with its tiny majority, was constantly at risk of being defeated on issues that had nothing to do with Northern Ireland. Wilson therefore met in January 1967 with Terence O'Neill, Prime Minister of Northern Ireland, and argued:

> [W]ithin a period of about three years one of two things must happen. Either (1) the Westminster Parliament would insist on interfering more and more with the internal affairs of Northern Ireland with the inevitable erosion of the 'division of powers' which formed the basis of the present arrangements or (2) an

259

INTERNAL EMPIRE

agreement would be reached whereby the British parliament and government would refrain from interfering at all in Northern Ireland affairs provided that Northern Ireland members of the Westminster Parliament observed the same discretion on voting on matters appertaining to Britain.[6]

Since Wilson knew that the UUP had no intention of voluntarily allowing any UK administration—least of all a Labour one—to meddle in Northern Ireland, this was a not very subtle attempt to remove UUP influence at Westminster over British affairs. Had it succeeded, discrimination in Northern Ireland would have continued just as before. However, civil unrest in Northern Ireland in 1968 against a wide range of injustices, followed by a violent Protestant reaction against the renewed IRA bombing campaign in favour of reunification, marked a dramatic change in the affairs of the six northern counties that no government at Westminster could ignore. And, although the Troubles began under a Labour government, it would be left at first to a Conservative administration, led by Edward Heath and supported by the UUP, to intervene.

Heath did not reverse the disbandment of the Ulster Special Constabulary (the decision had been taken just before the election that brought the Conservative Party to power). Two years later, his government suspended the Northern Ireland parliament, provoking the end of the formal alliance between the Conservative Party and the UUP. In May 1973, it then passed legislation to create a new assembly, with the elections held the following month designed to reassure the Catholic community that a peaceful path to reform was possible. In July of the same year, the Northern Ireland Constitution Act was introduced, abolishing not only the original Parliament of Northern Ireland, but also the post of governor—both in place since partition.

These were bold steps, in view of the history of the previous fifty years. Yet there was still no provision for a Northern Ireland

THE UNMAKING OF THE UK

executive that could bring together the different communities. This step was made possible by the Sunningdale Agreement, which Heath negotiated with his counterpart in Ireland and those leaders from Northern Ireland who shared its objectives. Sunningdale provided Anglo-Irish support for a cross-party executive. It began work on 1 January 1974, but had to be disbanded when Ulster unionists showed the limits of their loyalty to the British state through a general strike and widespread paramilitary activities. The 1974 Northern Ireland Act then dissolved the short-lived assembly—Northern Ireland would now be ruled directly by the British government, with only short interludes, until the Good Friday Agreement (GFA) in 1998.

The GFA marked the end of the Troubles, but it also signalled a new beginning which reflected the changes that had taken place, and would continue to take place, in Northern Ireland since the start of civil unrest and, indeed, since partition. While the population of Northern Ireland itself had not grown particularly fast (it was still only 1.9 million in 2021, according to the latest census), its religious affiliations, self-declared identities and ties with Great Britain had changed significantly. Meanwhile, in the neighbouring republic, population and living standards had grown rapidly, the Catholic Church had lost much of its influence, and Ireland was becoming much more socially liberal. The chasm between the Republic of Ireland and Northern Ireland, so marked at the time of partition, had not disappeared a century later—but it had narrowed considerably.

While the best-known change in Northern Ireland has been the increase in the proportion of the population describing itself as Catholic,[7] almost 20 per cent now describe themselves as having no religion or refuse to answer the question. Meanwhile, the proportion self-describing as either Presbyterian, Church of Ireland, Methodist or 'Other Christian' declines sharply with age, as was made clear by official comments after the 2011 census:

261

INTERNAL EMPIRE

> People who are or have been brought up as Catholics, in Other religions or who have no religion have younger age distributions than those who are or have been brought up as Protestants. In 2011, over half (52 per cent) of usual residents who were or had been brought up as Catholics were aged under 35, compared with two-fifths (40 per cent) of those who belonged to or had been brought up in Protestant denominations.[8]

Reflecting these changes in religious affiliation, there has been an important change in self-identification. At the time of partition, the only question of interest was whether a person identified as 'British' or 'Irish'. Since 1989, however, surveys have included the label 'Northern Irish', and an increasing number of respondents now choose this demonym to describe themselves. In the 2021 census, for example, the proportion calling themselves 'Northern Irish' rose to 31.5 per cent. This was still lower than those who identified as 'British' (42.8 per cent), but it was almost as high as those who claimed to be 'Irish' (33.3 per cent).[9] In other words, Northern Ireland was acquiring the characteristics of a nation, a proto-nation if you will, in which the primary identifier for a majority was no longer 'British'—since almost two thirds, including some unionists, preferred to describe themselves as 'Northern Irish' or 'Irish'.[10]

It has taken a long time for these societal changes to be fully reflected in politics. The outbreak of the Troubles did lead to the creation of the Social Democratic Labour Party (SDLP), giving nationalists a legal alternative to Sinn Féin, which was banned in Northern Ireland and the rest of the UK until 1974, after which it gradually replaced the SDLP as the main voice of nationalism. The focus at first, however, was on splits in the unionist movement, with the Reverend Ian Paisley's hardline Democratic Unionist Party (DUP) eventually emerging as the most successful branch of unionism during and after the Troubles.[11]

THE UNMAKING OF THE UK

The DUP and Sinn Féin dominated elections to the Northern Ireland Assembly after the GFA was signed and therefore had to work together (when the assembly was not suspended)[12] in a cross-party executive, according to the rules of the agreement. The DUP, as the party with the most seats until 2022, took the post of First Minister (no longer Prime Minister), while Sinn Féin occupied the position of Deputy First Minister. The success of the two parties in working together, to the surprise of many, contributed to the sense that a Northern Irish nation was indeed in the making. Yet, with the DUP committed to the UK and to maintaining strong links between Northern Ireland and Great Britain, there was little chance of the border poll envisioned by the GFA—and therefore no prospect of reunification on the island of Ireland.

All these calculations were changed by Brexit, when the Northern Irish electorate voted strongly in favour of remaining in the EU despite the campaign by both the DUP and the harder-line Traditional Unionist Voice to leave. However, unionist parties as a whole had been split on the issue of Brexit, with the UUP in support and the Alliance Party, a non-sectarian movement with its origins in unionism, strongly in favour of remain. The assembly elections in March 2017 were the first real test of public opinion after Brexit, and the results suggested a sea change was underway. They left the DUP and Sinn Féin on almost the same number of seats, while unionist parties secured only thirty-nine out of ninety seats.[13] The prospect of a future border poll leading to Irish reunification was no longer idle speculation.

These trends in Northern Ireland were confirmed by the results of the May 2022 elections for the assembly. By this time, the Northern Ireland protocol of the EU–UK Trade and Cooperation Agreement was in operation, leading to the diversion of Northern Irish trade from the rest of the UK to the Republic of Ireland, and a much closer economic relationship

INTERNAL EMPIRE

between the two parts of the island. Sinn Féin now emerged ahead of the DUP as the largest party, in terms of both votes and seats,[14] a result that entitled it to the post of First Minister—provided the DUP agreed to accept the position of Deputy First Minister. (It did not, in protest at the continued imposition of the Northern Ireland protocol, and at first boycotted the power-sharing executive.)[15] Furthermore, a strong showing by the Alliance Party, which came third, meant that unionist parties continued to have only a minority of seats in the assembly.

These results did not mean reunification was assured, as opinion polls suggested that a significant minority in the Catholic community wanted to remain part of the UK. However, Northern Ireland was definitely moving out of the British orbit and moving closer to the republic, with or without a border poll. Moreover, Sinn Féin's strong showing in opinion polls inside the republic raised the possibility of the party—the leading advocate of reunification—being in power in both parts of Ireland. If this happened, it would therefore be in a strong position to demand a border poll in the north and south.

Scotland

Scotland had formed a union with England and Wales voluntarily in 1707. Scottish nationalism, unlike what happened in conquered Wales, should not therefore have been under threat. However, the Jacobite rebellions and their aftermath had created suspicions about Scottish nationalism not only among the English, but also among some Scots themselves. Highland cultural practices were therefore suppressed, the lowland Scots language was discouraged, and Scottish nationalism lost its way—despite the eighteenth-century success of James Macpherson's *Poems of Ossian* in celebrating the national mythology of the poet's native land.[16]

THE UNMAKING OF THE UK

The memory of the Jacobite rebellions would eventually fade, to be followed by the enormous achievements of Enlightenment authors in Scotland such as David Hume and Adam Smith. Yet, despite their strong impact, these authors were not seeking to (re)create Scottish nationalism, since their focus was much more global. Nor were they interested in the notions that were propelling nationalism across continental Europe. In the words of John Gibson Lockhart, a Tory unionist writing in 1819:

> The generation of Hume, Smith, &c., left matters of feeling very much unexplored, and probably considered Poetry merely as an elegant and tasteful appendage to the other branches of literature, with which they themselves were more conversant. Their disquisitions on morals were meant to be the vehicles of ingenious theories—not of convictions of sentiment. They employed, therefore, even in them, only the national intellect, and not the national modes of feeling.[17]

That gap in Scottish nationalism would be filled in the nineteenth century, but—to his immense chagrin—not by Lockhart himself. Instead, its creator was Walter Scott. Widely considered the inventor of the historical novel, Scott had already played a large part in defining not only a Scottish nationalism, but an English one as well, through his immensely popular book *Waverley*. Indeed, it was George IV's reading of the novel that apparently persuaded the monarch to respond positively to Scott's proposal for a royal pageant in Edinburgh in 1822. That spectacular event created a bowdlerised version of Scottish nationalism with which Scots have had to live ever since.

Scott's nationalism placed the highlanders centre-stage and, with the exception of military officers, no gentleman could appear before the king except in traditional highland costume. This meant, as John Sutherland pointed out in his biography of Scott: '[A]n item of clothing for the wearing of which a

265

INTERNAL EMPIRE

Scotsman could face execution until 1782 became the uniform of a Lowland gentleman who before 1822 would no more have thought of wearing a kilt than a suit of medieval armour.'[18]

The Scottish nationalism invented by Sir Walter Scott may have been absurd, and there has been a long tradition in the centuries since deriding it as such.[19] However, it was strictly limited in scope and essentially established a cultural nationalism. There was no hint of any other kind in the pageant and this movement—unlike nationalism in nineteenth-century Ireland—was intended to be consistent with a unionism in which English rule would remain hegemonic. Scottish cultural nationalism therefore left a large vacuum that would only start to be filled towards the end of the century; even then, the trigger was not events in Scotland, but those in Ireland.

The campaign for Irish home rule, leading to an Irish parliament, had been gathering strength in Ireland in the 1870s. Scottish Conservatives, like their counterparts in England, were opposed and resisted the very idea of a similar outcome in Scotland. Yet an important faction of Scottish Liberals, a party dominant in Scotland from 1832 onwards,[20] not only saw home rule for Scotland as a desirable outcome in its own right, but also as a safeguard against the possibility that constitutional change in Ireland might disadvantage Scotland itself.

Their chance came in 1886, when the Liberal Prime Minister William Gladstone—having won an election the previous year—presented the first Irish home rule bill to the House of Commons. A Scottish Home Rule Association (SHRA) was established and demanded a Scottish parliament. Gladstone refused to concede the parallels with Ireland, and the defeat of his own bills for the island—first in 1886 and then in 1893—eventually led to the dissolution of the SHRA.[21]

However, the work of the SHRA, never anti-unionist, had not been entirely in vain. The special interests of Scotland had

THE UNMAKING OF THE UK

been highlighted, the cumbersome nature of resolving almost all Scottish matters in London had been emphasised, and the nation had at least regained in 1885 the post of Secretary of State for Scotland (abolished in 1745).[22] The accompanying Scottish Office would now be responsible for overseeing all legislation passed by the Westminster parliament that applied in Scotland, as well as administering that part of the UK budget dealing with Scottish affairs. To do so, it employed the Goschen formula, named after the Chancellor of the Exchequer at the time, which allocated 11 per cent of public spending to Scotland.[23]

Yet the post of Secretary of State for Scotland, upgraded in 1926 to a more senior role in the cabinet, was no substitute for a Scottish parliament. The creation of the Scottish National Party (SNP) in 1934, an amalgam of preexisting nationalist groups, pointed to dissatisfaction with the status quo in which Scotland was administered from the top down, like an English region.[24] A *Report of the Committee on Scottish Administration,* chaired by the Tory grandee Sir John Gilmour, addressed this in 1936, and the Scottish Office moved to Edinburgh in 1939—but after the war, it was still deemed necessary to establish a Royal Commission on Scottish Affairs, chaired by another Tory grandee, in view of continued dissatisfaction with the constitutional arrangements.[25]

Throughout the long period since the union, Scotland's share of the UK population had been in decline, with net emigration. Its unemployment rate after the Second World War was consistently higher than that of the rest of the UK, and its GDP per head was lower. This was the background when the Royal Commission on the Constitution was formed in 1969—but, by the time it reported in 1973, oil had been discovered off the coast of Scotland. A stream of books and articles would now point to a very different future for the Scottish economy,[26] and the SNP surged in the polls. A more dramatic response was needed from London, and that is exactly what happened.

INTERNAL EMPIRE

The royal commission recommended a devolved Scottish parliament, almost a century after the SHRA had called for the same thing. Labour, returned to power in 1974, agreed, and draft legislation was introduced in 1978 to set up a Scottish assembly, subject to a confirmatory referendum the following year. However, the legislation was amended before final approval, requiring at least 40 per cent of the registered electorate to vote in favour.[27] Although the referendum in 1979 produced a majority in favour of a Scottish assembly on a turnout of nearly 65 per cent, less than 40 per cent of the total electorate voted in favour, and the plans therefore had to be abandoned. The members of the commission, it seemed, had been premature when they had concluded that 'support for an assembly is growing ... and will continue to grow.'[28]

Premature perhaps, but not by much. A Campaign for a Scottish Assembly was soon formed by a combination of political parties, churches and civic groups. It was given strong impetus by the perceived negative impact on Scotland of the Conservative governments led by Margaret Thatcher (1979–90) and John Major (1990–7), both of whom were opposed to devolution. The Labour Party, with around 70 per cent of Scottish seats at Westminster throughout this period, could not fail to sense the change of mood, and committed in its 1997 manifesto to a new referendum.

Labour won the election. The vote was therefore held in September 1997 and consisted of two questions. The first was on the establishment of a Scottish parliament, and the second on whether such an institution should have tax-raising powers. The response to both questions was overwhelming. Nearly 75 per cent answered 'yes' to the first question and nearly 65 per cent to the second.[29] Every single voting area in Scotland was in favour of a Scottish assembly, and all but two supported giving it tax-raising powers.[30] Something dramatic had clearly happened

THE UNMAKING OF THE UK

in Scotland since 1979, and indeed since 1707, with a parliament now seen by the vast majority of Scots as the correct response to national issues.

The Labour government under Prime Minister Tony Blair, with many Scots in the cabinet, moved swiftly to introduce legislation, which paved the way for elections to a Scottish assembly with 129 seats. The elections were held in 1999 under a mix of constituency and regional seats, the former (seventy-three constituencies) using 'first past the post' as at Westminster and the latter based on eight regions each, with seven seats (fifty-six in total) and using a form of proportional representation. So far so good, it might be argued—but there was a sting in the tail, as the regional list used a modified voting system never previously applied.[31] This made it very difficult for the party winning the largest number of constituency seats to perform well in the regional list, and the results of the first election confirmed this. Labour, with fifty-six out of seventy-three constituency seats, won only three out of fifty-six seats in the regional list, despite gaining a third of the vote.

The electoral system was designed to ensure that no one party could dominate the new assembly, thereby ensuring that Scottish governance would require cross-party agreement to pass legislation. In doing so, it avoided an assembly dominated by the Labour Party, as happened with Scottish seats at Westminster, but it also had the (not unintended) effect of reducing the chances that the SNP would be able to push for a referendum on independence. Yet the setup failed to take into account the impact of rising Scottish nationalism and support for independence: by 2011, the SNP had secured not only a plurality of votes, but also an absolute majority of seats in the Scottish Parliament.

Given the voting arrangements, this was an extraordinary achievement. The SNP had won fifty-three out of seventy-three

269

constituency seats and, despite the skewed electoral system, an unexpected sixteen on the regional list. This meant that, for the first time, the Scottish nationalists could govern on their own (they had formed a minority government in 2007); and this implied that they could pursue their ambitions for Scottish independence. An outright majority for any party, least of all the SNP, was not supposed to happen and—not for the first or last time—tampering with an electoral system had proven to have unintended consequences.

The 1998 Scotland Act establishing the Scottish Parliament had not directly addressed the question of a referendum on independence. However, Section 30 did allow for the temporary transfer of legal authority to Scotland by the Westminster parliament in the case of 'reserved' matters. This was duly granted by the Conservative–Liberal Democrat coalition government that came to power in 2010, when David Cameron replaced Gordon Brown as Prime Minister. A bill was then passed in the Scottish Parliament in 2013 authorising a referendum to take place in September 2014. The campaign started immediately, and the SNP government published its blueprint for independence—a white paper entitled *Scotland's Future*.

The white paper was an impressive document, addressing in some detail the shape and character of an independent Scotland. In doing so, however, it had to give specific answers to perennial questions—such as the currency to be adopted, the fiscal 'hole' that might be left after transfers from the UK government ended, and how Scotland would retain membership of the EU.[32] This gave opponents of independence plenty of ammunition to question the viability of the independence proposition, and they used it effectively, arguing, for example, that what remained of the UK would never give its blessing to Scotland keeping the pound sterling. In addition, the leaders of the three main UK parties signed 'the Vow' a few days before the referendum,

THE UNMAKING OF THE UK

promising increased devolved powers if Scotland voted to remain part of the UK.

The strong sense of Scottishness among the voters was never in doubt, with not many giving 'British' as their primary identifier.[33] Furthermore, this identity with Scotland was particularly strong among the young, for whom the voting age was lowered to sixteen.[34] In the end, however, the perceived economic risks of independence proved a bridge too far and Scotland—on a massive turnout of 85 per cent—voted 55:45 to stay in the UK. Only four out of thirty-two voting regions—Dundee, Glasgow, North Lanarkshire and West Dunbartonshire—had majorities in favour of independence, while ten had voted to stay in the UK by more than 60 per cent. It was a transactional vote to stay, rather than one based on ties of 'Britishness'.

Nor, of course, was it the end of the story. Just as had happened when the SNP first formed a government in Scotland, more powers would again be devolved. The Calman Commission had been set up in December 2007 and had reported in 2009. Although the SNP originally opposed the establishment of the commission, which was set up following a vote on an opposition amendment, the SNP had broadly supported its recommendations. The UK government had then amended the 1998 Scotland Act in 2012 to give more powers (especially fiscal) to the Scottish government. Now, after the referendum, the Smith Commission was established. It reported in November 2014 and the Scotland Act was amended again in 2016, although the devolution of additional powers fell short of those promised in 'the Vow'.

Scotland was now drifting away from the rest of the UK, with or without independence. With the empire gone and the Commonwealth fading into irrelevance, one of the main factors holding Scotland inside the union was Europe. Yet Brexit ended that as well. In 2014 Scotland had been promised that a vote to

INTERNAL EMPIRE

remain in the UK was the way to ensure that it stayed in the EU, but the opposite had happened. This gave a huge boost to the independence cause, support for which often exceeded 50 per cent in opinion polls.[35] However, it also raised uncomfortable questions about the impact on the Scottish economy, if an independent Scotland rejoined the EU and the rest of the UK remained outside, since England, not the EU, is the main market by far for Scotland's exports.[36] In such an environment, trade would be far from frictionless—as the UK's experience with the EU from January 2021 onwards has demonstrated.

Independence was seen by many as a binary choice, but it was not. Scotland was now moving away from England's orbit, regardless of whether a second referendum on independence took place or how the electorate might vote in it. Despite a series of well-documented problems in its governance of Scotland, the SNP still managed in 2021 to win sixty-two out of seventy-three constituency seats. With two more from the regional list and a coalition with the Scottish Green Party, this gave the SNP the majority it needed to demand a second referendum on independence. This it did in 2021, and the Scottish government spelt out in a series of position papers the following year what independence would mean for Scotland. Even if a vote on independence might not be achieved for some years, as a result of resistance from the UK government,[37] the alternative was bound to be more devolution, and with it the further unravelling of the ties that had held Scotland inside Great Britain since 1707.

Of course, if a vote were held, it was not a guarantee that a majority of voters in Scotland would support independence. Yet two events in September 2022 gave the independence cause a boost. First, surveys done before and after the appointment of a new Prime Minister (Liz Truss—another quintessentially English politician—who replaced Boris Johnson) suggested that support for independence might rise as a result of the change. Secondly,

THE UNMAKING OF THE UK

the death of Queen Elizabeth raised questions about whether her successor (King Charles III) would command the same respect from Scottish voters as had been shown to his mother. If not, as seemed likely, it would mean that one of the 'glues' holding the union together in a post-Imperial world was becoming unstuck.

Wales

Wales had been finally conquered by England in 1284 and, despite a major rebellion led by Owain Glyndŵr at the start of the fifteenth century, it would never regain independence. If we exclude the 'inherited' province of Gascony, it was England's first colony. However, its language—spoken by almost all the population—allowed a cultural nationalism to flourish, despite English colonialism, which found its expression in scholarship, poetry and music. It was not until Wales was annexed in 1535 by England—ruled by Henry VIII, a Tudor king of impeccable Welsh descent—that this tradition began to be threatened.

Henry VIII and his Protestant successors, nervous of a Welsh nation that still had strong links to Catholic Europe even after the creation of an Anglican Church, wanted to erase the differences between England and Wales. There would be one legal jurisdiction for both countries and no new name for the expanded state. Over the next 250 years, the Welsh nobility declined in importance, the bardic profession disappeared and the *eisteddfodau*—the great celebrations of Welsh culture held since the twelfth century—withered away. Starting in the nineteenth century, even the language came under threat, through both the anglicisation of education and the migration into Wales of non–Welsh speakers, pulled in by the growth of mining everywhere, new industries in the Welsh south and the expansion of market towns in the north. Wales, once the cradle of a cultural nationalism that was the envy of Europe, was starting to look more and more like

INTERNAL EMPIRE

a region of England—and a very backward one at that. Welsh nationalists took note and were appalled.

Their efforts to revive Welsh nationalism were not at first very promising.[38] The *eisteddfod* did start to be celebrated again every year from 1880 onwards (except 1914 and 1940), and there was a growth in Welsh choral societies and a Welsh-language press. However, the campaign for Welsh home rule, modelled on those in Ireland and Scotland, failed to make much headway.[39] More successful was the campaign to secure recognition of the special circumstances of education in Wales, leading to a Welsh department of the Board of Education in 1907 that went some of the way to correct the bias revealed in *The Treachery of the Blue Books,* the notorious 1847 report by English commissioners.[40] There was also the long-running struggle, finally achieving success in 1920, to disestablish the Anglican Church, in a nation where the vast majority were Nonconformists.

It was the language issue with which Welsh nationalism finally chose to nail its colours to the mast. Plaid Cymru had been formed in 1925, soon after the 1921 census had revealed that Welsh-speakers among the population had fallen to 38.7 per cent. Although much lower than the figure given in previous censuses, this might still seem high for the national language when compared with Ireland and Scotland. Yet the census also revealed that only 6.6 per cent of the population were *solely* Welsh-speaking. For Saunders Lewis—one of the founders of Plaid Cymru and for decades the dominant force in Welsh nationalism, for better or worse[41]—this was a major concern, as he made clear in an article in 1933:

> [E]ven in the Nationalist Party [Plaid Cymru] I fear that some still do not understand that 'bilingual Wales' is something to fear and avoid, that the lessening in number of monoglot Welsh-speakers is a disaster, and that it is only a monoglot Welsh-speaking Wales that is consistent with the

THE UNMAKING OF THE UK

> aims and philosophies of Welsh nationalism ... To believe otherwise is self-deceit and a refusal to face the truth. Therefore if we wish to fight at all for the Welsh language, we must fight seriously for the continuance of the monoglot Welsh-speakers. There is only one method of ensuring a monoglot *Welsh people,* and that is to create a monoglot *Wales.* Nothing else is practicable.[42] (Emphasis original.)

Needless to say, these ideas did not go down well with the many English-speakers in the industrial heartlands of Wales, who were switching their political allegiance from the Liberal Party to Labour in droves after the First World War. By the time of the 1922 general election, the Labour Party's share of the vote in Wales was above 40 per cent, where it would stay (with rare exceptions) for the next century.[43] By contrast, Plaid Cymru's share was less than 5 per cent in every election before 1970 but one (in 1959).

Plaid Cymru's views in general, and on the Welsh language in particular, seemed to fall on stony ground. However, Labour—like the Liberal Party before it—contained a large number of influential Welsh politicians who were deeply conscious of the disregard, some would say contempt, shown towards Wales by so many UK governments. These men and women were not nationalists, committed as they were to a class-based analysis of British politics, but they recognised injustice, and believed in social equality, between Wales and England. Their chance came with Labour's victory in the 1964 election.

One of the first acts of the Wilson government, in October that year, was to establish the post of Secretary of State for Wales. The following year, a Welsh Office was created with responsibility for housing, local government and roads; later other duties—education and training, health, trade and industry, environment, planning, transport and agriculture—were added. In 1967, the Welsh Language Act gave legal status to the use of

275

INTERNAL EMPIRE

Welsh in the law courts for the first time since the Laws in Wales Acts of 1535 and 1542.

These changes were welcomed by Welsh nationalists, but they represented reform from the top down. The first real test of popular support would come after the publication in 1973 of the Royal Commission on the Constitution, recommending that a Welsh assembly should be established, on the relatively uncontroversial grounds that:

> Welsh nationalism has served to focus attention on the strong desire which the people of Wales have to preserve and foster their own identity and special interests, and this desire seems to evoke considerable sympathy even among Welshmen in the industrial and border areas, whose general attitudes otherwise seem to be more akin to those of English people. It seems that, for a good many people in Wales, the distinctive Welsh culture and language has come to assume the degree of importance which is attached to the idea of Scottish sovereignty in the minds of people in Scotland.[44]

At first the omens for Welsh nationalism were good. Plaid Cymru had won more than 10 per cent of the Welsh vote in both general elections in 1974 and ended with three seats in the Westminster parliament where Labour had formed a government. Prime Minister Wilson accepted the commission's recommendations for a Welsh assembly, which was then contained within the Wales Act 1978. A referendum was duly held on 1 March 1979, but—despite being St. David's Day—the results were disastrous for the cause of Welsh nationalism. The question 'Do you want the Provisions of the Wales Act 1978 to be put into effect?' was rejected by nearly 80 per cent of the electorate. Not a single council area came close to supporting it.

From this low point, Welsh nationalism quickly recovered, and it was driven by the election of a Conservative government

276

THE UNMAKING OF THE UK

led by Margaret Thatcher in May 1979. The Conservatives had not been popular in Wales since the widening of the franchise in 1868, when Liberals swept to power in most seats. They managed to secure 32.2 per cent of the Welsh vote in 1979, almost their best performance since the Liberal surge, but during the next eighteen years of Conservative rule the party's share steadily fell. In 1992 it won only six Welsh seats out of thirty-eight at the Westminster parliament, and only forty-two out of 1,273 council seats. Thatcher was eventually obliged to appoint as Secretary of State for Wales English MPs from English constituencies, with no knowledge of, or empathy with, the nation at all. In 1997, when it was defeated nationally by Labour, the Conservative Party secured less than 20 per cent of the vote in Wales and failed to win a single seat.

The reasons for the Conservatives' growing unpopularity in Wales were not hard to fathom. The assault on the miners, culminating in the 1984 miners' strike, left a bitter memory, with communities destroyed and no effort made to rebuild them. The miners may have lost, but there was broad sympathy for their cause in Wales and disgust at the lack of official response to their plight. And when John Redwood was appointed as Secretary of State for Wales in 1993, a man strongly associated with the Thatcherite policies that had led to the miners' strike in the first place, disgust turned to anger, as Redwood used his position to undermine what little autonomy Wales had achieved since the establishment of the Welsh Office in 1964.

The answer for a growing number of Welsh voters was their own assembly, one that would protect Wales from this kind of behaviour in the future—the very assembly they had overwhelmingly rejected in 1979. A second chance came in 1997, when the new Labour government of Tony Blair met its manifesto promise by offering an either/or referendum offering two alternative statements. As the 1993 Welsh Language Act

277

INTERNAL EMPIRE

had put the Welsh language on an equal footing with English in Wales, the statements were put in two languages:

I agree that there should be a Welsh Assembly
Yr wyf yn cytuno y dylid cael Cynulliad i Gymru
I do not agree that there should be a Welsh Assembly
Nid wyf yn cytuno y dylid cael Cynulliad i Gymru

Only half the electorate voted, but this time there was a small majority for an assembly (50.3 per cent in favour), with the twenty-two voting areas (the local councils) split down the middle. Compared with the result in Scotland, it was hardly an overwhelming vote. However, by contrast with what had happened in 1979, it was a big change.

The Blair government soon introduced the Government of Wales Act 1998, elections were held the following year, and the National Assembly for Wales met for the first time on 12 May 1999—the first time in nearly 600 years that a Welsh parliament had been convened. Held under the same system as in Scotland, the elections delivered twenty-eight out of sixty seats to Labour, twenty-seven of them constituency seats. Plaid Cymru performed spectacularly well, winning nearly 30 per cent of the popular vote and gaining seventeen seats. The Conservative Party came third with nine seats and 15 per cent of the vote, but Labour preferred to ally at first with the Liberal Democrats to form a Welsh government.[45]

Reflecting the narrow vote in support, at the beginning the Welsh assembly had much more limited powers than its equivalent in Scotland. There was no separation of the executive from the legislature and very restricted rights to pass secondary legislation. This was soon changed, and the assembly—renamed as a 'Parliament' in 2020 with the voting age reduced to 16—acquired new powers under three Westminster acts in 2006, 2014 and 2017, as well as operating with a separate executive and

THE UNMAKING OF THE UK

legislature from 2007. Devolution was clearly popular, as was confirmed by the results of a referendum in 2011 asking voters if they wanted the assembly 'to be able to make laws on all matters in the 20 subject areas it has powers for'.[46]

One of those devolved areas was health, and the pandemic that started in early 2020 brought home to many, inside and outside Wales, the considerable powers of the Welsh Parliament (known as the Senedd in Wales) and the Welsh government. UK ministers were now obliged to refer to differences in policies on health, coordinating—as far as possible—pandemic policies for the four nations through consultation. This was straightforward with Northern Ireland, Scotland and Wales, as they all had devolved administrations with responsibility for health—but it meant of course that, in the case of England, UK ministers at times had to consult themselves, as the English nation has no government.

The success of devolution in Wales was bound to have consequences both for the self-identification of the Welsh people and for their views on independence, and so it proved. Brexit, of course, complicated responses, but by the time of the 2021 Welsh Parliament elections a multitude of surveys were pointing in the same direction. Two thirds of people in Wales identified as Welsh, one third were in favour of independence and a majority of Welsh voters wanted either independence or greater powers for their parliament. Furthermore, there was a significant age profile to responses, with younger voters identifying more strongly as Welsh and being more supportive of independence.

Wales, it would seem, is moving away from the long English embrace without necessarily wishing to leave the UK. Clearly the constitutional implications are enormous, and Welsh political parties have had to address them. Plaid Cymru, for example, set up an Independence Commission that reported in September 2020 and set out a pathway towards greater autonomy.[47] Not to

279

be outdone, in 2021 the Welsh government—led by Labour—created an Independent Commission on the Constitutional Future of Wales and joined as a core member the Beyond Oil and Gas Alliance, an international body of like-minded governments to which the UK does not belong.[48]

Whatever the outcome of this constitutional debate, it is clear that Wales will become more autonomous, with greater responsibility for its own affairs. And, if Scotland were to become independent, and Ireland to reunite, it is hard to believe this would not have major repercussions on the campaign for independence in Wales itself. Yet the most important consideration is likely to be the reaction of England, the former colonial power, to Wales' search for greater autonomy—and her degree of willingness to accommodate greater constitutional equality between the four nations. It is to this that we now turn.

England

Just before the 1284 conquest of Wales, there was no English empire—if we exclude the scattered remnants of the former Norman Empire still held abroad by English kings, including Gascony and a part of Ireland. Instead, there was a nation-state called England that lived side by side with Scotland and Wales, and which was adapting to an Ireland where most of the 'old' English had largely been absorbed into the numerous Irish kingdoms. It was the conquest of Wales, a military campaign led by an English king with an English army, that finally launched England on an imperial path.

The full annexation of Wales in 1535 did not end English imperialism, but it did change it. Instead of becoming an equal partner in a new state with a new parliament, Wales was now considered a 'dominion' of England whose inhabitants were expected to participate in new imperial adventures. These

THE UNMAKING OF THE UK

included the conquest and colonisation of the rest of Ireland, which began under the Tudors, as well as the numerous attempts to subordinate Scotland to England's will.

Wales' status after annexation was taken for granted by the English, but the union with Scotland in 1707, leading to the creation of Great Britain, required that the relationship between England and Wales be made more explicit. A statute, the Wales and Berwick Act, was therefore passed by the Westminster parliament in 1746, with Article III stating: 'In all cases where the kingdom of *England*, or that part of *Great Britain* called *England*, hath been or shall be mentioned in any act of parliament, the same has been and shall from henceforth be deemed and taken to comprehend and include the dominion of *Wales*' (original emphasis). This act, confirming the subordinate status of Wales as part of England, remained on the statute book for centuries. It was finally amended in 1967, when Article III was revoked as part of the Welsh Language Act passed in that same year.[49]

The union of England (and Wales) with Scotland in 1707 was significantly different. Although Scotland sent a small number of MPs to join a parliament that was still essentially an English one, the enlarged country did change its name to Great Britain, and its subjects became British. Yet there was no doubt in the minds of the English which part of Great Britain was more important and which British people had made the greater contribution to this joint venture. When building his Temple of British Worthies at Stowe in the 1730s, for example, William Kent included sixteen busts—fifteen of which represented English heroes. Yet even in the case of the sixteenth (William of Orange), Kent made clear his English prejudices, since the bust is inscribed as 'William III'—this was the king's title in England, but in Scotland he had been William II.[50]

English hegemony also survived the union with Ireland in 1801, when the Kingdom of Ireland (an English colony) was

281

INTERNAL EMPIRE

added to Great Britain to form the United Kingdom. England now had just over 50 per cent of the UK population, but nearly 75 per cent of the seats in the House of Commons. So dominant was England and its de facto parliament at Westminster that the Irish drumbeat in support of home rule became louder and louder (with echoes, as we have seen, in Scotland and Wales). And if Ireland was to have its own parliament, then—as was assumed in the first home rule bill—its MPs would have to be excluded from Westminster, giving England an even bigger share of the seats in the UK parliament.

The Irish Free State created in 1922 could have been a mortal blow against English hegemony within a UK now reduced in size, uniting Great Britain only with Northern Ireland. However, the free state (at first a dominion within the British Empire) lost all its representatives at Westminster, the number of MPs from Northern Ireland was reduced to twelve and England found itself with nearly 80 per cent of all House of Commons seats.

England's hegemony therefore survived even the loss of Ireland's south. To most English, and nearly all foreigners, 'England' still meant 'Great Britain' or even 'the UK'. Indeed, during the negotiations for the Anglo-Irish Treaty in 1921, the Irish side had passed each other secret notes referring to the team on the other side of the table as the 'English government'. Meanwhile, the English share of the UK population kept on rising, since net migration tended to be concentrated in England rather than the other three nations. By the time of the 2021 census, published in mid-2022, the population of England was nearly 90 per cent of the UK total—even higher than England's share of seats at Westminster (82 per cent).

England's hegemony within the UK was so powerful that the English population could afford to take a relaxed view of devolution in Northern Ireland, Scotland and Wales. A unionist

282

THE UNMAKING OF THE UK

MP from Scotland, Tam Dalyell, raised in 1977 what later became known as the 'West Lothian question'—why, after devolution, should Westminster MPs from the other three nations have the right to vote on English matters, when Westminster MPs for England could no longer vote on Scottish, Welsh and Northern Irish matters? At first, however, the question received no more attention than when the issue had first been raised in 1886 in relation to Gladstone's home rule bill or, indeed, by Harold Wilson in 1967 in the context of Ulster votes at Westminster. An assembly therefore went ahead in both Scotland and Wales in 1999 without much English dissent, and was revived in Northern Ireland in 1998 after the Good Friday Agreement, cosigned by the government in London.

Indeed, English attention at first was much more focused on the need for decentralisation of England itself—something that had been identified as a serious problem in a memorandum of dissent published in 1973 by two members of the Royal Commission on the Constitution.[51] They had recommended the establishment of five assemblies in England, but their ideas had been largely forgotten until devolution was approved in 1997. The Blair government then addressed the issue of English decentralisation, and a referendum was held in London in 1998 asking voters: 'Are you in favour of the government's proposals for a Greater London Authority, made up of an elected mayor and a separately elected assembly?'

Those who voted (turnout was only 34.6 per cent) enthusiastically supported the idea, and the government then pressed ahead with plans to decentralise the rest of England, hoping to establish elected assemblies in three English regions. However, the proposal for an elected assembly in North East England, held in 2004, was so overwhelmingly rejected by voters that the other two public consultations never went ahead. The Labour government, as well as its successors, then pressed ahead

INTERNAL EMPIRE

with plans for directly elected mayors, although the majority of referendums on creating elected mayors resulted in 'no' votes.[52]

Support for decentralisation in England was therefore decidedly mixed—even if there were signs in those cities or large administrative regions where it had gone ahead, such as Greater Manchester, that it would prove to be popular in the long term.[53] Yet it was never going to be an answer to the 'English question', i.e. the dominance of England within a four-nation model. Nor could it be a response to the West Lothian question itself, which had remained unanswered for so many decades.

It was the SNP victories in elections for the Scottish Parliament from 2007 onwards, as well as the Scottish independence referendum in 2014, that forced the West Lothian question up the political agenda. With almost all of its MPs coming from English constituencies (100 per cent between 1997 and 2001), it was to be expected that the Conservative Party would be the most troubled by the issue. On the day following the Scottish referendum, therefore, Prime Minister Cameron stood outside 10 Downing Street and told assembled journalists:

> I have long believed that a crucial part missing from this national discussion is England. We have heard the voice of Scotland—and now the millions of voices of England must also be heard. The question of English votes for English laws [EVEL]—the so-called West Lothian Question—requires a decisive answer.[54]

Following the 2015 general election, once the Conservative Party was no longer dependent on its Liberal Democrat coalition partner, EVEL was put into practice, with standing orders designed to ensure that no 'England-only' bill could be passed without the support of a majority of English MPs. Yet it proved both unpopular and unnecessary. The procedures were complex, and after 2015 the Conservative government had more than enough English MPs to secure an English majority in any case.

THE UNMAKING OF THE UK

EVEL was therefore suspended in 2020 and abolished in 2021. The West Lothian question once again went unanswered.

The aftermath of Brexit finally focused attention on English hegemony, the issue that had overshadowed the relationship between the four nations for centuries, and which was far more important than the West Lothian question. EVEL, after all, had been no more than a tactic to address the minor discrimination against English MPs brought about by devolution. Brexit, on the other hand, was a strategic act of English imperialism that had demonstrated the weakness of the other three nations and which had far-reaching consequences for them.

Parts of the elites, invariably English, saw Brexit as an opportunity to exercise 'muscular unionism' in support of England's continued hegemony within the UK. An internal market bill was therefore forced through parliament in 2020, in the face of strong opposition from the devolved nations, giving England de facto powers that it had never enjoyed while in the EU. One constitutional expert, explaining how the new rules worked, stated:

> For example, England might authorise a new active substance for pesticides, or a new GMO [genetically modified organism], and would then be able to freely export those products to devolved nations, even if they had controls domestically. In so doing, England could competitively undercut producers and in effect undermine permitted divergence.[55]

The United Kingdom Internal Market Act was then followed by a Shared Prosperity Fund.[56] Designed to replace the European Structural and Investment Funds that were no longer spent in the UK after withdrawal from the EU, it gave the British government (i.e. the English administration) the power to spend money on projects that had previously been the preserve of the devolved nations and to brand them with the Union Jack. And,

INTERNAL EMPIRE

just to make sure nobody missed the point, UK civil servants were asked to refrain as far as possible from referring to 'the four nations' and refer instead to one country, the UK.

The devolved assemblies and their governments soon saw through this 'power grab' and were just as quick to denounce it. Alison Thewliss addressed their joint concerns in a debate in the House of Commons on the internal markets bill, when she stated:

> It is perfectly clear that this [is] an attack and an undermining of devolution. That is not just my opinion, but an opinion shared by legal experts around the world ... Clauses [in the bill] grant sweeping authority to Ministers to spend money in areas that are devolved to the Scottish Parliament, the Welsh Assembly and the Northern Ireland Assembly, allowing discretionary funding of any activities that UK Ministers judge directly or indirectly to benefit the United Kingdom.[57]

Table 9.1: English Responses on the Survival of the Union, 2020

	% agreeing 'Northern Ireland should stay part of the UK'	% agreeing 'Scotland should stay part of the UK'	% agreeing 'Wales should stay part of the UK'
London	23	40	43
Rest of South	28	49	53
Midlands (incl. Wales)	26	45	54
North	25	44	49
England	26	46	51

Source: Kenny et al. (2021)

286

THE UNMAKING OF THE UK

With the passage of the United Kingdom Internal Market Act and the introduction of the Shared Prosperity Fund, the UK government had won the battle, but it was far from winning the war. Not only was public opinion in the devolved nations inflamed, but also the English public itself showed very little interest in keeping the union together. Poll after poll showed a lack of concern over the affairs of the other three nations by English voters and this *insouciance* was spread across every region of England (see Table 9.1). So indifferent, it seems, were English voters—and so focused on Brexit—that almost half were prepared to risk the unravelling of the Northern Ireland peace process, while nearly two thirds were prepared to countenance independence for England in the event that Brexit should be stopped.[58]

A union where voters in its hegemonic country are seemingly indifferent to its fate is never going to last long—at least in its present form. The UK, as a union of four nations dominated by England, is unravelling. The glue that has held it together for so long—empire, Commonwealth and Europe—has come unstuck, while the centrifugal forces unleashed by devolution are gathering strength after Brexit. This 'English question' now needs to be addressed as a matter of urgency, since the status quo has become unsustainable.

10

ENGLISH QUESTIONS

In the twenty-first century, an old English question has resurfaced—namely, how to adjust the constitutional relationship between the four nations, now that English MPs cannot vote on devolved matters in Northern Ireland, Scotland and Wales. Yet this is just one, and not even the most recent, in a series of 'English questions' that have been posed since the Venerable Bede wrote his ecclesiastical history of the English people some 1,300 years ago. Each question, and the answers provided, has given insight into the changing nature of Englishness. Far from being immutable, therefore, Englishness has been constantly evolving, and the process is still continuing.

Bede's book, written c. 730, had posed the question of whether the English people—already a nation—were capable of overcoming their political differences to form a nation-state. No sooner was that question answered in the affirmative than a second question was posed, namely whether Englishness could survive colonisation by a foreign power. And when that question was also answered in the affirmative, the English question changed again, to the very contemporary one of whether England could coexist peacefully with its neighbours in the Hiberno-British Isles, or whether it would seek to dominate them—by force if necessary.

The conquest of Wales at the end of the thirteenth century and the birth of the English Empire provided the answer. Yet, when the colony of Wales was annexed to England by the Tudor king Henry VIII 250 years later, a new question arose: what would happen to Englishness as the other nations of the Isles were absorbed into the expanding English state? And, as an external empire grew up alongside the internal one, creating in the process a Britishness that had not existed for more than a thousand years, the English question changed again: what did it mean to be English when so many people were proud to be British?

The answer was provided by a growing belief in English exceptionalism, which was used to explain both the internal and external empires and to give the people of England attributes that distinguished them from their UK neighbours. The end of the Second World War, however, saw the unravelling of the British Empire and once again, therefore, the need to redefine Englishness. This time, instead of the comforting assumption of place, a racial definition started to rear its ugly head. Although *British* citizens and subjects could be of any colour, *Englishness*—in the eyes of many—now implied whiteness. As a result, Englishness became associated with white supremacy and the right-wing political groups that espoused it.

This dimension of Englishness has not entirely disappeared, but it has diminished. And, as devolution and Brexit have started to take their toll on the internal empire, Englishness has started to change again, along with the English question itself. Indeed, no fewer than three English questions have emerged in this post-Imperial phase of English history, of which the most important revolves around the nature of Englishness as an English nation-

ENGLISH QUESTIONS

state is recreated. No one can predict with accuracy the answers at this stage, but there is no need for pessimism or fatalism. An independent England does not have to be the reactionary caricature depicted by some, as there is also a long progressive tradition on which a reborn Englishness could draw. Time will tell, but there are many reasons to be optimistic.[1]

Pre-Imperial Englishness

Englishness first emerged after the creation of an English people with an ethnicity distinct from that of the Britons, Picts, Scots and Irish. There is no hint of such a group in Gildas, who c. 540 CE considered 'the fierce and impious Saxons, a race hateful to both God and men' to be a mortal threat to his beloved native country.[2] That these Germanic invaders—a rabble of squabbling Jutes, Angles, Frisians, Saxons and others—should be considered a distinct ethnic group would never have occurred to Gildas, who still hoped the beast could be strangled at birth if only the godless Britons would follow the true ecclesiastical path and unite politically.

It would be another 200 years before any widely read writer would be bold enough to refer to the Germanic invaders and their descendants as an English people, which the Venerable Bede did in his *Historia Ecclesiastica Gentis Anglorum*. Yet Bede, a much better scholar than Gildas, was all too aware that those who would become English had not been a single people when they had arrived in the fifth century CE:

> Those who came over were of the three most powerful nations of Germany—Saxons, Angles and Jutes. From the Jutes [in Jutland] are descended the people of Kent and of the Isle of Wight ... From the Saxons, that is, the country that is now called Old Saxony, came the East Saxons [Essex], the South

INTERNAL EMPIRE

Saxons [Sussex] and the West Saxons [Wessex]. From the Angles, that is ... the country between the Jutes and Saxons, are descended the East Angles [East Anglia], the Midland Angles, the Mercians, all the race of the Northumbrians, that is, of those nations that dwell on the north side of the river Humber, and the other nations of the Angles.[3]

In this passage, Bede drew attention not only to the differences among the Germanic tribes, but their distinct points of settlement in Britain. His book is then largely devoted to explaining how a single people was forged out of this ethnic, linguistic and geographic diversity, as a result of victories over the Britons, conversion to Christianity without the help of the natives and the spread of a vernacular language (Old English). Englishness, in Bede's view, therefore owed nothing to the Britishness it replaced, which instead was driven to the margins of Britain.[4] Rather, Englishness had evolved from the 'Anglo-Saxon' communities themselves after settlements were first established.[5]

Englishness may have come into existence by the time Bede wrote his magnum opus, but this did not mean political union, despite the habit of kings and their acolytes to refer to themselves as *Rex Anglorum*. On the contrary, Bede drew attention to the persistent conflicts among English rulers throughout the period when Englishness was being created. Thus, the first 'English question' was whether the different kingdoms could ever form a single nation-state of England—a question that became even more pressing and difficult to answer in the affirmative after the appearance of the Vikings at the end of the eighth century.

Another 200 years would pass after Bede before the question could be answered at all, and even then the response at first had to be a tentative one. Alfred may have prevented a total victory of the Viking Great Army at the Battle of Edington in 878,[6] but it was left to his grandson Æthelstan to unite all of

ENGLISH QUESTIONS

future England—at least temporarily.[7] To other kingdoms in the Hiberno-British Isles, political unity amongst the English was potentially a mortal threat. As the most populous and richest of the kingdoms in the Isles, England needed to be broken up before it could begin if these other kingdoms were to be secure, and leaders from Ireland, Scotland and Strathclyde (the Welsh stayed out) came together at the Battle of Brunanburh in 937 to try and defeat Æthelstan, already the dominant figure south of the Humber. However, Æthelstan's army won, and he could claim with some justification to have become the first King of the Anglo-Saxons. He even claimed, with much less justification, to be *Rex totius Brittaniae* (King of All Britain). The English had presented a united front in the battle and it paid off. The first English question appeared to have been answered in the affirmative.

It was, of course, a fragile unity. The north–south divide, hinted at by Bede in his description of the Humber as a line of political separation, reemerged as soon as Æthelstan died in 939. A Viking was restored to the kingship of Northumbria, and it was not until 954 that all of England was once again united under a single monarch. Even then, there was constant squabbling among the elites ruling England, and this political disunity could only encourage those foreign rulers who harboured ambitions to rule the young Kingdom of England for themselves. Yet a strong sense of Englishness always survived,[8] and there were limits to the struggles, as this quotation from the *Anglo-Saxon Chronicle* makes clear when referring to one of the many internal disputes among the English:

> The King had a great land-force on his side; but they were most of them loath to fight with their own kinsmen—for there was little else of any great importance but Englishmen on either side; and they were also unwilling that this land [England] should be the more exposed to outlandish people, because they destroyed each other.[9]

293

INTERNAL EMPIRE

The 'outlandish' people included the Vikings, and the successful invasion of England by the Danes in the early eleventh century raised a second English question, namely whether Englishness would survive if England were colonised by foreigners. King Cnut was quick to execute several of the leading English nobles who had opposed the Danish invasion, and removed others from positions of influence. Yet he was content to leave it at that, marrying the widow of the previous English king (Æthelred the Unready) and allowing the structures of English society to remain largely intact. Although Danish rule lasted until 1042, when Edward the Confessor became King of England, Englishness hardly changed at all.[10]

The Norman invasion in 1066 would be a much more serious threat to Englishness. The Normans, of Norse descent, had adopted the French language in the 150 years since their arrival from Scandinavia, but they had preserved a distinct identity (*Normanitas*) that was quite different from Frenchness (or, strictly speaking, Frankishness). Despite acknowledging the Frankish king as their overlord, the Normans had nothing but contempt for the 'French', unlike the Danes' grudging respect for the English. Their society operated according to different laws and customs, although they did share a common religion as well as language.

If the Normans succeeded in colonising England, would Englishness be eclipsed? This, after all, is what had happened to the original Britishness in the lands seized by Germanic invaders in the three centuries before Bede. Or would Englishness survive a Norman occupation, as had happened after the more recent Danish invasion? Or, perhaps, would some Anglo-Norman fusion emerge through a process of acculturation, as appeared to have happened in Scotland with the merging of the Picts and Scots? Following the Battle of Hastings, this new English question was about to find an answer.

294

ENGLISH QUESTIONS

The first acts of the Normans suggested that *Normanitas* would triumph. Many of the English leaders were executed, the lands of most English nobles were seized, and all resistance was crushed through a scorched-earth policy. And yet there were limits. Few peasants arrived from the continent, so that the serfs and slaves remained almost entirely English. Wealthier Norman settlers arrived and—together with those in the invading army, which also included Bretons and Flemish—were given the best lands. However, as settler colonialism goes, this was quite limited. As a result, so few Normans were available for the top jobs that William the Conqueror and his successors were forced to use native-born English in many key positions.

Just as important was the lack of Norman women among the settlers. Normans, with the important exception of the royal family, therefore tended to marry English women, and many of the historians of this period were products of these 'Anglo-Norman' unions. Yet a process of acculturation never took place.[11] Instead, Englishness survived and gradually came to displace the *Normanitas* that had threatened its existence. By the time France (as it had now become) recovered its Norman lands in 1204, almost all levels of society in England were thoroughly English. The one exception was the royal family, which maintained a delusional attachment to *Normanitas* until Henry III (King John's successor) was eventually forced to accept the inevitable.

The English question would now change again. England was once more a nation-state, but it was much more populous, more powerful and richer than the other nation-states in the Isles. Would this newly independent England be able to live side by side with its neighbours, or would it be tempted to impose its will on the weaker states? This new version of the English question would not be posed immediately, as it took some time for the kings of England to abandon their dream of recovering

INTERNAL EMPIRE

Norman possessions on the European continent, but it could not be postponed indefinitely.

Although we now know that the answer would be English domination, this was not obvious to contemporaries. England in the thirteenth century had enough problems of its own and had even endured an invasion by French troops under Prince Louis at the end of the reign of King John. This, together with the failure to take back continental possessions during the long reign of Henry III (1216–72), generated a certain humility among the English elites. Indeed, English exceptionalism—the notion of the English as a people chosen by God for special favour—does not seem to have been much in evidence at this time, whatever the claims of later scholars.[12]

Furthermore, although contempt for the Irish never diminished, attitudes among the English towards the peoples of Scotland and Wales had softened since the 1100s, when William of Malmesbury had referred to the Welsh as 'all that barbarianage' while William of Newburgh had considered the Scots to be 'a barbarous nation'. By the middle of the thirteenth century, the English monk Matthew Paris was able to describe Alexander, King of Scotland, as 'good, just, pious, bountiful, and loved by everyone, both the English and his own subjects', while the Tewkesbury chronicler could write about Llywelyn ap Gruffydd, the future (and 'last') Prince of Wales, as fighting vigorously to preserve his 'paternal liberties'.[13]

Yet it was difficult to imagine that the unequal relationship between the nation-states of the Isles would not lead the largest at some point to seek to impose its will on the others. Indeed, the Lordship of Ireland, with perhaps half the population of the island, was already in place before the loss of Normandy to France, and the imbalance between England and the rest seemed to be growing larger with time. Towards the end of the 1200s, for example, England's population is estimated at 3.5 to 5.5 million,

ENGLISH QUESTIONS

while Wales was between 0.2 and 0.3 million, Scotland between 0.5 and 1 million, and Ireland (including the Lordship) about 1.3 million.[14]

Not only was England more populous, but it was also more urbanised and more open to trade and therefore richer. England's urban population at this time (c. 1290) has been estimated at nearly 80 per cent of all those living in towns across the Isles, while the proportion was even higher for large towns of 2,000 inhabitants or more. Only in exports per head did any of the other nation-states come close to the English figure, and that was in Scotland. However, the northern kingdom's smaller population meant that total exports, imports and taxes collected were much lower.[15]

The colonisation of Wales under Edward I, followed by the invasion of Scotland a few years later and settler colonialism in Ireland under the Tudors and Stuarts, launched England on its imperialist path. With the birth of this insular or internal empire, Englishness would now change. The last of the pre-imperial English questions—could England enjoy peaceful co-existence with other nation-states in the Isles?—had been definitively answered in the negative, but other English questions would soon arise, as empire started to have its impact on the nature of Englishness.

Imperial Englishness

England's Welsh colony made no difference to Englishness. Language and geography ensured that this imperial possession remained distinct from England, and the long colonial war against Owain Glyndŵr at the start of the fifteenth century even strengthened anti-Welsh feeling among the English. There was, therefore, no legal, cultural or political reason for Englishness to change.

INTERNAL EMPIRE

More challenging was the decision of Henry VIII to annex Wales and absorb it into England. The timing of the two acts of annexation (1535 and 1542) made clear that this was not explained by the Tudors' cultural affection for their ancestral land, but had everything to do with the threat of a foreign invasion following the break with the Church of Rome. This, however, raised the question of whether this greater England would change Englishness in some way, now that it was supposed to reflect the interests of the Welsh people as well.

The answer was a resounding no. The name of the expanded state remained 'England', English became the language of the Welsh courts, and laws passed by the English parliament automatically applied to Wales as well. All that remained of Wales, apart from its language and later its Nonconformist version of Christianity, was a handful of MPs at Westminster. Even the Welsh Court of Great Sessions, established in 1542 to prosecute felonies and serious misdemeanours in Wales, was abolished in 1830.

A more serious challenge to Englishness was provided by the union of the two crowns in 1603. James I of England and VI of Scotland may have been content to live most of his time at court in London, but he had ambitions to build a bigger state, with a new name and administrative input from both Scotland and England. He explained to the English parliament that he hoped 'no man would be so unreasonable' as to ask him to be 'a husband to two wives' and on 20 October 1604 issued a royal proclamation stating:

> Wherefore wee have thought to discontinue the divided names of England and Scotland out of our Regall Stile, and doe intend and resolve to take and assume unto Us in maner and forme hereafter expressed, the Name and Stile of KING OF GREAT BRITTAINE, including therein according to the trueth, the whole Island.

298

ENGLISH QUESTIONS

Despite James' pleading, the English parliament was unimpressed and refused to allow James to use the title 'King of Great Britain'. James therefore sought legal opinion and was shocked to find that the English judges concurred with the view of parliamentarians. Englishness, it seems, was not going to be abandoned easily or quickly.

James was calling not just for a change in royal title, but also for a full political and legal union between his two kingdoms (a 'perfect' union). A commission of English and Scottish MPs was therefore established after the proclamation to see how the plan might be carried out and, in 1606, anticipating a favourable outcome, James ordered a 'British' flag to be created including the crosses of both St. George (England) and St. Andrew (Scotland).[16] Yet when the commissioners' recommendations were presented to the English parliament, they found insufficient support for numerous reasons, including the threat to the survival of English common law (a key component of Englishness). By 1607, the idea of a perfect union was dead and Englishness continued unscathed, although parliament did agree to repeal those laws that were hostile to the Scots.

The Acts of Union in 1707 may not have introduced a perfect union (Scotland, for example, preserved its legal system), but it still presented a potentially mortal threat to Englishness. 'North Britain' (Scotland) and 'South Britain' (England and Wales) were now one state, and its citizens and subjects were British. Furthermore, the external empire that was now rapidly expanding was British, not English, and its subjects were therefore legally British. What room was there for Englishness in this new state, with its far-flung imperial possessions?

The simplest answer to this new version of the English question was just to equate Englishness and Britishness. If they were one and the same, then the survival of Englishness was secure. This may have been sufficient for the rest of the world, for

299

INTERNAL EMPIRE

whom 'English' and 'British' now became interchangeable, since they were already accustomed to the idea of English hegemony within the Isles.[17] However, it was problematic for those English people who gave any thought to the issue, since 'Britishness' was not yet defined. And for those British who were not English, it clearly made no sense to consider the two as being the same.

The inhabitants of England never agreed that they lived in a place called South Britain, but gradually they came to accept that they were British. This is because the empire was British and they wished to identify with it (and continued to do so even after the loss of the thirteen colonies in North America). Britishness, which had been crushed in England by the English even before Bede, was therefore resurrected, as an imperial exercise in which all those who lived in Great Britain could participate. Meanwhile imperial subjects, such as those in the Caribbean, were also British—together with their slaves.

Within this shared definition of Britishness, there was still room for at least some elements of Englishness, since England had not merged its legal system with Scotland. This was demonstrated very clearly in the *Somerset v. Stewart* dispute in 1772. The case was brought on behalf of James Somerset, an enslaved African who argued that neither English common law nor parliamentary statute permitted slavery on English soil. Lord Chief Justice Mansfield did not rule against slavery in England, but he did judge that 'no master ever was allowed here [England] to take a slave by force to be sold abroad because he had deserted from his service.'[18]

Somerset won the case, but Mansfield's ruling had no bearing on what happened in Scotland. It would be another six years before a different case (*Knight v. Wedderburn*) was settled there, bringing into sharp relief some of the many differences between Englishness and Scottishness. Joseph Knight, a slave purchased in Jamaica, demanded his freedom once in Scotland,

ENGLISH QUESTIONS

but the Justices of the Peace sided with his master. On appeal, however, the Sheriff of Perth concluded that 'the state of slavery is not recognized by the laws of this kingdom [Scotland] and is inconsistent with the principles thereof', a judgement that was later upheld by the Court of Session (Scotland's supreme civil court). This judgement, by outlawing slavery in Scotland, went far beyond the more limited Mansfield ruling in England.[19]

These two rulings would come to have an important bearing on British debates over the slave trade, but before abolition was achieved Englishness faced a new challenge. This was the Acts of Union, which in 1801 brought England's Irish colony into a United Kingdom of Great Britain and Ireland.[20] The population of the western island was large, but most were Catholic and did not identify as British (yet alone English), despite their willingness to participate in the external empire. The need to clarify the meaning of Englishness, and to distinguish it from Britishness (and Irishness), was now greater than ever; and the nineteenth and early twentieth centuries would be the moment when a concerted effort was made in this regard.

The first reference to Englishness in the *Oxford English Dictionary* is for the year 1804.[21] By then, however, an ideology of English exceptionalism was starting to take shape—one that would grow in popularity in the next decades and allegedly stood in sharp contrast to what had happened on the European continent. It traced its roots to England before the Norman invasion and considered the Anglo-Saxons to be the original freedom-loving people. They had thrown off the 'Norman yoke' to establish an unbroken parliamentary tradition resulting in the sovereignty of the House of Commons—a sovereignty that had been confirmed by revolution in 1642 and 1688.[22]

English exceptionalism, seen by some as the product of divine intervention,[23] had then produced an external empire to complement the internal one. This new empire was British, but there would be no British exceptionalism to explain its apparent successes—how could there be when Great Britain was such a recent creation? Imperial triumph was due to *English* exceptionalism, marshalled by an 'island race' (despite England not being an island and the English not a race) that increasingly drew parallels between itself and the Romans who had forged a vast empire centuries before. History, at least in its 'Whig interpretation', began to acquire an almost predetermined character that allowed one triumph to be followed by another:

> Let us praise as a living thing the continuity of our history, and praise the whigs who taught us that we must nurse this blessing—reconciling continuity with change, discovering mediations between past and present, and showing what can be achieved by man's reconciling mind. Perhaps it is not even the whigs that we should praise, but rather something in our traditions which captured the party at the moment when it seemed ready to drift into unmeasurable waters. Perhaps we owe most in fact to the solid body of Englishmen, who throughout the centuries have resisted the wildest aberrations, determined never for the sake of speculative ends to lose the good they already possessed; anxious not to destroy those virtues in their national life which need long periods of time for their development; but waiting to steal for the whole nation [England] what they could appropriate in the traditions of monarchy, aristocracy, bourgeoisie and church.[24]

If this was the ideology of Englishness, what were its attributes? Here there was no consensus, some writers finding it in 'place' and others in 'race'—a confusion that was to cause endless trouble after the Second World War. Before the war, however, most writers took comfort from location as the defining feature of being English. In *The Spirit of the People: An Analysis of the English Mind,* written in 1907, Ford Madox Ford explained, 'It is

ENGLISH QUESTIONS

not—the whole of Anglo-Saxondom—a matter of race, but one, quite simply, of place—of place, and of spirit, the spirit being born of the environment.'[25]

The notion of place defining Englishness has been taken up by hundreds of writers, including in our own time.[26] It served poets well, with Wordsworth, Tennyson and others waxing lyrical on the features of England's landscape that helped to define Englishness. Yet place could be rendered elastic, with John Ruskin in particular pointing to architecture as a way of reproducing Englishness in the colonies and helping to forge among the colonial population a people who, in the words of the Whig historian Thomas Babington Macaulay, would be 'English in taste, in opinions, in morals and in intellect.'[27]

Many of the stories of English exceptionalism and of the attributes of Englishness were mythical, but not necessarily any more so than the myths with which other peoples comforted themselves on their origins and characteristics. More important was the way the story reconciled Englishness with Britishness, during a time when most people in Great Britain, and some in Ireland, were proud to be British. The English question had been answered emphatically, and Englishness had once again survived. In the words of George Orwell, that keen observer of the English class and social scene:

> It is not easy to discover the connecting thread that runs through English life from the sixteenth century onwards, but all English people who bother about such subjects feel that it exists. They feel that they understand the institutions that have come to them out of the past—Parliament, for instance, or sabbatarianism, or the subtle grading of the class system—with an inherited knowledge impossible to a foreigner. Individuals too are felt to conform to a national pattern. D.H. Lawrence is felt to be 'very English', but so is Blake; Dr. Johnson and G.K. Chesterton are somehow the same kind of person. The

303

INTERNAL EMPIRE

belief that we resemble our ancestors—that Shakespeare, say, is more like a modern Englishman than a modern Frenchman or German—may be unreasonable, but by existing it influences conduct. Myths which are believed in tend to become true, because they set up a type, or 'persona', which the average person will do his best to resemble.[28]

Postwar Englishness

Orwell published his essay in 1947, but the English world he was describing had already changed dramatically as a result of the Second World War. Until then, almost all peoples in the empire, both its colonies and its dominions, had the legal status of British subjects. In 1946, however, Canada had introduced a Canadian citizenship law; in 1947 Ceylon (Sri Lanka), India and Pakistan had become independent (Burma a year later); and the following year Ireland announced it was leaving the Commonwealth.[29] Britishness based on imperial links was now under threat and, in an effort to confront this, the Commonwealth meeting in 1948 agreed that the UK and the dominions would enact legislation to create separate categories of national citizenships while retaining the common status of British subjects.

The British Nationality Act 1948 was an attempt to keep alive the old meaning of Britishness, as the first few clauses made clear:

1(1) Every person who under this Act is a citizen of the United Kingdom and Colonies or [the dominions] shall by virtue of that citizenship have the status of a British subject.

1(2) Any person having the status aforesaid may be known either as a British subject or as a Commonwealth citizen ... accordingly ... the expression 'British subject' and the expression 'Commonwealth citizen' shall have the same meaning ...

ENGLISH QUESTIONS

2(1) Any citizen of [Ireland] who immediately before the commencement of this Act was also a British subject shall not ... be deemed to have ceased to be a British subject...

Yet as soon as dominions and former colonies created their own citizenships, it should have been obvious that the concept of Britishness was going to change. The 1948 act was therefore an attempt to postpone the inevitable, but in the meantime it provided protection for those British subjects who wished to come to the UK to settle and work—a right they had always enjoyed, although not many had taken advantage of it.[30] The desperate labour shortage that the British economy faced after the war meant that, this time, they received official encouragement to do so.

Although the *Empire Windrush* in 1948 was not the first to bring people from the Caribbean, it is the ship most closely associated in the public imagination with the postwar arrival in Great Britain of foreign-born British subjects.[31] Many came from the West Indies and the Indian subcontinent, less so at first from Africa or other parts of Asia. The non-white population then rose to an estimated 1.3 million by 1971 and 2.1 million a decade later, with most settling in England and taking advantage of a tight labour market with large numbers of vacancies in both the public and private sectors. The composition of the English population, some 46 million in 1971, was now changing rapidly.

The main English ports (including London) had for centuries included small concentrations of non-white people. Since Englishness was widely accepted as being defined by place, they were as English as anyone else. Non-white people had become part of English society as lawyers, politicians, writers, traders, restaurateurs, skilled workers, professional sportsmen and so on, often finding and marrying white partners.[32] Yet the increase in their numbers after the Second World War sparked a backlash

305

INTERNAL EMPIRE

that included discrimination in jobs, housing and education, threats to personal safety, and riots against their presence by white mobs.

Governments, fearful of the possible electoral implications of this backlash, responded with changes to immigration laws. In 1962 a Conservative administration passed the Commonwealth Immigrants Act, designed to 'control the immigration into the UK of Commonwealth citizens' by restricting entry, among other things, to those holding employment vouchers issued by the Minister of Labour. Not to be outdone, a Labour government in 1968 then passed its own Commonwealth Immigrants Act, further restricting access and taking aim in particular at East Africans of Asian descent.

These laws were not de jure discriminatory—the words 'white' or 'black', for example, never appear—but de facto they were, as many commentators pointed out at the time. Indeed, even the leader of the Labour opposition, Hugh Gaitskell, described the 1962 act as 'cruel and brutal anti-colour legislation' shortly before he died. The law was much harsher on immigration by non-white people, and that was the clear intent. The message, heard loud and clear, was that immigration from the 'white' Commonwealth would be treated differently from immigration from elsewhere.

This meant, however, that the previous interpretation of Englishness as defined by place, not colour, was now under threat. A British subject might be non-white—millions clearly were, outside and inside the UK—but the new laws, and the bigotry that had led to them, seemed to suggest that to be English one had to be white. On this interpretation, those non-white people in England who had acquired UK citizenship might be British, but they could not be English. The English question had now been reframed, and the answer at first was to take England and Englishness into a very dark place indeed.

306

ENGLISH QUESTIONS

Many mainstream English politicians had addressed this new English question in a roundabout sort of way, but the first to offer an answer explicitly based on colour was Enoch Powell. A member of the Conservative shadow cabinet, Powell had made speeches attacking immigration on many occasions and had not been the subject of any opprobrium from his party.[33] However, his speech in Birmingham on 20 April 1968, including its literary reference to 'the River Tiber foaming with much blood', was considered to have gone too far and he was sacked by his party leader.[34] This then left Powell free to say what he really thought, and his most incendiary speech was delivered on 16 November of the same year at the London Rotary Club in Eastbourne:

> At present large numbers of the offspring of immigrants, even those born here in Britain, remain integrated in the immigrant community which links them with their homeland overseas. With every passing year this will diminish. Sometimes people point to the increasing proportion of immigrant offspring born in this country as if the fact contained within itself the ultimate solution. The truth is the opposite. *The West Indian or Asian does not, by being born in England, become an Englishman.* In law he becomes a United Kingdom citizen by birth; in fact he is a West Indian or Asian still ... he will have lost one country without gaining another, lost one nationality without acquiring a new one. (Author's emphasis.)

Powell had been shunned by the leadership of his own party. Yet he was popular among much of the white population, many of whom marched in support of his ideas—including the notion that one could not be 'Black' and 'English'. It was no surprise, therefore, that three years after his speech another Conservative administration passed the Immigration Act 1971, which not only targeted entry into the UK, but also introduced a distinction between immigration and the 'right of abode' (a person with

INTERNAL EMPIRE

such a right now being described as 'patrial'). The act even encouraged repatriation, a key demand of Enoch Powell: 'The Secretary of State may ... make payments of such amount as may be determined to meet or provide for expenses of those persons who are not patrial in leaving the United Kingdom for a country or territory where they intend to reside permanently...'.

Ten years later, in 1981, Britishness was then almost entirely separated from its imperial roots with the passing of the British Nationality Act. Although introduced by a Conservative administration, it had its origins in the previous Labour government (1974–9). British citizens now had automatic right of abode in the UK, but to be a British citizen it was no longer sufficient to have been born in a former British colony. Instead, one had to prove a close connection to the 'mother' country, so that 'a person born in the United Kingdom ... shall be a British citizen if at the time of the birth his father or mother is (a) British citizen or (b) settled in the United Kingdom'.

The meaning of Britishness had now changed completely, and this was bound to have implications for Englishness. However, the wrong lessons were drawn. Instead, the 1991 census introduced questions on ethnicity that were expanded in 2001 and caused great confusion. In those and subsequent years, individuals who gave their ethnic group as 'Asian or Asian British' or 'Black or Black British' had to tick an additional box that did not allow them to identify as English.[35] The non-white population of England, which had reached nearly 4.5 million (or 9 per cent) in 2001, could identify as British, but not as English—a flaw in the census form that continues to this day.[36]

Englishness had therefore been defined by default as associated with whiteness—something Enoch Powell had campaigned for all along. This delighted the white-supremacist groups that were becoming increasingly vocal on the fringes of English politics. With their origin in the interwar British Union of Fascists,

ENGLISH QUESTIONS

these groups may not always have had 'English' in their names, but their focus was definitely the white population of England. The League of Empire Loyalists, the White Defence League, the Racial Preservation Society, the British National Party and the National Front—to name but a few—may have disagreed on many things in the postwar decades, but they all agreed that whiteness was a *sine qua non* for Englishness. Like their ideological heirs of the twenty-first century, the England First Party and the English Defence League, they promoted the flag of St. George as the national flag of England, thereby making it repellent not only to the non-white population, but to many of the white population as well.

Mainstream political parties did little to challenge the idea that Englishness was associated with whiteness. They did, however, put considerable effort into recruiting representatives who would come to be labelled 'Black, Asian and Minority Ethnic' (BAME) or simply 'minority ethnic'. The Labour Party, as a result of its history and trade union links, was for many years the most successful, but those Labour MPs elected in the 1980s tended to define themselves as 'British' not 'English'.[37] The same was true of the non-white population at large, which by the end of the 1990s was largely content to use 'British', but not 'English', alongside ethnic identifiers such as 'Afro-Caribbean, 'Indian' or 'Chinese'.[38]

For the Conservative Party, the embrace of the non-white English electorate was a more tortuous affair. The party had historically included many racists, and some of the white supremacy groups had been started by politicians who had broken away from Conservatism. As a result, it had struggled to win support among non-white voters; but that began to change under Prime Minister Margaret Thatcher (1979–90), whose policies expanded the size of the ethnic-minority middle class. And, as the party increasingly became an 'English national

INTERNAL EMPIRE

party' (see Chapter 8), it could not afford to ignore a group that, by 2021, constituted 19 per cent of the English population.[39] Furthermore, the Conservatives needed to find not just votes, but also representation among the non-white population. This they did with some success and, since returning to power in 2010, the party has been energetic (along with the Liberal Democrats) in securing the election of non-white English MPs and local councillors.[40] Indeed, following the resignation of Liz Truss as Prime Minister in October 2022 after a mere six weeks, Conservative MPs supported Rishi Sunak (a British Asian) in such large numbers that party members were not required to vote in a leadership contest; Sunak then became Prime Minister.

These changes have helped to break the link between Englishness and whiteness.[41] And, with English teams in international sport usually including significant numbers of non-white members, it has become more common for prominent individuals to self-identify as English. This has arguably made it easier for the mass of the ethnic-minority population in England to do the same. Meanwhile, the flag of St. George is starting to lose its racist overtones and has become a familiar sight at England's sporting events, where in previous decades the union flag would have been waved, because of the English flag's association with white supremacy—England supporters at the FIFA World Cup final in 1966, for instance, were waving the Union Jack, not the flag of St. George.

The English question posed at the beginning of this section is now being given a different answer—not before time. Englishness this time does not necessarily imply whiteness, even if it is no longer explained by place in the way that was understood before the Second World War. This new version of Englishness is still evolving, still raw and often hard to understand, but it is exciting and full of potential. Such a radical change has inevitably generated a wave of nostalgic literature, which ranges from the apoplectic

ENGLISH QUESTIONS

to the romantic, but in fairness has always recognised that the clock cannot be turned back.[42] Yet, in truth, the transformation of Englishness is something to celebrate. And, in the process, England is acquiring national attributes that will be needed if it once again becomes a nation-state.

Post-Imperial Englishness

Since modern Britishness was largely defined and explained by global imperialism, it is hardly surprising that the end of the British Empire has been associated with a decline in the proportion of those in England identifying strongly as British. Just as this external empire was coming to an end, however, the internal empire—stretching back to the conquest of Wales— was coming under threat from the rise in Scottish and Welsh nationalism, as well as its growing intensity in Northern Ireland. This threat was then elevated by devolution. Identifying strongly as British became even more challenging for those living in England when so many in the other parts of the Isles were rejecting the British label.

The collapse of one empire and the fall of the other has been a challenge for the English, and the tradition over centuries of conflating English and British has made self-identification very perplexing for many people in England today. Surveys and opinion polls have captured these complexities.[43] Yet they cannot resolve the conundrums, as these are of such long standing and reflect a moment in time when opinions are starting to shift. The authors of the most thorough analysis of Englishness to date were surely right, however, to conclude:

> The history of the establishment of the British state—whereby an English core expanded through either treaty or conquest— means that institutions, symbols, and values that in the rest

311

INTERNAL EMPIRE

of the state are regarded as quintessentially British are viewed by those who ascribe to a sense of English identity as theirs— English in all but name.[44]

As Britishness came under threat, it was inevitable that those in favour of the union would make a serious effort to redefine it for a post-Imperial age (in both senses). No one has been more associated with this task than Gordon Brown, a Scot and the former Chancellor of the Exchequer (1997–2007) and Prime Minister (2007–10). Brown, a historian by training with a doctorate entitled *The Labour Party and Political Change in Scotland 1918–1929,* gave a major speech on the topic in 2007, in which he claimed:

> Britain has a unique history—and what has emerged ... is I believe a distinctive set of British values which influence British institutions ... British tolerance, the British belief in liberty and the British sense of fair play ... Out of the necessity of finding a way to live together in a multinational state came the practice of tolerance, then the pursuit of liberty and the principle of fairness to all.[45]

Brown returned to the theme of British values after leaving office, and it became a key part of the work at his think tank Our Scottish Future.[46] Yet he could never circumnavigate two problems: first, his reading of British history, and in particular the construction of the two empires, was highly selective and in many respects wrong;[47] second, the values he outlined were not peculiarly British, but could easily be accepted by citizens in many countries around the world.

Despite the heroic efforts to assert a unique set of British values, the campaign by Brown and other unionists could not, in the end, reverse the decline of Britishness and the rise in England of Englishness—a change that contributed so much

312

ENGLISH QUESTIONS

to the result of the Brexit referendum in 2016. Englishness continued to advance, and the old English question—the West Lothian one—refused to go away, even after the Conservative administration led by David Cameron introduced English Votes for English Laws (EVEL).

EVEL withered away during the pandemic, but there was still no consensus on the answer to the English question that the EVEL procedures had been designed to address. The most logical response would have been the creation of an English parliament to complement those in the other three nations, leaving the House of Commons and House of Lords at Westminster as the institutions to address union-wide issues. Indeed, the Campaign for an English Parliament had been started in 1998, and the Constitution Unit at University College London had explored in detail how such a body might work.[48] Yet the proposal never gained traction, for the simple reason that the English refuse to accept that the Westminster parliament is anything other than their own and are unwilling to accept any diminution of parliamentary sovereignty.[49]

Meanwhile, the 2016 referendum and the implementation of its result, especially the repatriation of powers from Brussels, meant that an even older English question had resurfaced: was it possible to reform the constitution in such a way as to diminish the hegemonic role of England in the United Kingdom? Devolution was supposed to have solved this question, especially when the experiment proved so popular in Scotland and more popular than expected in Wales.[50] Yet the result of the Brexit referendum had shown the dominant force of the English vote, and the repatriation of powers from Brussels has subsequently shown the hegemonic role of a government whose formation depended on English MPs.[51]

One obvious answer to this English question was federalism: a union of four nations that would provide constitutional

313

guarantees for the smaller nations. Yet this proposal, attractive as it seemed to some outside England, would have required either the creation of an English parliament or the establishment of a series of regional assemblies—both options being deeply unpopular with English voters, as demonstrated by the vote on a regional assembly for the northeast in 2004. The establishment of more directly elected regional mayors, as proposed in the 2022 white paper *Levelling Up the United Kingdom*, might help to decentralise England, but it could never be a substitute for federalism.

Some constitutional experts have argued that devolution brought a de facto form of federalism without the need to call it such. Vernon Bogdanor, one of the leading experts on the British constitution, claimed in 1998:

> It is in constitutional theory alone that the supremacy of Parliament is preserved. For power devolved, far from being power retained, will be power transferred; and it will not be possible to recover those powers except under pathological circumstances ... Thus, the relationship between Westminster and Edinburgh [and Cardiff and Belfast] will be quasi-federal in normal times.[52]

Unfortunately, although Bogdanor himself could not have anticipated it when he wrote these words, 'pathological circumstances' have turned out to include Brexit. The repatriation of powers from Brussels has involved the use of muscular unionism by the British government that undermines 'quasi-federalism'. Yet all efforts to establish federalism on a constitutional basis have been met with English resistance. And when the leader of Plaid Cymru went further in 2019, proposing that the three nations of Britain—England, Scotland and Wales—establish a confederation, the idea was greeted with resounding silence by the English.[53]

314

ENGLISH QUESTIONS

Nero fiddled, it is said, while Rome burned. As the debates over these two English questions have gone round in circles, the United Kingdom has headed towards disintegration. A united Ireland became an even more serious prospect following the elections for the Northern Irish assembly in May 2022, in which Sinn Féin emerged as the largest party. By then, a second referendum on Scottish independence had already been promised by the government in Scotland—a vote that can be blocked or delayed by the UK administration, but only at the risk of increasing support for independence. And if Northern Ireland and Scotland left the UK, Wales could be expected to push for greater autonomy, even if it fell short of independence.

Far from being appalled, English public opinion seems largely indifferent to the possibility of the breakup of the UK (see Table 9.1). The end of the internal empire, for that is what disintegration implied, apparently means very little to people in England. The more far-sighted have even begun to consider the prospect of England (with or without Wales) once again operating as a nation-state—as it had done for centuries before 1707. New English questions have now surfaced.[54] How would Englishness change if this happened? Would England be treated as the 'continuing' state to the UK by the rest of the world, as with the Russian Federation after the collapse of the Soviet Union? Or would England be considered a 'successor' state, as with the Czech Republic and Slovakia after the breakup of Czechoslovakia? And would the newly sovereign England find a way of rebuilding the internal empire, by virtue of its relative size and economic strength?

The last question was the easiest to answer and in the negative. Within a united Ireland, the former Northern Ireland would be part of the EU and therefore relatively safe from English pressure. Any matters that could not be settled bilaterally through institutions, such as whatever replaced the British–Irish Council,

INTERNAL EMPIRE

would soon end up as disputes between the UK and the EU. And the aftermath of Brexit has already shown the considerable power of the EU in such episodes. Furthermore, English governments can be expected to be relieved at the prospect of not having to address Northern Ireland questions, although there are bound to be some legacy issues surrounding that part of the population currently identifying as British.

Scotland would, it is often assumed, become a member of the EU soon after independence. It would first need a broad trade and cooperation agreement with England in order to safeguard its interests, especially the high proportion of Scottish goods and services destined for export south of the border—in 2019, some 60 per cent went to the rest of the UK, of which by far the largest share can be assumed to go to England.[55] By contrast, the share of English exports going to Scotland is small (less than 10 per cent). The need for Scotland to avoid English tariffs on its exports of goods, and non-tariff barriers on its exports of services, would give England considerable leverage in negotiations—but this is similar (in reverse) to the situation the UK faced when negotiating the Trade and Cooperation Agreement with the EU in 2020. For reasons explained below, it is likely that a solution would eventually be found acceptable to both sides.

The internal empire will not therefore be revived, although Wales is likely to find itself as a very junior partner in the new state if it does not choose independence. Yet what will be the international standing of this new state? In particular, will England & Wales (E&W) be a permanent member of the United Nations Security Council as the UK has been since its creation, with a right to nuclear weapons? Simon Heffer, addressing the possibility of Scottish independence some years ago, thought the answer was obvious:

ENGLISH QUESTIONS

> Scotland, with its five million people out of a United Kingdom total of 58 million, would only be a marginal loss to England, and no loss at all in economic terms. England would still be as much of a power in the European Union and in NATO as Britain was before it. Its permanent place on the United Nations Security Council is not dependent on the Union with Scotland.[56]

It is true that England, even without Wales, would still be a very large economy. It would drop below France and India, but would remain in the top ten (if official exchange rates are used) and therefore would easily qualify for membership of the G20. Yet would it inherit the privileged position formerly occupied by the UK in the international system, especially at the UN? If E&W claimed to be a successor state, it would acquire a new international legal personality and would not be bound by treaties previously ratified by the UK.[57] If, on the other hand, it claimed to be a continuing state, and therefore the inheritor of the UK's previous position, it might need the support of Scotland (and possibly Ireland) to avoid disputes over how to distribute the privileged position assigned to the UK in the global system after the Second World War. Since England would presumably prefer to be a continuing state, in accordance with the precepts of English exceptionalism and in view of the geopolitical importance it would thereby hope to retain, Scotland would then acquire considerable leverage of its own over E&W—and would be expected to use this to secure a satisfactory outcome in bilateral negotiations with its southern neighbour.

This then brings us to the final, and perhaps most intriguing, English question: what will be the nature of Englishness in a future nation-state of E&W? Englishness, it has been argued, contains a community-based strand ideally placed to resist the drive towards social inequality that is inherent in neoliberalism. On the other hand, Englishness has also been associated with racism, classism and right-wing views.[58] Which of these two very

INTERNAL EMPIRE

different kinds of Englishness—progressive or reactionary, if you will—is likely to prevail?

At first glance, it might seem that reactionary Englishness will have the edge. One study published in 2018, for example, showed that, if Englishness is ranked on a scale of 1 (not at all English) to 7 (very strongly English), 50 per cent identified as 'strongly English', and there was a high correlation between strength of feeling and right-wing views.[59] Furthermore, the only mainstream organisation so far to have successfully positioned itself as an English national party is the Conservative Party—which is not afraid to identify as right-wing.[60] This would suggest that the Conservatives are in pole position to form the government in a post-imperial nation-state of E&W, even without much support in Wales. And, as an English national party in all but name, the Conservatives might even hope to enjoy for decades the hegemonic position occupied by other nationalist parties, such as the SNP in Scotland or the ANC in democratic South Africa.

Yet this is too simplistic. The Conservatives would suffer reputational damage if the UK breaks up—the clue is in its official name of the Conservative and Unionist Party. New faultlines would soon emerge in English politics, and the progressive strand would find its voice. All parties could now claim to represent English nationalism, so that electoral competition, with or without a change to the voting system, would quickly throw up a challenger to Conservative hegemony. It might even be a new party, given the close historical association of both Labour and the Liberal Democrats with the union. And the 50 per cent of English voters who do not currently identify as 'strongly English', and whose views are more closely correlated with progressive causes, would need to find a new identity in England after they had ceased to be legally British.

All of this is speculation, and there is a limit to how far it should be taken. However, there is no need for pessimism, or

ENGLISH QUESTIONS

indeed fatalism, as we approach the end of the United Kingdom of Great Britain and Northern Ireland. It is, after all, only a century old in its current form, and during that time many other states have broken up without irreparable damage to their constituent parts. If the UK can avoid the period of turbulence associated with the end of British India, the Soviet Union or Yugoslavia, while matching the peaceful end of Czechoslovakia or Serbia and Montenegro, so much the better. The people of England do not appear to be fazed by the prospect of independence, so their political leaders can draw some comfort as the end of the UK approaches.

pp. [1–4]

NOTES

INTRODUCTION

1. There are a few imperial possessions still in existence. Grouped together as British Overseas Territories, they include a number of important tax havens such as the British Virgin Islands and the Cayman Islands.
2. 'Hibernia' was the Roman name for Ireland and 'Britannia' for [Great] Britain. Norman Davies also uses 'the Isles' throughout his magisterial study of the two islands. See Davies, N. (1999), p. xxii.
3. Even longer if we take into account the territories inherited by England from the Normans after their defeat by France in 1204 (Gascony, the Channel Islands and the Lordship of Ireland).
4. From 1922, the name would be changed to the United Kingdom of Great Britain and *Northern* Ireland, but still abbreviated to the 'UK'.
5. Northern Ireland did in fact have a governor appointed by the British government for the first fifty years after its creation in 1921.
6. See Maier (2007), p. 7.
7. See Paxman (1998), p. 53. Andrew Bonar Law was Prime Minister of the UK from October 1922 to May 1923.
8. The Commonwealth still has purpose and meaning for many of its members, especially the smaller ones, who find in it an opportunity to raise issues that barely receive a hearing elsewhere. However, this is irrelevant to the strength of Britishness among the UK population.

NOTES

pp. [5–19]

9. To those who argue that the decision to leave the EU was simply the result of a democratic vote by the UK electorate, one need only consider what would have happened if the overall result had been the same, but with England voting to remain while the other three nations voted to leave. It is not idle speculation to assume that the UK would have found a way to stay.

10. There has been a huge amount of work published in recent years on many of these themes. Some of these make an important contribution and have helped me greatly in writing this book, although none adopt the same perspective I do. Among these books are Ali (2022), Bogdanor (2019), Dorling & Tomlinson (2019), Morgan & Patomäki (2018), Keating (2021), Olusoga (2021), O'Toole (2018), Reynolds (2019), Tombs (2021) and Wellings (2019). Many other recent books are referenced in the text itself.

11. See Heffer (1999), p. 19.

12. See Henderson & Wyn Jones (2021). This emphasis on Englishness might at first sight appear to be contradicted by the results of the 2021 Census, which found a big rise compared with 2011 in England and Wales in those identifying as 'British only' and an equivalent fall in those identifying as 'English only'. However, as the Office for National Statistics was quick to point out when publishing the results, this change 'most likely [is] a result of the changes to the question structure where "British" became the top response option in 2021 for England only'. See ONS (2022), Footnote 1.

1. BIRTH OF THE FOUR NATIONS

1. See Raftery (2005), pp. 140–5.

2. See Russell (2005), pp. 405–50.

3. See Cróinín (1995), pp. 14–15. Patrick was born in Wales, but had been enslaved by Irish pirates and taken to Ireland as a boy before escaping.

4. See Byrne, F. J. (1973), pp. 70–86.

5. See MacManus (2018), pp. 280–1.

6. There is a detailed description of the battle in Chatterton-Newman (1983), Chapter 9.

322

pp. [19–32]

NOTES

7. See the special issue of *History Ireland* (March/April 2014) devoted to the 1000th anniversary of the Battle of Clontarf.

8. See Avakov (2010), Table 1.2.

9. The Arthurian legend has acquired a life of its own, but it was given huge impetus by the publication c.1136 of *The History of the Kings of Britain* by Geoffrey of Monmouth.

10. The same is true of the historical figure Cadwallon ap Cadfan, ruler of one Welsh kingdom, who invaded the Germanic kingdom of Northumbria and ruled it until his death in 634. Cadwallon was fighting for all Britons and not just those of Wales.

11. While *Cymru* and *Cymry* are derived from Celtic, 'Wales' and 'Welsh' were used by Germanic invaders to describe all peoples other than themselves. Eventually, the word *wealas* (modern Welsh) came to refer only to the Britons of modern Wales.

12. See Maund (1991), pp. 132–9.

13. Harold at this time married Ealdgyth, the widow of Gruffydd ap Llywelyn, who then briefly (until Harold's death) became Queen of England, having already been Queen of Wales.

14. See Davies, J. (2007), p. 103.

15. Ptolemy's atlas was published c. 150 CE, but its map of the land was based on information that dated from the time of the first Roman invasion of Britain.

16. See Ravilious (2021), pp. 55–65.

17. Hadrian's successor (Emperor Antoninus Pius) was more ambitious and built the Antonine Wall further north, but the Romans soon abandoned it, leaving Hadrian's Wall as the de facto southernmost boundary.

18. After the Roman name for Irish people, *Scoti*.

19. See Benner (2021), pp. 64–72.

20. See Duncan (2002), pp. 8–26.

21. York at that time was the name not just for the town, but also the surrounding lands that corresponded to the old kingdom of Deira.

22. See Gildas (1999), p. 37.

23. Augustine, a Benedictine monk in Rome, was selected in 595 by Pope Gregory the Great to lead an evangelical mission to Anglo-Saxon England. He became the first Archbishop of Canterbury.

NOTES

pp. [32–42]

24. See John (1996), p. 59.
25. Alfred was therefore the first, but by no means the last, to pay Danegeld—as the bribes were known—to the Vikings.
26. See John (1996), p. 97.
27. Charles the Simple had agreed to allow Viking warriors led by Rollo to establish a Danelaw in Normandy after the siege of Chartres.
28. Æthelred could not literally have killed all Danes in England, but he killed enough for the day to be forever remembered as the Massacre of St. Brice's Day.

2. FOUR NATIONS, FOUR STATES

1. See Davies, R. R. (1990), p. 67.
2. Henry II, who came to the throne in 1154, was the grandson of Henry I and the great-grandson of William the Conqueror. He was Duke of Normandy from 1150—even before he became King of England. He could hardly have been more Norman, and the subsequent addition of other titles such as Count of Anjou and Duke of Aquitaine did not alter the facts.
3. It is often said that Henry I married an English woman because her mother was Anglo-Saxon, but his wife was born in Scotland and her father was the Scottish king. She was therefore Scottish and not English.
4. Orderic Vitalis was born in 1075. His monumental *Historia Ecclesiastica* consisted of six volumes.
5. See Carpenter (2003), p. 8.
6. The population of England c. 1300 has been estimated at around 3 million. A few historians have been sufficiently impressed by this demographic increase, and the related economic changes, to argue that England had ceased to be a Norman colony within a few generations of the conquest in 1066. See, for example, Gillingham (2000), p. 4.
7. The English Channel Islands (the Bailiwicks of Guernsey and Jersey, including smaller islands such as Sark and Alderney) should not be confused with the French Channel Islands, which lie close by.

324

pp. [42–56]

NOTES

8. Given that the king's annual revenue was probably no more than £30,000, this was a huge sum.

9. Quoted in Carpenter (2020), p. 97.

10. See Cróinín (1995), p. 211.

11. Brian's son Donnchadh did marry Driella, daughter of Earl Godwin of Wessex. She was the sister of Harold Godwinson, who would be the last pre-Norman King of England.

12. See Hudson (1994), p. 153.

13. Quoted in Cróinín (1995), p. 281. The son-in-law was Arnulf de Montgomery.

14. See Gillingham (2014), p. 135.

15. This would have been a joint decision by the two brothers. The English capture of the Isle of Man in the same year had made it imperative to prevent Ireland from becoming the base for an English invasion of Scotland.

16. See *Remonstrance of the Irish Chiefs to Pope John XXII*, p. 42 (available at https://celt.ucc.ie//published/T310000-001/).

17. See Frame (1989), pp. 151–2.

18. Gerald of Wales, a clergyman and historian of mixed Welsh and Norman heritage, quoted in his famous *Description of Wales* a letter from Henry II of England to Emanuel, Emperor at Constantinople, claiming that the Welsh were: 'So bold and ferocious that, when unarmed, they [do] not fear to encounter an armed force; being ready to shed their blood in defence of their country and to sacrifice their lives for renown.'

19. The payment was recorded in the Domesday Book in 1086.

20. See Carpenter (2003), p. 112.

21. See Walker, D. (1991), p. 73.

22. See Pryce (1998), pp. 4-11.

23. See Turvey (2013), p. 94.

24. See Carr (1995), p. 45; and Carr (1989), pp. 125–6.

25. See Stephenson (2019), p. 16.

26. Joan was his 'natural' daughter, but still a huge 'catch' for Llywelyn. John later persuaded the Pope to legitimise her birth.

325

NOTES

pp. [57–67]

27. See Smith (1984), pp. 344–62. Three articles of Magna Carta (56–8) refer to Wales, of which the first is perhaps the most important, as it recognises the primacy of Welsh law in Wales.
28. See Carpenter (2020), pp. 7–13.
29. See Walker, R. F. (1972), p. 469.
30. Henry was in fact Dafydd's uncle, since his sister Joan was Dafydd's mother. Dafydd had an elder half-brother, but Llywelyn had not married the mother, and so Dafydd's claim to the throne was considered stronger.
31. Quoted by the English monk Matthew Paris (d. 1259) in his famous *Chronica Majora.*
32. With one exception. However, the treaty allowed Llywelyn to purchase this baron's homage from Henry III at a later date, which is what happened.
33. In 1273, shortly after Henry III's death, he wrote in a letter (referring to himself in the third person) that 'The king knows well that the rights of [my] principality are totally separate from the rights of the [King of England's] kingdom ... Llywelyn and his predecessors have had the power to build castles, fortresses and markets within their borders without the favour of anyone.'
34. See Anderson, A. O. (1963), pp. 6–7.
35. See Green (1989), p. 59.
36. See Lynch (1992), p. 53.
37. Subsequently, the only significant change to the border has been the annexation of Berwick-upon-Tweed by England in 1482.
38. See Duncan (1975), p. 580.
39. Orkney and Shetland, however, remained Norwegian until 1472.
40. See Barrow (1976), p. 63. Quoted in Bonner (1999), p. 12.
41. See Nicholson (1959), pp. 114–32.
42. See Bonner (1999), p. 5.

3. THE RISE OF ENGLISH IMPERIALISM

1. The one queen among the Norman kings was Matilda, the daughter of Henry I, who ruled England briefly during the Anarchy, but was never crowned.

pp. [68–89]   NOTES

2. See Davies, R. R. (2000), p. 2.

3. See Carpenter (2003), pp. 16–24.

4. See Gerald of Wales (1978), *The Description of Wales*, Book II, Chapter 1.

5. See Smith (2007), pp. 139–52.

6. See Stephenson (2019), p. 27.

7. See Carpenter (2003), p. 512.

8. Since much of South Wales was already administered in this way by the descendants of Norman lords, the practical effect of this part of the Statute was felt above all in north Wales.

9. See Davies, R. R. (1978), p. 272.

10. See Bowen, I. (1908), pp. 164–5.

11. Edward approached parliament shortly before the expulsion, but the decision to support his request was not taken until after the Jews had been expelled.

12. See Brough (2017), pp. 217–29.

13. See Gillingham (2014), pp. 136–8.

14. See Frame (1998), p. 204.

15. See McGrath (2006), p. 161.

16. The policy was so named by William Butler. See Butler (1913), pp. 47–65.

17. Quoted in Maginn (2007), p. 957.

18. Presbyterians were not only opposed to Catholicism, but also to the established (Protestant) Church of Ireland.

19. See Hegarty (2011), p. 123.

20. Cromwell was made Lord Protector in 1653.

21. See, for example, McDonnell (1906).

22. Scotland followed suit the following year, when William and Mary became joint monarchs of the northern kingdom as well.

23. See Prestwich (1989), p. 183.

24. He was first imprisoned in the Tower of London and then allowed to retire to his estates in France.

25. See Lynch (1992), p. 124.

26. See Nicholson (1965), pp. 75–99.

27. Quoted in Mason (1987), p. 63.

327

NOTES

pp. [90–108]

28. See Vergilius (1534), Chapter XXVI, p. 41.

29. Charles wanted to make the Church of Scotland episcopalian, with the monarch as head of the Church, as in England. See Jackson, L. C. (2015), Chapter 2.

30. See Gillingham (2001), pp. 50-1.

31. See Crooks (2011), pp. 11–13.

32. See Labarge (1980), p. 206.

33. The Treaty of Troyes in 1420 stated that Henry V of England would become King of France on the death of Charles VI, but Henry died before he could accede. His son, Henry VI, was crowned as King of France in 1431, but English control was always disputed, and Henry never ruled the entire country.

34. See Biggar (2010), p. 8.

35. Quoted in Crooks (2011), p. 40.

4. FOUR NATIONS, ONE STATE

1. The act is sometimes dated as 1536 as it received the royal assent in that year. At the time, New Year's Day was 25 March (Scotland moved to 1 January in 1600 and England—including Wales and Ireland—in 1752).

2. On England's 'racial' discrimination against the Welsh during the colonial period, see Stevens & Phipps (2020), pp. 290–331.

3. See Hechter (1975), pp. 110–11.

4. The Welsh not (sometimes spelt as 'note' or 'knot') was a stick used in schools to discourage the use of the language. Given to the first person heard speaking Welsh, it was passed round the classroom until the end of the day, when the last person holding it was punished. The practice only ended in the twentieth century.

5. See Davies, J. (2007), p. 242.

6. See Williams (1960), p. 72.

7. *Hansard*, HC Deb. 5 February 1913, vol. 47, col. 2251.

8. See Stephen (2007), pp. 1-4.

9. This was the War of the Spanish Succession, which the Scottish privy council reluctantly endorsed after England had already declared war.

pp. [108–121] NOTES

10. There is a vast literature on the union. On the economic factors, see Whatley (1989), Riley (1969) and Harris (2010).

11. The behaviour of Hamilton has been the subject of much speculation. See Fry (2006), pp. 188–9.

12. For a detailed analysis of the votes on the Articles of Union in the Scottish parliament, see MacInnes (1989).

13. The privileges of the Church of Scotland, established by parliament in 1690, were confirmed by the Articles of Union, which also banned the ascent to the throne of any Catholic.

14. Defoe (1709), quoted in Lynch (1992), p. 310. Defoe was a propagandist for union, but he could see the problems very clearly from his time in Scotland.

15. Scotland would be given sixteen seats in an expanded House of Lords.

16. One of the most articulate opponents of union was Andrew Fletcher of Saltoun. See Scott (1992).

17. On the day itself (1 May 1707), there was a service in London at St. Paul's Cathedral to commemorate the event, which was attended by Queen Anne—but almost nothing in Scotland. See Devine (2016), p. 2.

18. Quoted in Hayton (2007), p. 45.

19. Quoted in McGrath (2008), p. 20.

20. See Kelly (2001), p. 56.

21. See Hegarty (2011), p. 158.

22. Quoted in Geoghegan (2001), p. 4.

23. Tone was an atheist, but he had been raised in the (Protestant) Church of Ireland, while his mother had only converted from Catholicism after he was born. His pamphlet focused heavily on the need to end sectarian divisions on the island.

24. Quoted in Geoghegan (2001), p. 115.

25. The expanded House of Commons had 558 members. In addition, Ireland was allocated four Lords spiritual and twenty-eight Lords temporal.

26. Assuming an Irish population of around 4.5 million, the total for both islands was 15 million—giving an Irish share of around 30 per cent. Adding in the 500,000 military and naval personnel and convicts,

329

NOTES pp. [123–137]

who were not included in the 1801 census for England and Wales, would reduce the Irish share to 29 per cent.

27. Like the inhabitants of the Isle of Man, the Channel Islanders became British citizens, but neither people became members of the European Union.

28. See Goodare (1998), pp. 31–57.

29. See Coupland (1954), p. 190.

30. See Morgan (1981), p. 20.

31. Quoted in Davis (1998), p. 1.

32. His name was James Thomson and his poem was set to music by Thomas Arne in order to be performed in 1740 for Frederick, son of George II. Since Frederick (like his father) was a Hanoverian, the references to the subjects of Great Britain as 'Britons' rather than 'English' and/or 'Scottish' in the poem must have held some attraction.

33. See Colley (1996), pp. 11–58.

34. See Bulmer-Thomas, I. (1965), Vol. I, pp. 17–30.

35. See Colley (1996), pp. 126–7.

36. This was David Lloyd George, who served as Prime Minister from 1916 to 1922.

5. THE BRITISH EMPIRE

1. See Colley (1996).

2. Leaving aside the Channel Islands and the Isle of Man.

3. See Pettigrew (2013), p. 11.

4. There were several treaties signed between 1713 and 1715, but they are usually grouped together as the 1713 Treaty of Utrecht.

5. See Scanlan (2020), pp. 331–73.

6. See Marshall (1996), p. 17.

7. Exactly as had been predicted by Adam Smith in *The Wealth of Nations*, which was first published in 1776.

8. The slaves were expected to come from other British colonies in the Caribbean, but there was no way to be sure. See Bulmer-Thomas, V. (2012), pp. 65–9.

330

pp. [137–147] NOTES

9. Slavery continued until the 1840s in those parts ruled by the East India Company.
10. The indentured labourers came in the main from British India, and their conditions of work during the period of indenture (normally seven years) were not unlike those that prevailed under slavery. However, at the end of this period, they were free to return to their country of origin if they wanted.
11. Quoted in Schuyler (1922), p. 546.
12. See, however, some reservations in MacKenzie (2008), pp. 1253–5.
13. See Kumar (2000), p. 592.
14. See Morris (2014), pp. 293–314.
15. See Bulmer-Thomas, I. (1965), p. 141.
16. See Llwyd (2002), pp. 167–8.
17. See Williams (1982), pp. 13–18.
18. The phrase 'Brytish Impire' appears no fewer than thirteen times in Dee's book.
19. See Evans (2010), pp. 14–15.
20. See Philipps (1746).
21. See Evans (2016), pp. 52–5, for a detailed treatment.
22. See Evans (2010), p. 63.
23. 'New South Wales' in Australia, however, was not named in honour of Welsh settlers; it was designated as such by Captain James Cook, on account of its alleged topographical similarity to south Wales.
24. See Mackillop (2016), p. 145.
25. See Bowen, H. V. (2016), pp. 174–6.
26. See Evans (2010), pp. 65–72.
27. See the entry for Richard Pennant at historyofparliamentonline.org.
28. See, in particular, Williams (1985), Chapters 6, 7.
29. A good example is the detailed record of a Scottish slave-owning family in the Caribbean written by a modern descendant. See Renton (2021).
30. See Duffill (2004), pp. 102–3.
31. See Devine & Rössner (2011), p. 48.
32. See Long (1774), Vol. 2, pp. 286–7.
33. See Hamilton (2005), pp. 55–78.

331

NOTES

34. See Whyte (2006), pp. 45–6.
35. See Devine (2015), p. 229.
36. Ibid., p. 235. Excluding reexports.
37. See Naismith (1790), p. 93.
38. See Schmitz (1997), pp. 42–68.
39. See Marshall (1996), p. 265. The figure for South Africa is from the 1911 census.
40. See also Fry (2001) and Devine (2003).
41. See Gibb (1937), pp. 311–12.
42. The ambiguities for Ireland of being both a kingdom and a colony are well described in Bartlett (2005), pp. 61–89.
43. See Ohlmeyer (2004), p. 54.
44. See Akenson (1997).
45. The Montserrat flag today contains an Irish harp, in recognition of the past role played by settlers from Ireland.
46. See Beckles (1990), p. 519.
47. See Evans (2016), p. 45.
48. See Cullen (1994), pp. 112–49.
49. See Dickson (2005), p. 133.
50. See Bartlett (2005), p. 64.
51. The story is well told in Jay (2019). More recently, and suitably embellished, it was turned into a television drama as part of the series *Poldark*.
52. Quoted in Bartlett (2005), p. 85.
53. See Hegarty (2011), p. 248.

6. THE COMMONWEALTH

1. See Durham (1839), p. 132.
2. Ibid., p. 128.
3. 'Responsible government' meant that the executive reported to an elected assembly and could not function without support in the legislature. This was very different from 'representative government', under which elected assemblies could only advise the executive.
4. Quoted in Zimmern (1941), p. 26.

332

pp. [165–174]   NOTES

5. Newfoundland finally joined in 1949.

6. It was not until the Constitution of 1982 that Canada's independence was written into law.

7. Newfoundland, however, abandoned self-government in 1934, as a result of a financial crisis; it therefore de facto ceased to be a dominion. Its dominion status formally ended when it joined the Dominion of Canada fifteen years later.

8. See Marshall (1996), p. 68.

9. In addition, the dominions were allowed to join the League of Nations as founder-members, and three of them (Australia, New Zealand and South Africa) were awarded mandates consisting of former German colonies. This effectively enlarged the British Empire without the need for Great Britain to do anything.

10. India was, however, allowed to join the League of Nations on its foundation in 1920, together with the dominions.

11. In other words, each parliament was to consist of two legislative chambers (as at Westminster), but with an upper house consisting of a Senate rather than a House of Lords.

12. Sinn Féin ('we ourselves') had been founded in 1905 in opposition to the programme of home rule favoured by the Irish Parliamentary Party. By 1918, Sinn Féin was seeking to leave the UK altogether and establish an independent state.

13. Balfour, a Conservative politician, had been Prime Minister from 1902 to 1905. He authored the report in 1926 in his capacity as Lord President of the Council, by which time he had become Lord Balfour.

14. See Balfour Report (1926), p. 2. So important were these words deemed to be that they appear in the original in italics.

15. Joseph Chamberlain had split the Liberal Party in 1886 over the issue of home rule, and had formed the Liberal Unionist Party, which worked closely with the Conservative Party. He then split the Conservative Party in 1903 through his advocacy of imperial preference. The Liberal Unionist Party finally merged with the Conservative Party in 1912 to create the Conservative and Unionist Party—the official name of the Conservative Party today.

333

NOTES

pp. [174–182]

16. With its large group of white settlers (albeit only a minority of the population), Southern Rhodesia was being groomed to become a dominion along the lines of South Africa.

17. See Mansergh (1953), Vol. I, p. 122.

18. De Valera had led opposition to the Anglo-Irish Treaty after it was signed. When Sinn Féin split over the issue of the treaty, de Valera's faction pursued a policy of abstention until 1926, when he formed Fianna Fáil ('Soldiers of Destiny') to fight elections, with successful candidates committed to taking their seats without speaking the oath.

19. See Mansergh (1953),Vol. I, p. 303.

20. See Coffey (2018), pp. 126–9.

21. See Mansergh (1948), p. 208.

22. It might be thought that a declaration of neutrality, when Great Britain was at war, was inconsistent with dominion status. Yet declarations of war were now a dominion matter, and in 1939 the South African parliament had only narrowly rejected a motion in favour of neutrality—a motion that had been supported by the Afrikaner Prime Minister J. B. M. Hertzog himself.

23. Churchill himself had gone out of his way to try and block the Government of India Act in 1935, which granted a measure of autonomy to the Indian provinces.

24. See Catterall (2018), p. 831.

25. See India Office (1942), p. 1.

26. See *Hansard*, HL Deb. 18 November 1947, vol. 152, col. 752.

27. See Longford & O'Neill (1970), pp. 432–3.

28. See Mansergh (1953), Vol. II, p. 1210.

29. Ceylon was the last colony to become a dominion, in 1948. (It too would become a republic within the Commonwealth, in 1972 and under the name Sri Lanka.)

30. This would then be merged with Foreign Affairs in 1968, with a Secretary of State for Foreign and Commonwealth Affairs.

31. It had already changed its name in 1948 to the Association of Universities of the British Commonwealth.

32. Southern Rhodesia declared independence unilaterally the following year as Rhodesia, in the hope of preserving white supremacy—

NOTES

leading to a civil war that ended when it became independent in 1980 as Zimbabwe.

33. Today it even includes four former colonies (Gabon, Mozambique, Togo and Rwanda) which had not even been British.

34. See Gaitskell (1962), p. 3.

35. See Gaitskell (1962), p. 7; and McDermott (1972), p. 250.

36. Harold Wilson had ceased to be Prime Minister, following the victory of the Conservative Party in the 1970 elections, but the groundwork for CHOGM was done during the Labour government.

37. There had never been a requirement that the British monarch should be the Head of the Commonwealth, but it was agreed in 2018 that the next head should be the queen's eldest son and heir to the throne (then Prince Charles, now King Charles III).

38. See Prior (2019).

39. Mahatma Gandhi himself, who had led India to independence before his assassination, had been part of this community for over twenty years.

40. Per the 1931 Statute of Westminster agreed by all Commonwealth members at the time.

41. Powell's speech was delivered at Camborne on 14 January 1966.

42. France, however, had faced the same problem, and found a solution by persuading the other five founding members to accept its former colonies as 'associated states' of the EEC, with preferential trade arrangements.

43. Author's calculations using annual data from the IMF's 'Direction of Trade Statistics'.

44. This is the strapline that would be adopted by the Commonwealth in due course.

45. The very first SNP representation at Westminster had been a brief wartime spell in 1945; the seat, won in a byelection, was lost again in the general election later that year. Ewing's victory in 1967 marked the beginning of the party's continuous presence in the Commons.

46. See Petrie (2018), p. 210.

47. See Kilbrandon Report (1973), Vol. 1.

NOTES

pp. [189–196]

48. A minority opinion, written by two members, argued in favour of federalism and was published as a separate volume. See ibid., Vol. 2.

49. The report was equally silent on the Channel Islands and the Isle of Man—both of which had been included in the terms of reference.

7. EUROPE

1. An integration scheme with a common external tariff is known as a customs union. If it also includes free movement of labour and capital, it is known as a common market.

2. The British government had been invited to participate in the negotiations leading to the ECSC, but had not accepted. It was therefore not invited to Messina. See Ludlow (1997), pp. 12–20.

3. See Steinnes (1998), p. 62, n. 4.

4. There were European institutions shared by France and the UK, such as the Council of Europe and the Western European Union, but these were primarily concerned with human rights and security respectively, rather than economics.

5. See Anderson & Hecht (2018), Fig. 5. See also Spence (1976), pp. 18–36.

6. The Ulster Unionist Party, although independent, almost always supported the Conservative [and Unionist] Party in the UK parliament during its own period of hegemony in Northern Ireland, which ended in 1972. The Scottish Unionist Party, formed in 1912, was in effect the Scottish arm of the Conservative Party until the two merged in 1965.

7. Quoted in Gaitskell (1962), p. 2.

8. The Treaty of Rome had created not just the European Economic Community (EEC), but also the European Atomic Energy Community (Euratom). As the European Coal and Steel Community (ECSC) had started in 1952, the application of any new state was in fact to join the three European Communities—not just the EEC.

9. See Macmillan (1972), p. 5.

10. The common external tariff of the EEC was bound to bring some trade diversion at the expense of the US, since the US was such

336

pp. [196–204]   NOTES

a large provider of imports. And this problem for the US would increase every time new members joined the EEC.

11. See Steinnes (1998), p. 62.

12. The CAP was particularly problematic for Commonwealth member-states that supplied food to the UK. The CAP set a minimum domestic price for EEC producers, which then required a high (variable) tariff on imports to the EEC, to protect the local market.

13. Wilson's position while Labour was still in opposition is explained in his long speech to the House of Commons on 7 June 1962. See Kitzinger (1968), pp. 83–99.

14. Temporary concessions were, however, sought for food imports from Australia and New Zealand, while the developing countries in the Commonwealth were allowed to join the preferential trading scheme already in place for former colonies of EEC members.

15. The vote on the second reading (the most important one) was 309 to 301.

16. Norway had completed negotiations along with the other three applicants, but then put membership to a referendum in 1972, when it was rejected by 53.5 per cent.

17. See Kitzinger (1968), p. 19.

18. Quoted in Reith (1966), p. 8.

19. See Hedges (1976), p. 37.

20. See Spence (1976), p. 29.

21. Quoted in Butler & Kitzinger (1976), p. 50.

22. In 1970, the last election before the successful negotiations to join the EC, the Conservative Party had won 292 seats in England, compared with 216 won by the Labour Party. See Pilling & Cracknell (2021).

23. Even the Ulster Unionist Party, now independent of the Conservative Party, opposed membership, as did its upstart rival the Democratic Unionist Party.

24. These survey results are summarised in Hedges (1976), p. 59.

25. See Butler & Kitzinger (1976), pp. 80, 91.

26. See Fusaro (1979), pp. 362–86.

27. See Saunders (2018), pp. 324–44.

NOTES pp. [205–217]

28. Although the origins of the Alliance Party lie in unionism, it now refuses to be drawn on the issue of unionism versus reunification and presents itself to the electorate with considerable success as a non-sectarian movement.

29. This included eight UUP seats, as they took the Conservative whip in the House of Commons until 1972.

30. There was then a small recovery, but even in 2019 only 5.5 per cent of Conservative seats came from outside England. See Pilling & Cracknell (2021).

31. See Saunders (2018), p. 80.

32. See Butler & Kitzinger (1976), p. 38.

33. *Hansard*, HC Deb. 18 March 1975, vol. 888, col. 1460.

34. See Ward (2021), p. 10.

35. See HMRC (n.d.). No regional breakdown of export of services was published.

36. See Ward (2020), p. 14.

37. See Brien (2020), p. 15.

38. See Crowson (2007), p. 51.

39. The last to join was Croatia in 2013. Others are still in negotiation.

40. Quoted in Saunders (2018), p. 254.

41. The comments on the inhabitants of the other three nations received the biggest laughs from English audiences when the song was performed. They included 'gems' such as referring to Welshmen as untrustworthy miner-monkeys.

42. Neither Ireland nor Scotland were part of the Roman Empire; Norman rule did not extend to Scotland, Ireland or most of Wales; nor did Angevin rule, although a small part of Ireland was affected after 1169 (none of it in Northern Ireland); in 1688 the English parliament offered the English crown to William and Mary, while the Scottish parliament awarded them the Scottish crown (there was no British crown at that time). The speech was delivered on 20 September 1988 at the College of Europe. It can be found at https://www.margaretthatcher.org/document/107332 (accessed 1 November 2022).

43. See Carter et al. (1998), p. 472.

pp. [219–226]

NOTES

44. In 2010 the population of England was 52.64 million, while that of the UK was 62.51 million. Net migration at this time, very high by historical standards, averaged around 300,000. This number was in fact exceeded in 2022, when net migration in the 12 months to June was recorded as 504,000. However, this very high figure was mainly due to one-off factors including the return of overseas students after COVID together with refugees from Ukraine and Hong Kong.

45. See the annual reports of British Social Attitudes, available at https://www.bsa.natcen.ac.uk. In these years, England's population was roughly 84 per cent of the UK total, so any random survey result was bound to be heavily biased towards the responses in England.

46. See Curtice et al. (2018), p. 17.

47. Nigel Farage became UKIP's leader in 2006. An effective public speaker, he focused relentlessly on the immigration figures.

48. The Liberal Party had merged with the Social Democratic Party in 1988 to form the Liberal Democrats.

49. UKIP also took almost all the votes of the British National Party (BNP), a neo-fascist party that—despite its name—had received 98.4 per cent of its support from English voters in the 2005 elections. The BNP electorate itself included many who had previously voted Conservative.

50. UKIP also performed well in Wales, but it did not succeed in replacing Labour as the party with the most votes.

51. Assuming a 70 per cent turnout, even a tiny 2 per cent margin in England could not be overturned without an unlikely 13 per cent margin in the three other nations combined.

8. BREXIT

1. See Cameron (2013), p. 7. See also Shipman (2016), pp. 7–8.

2. See *The Times*, 1 October 2015.

3. The others were (a) economic governance, (b) competitiveness and (c) sovereignty.

4. Letter from the Prime Minister of the UK to the President of the European Council, 10 November 2015.

339

NOTES

pp. [227–237]

5. See European Council, 'Concerning a New Settlement for the United Kingdom within the European Union', European Council Meeting, 18–19 February 2016, EUCO 1/16, Annex 1, p. 23.

6. There was also an agreement that child benefit paid to children outside the UK could be indexed to the cost of living in those member-states, thereby reducing the cost to the British government.

7. See Jones, M. (2017), pp. 1–5.

8. This number uses the official figure of one counting area for all of Northern Ireland, rather than the unofficial figure of eighteen.

9. Conservative Party rules for choosing a new leader require a ballot of sitting MPs, in rounds of voting until only two names are left. Unless there is an indisputable frontrunner, these are then given to the party membership for a final selection. May and Andrea Leadsom were the final two in 2016, but Leadsom withdrew before the members could vote. This left May as the winner.

10. See YouGov (2018).

11. 'Confidence and supply' avoided the need for a formal coalition, but guaranteed Prime Minister May the votes needed for crucial measures. With its ten seats following the 2017 election, the DUP provided just enough to take the Conservatives past 50 per cent of the 650 seats in parliament.

12. See Joint Report (2017), para 49.

13. All chairpersons have represented English constituencies, as have all but one of the deputy chairpersons. The exception is David Jones, who was appointed in 2020 while representing a Welsh constituency.

14. Johnson was initially undecided on whether to support Brexit and had actually drafted an article on 19 February arguing for remain, which is reproduced in Shipman (2016), pp. 616–18. Two days later, however, he declared for Brexit, and his participation in the campaign was judged to be crucial by Conservative Party members.

15. See *Hansard*, HC Deb. 25 July 2019, vol. 663, col. 1458.

16. Even without their twenty MPs in London, English constituencies gave the Conservative Party 325 seats—just enough for a majority in the Commons, assuming the speaker did not vote.

340

NOTES

17. In theory, the transition period could have been extended if both sides agreed to do so by July 2020, but the UK showed no interest.

18. See European Commission (2021), p. 2.

19. See Paun (2018), pp. 1–23, and Cabinet Office (2020), p. 5.

20. The original draft was in conflict with that part of the withdrawal agreement dealing with Northern Ireland, leading the British government to state that it was prepared to break international law 'in a very specific and limited way'. See *Hansard*, HC Deb. 8 September 2020, vol. 679, col. 509.

21. It also created a new body (British–Irish Council) to improve relations between the UK and the Republic of Ireland.

22. The new articles of the constitution were put to a referendum in Ireland in June 1998 and were supported by 94 per cent of those who voted.

23. See D'Arcy & Ruane (2018), pp. 3–14.

24. The London School of Economics has a large collection of leaflets and pamphlets relating to the 2016 referendum, available at https://digital.library.lse.ac.uk/collections/brexit.

25. At the time, Johnson was still Mayor of London and had just committed to the Brexit campaign. See BBC News, 'Boris Johnson: Brexit would not affect Irish border', 29 February 2016.

26. See UK Prime Minister's Office & Department for Exiting the European Union, 'The government's negotiating objectives for exiting the EU: PM speech', 17 January 2017.

27. Senator Mitchell, President Clinton's Special Envoy for Northern Ireland, had chaired the talks leading to the GFA in 1998.

28. Not, however, the other way round. The preamble to the protocol had noted that 'nothing in this Protocol prevents the United Kingdom from ensuring unfettered market access for goods moving from Northern Ireland to the rest of the United Kingdom's internal market.'

29. The DUP First Minister did withdraw in February 2022, leading to a collapse in the power-sharing Northern Ireland executive.

30. See HM Government (2021).

31. Trade data subsequently released by the Central Statistics Office of Ireland confirmed these shifts. Exports of goods from the Republic

to Northern Ireland in 2021 rose by 54 per cent compared with 2020 volumes, while imports to the Republic from Northern Ireland rose by 65 per cent over the same period.

32. The process would then need to be repeated subsequently (four years if consent was given by a simple majority and eight years if it had cross-community support).

33. The other possibility (that the Assembly might withhold consent) would lead to a two-year period during which all parties would be committed to finding a solution that would not lead to a hard border on the island of Ireland. Given the difficulty of achieving that without the trade provisions of the Protocol, a cynic might be forgiven for assuming the British government would not wish to see the DUP and its allies holding a majority in the Northern Ireland Assembly in December 2024.

34. According to the Office of National Statistics (ONS), net births were barely positive in England and Northern Ireland and substantially negative in Scotland and Wales, leading to deaths exceeding births for the whole of the UK. See ONS (2015); and ONS (2021).

35. Strictly speaking, the new rules applied to European Economic Area (EEA) states plus Switzerland. The EEA consists of all EU states plus Iceland, Liechtenstein and Norway.

36. This was especially the case for so-called Tier 2 immigration (skilled workers), which was no longer capped.

37. The other possibility to sustain population growth was migration from England to the other three nations, but this was not something that the devolved governments could easily influence.

38. See UK Trade Policy Observatory (2021).

39. There was also an agreement with Japan (the Comprehensive Economic Partnership Agreement, or CEPA), which was touted as 'new' when signed, as the EU–Japan free trade agreement had not yet become operational. However, there are very few differences between the CEPA and the EU version, so it is similar to the UK's other 'grandfathered' trade deals.

40. See Office for Budget Responsibility (2021), p. 1.

41. Calculated at purchasing power parity (PPP) exchange rates.

pp. [254–262]   NOTES

42. See World Bank, 'World Development Indicators: GDP, PPP (current international $) for 2020'.

9.   THE UNMAKING OF THE UK

1. The assumption that all those of Catholic heritage in Northern Ireland were in favour of reunification was probably a fair reflection of reality in the 1920s, but would need to be challenged in due course. By contrast, the assumption that almost all those of Protestant heritage are in favour of union with Great Britain is still, broadly speaking, correct.

2. Excepted powers, such as foreign affairs, could never be devolved. Reserved powers, such as broadcasting, could in future be devolved.

3. When a new building was completed in 1932, parliament met at Stormont on the outskirts of Belfast; therefore the Northern Irish legislature is often known simply as Stormont.

4. See Walker, G. S. (2004), pp. 54–80.

5. See Newman (2020), pp. 166–241.

6. Quoted in Jackson, A. (2011), p. 468.

7. It was 42.3% according to the 2021 census, far ahead of the combined figure for those giving their religion as either Presbyterian Church in Ireland (16.7%), Church of Ireland (11.5%), or Methodist Church in Ireland (2.3%). Even with 'Other Christian' added (6.8%), the non-Catholic community (37.4%) was still smaller than the Catholic one.

8. See NISRA (2013), p. 1. 'Other Christian' excludes Catholics.

9. These numbers add up to more than 100, because some respondents prefer to use multiple identities. The categories for 'Northern Irish' were 'Northern Irish only' (19.78%), 'British and Northern Irish only' (7.95%), 'Irish and Northern Irish only' (1.76%), 'British, Irish and Northern Irish only' (1.47%) and 'other combination of British/Irish/Northern Irish/English/Scottish/Welsh only' (0.62%). The proportion calling themselves 'British only' was 31.86%, while 'Irish only' was 29.13%.

10. A significant minority of supporters of the UUP gave 'Northern Irish' as their primary identifier. See Hennessey et al. (2019), p. 133.

343

NOTES

pp. [262–267]

11. That is, until the DUP itself was challenged after Brexit by both the revival of the UUP and the emergence of an even harder version of unionism, the Traditional Unionist Voice (TUV).

12. Since the GFA, the assembly has been suspended by the British government on several occasions. The most serious suspension was October 2002 to May 2007, when the DUP withdrew from the Northern Ireland executive.

13. As the DUP won twenty-eight seats to Sinn Féin's twenty-seven, it did retain the post of First Minister. Compared with the previous election in May 2016, the DUP had lost ten seats, but the number of seats in that election was larger (108 in 2016; ninety in 2017). On a 'like-for-like' basis, the loss was still five seats.

14. The share of votes refers to first preferences, as Northern Ireland uses a system of proportional representation for its assembly elections.

15. The party's official position was that it would only enter the executive (without which the assembly cannot function) if the protocol were scrapped.

16. Macpherson claimed to have 'discovered' the original poems and translated them himself, but it was an open secret that he was the author.

17. Quoted in Duncan, I. (2007), p. 60.

18. See Sutherland (1995), p. 258.

19. See, for example, Arata (2001), Craig (2001) and Nairn (1977), pp. 114–17.

20. Liberals won a majority of seats in Scotland in every election from 1832 to 1895. See Torrance (2021), Appendix 2.

21. See Lloyd-Jones (2014), pp. 862–87, and Finlay (1994), Chapter 1.

22. See Torrance (2020), pp. 1–5.

23. The Goschen formula, drawn up in 1888, used population shares to allocate 80 per cent to England and Wales, 9 per cent to Ireland and the rest to Scotland. It was not updated until 1978, when Joel Barnett, a civil servant at the Treasury, introduced a different formula that allocated increases or decreases in public spending according to population shares, while leaving the baseline unchanged. See House of Lords (2009), Chapter 3.

pp. [267–270]　　　NOTES

24. See Jackson, B. (2020), Chapter 1.
25. This was Robert Balfour, 3rd Earl of Balfour and the nephew of former Conservative Prime Minister Arthur Balfour.
26. The Fraser of Allander Institute for research on the Scottish economy, based in Glasgow, was created to take advantage of this change in mood, and the sophistication of work on the Scottish economy increased considerably as a result. See, for example, Fraser of Allander Institute (1978).
27. This was not as innocent as it might sound. The electoral register in Scotland was notoriously unreliable, with many dead people still on the list. In addition, the amendment had the effect of counting every abstention as a 'no' vote.
28. Kilbrandon Report (1973), Vol. I, p. 335.
29. This referendum was not subject to the infamous condition that 40 per cent of the registered electorate vote in favour. This was just as well, as the hurdle was met for the first question, but not the second. (The turnout was the same, at 60 per cent, but the majority was smaller.)
30. The exceptions were Orkney (47.4 per cent in favour) and Dumfries & Galloway (48.8 per cent in favour).
31. The D'Hondt system, developed by a Belgian statistician in the nineteenth century, allocates the quota (Q) of seats according to the formula $Q=V/(S+1)$, where 'V' stands for party votes and 'S' the number of seats at the start of each 'round'. Since 'S' should be zero at the start of the process, the formula in the first round collapses to $Q=V$ and the first seat in each region goes to the party with the most votes (in the second round, the denominator for the winning party is now '2', so that its vote is halved and the next most popular party has a good chance of winning a seat). In Scotland, however, the act establishing a Scottish assembly ruled that 'S' in the first round should be equal to the number of constituency seats won by each party.
32. The white paper asserted that Scotland would retain the pound sterling; that fiscal resources, including those from North Sea oil, would be sufficient to cover the fiscal gap; and that Scotland would 'automatically' become a new state within the EU.

345

pp. [271–275]

33. In a survey conducted by Deltapoll in 2021, nearly two thirds gave their primary identity as 'Scottish' and less than 30 per cent as 'British'. The trends in response to this question from 1979 to 2012 can be found in *British Social Attitudes Survey 30*.

34. The referendum was the first time that this younger voting age was used; it was subsequently widened to apply to all Scottish elections.

35. The trends in support for independence since 1999 can be found in the *Scottish Social Attitudes Survey*. The results are summarised in Curtice & Montagu (2020), p. 2.

36. See Hayward & McEwen (2022), pp. 1–29.

37. The Scottish government in 2022 had asked the UK supreme court to rule on the legality of an independence referendum that did not have UK government approval, but had anticipated an unfavourable response by declaring that—if necessary—it would fight the next general election on a platform containing only one policy (independence for Scotland), thus hoping to convert the election itself into a referendum.

38. See Morgan (1971), pp. 153–71.

39. The Cymru Fydd (New Wales) movement had been founded in 1886 and gained enough support in parliament among Welsh and Scottish MPs to introduce a Government of Wales bill in 1922, but it failed to pass. For the debate, see *Hansard*, HC Deb. 28 April 1922, vol. 153, cols 929–42.

40. The first specifically Welsh act of the Westminster parliament was the 1881 Sunday Closing (Wales) Act, in recognition of the opposition to alcohol consumption among many Nonconformists.

41. A convert to Catholicism, Saunders Lewis was a controversial figure. Born in England to a Welsh-speaking family, he had deeply conservative views, flirted with fascism before and even during the Second World War, and was uninterested in socioeconomic conditions. Yet he was a brilliant writer and orator, whose powers of persuasion were considerable. See Brooks (2017), pp. 119–25.

42. Quoted in Jones, D. (1996), p. 31.

43. Only in 1983, 2010 and 2015 did the share fall below 40 per cent, while between 1945 and 1966 it was close to 60 per cent. See Pilling & Cracknell (2021).

pp. [276–287]   NOTES

44. See Kilbrandon Report (1973), Vol. I, p. 110.

45. This would be the pattern of all future elections, with Labour winning half or nearly half of all seats, while Plaid Cymru and the Conservative Party competed for second place. Labour would then form the government, either in coalition or as a minority, and hold the post of First Minister.

46. Although the turnout was low (35.6 per cent), nearly two thirds voted in favour of the change.

47. See Independence Commission (2020).

48. Wales signed the BOGA declaration at the COP-26 summit in Glasgow, hosted by the British government.

49. The act also included Berwick-upon-Tweed in the definition of England, but that part has never been revoked.

50. The list included Alexander Pope, Sir Thomas Gresham, Inigo Jones, Milton, Shakespeare, John Locke, Sir Isaac Newton, Francis Bacon, King Alfred, the Black Prince, Elizabeth I, William III, Raleigh, Drake, John Hampden and Sir John Barnard. Strictly speaking, none of these heroes were 'British', since they had all died before the creation of Great Britain, but this is unlikely to have troubled William Kent.

51. See Kilbrandon Report (1973), Vol. II, pp. 84–108.

52. See Sandford (2021), p. 3.

53. A white paper in 2022 outlined the UK government's plans to push ahead with further directly elected 'metro' mayors in England. See HM Government (2022), pp. 234–44.

54. UK Prime Minister's Office & Office of the Secretary of State for Scotland, 'Scottish Independence Referendum: statement by the Prime Minister', 19 September 2014.

55. The Scottish Parliament, 'Finance and Constitution Committee: Session 5', 23 September 2020. This was evidence given by Dr. Emily Lydgate.

56. See Brien (2022), pp. 5–37.

57. See *Hansard*, HC Deb. 16 September 2020, vol. 680, col. 348.

58. See YouGov (2019).

347

NOTES

pp. [291–301]

10. ENGLISH QUESTIONS

1. See, for example, Kagarlitsky (2018).
2. See Gildas (1999), Part II, p. 23.
3. See Bede (1907), p. 35.
4. Britishness may have been driven out of England, but not the Britons. See Ward-Perkins (2000), pp. 513–33.
5. The use of the term 'Anglo-Saxon' seems to have originated abroad in order to distinguish the Saxons of England from the Saxons on the Continent. See Reynolds, S. (1985), pp. 395–414.
6. See Hadley & Richards (2021), p. 227.
7. Alfred did, however, advance significantly Bede's notion of Englishness. See Foot (1996), pp. 25–49.
8. See Wormald (1983), pp. 120–3.
9. See Savage (1996), 1052 CE.
10. On the strength of Englishness before the Norman conquest, see Thomas (2003), pp. 20–31.
11. Ibid., pp. 70–82.
12. See Molyneaux (2014), pp. 721–37.
13. See Carpenter (2003), p. 15.
14. See Campbell (2008), Tables 15 and 16, pp. 927, 931.
15. Ibid., Table 16, p. 931.
16. This is the origin of the Union Jack, which would later have the cross of St. Patrick incorporated into it after the Act of Union with Ireland; Wales was never included.
17. In 1943, for example, Denis Brogan (himself a Scot) published a book entitled *The English People: Impressions and Observations.* On reading it, however, it soon becomes clear—despite its title—that it is designed to reduce the hostility towards Great Britain and its empire on the part of a US population sceptical of joining the war effort. In his own words (p. 12), 'An American might wish for a better, more powerful, more amiable and more understandable ally. But what he has got is England...'
18. See Fryer (1984), pp. 120–6.
19. See Whyte (2006), pp. 16–18.

pp. [301–308] NOTES

20. Strictly speaking, it was a British colony at the time. However, it had been an English colony for a very long time before 1707.
21. See Sherwood (2013), p. 174.
22. See Kumar (2015), p. 81.
23. See Kumar (2003), p. 202; Paxman (1998), Chapter 6.
24. See Butterfield (1945), pp. 138–9.
25. See Ford (1907), p. 43.
26. See, for example, Winder (2017).
27. Quoted in Baucom (1999), p. 20.
28. See Orwell (1947), p. 12.
29. With effect from 18 April 1949.
30. The non-white population just after the Second World War was around 100,000. See Owen (1995), p. 1.
31. The first postwar ship to bring large numbers of migrants was SS *Ormonde*, which sailed from Jamaica to Liverpool in March 1947. Dealing with eleven stowaways on board, a Liverpool magistrate said, 'It is a thousand pities that Mr. Isaacs [Minister of Labour] is not here this morning, seeing that they have to import Italian labour into this country while there are British subjects still unemployed in the Dominions.' (*The Times*, 2 April 1947, p. 2). The men were sentenced to one day in prison, after which they were free to look for work.
32. See Fryer (1984).
33. Powell had also written an anonymous letter to *The Times* in 1964, in which he referred to 'coloured immigration in the last decade [having] inflicted social and political damage that will take decades to obliterate'. See Webster (2005), pp. 171–8.
34. Powell, who had been a classical scholar, was referencing a prophecy in Virgil's *Aeneid*.
35. Those who identified as 'Asian or British Asian' were given a choice of Indian, Pakistani, Bangladeshi or 'Any other Asian background'. Those who identified as 'Black or Black British' had the choice of 'Caribbean', 'African' or 'any other Black background'.
36. Not, however, in Wales, where in the 2021 census it became possible to identify as 'Black Welsh' or 'Asian Welsh', while in Scotland (which

349

NOTES

pp. [309–314]

held the census late, in 2022) it was possible to identify as 'Scottish Asian', 'Scottish African', 'Scottish Caribbean', 'Black Scottish' or 'Scottish Arab'.

37. For the case of Bernie Grant, see Paxman (1998), p. 74.
38. See Modood (1997), pp. 328–31.
39. These are the estimates of the Office of National Statistics. See ONS (2022).
40. See Uberoi & Tunnicliffe (2021), pp. 1–23.
41. See Byrne, B. (2007), pp. 139–55.
42. See, for example, Hitchens (1999) and Scruton (2000).
43. The most important have been the British Election Study since 1964, the British Social Attitudes Survey since 1992 and YouGov's Future of England Survey since 2011.
44. See Henderson & Wyn Jones (2021), p. 56.
45. Speech delivered at the Commonwealth Club, London, 27 February 2007.
46. Brown also chaired a commission on Britain's future that published a report in December 2022 with a series of recommendations designed to strength the Union. See Report of the Commission on Britain's Future (2022).
47. Brown, for example, claimed that 'Britain led the world in abolishing the slave trade' by passing legislation in support of abolition in 1807, ignoring (or conveniently forgetting?) that Denmark had done the same in 1793, France in 1794 (reversed in 1802) and the United States in 1807 (three weeks before the UK). Haiti, of course, had abolished both slavery and the slave trade long before then.
48. See Russell & Sheldon (2018).
49. See Schütze (2018), pp. 1–26.
50. Northern Ireland was much more complicated in view of the sectarian history of the parliament established in 1921. However, the assembly established by the Good Friday Agreement in 1998, with its power-sharing executive, has been broadly welcomed.
51. These constitutional questions are tackled head-on in Bogdanor (2019).
52. See Bogdanor (1998), p. 291, n. 131.

NOTES

53. See speech by Adam Price to the Centre on Constitutional Change, University of Edinburgh, 26 June 2019, in which he argued for a pooling of sovereignty by the three nations, similar to that adopted since 1944 by the Benelux countries (Belgium, Netherlands, Luxembourg).

54. Many books and articles since Brexit have been devoted to this theme. See, in particular, Dorling & Tomlinson (2019), Wellings (2019) and Ali (2022).

55. See Scottish Government (2021), pp. 1–36. The most important exports to the rest of the UK in 2019 were financial & insurance services (£9bn); utilities (£7.3bn—mainly electricity); wholesale & retail (£6.6bn); professional, scientific & technical (£4.1bn); and food & beverages (£3.4bn). Official statistics on Scottish exports do not currently include oil and gas from the North Sea, although this would change after independence.

56. See Heffer (1999), p. 12.

57. As explained in the 1978 Vienna Convention on Succession of States in Respect of Treaties.

58. For a good summary of both views of Englishness, see Leddy-Owen (2014), pp. 1123–38.

59. See Denham & Devine (2018), pp. 621–30.

60. UKIP, of course, did position itself as an English national party, but as of the early 2020s is almost defunct.

BIBLIOGRAPHY

Akenson, D. H. (1997). *If the Irish Ran the World: Montserrat, 1630–1730.* Montreal: McGill-Queen's University Press.

Ali, A. (2022). *Brexit and Liberal Democracy: Populism, Sovereignty, and the Nation-State.* London: Routledge.

Anderson, A. O. (1963). 'Anglo-Scottish Relations from Constantine to William', *The Scottish Historical Review,* 42.133: 1–20.

Anderson, C. J., and Hecht, J. D. (2018). 'The Preference for Europe: Public Opinion about European Integration since 1952', *European Union Politics,* 19.4: 617–38.

Arata, S. (2001). 'Scott's Pageants: The Example of "Kenilworth"', *Studies in Romanticism,* 40.1: 99–107.

Avakov, A. V. (2010). *Two Thousand Years of Economic Statistics: World Population, GDP and PPP.* New York, NY: Algora.

Balfour Report (1926). *The Imperial Conference of 1926.* London: HMSO.

Barrow, G. W. S. (1976). *Robert Bruce and the Community of the Realm of Scotland.* Edinburgh: Edinburgh University Press.

Bartlett, T. (2005). 'Ireland, Empire, and Union, 1690–1801', in Kenny, K. (ed.), *Ireland and the British Empire.* Oxford: Oxford University Press.

Baucom, I. (1999). *Out of Place: Englishness, Empire, and the Locations of Identity.* Princeton, NJ: Princeton University Press.

BIBLIOGRAPHY

Beckles, H. (1990). 'A "riotous and unruly lot": Irish Indentured Servants and Freemen in the English West Indies, 1644–1713', *The William and Mary Quarterly*, 47.4: 503–22.

Bede (1907). *Ecclesiastical History of England*. London: Bell.

Benner, D. (2021). 'King of the Hill', *HistoryNet* (November): 63–71.

Biggar, H. P. (2010). *Precursors of Jacques Cartier*. Charleston, NC: Nabu Press.

Bogdanor, V. (1998). 'Devolution: The Constitutional Aspects', in Beatson, J. (ed.), *Constitutional Reform in the United Kingdom: Practice and Principles*. Oxford: Hart.

——— (2019). *Beyond Brexit: Britain's Unprotected Constitution*. London: I. B. Tauris.

Bonner, E. (1999). 'Scotland's "Auld Alliance" with France, 1295–1560', *History*, 84.273: 5–30.

Bowen, H. V. (2016). 'Asiatic interactions: India, the East India Company, and the Welsh economy, c.1750–1830', in Bowen, H. V. (ed.), *Wales and the British Overseas Empire: Interactions and Influences, 1650–1830*. Manchester: Manchester University Press.

Bowen, I. (1908). *The Statutes of Wales*. London: Fisher Unwin.

Brien, P. (2020). 'EU Funding in the UK', House of Commons Library Briefing Paper 7847: 1–45.

——— (2022). 'The UK Shared Prosperity Fund', House of Commons Library Research Briefing 08597: 1–41.

Brogan, D. W. (1943). *The English People*. New York, NY: Knopf.

Brooks, S. (2017). *Why Wales Never Was: The Failure of Welsh Nationalism*. Cardiff: University of Wales Press.

Brough, G. (2017). *Rise and Fall of Owain Glyndŵr—England, France and the Welsh Rebellion in the Late Middle Ages*. London: I. B. Tauris.

Bulmer-Thomas, I. (1965). *The Growth of the British Party System: Vol. 1*. London: John Baker.

Bulmer-Thomas, V. (2012). *The Economic History of the Caribbean since the Napoleonic Wars*. Cambridge: Cambridge University Press.

Butler, W. F. (1913). *Sir William Butler: An Autobiography*. New York, NY: Scribner's.

Butler, D. and Kitzinger, U. (1976). *The 1975 Referendum*. London: Palgrave Macmillan.

BIBLIOGRAPHY

Butterfield, H. (1945). *The Englishman and his History*. Cambridge: Cambridge University Press.

Byrne, B. (2007). 'Crisis of Identity? Englishness, Britishness, and Whiteness', in MacPhee, G. and Poddar, P. (eds), *Empire and After: Englishness in Postcolonial Perspective*. Oxford: Berghahn.

Byrne, F. J. (1973). *Irish Kings and High-Kings*. London: Batsford.

Cabinet Office (2020). *Frameworks Analysis 2020: Breakdown of areas of EU law that intersect with devolved competence in Scotland, Wales and Northern Ireland*. London: HMSO.

Cameron, D. (2013). *EU Speech at Bloomberg*. Cabinet Office: HMSO.

Campbell, B. (2008). 'Benchmarking Medieval Economic Development: England, Wales, Scotland, and Ireland, c.1290', *The Economic History Review*, 61.4: 896–945.

Carpenter, D. (2003). *The Struggle for Mastery: Britain 1066–1284*. London: Allen Lane.

—— (2020). *Henry III*. New Haven, CT: Yale University Press.

Carr, A. D. (1989). 'Anglo-Welsh Relations', in Jones, M. and Vale, M. G. A. (eds), *England and her Neighbours, 1066–1453: Essays in Honour of Pierre Chaplais*. London: Hambledon.

—— (1995). *Medieval Wales*. Basingstoke: Macmillan.

Carter, N., Evans, M., Alderman, K. and Gorham, S. (1998). 'Europe, Goldsmith and the Referendum Party', *Parliamentary Affairs*, 51.3: 470–86.

Catterall, P. (2018). 'The Plural Society: Labour and the Commonwealth Idea 1900–1964', *The Journal of Imperial and Commonwealth History*, 46.5: 821–44.

Chatterton-Newman, R. (1983). *Brian Boru, King of Ireland*. Dublin: Anvil Books.

Coffey, D. (2018). '"The Right to Shoot Himself": Secession in the British Commonwealth of Nations', *The Journal of Legal History*, 39.2: 117–39.

Colley, L. (1996). *Britons: Forging the Nation, 1707–1837*. London: Vintage.

Coupland, R. (1954). *Welsh and Scottish Nationalism: A Study*. London: Collins.

BIBLIOGRAPHY

Craig, C. (2001). 'Scott's Staging of the Nation', *Studies in Romanticism*, 40.1: 13–28.

Cróinín, D. O. (1995). *Early Medieval Ireland, 400–1200*. London: Longman.

Crooks, P. (2011). 'State of the Union: Perspectives on English Imperialism in the Late Middle Ages', *Past & Present*, 212: 3–42.

Crowson, N. J. (2007). *The Conservative Party and European Integration since 1945: At the Heart of Europe*. London: Routledge.

Cullen, L. M. (1994). 'The Irish Diaspora of the Seventeenth and Eighteenth Centuries', in Canny, N. P. (1994), *Europeans on the Move: Studies on European Migration, 1500–1800*. Oxford: Oxford University Press.

Curtice, J. and Montagu, I. (2020). *Is Brexit fuelling support for independence?*. Edinburgh: ScotCen Social Research.

Curtice, J., Phillips, D., Phillips, M. and Perry, J. (2018). *British Social Attitudes: The 35th Report*. London: The National Centre for Social Research.

D'Arcy, M., and Ruane, F. (2018). *The Belfast/Good Friday Agreement, the Island of Ireland Economy and Brexit,* London: British Academy.

Davies, J. (2007). *A History of Wales*. London: Penguin.

Davies, N. (1999). *The Isles: A History*. London: Papermac.

Davies, R. R. (1978). *Lordship and Society in the March of Wales, 1282–1400*. Oxford: Clarendon.

———— (1990). *Domination and Conquest: The Experience of Ireland, Scotland and Wales 1100–1300*. Cambridge: Cambridge University Press.

———— (2000). *The First English Empire: Power and Identity in the British Isles 1093–1343*. Oxford: Oxford University Press.

Davis, L. (1998). *Acts of Union: Scotland and the Literary Negotiation of the British Nation, 1707–1830*. Stanford, CA: Stanford University Press.

Defoe, D. (1709). *The History of the Union of Great Britain*. Edinburgh: printed by the heirs and successors of Andrew Anderson.

Denham, J. and Devine, D. (2018). 'England, Englishness and the Labour Party', *The Political Quarterly*, 89.4: 621–30.

BIBLIOGRAPHY

Devine, T. M. (2003). *Scotland's Empire, 1600–1815*. London: Allen Lane.

———— (2015). 'Did Slavery make Scotia Great?', in Devine, T. M. (ed.), *Recovering Scotland's Slavery Past: The Caribbean Connection*. Edinburgh: Edinburgh University Press.

———— (2016). *Independence or Union: Scotland's Past and Scotland's Present*. London: Allen Lane.

Devine, T. M. and Rössner, P. R. (2011). 'Scots in the Atlantic Economy, 1600–1800', in MacKenzie, J. M. and Devine, T. M. (eds), *Scotland and the British Empire*. Oxford: Oxford University Press.

Dickson, D. (2005). *Old World Colony: Cork and South Munster, 1630–1830*. Madison, WI: University of Wisconsin Press.

Dorling, D. and Tomlinson, S. (2019). *Rule Britannia: Brexit and the End of Empire*. London: Biteback.

Duffill, M. (2004). 'The Africa trade from the ports of Scotland, 1706–66', *Slavery & Abolition*, 25.3: 102–22.

Duncan, A. A. M. (1975). *Scotland: The Making of the Kingdom*. New York: Barnes & Noble.

———— (2002). *The Kingship of the Scots, 842–1292: Succession and Independence*. Edinburgh: Edinburgh University Press.

Duncan, I. (2007). *Scott's Shadow: The Novel in Romantic Edinburgh*. Princeton, NJ: Princeton University Press.

Durham, J. G. (1839). *Report on the Affairs of British North America*. London: HMSO.

Electoral Commission (2019). 'Results and Turnout at the 2014 European Parliamentary Elections. London' (6 Aug. 2019).

Elkins, C. (2022). *Legacy of Violence: A History of the British Empire*. New York, NY: Knopf.

Esler, G. (2021). *How Britain Ends: English Nationalism and the Rebirth of Four Nations*. London: Head of Zeus.

European Commission (2021). 'UK–EU Trade and Cooperation Agreement' (30 Apr. 2021).

Evans, C. P. (2010). *Slave Wales: The Welsh and Atlantic Slavery, 1660–1850*. Cardiff: University of Wales Press.

———— (2016). 'Wales, Munster and the English South West: contrasting articulations with the Atlantic world', in Bowen, H. V. (ed.), *Wales*

BIBLIOGRAPHY

and the British overseas empire: Interactions and influences, 1650–1830, Manchester: Manchester University Press.

Finlay, R. J. (1994). *Independent and Free: Scottish Politics and the Origins of the Scottish National Party 1918–1945.* Edinburgh: J. Donald.

Foot, S. (1996). 'The Making of Angelcynn: English Identity before the Norman Conquest', *Transactions of the Royal Historical Society,* 6: 25–49.

Ford, F. M. (1907). *The Spirit of the People: An Analysis of the English Mind.* London: Rivers.

Frame, R. (1989). 'England and Ireland, 1171–1399', in Jones, M. and Vale, M. G. A. (eds), *England and her Neighbours, 1066–1453: Essays in Honour of Pierre Chaplais.* London: Hambledon.

——— (1998). *Ireland and Britain: 1170–1450.* London: Hambledon.

Fraser of Allander Institute (1978). *Input–Output Tables of the Scottish Economy.* Glasgow: Fraser of Allander Institute.

Fry, M. (2001). *The Scottish Empire.* East Linton: Tuckwell.

——— (2006). *The Union: England, Scotland and the Treaty of 1707.* Edinburgh: Birlinn.

Fryer, P. (1984). *Staying Power: The History of Black People in Britain.* London: Pluto.

Fusaro, A. (1979). 'Two Faces of British Nationalism: The Scottish National Party & Plaid Cymru Compared', *Polity,* 11.3: 362–86.

Gaitskell, H. (1962). 'Speech by Hugh Gaitskell against UK membership of the Common Market', in Labour Party, *Texts of speeches made at the 1962 Labour Party Conference by the Rt. Hon. Hugh Gaitskell M.P. and the Rt. Hon. George Brown M.P. together with the policy statement accepted by Conference,* 40: 3–23.

Geoghegan, P. M. (2001). *The Irish Act of Union: A Study in High Politics, 1798–1801.* Dublin: Gill & Macmillan.

Gerald of Wales (1978). *The Journey through Wales and the Description of Wales.* Harmondsworth: Penguin.

Gibb, A. D. (1937). *Scottish Empire.* London: MacLehose.

Gildas (1999). *On the Ruin of Britain.* Champaign, IL: Project Gutenberg.

Gillingham, J. (2000). *The English in the Twelfth Century: Imperialism, National Identity, and Political Values.* Woodbridge: Boydell.

BIBLIOGRAPHY

———— (2001). *The Angevin Empire*. London: Arnold.

———— (2014). *Conquests, Catastrophe and Recovery: Britain and Ireland 1066–1485*. London: Vintage.

Goodare, J. (1998). 'The Statutes of Iona in Context', *Scottish Historical Review*, 77.203: 31–57.

Green, J. (1989). 'Anglo-Scottish Relations, 1066–1174', in Jones, M. and Vale, M. G. A. (eds), *England and her Neighbours, 1066–1453: Essays in Honour of Pierre Chaplais*. London: Hambledon.

Hadley, D. M. and Richards, J. (2021). *The Viking Great Army and the Making of England*. London: Thames and Hudson.

Hamilton, D. J. (2005). *Scotland, the Caribbean and the Atlantic World, 1750–1820*. Manchester: Manchester University Press.

Harris, B. (2010). 'The Anglo-Scottish Treaty of Union, 1707 in 2007: Defending the Revolution, Defeating the Jacobites', *Journal of British Studies*, 49.1: 28–46.

Hayton, D. W. (2007). 'Henry Maxwell, M.P., Author of "An Essay upon an Union of Ireland with England (1703)"', *Eighteenth-Century Ireland / Iris an dá chultúr*, 22: 28–63.

Hayward, K. and McEwen, N. (2022). *An EU Border across Britain: Scotland's Borders after Independence*. London: UK in a Changing Europe.

Hechter, M. (1975). *Internal Colonialism: The Celtic Fringe in British National Development, 1536–1966*. Berkeley, CA: University of California Press.

Hedges, B. (1976). 'The Final Four Years: from Opposition to Endorsement', in Hoinville, G. and Jowell, R. (eds), *Britain into Europe*. London: Croom-Helm.

Heffer, S. (1999). *Nor Shall my Sword: The Reinvention of England*. London: Weidenfeld & Nicolson.

Hegarty, N. (2011). *The Story of Ireland: A History of the Irish People*. New York, NY: Thomas Dunne.

Henderson, A. and Wyn Jones, R. (2021). *Englishness: The Political Force Transforming Britain*. Oxford: Oxford University Press.

Hennessey, T., Braniff, M., McAuley, J. W., Tonge, J. and Whiting, S. A. (2019). *The Ulster Unionist Party: Country before Party?*. Oxford: Oxford University Press.

BIBLIOGRAPHY

Hitchens, P. (1999). *The Abolition of Britain: The British Cultural Revolution from Lady Chatterley to Tony Blair.* London: Quartet.

HM Government (2021). *Northern Ireland Protocol: the way forward.* Command Paper 502, July 2021.

HM Government (2022). *Levelling Up the United Kingdom.* Command Paper 604, Feb. 2022.

HMRC (n.d.). *Regional Trade Statistics.* London: HMSO.

House of Lords (2009). *Select Committee on the Barnett Formula – First Report.* Select Committee on the Barnett Formula Committee Publications, Session 2008–9.

Hudson, B. (1994). 'William the Conqueror and Ireland', *Irish Historical Studies*, 29.114: 145–58.

Independence Commission (2020). *Towards an Independent Wales,* Talybont: Y Lolfa Cyf.

India Office (1942). *Draft Declaration on India (Cripps Mission).* London: HMSO.

Jackson, A. (2011). '"Tame Tory Hacks"? The Ulster Party at Westminster, 1922–1972', *The Historical Journal*, 54.2: 453–75.

Jackson, B. (2020). *The Case for Scottish Independence: A History of Nationalist Political Thought in Modern Scotland.* Cambridge: Cambridge University Press.

Jackson, L. C. (2015). *Riots, Revolutions, and the Scottish Covenanters: The Work of Alexander Henderson.* Grand Rapids, MI: Reformation Heritage.

Jay, M. (2019). *The Unfortunate Colonel Despard and the British Revolution that Never Happened.* London: Robinson.

John, E. (1996). *Reassessing Anglo-Saxon England.* Manchester: Manchester University Press.

Joint Report (2017). *Joint Report from the Negotiators of the European Union and the UK government.* London: HMSO.

Jones, D. (1996). '"I Failed Utterly": Saunders Lewis and the Cultural Politics of Welsh Modernism', *The Irish Review*, 19: 22–43.

Jones, M. (2017). 'Wales and the Brexit Vote', *Revue Française de Civilisation Britannique*, XXII-2: 1–10.

BIBLIOGRAPHY

Kagarlitsky, B. (2018). 'Brexit and the Future of the Left', in Morgan, J. and Patomäki, H. (eds), *Brexit and the Political Economy of Fragmentation*. London: Routledge.

Keating, M. (2021). *State and Nation in the United Kingdom: The Fractured Union*. Oxford: Oxford University Press.

Keating, M. and McEwen, N. (2017). *Debating Scotland: Issues of Independence and Union in the 2014 Referendum*. Oxford: Oxford Academic (online edn), https://doi.org/10.1093/acprof:oso/9780198789819.001.0001.

Kelly, J. (2001). 'The Acts of Union: its origin and background', in Keogh, D. and Whelan, K. (2001). *Acts of Union: The Causes, Contexts, and Consequences of the Act of Union*. Dublin: Four Courts.

Kenny, M., Rogers de Waal, J. and Kelsey, T. (2021). *What Matters to the English after Covid?* Cambridge: Barnett Institute for Public Policy.

Kilbrandon Report (1973). *Royal Commission on the Constitution: 1969–1973, Vols I and II*. London: HMSO.

King, R. (2022). *Brittle with Relics: A History of Wales, 1962–1997*. London: Faber.

Kitzinger, U. W. (1968). *The Second Try: Labour and the EEC*. Oxford: Pergamon.

Kumar, K. (2000). 'Nation and Empire: English and British National Identity in Comparative Perspective', *Theory and Society*, 29.5: 575–608.

——— (2003). *The Making of English National Identity*. New York, NY: Cambridge University Press.

——— (2015). *The Idea of Englishness*. London: Ashgate.

Labarge, M. W. (1980). *Gascony, England's First Colony, 1204–1453*. London: Hamish Hamilton.

Leddy-Owen, C. (2014). 'Reimagining Englishness: "Race", Class, Progressive English Identities and Disrupted English Communities', *Sociology*, 48.6: 1123–38.

Lloyd-Jones, N. (2014). 'Liberalism, Scottish Nationalism and the Home Rule Crisis, c.1886–93', *English Historical Review*, 129.539: 862–87.

Llwyd, H. (2002). *Cronica Walliae*. Cardiff: University of Wales Press.

Long, E. (1774). *The History of Jamaica*. London: Printed for T. Lowndes.

BIBLIOGRAPHY

Longford, F. P. and O'Neill, T. P. (1970). *Eamon de Valera*. London: Hutchinson.

Ludlow, N. P. (1997). *Dealing with Britain: The Six and the First UK Application to the EEC*. Cambridge: Cambridge University Press.

Lynch, M. (1992). *Scotland: A New History*. London: Pimlico.

Macinnes, A. (1989). 'Treaty of Union: Voting Patterns and Political Influence', *Historical Social Research / Historische Sozialforschung*, 14.3: 53–61.

MacKenzie, J. (2008). 'Irish, Scottish, Welsh and English Worlds? A Four-Nation Approach to the History of the British Empire', *History Compass*, 6.5: 1244–63.

Mackillop, A. (2016). 'A "reticent" people? The Welsh in Asia, c.1700-1815', in Bowen, H. V. (ed.), *Wales and the British Overseas Empire: Interactions and Influences, 1650–1830*. Manchester: Manchester University Press.

MacManus, S. (2018). *The Story of the Irish Race: A Popular History of Ireland*. New York, NY: Chartwell.

Macmillan, H. (1972). *Pointing the Way: Autobiography Vol. 5*. London: Macmillan.

Maginn, C. (2007). '"Surrender and Regrant" in the Historiography of Sixteenth-Century Ireland', *The Sixteenth Century Journal*, 38.4: 955–74.

Maier, C. S. (2007). *Among Empires: American Ascendancy and its Predecessors*. Cambridge, MA: Harvard University Press.

Mansergh, N. (1948). *The Commonwealth and the Nations: Studies in British Commonwealth Relations*. London: Royal Institute of International Affairs.

——— (1953). *Documents and Speeches on British Commonwealth Affairs 1931–1952: Vol. 1–2*. Oxford: Oxford University Press.

Marshall, P. J. (1996). *The Cambridge Illustrated History of the British Empire*. Cambridge: Cambridge University Press.

Mason, R. A. (1987). 'Scotching the Brut: Politics, History and National Myth in 16th Century Britain', in Mason, R. A. (ed.), *Scotland and England, 1286–1815*. Edinburgh: Donald.

Maund, K. L. (1991). *Ireland, Wales, and England in the Eleventh Century*. Woodbridge: Boydell.

BIBLIOGRAPHY

McDermott, G. (1972). *Leader Lost: A Biography of Hugh Gaitskell*. London: Frewin.

McDonnell, R. (1906). *When Cromwell came to Drogheda: A memory of 1649, edited from the record of Clarence Stranger, a captain in the army of Owen Roe O'Neill*. Dublin: Gill.

McGrath, C. (2006). 'Government, Parliament and the Constitution: The Reinterpretation of Poynings' Law, 1692–1714', *Irish Historical Studies*, 35.138: 160–72.

—— (2008). 'The "Union" Representation of 1703 in the Irish House of Commons: A case of mistaken identity?', *Eighteenth-Century Ireland / Iris an dá chultúr*, 23: 11–35.

Migration Observatory (2020). *UK Public Opinion toward Immigration: Overall Attitudes and Level of Concern*. Oxford: Migration Observatory.

Modood, T. (1997). 'Culture and Identity', in Modood, T. et al. (1997), *Ethnic Minorities in Britain: Diversity and Disadvantage*. London: Policy Studies Institute.

Molyneaux, G. (2014). 'Did the English Really Think They Were God's Elect in the Anglo-Saxon Period?', *Journal of Ecclesiastical History*, 65.4: 721–37.

Morgan, J. and Patomäki, H. (eds) (2018). *Brexit and the Political Economy of Fragmentation*. London: Routledge.

Morgan, K. O. (1971). 'Welsh Nationalism: The Historical Background', *Journal of Contemporary History*, 6.1: 153–72.

—— (1981). *Rebirth of a Nation: Wales 1880–1980*. Oxford: Clarendon.

Morris, M. (2014). 'From Anti-colonialism to Anti-imperialism: the Evolution of H. M. Hyndman's Critique of Empire, *c*.1875–1905', *Historical Research*, 87.236: 293–314.

Nairn, T. (1977). *The Break-Up of Britain: Crisis and Neo-nationalism*. London: NLB.

Naismith, J. (1790). *Thoughts on Various Objects of Industry Pursued in Scotland: With a view to enquire by what means the labour of the people may be directed to promote the public prosperity*. Edinburgh: Printed for the author.

Newman, S. (2020). *For God, Ulster and the "'B'-men": The Ulsterian Revolution, the Foundation of Northern Ireland and the Creation of*

BIBLIOGRAPHY

the Ulster Special Constabulary, 1910-1927. Birkbeck, University of London: Unpublished PhD thesis.

Nicholson, R. (1959). 'The Franco-Scottish and Franco-Norwegian Treaties of 1295', *Scottish Historical Review*, 38.126: 114–32.

——— (1965). *Edward III and the Scots: The Formative Years of a Military Career, 1327–1335*. Oxford: Oxford University Press.

NISRA—Northern Ireland Statistics and Research Agency (2013). *Statistics Bulletin*, 16 May 2013. Belfast: Northern Ireland Government.

Office for Budget Responsibility (2021). 'The Initial Impact of Brexit on UK Trade with the EU', *Economic and Fiscal Outlook*, October 2021.

Ohlmeyer, J. (2004). 'A Laboratory for Empire? Early Modern Ireland and English Imperialism', in Kenny, K. (ed.), *Ireland and the British Empire*. Oxford: Oxford University Press.

Olusoga, D. (2021). *Black and British: A Forgotten History*. London: Picador.

ONS (2015). 'Trends in Births and Deaths over the Last Century'.

——— (2021). 'Vital Statistics in the UK: Births, Deaths and Marriages'.

——— (2022). 'Ethnic Group, National Identity, Language and Religion: Census 2021 in England and Wales'.

Orwell, G. (1947). *The English People*. London: Collins.

O'Toole, F. (2018). *Heroic Failure: Brexit and the Politics of Pain*. London: Head of Zeus.

Owen, D. (1995). *Ethnic Minorities in Great Britain: Patterns of Population Change, 1981–1991*. Coventry: Centre for Research in Ethnic Relations, University of Warwick.

Paun, A. (2018). *Common UK Frameworks after Brexit*. Edinburgh: Scottish Parliament, Scottish Parliament Information Centre (SPICe) briefing 18-09.

Paxman, J. (1998). *The English: A Portrait of a People*. London: Michael Joseph.

Petrie, M. (2018). 'Anti-socialism, Liberalism and Individualism: Rethinking the Realignment of Scottish Politics, 1945–1970', *Transactions of the Royal Historical Society*, 28: 197–217.

Pettigrew, W. (2013). *Freedom's Debt: The Royal African Company and the Politics of the Atlantic Slave Trade, 1672–1752*. Chapel Hill, NC: University of North Carolina Press.

BIBLIOGRAPHY

Philipps, J. T. (1746). *A journal of a voyage made in the Hannibal of London, ann. 1693, 1694, from England, to Cape Monseradoe, in Africa, and thence along the coast of Guiney to Whidaw, the island of St. Thomas, and so forward to Barbadoes.* Printed for Henry Lintot and John Osborn.

Pilling, S. and Cracknell, R. (2021). 'UK Election Statistics, 1918–2021: A Century of Elections'. House of Commons Library, Commons Briefing Paper 7529.

Prestwich, M. (1989). 'England and Scotland during the Wars of Independence', in Jones, M. and Vale, M. G. A. (eds), *England and her Neighbours, 1066–1453: Essays in Honour of Pierre Chaplais.* London: Hambledon.

Prior, C. (2019). '"This Community Which Nobody Can Define": Meanings of Commonwealth in the Late 1940s and 1950s', *Journal of Imperial and Commonwealth History*, 47.3: 568–90.

Pryce, H. (1998). 'Owain Gwynedd and Louis VII: the Franco-Welsh Diplomacy of the First Prince of Wales', *Welsh History Review*, 19.1: 1–28.

Raftery, B. (2005). 'Iron-Age Ireland', in Cróinín, D. O. (ed.), *A New History of Ireland: Vol. 1.* Oxford: Oxford University Press.

Ravilious, K. (2021). 'Land of the Picts', *Archaeology*, September–October: 1–8.

Reith, J. C. W. R. (1966). *Days of Challenge.* Glasgow: Jackson.

Renton, A. (2021). *Blood Legacy: Reckoning with a Family's Story of Slavery.* London: Canongate.

Report of the Commission on Britain's Future (2022). *A New Britain: Renewing our Democracy and Rebuilding our Economy*, London: Labour Party.

Reynolds, D. (2019). *Island Stories: Britain and its History in the Age of Brexit.* London: William Collins.

Reynolds, S. (1985). 'What do we mean by "Anglo-Saxon" and "Anglo-Saxons"?', *Journal of British Studies*, 24.4: 395–414.

Riley, P. W. J. (1969). 'The Union of 1707 as an Episode in English Politics', *English Historical Review*, 84.332: 498–527.

Russell, M. and Sheldon, J. (2018). *Options for an English Parliament.* London: The Constitution Unit, University College London.

BIBLIOGRAPHY

Russell, P. (2005). '"What was Best of Every Language"? The Early History of the Irish Language', in Cróinín, D. O. (ed.), *A New History of Ireland: Vol. 1*. Oxford: Oxford University Press.

Sandford, M. (2021). 'Directly-elected Mayors'. House of Commons Library Briefing Paper 05000: 1–16.

Saunders, R. (2018). *Yes to Europe!: The 1975 Referendum and Seventies Britain*. New York, NY: Cambridge University Press.

Savage, A. (1996). *The Anglo-Saxon Chronicles*. Godalming: Coombe Books.

Scanlan, P. (2020). *Slave Empire: How Slavery Built Modern Britain*. London: Robinson.

Schmitz, J. (1997). 'The Nature and Dimensions of Scottish Foreign Investment, 1860–1914', *Business History*, 39.2: 42–68.

Schütze, R. (2018). 'Introduction: British "Federalism"?', in Schütze, R. and Tierney, S. (eds), *The United Kingdom and the Federal Idea*. Oxford: Hart.

Schuyler, R. L. (1922). 'The Rise of Anti-Imperialism in England', *Political Science Quarterly*, 37.3: 440–71.

Scott, P. H. (1992). *Andrew Fletcher and the Treaty of Union*. Edinburgh: Donald.

Scottish Government (2021). *Export Statistics Scotland 2019*. Edinburgh: National Statistics, 1–36.

Scruton, R. (2000). *England: An Elegy*. London: Chatto & Windus.

Sherwood, M. (2013). *Tennyson and the Fabrication of Englishness*. Basingstoke: Palgrave Macmillan.

Shipman, T. (2016). *All Out War: The Full Story of How Brexit Sank Britain's Political Class*. London: William Collins.

Smith, B. (1984). 'Magna Carta and the Charters of the Welsh Princes', *English Historical Review*, 99.391: 344–362.

——— (2007). 'Distinction and Diversity: the Common Lawyers and the Law of Wales', in Pryce, H. and Watts, J. (eds), *Power and Identity in the Middle Ages: Essays in Memory of Rees Davies*. Oxford: Oxford University Press.

Sobolewska, M. K. and Ford, R. A. (2020). *Brexitland: Identity, Diversity and the Reshaping of British Politics*. New York, NY: Cambridge University Press.

BIBLIOGRAPHY

Spence, J. (1976). 'Movements in the Public Mood: 1961–75', in Hoinville, G. and Jowell, R. (eds), *Britain into Europe*. London: Croom-Helm.

Steinnes, K. (1998). 'The European Challenge: Britain's EEC Application in 1961', *Contemporary European History*, 7.1: 61–79.

Stephen, J. (2007). *Scottish Presbyterians and the Act of Union 1707*. Edinburgh: Edinburgh University Press.

Stephenson, D. (2016). 'Empires in Wales: from Gruffudd ap Llywelyn to Llywelyn ap Gruffudd', *Welsh History Review / Cylchgrawn Hanes Cymru*, 28.1: 26–54.

———— (2019). *Medieval Wales c. 1050–1332: Centuries of Ambiguity*. Cardiff: University of Wales Press.

Stevens, M. F. and Phipps, T. (2020). 'Towards a Characterization of "Race Law" in Medieval Wales', *Journal of Legal History*, 41.3: 290–331.

Sutherland, J. (1995). *The Life of Walter Scott*. Cambridge, MA: Blackwell.

Thomas, H. M. (2003). *The English and the Normans: Ethnic Hostility, Assimilation, and Identity, 1066–c. 1220*. Oxford: Oxford University Press.

Tombs, R. (2021). *This Sovereign Isle: Britain In and Out of Europe*. London: Penguin.

Torrance, D. (2020). *Standing Up for Scotland*. Edinburgh: Edinburgh University Press.

———— (2021). *A History of the Scottish Liberals and Liberal Democrats*. Edinburgh: Edinburgh University Press.

Turvey, R. (2013). *Owain Gwynedd: Prince of the Welsh*. Talybont: Y Lolfa.

Uberoi, E. and Tunnicliffe, R. (2021). 'Ethnic Diversity in Politics and Public Life'. House of Commons Library Briefing Paper 01156: 1–47.

UK Trade Policy Observatory (2021). *The UK's New Trade Agreements: Curb Your Enthusiasm*. Falmer: University of Sussex.

Vergilius, P. (1534). *Anglica Historia*. Basileae: Bebel.

Walker, D. (1991). *A Guide to the Church in Wales*. Penarth: Church in Wales.

Walker, G. S. (2004). *A History of the Ulster Unionist Party: Protest, Pragmatism and Pessimism*. Manchester: Manchester University Press.

Walker, R. F. (1972). 'Hubert de Burgh and Wales, 1218–1232', *English Historical Review*, 87.344: 465–94.

BIBLIOGRAPHY

Ward, M. (2020). 'Statistics on UK–EU Trade'. House of Commons Library Briefing Paper 7851: 1–19.

——— (2021). *Statistics on UK Trade with the Commonwealth.* House of Commons Library Commons Briefing Paper 8282: 1–17.

Ward-Perkins, B. (2000). 'Why Did the Anglo-Saxons Not Become More British?', *English Historical Review*, 115.462: 513–33.

Webster, W. (2005). *Englishness and Empire, 1939–1965.* Oxford: Oxford University Press.

Wellings, B. (2019). *English Nationalism: Brexit and the Anglosphere.* Manchester: Manchester University Press.

Whatley, C. (1989). 'Economic Causes and Consequences of the Union of 1707: A Survey', *Scottish Historical Review*, 68.186: 150–81.

Whyte, I. (2006). *Scotland and the Abolition of Black Slavery, 1756–1838.* Edinburgh: Edinburgh University Press.

Williams, G. (1960). 'Wales and the Commonwealth', in Roderick, A. J. (ed.), *Wales through the Ages: Vol. 2.* Llandybie: Christopher Davies.

——— (1982). *The Welsh in their History.* London: Croom Helm.

——— (1985). *When Was Wales?: A History of the Welsh.* London: Penguin.

Winder, R. (2017). *Last Wolf: The Hidden Springs of Englishness.* London: Little, Brown.

Wormald, P. (1983). 'Bede, the *Bretwaldas* and the Origins of the *Gens Anglorum*', in Wormald, P., Bullough, D. and Collins, R. (eds), *Ideal and Reality in Frankish and Anglo-Saxon Society.* Oxford: Blackwell.

YouGov (2018). 'Future of England Survey Results', 1–13.

——— (2019). 'Future of England Survey Results', 1–10.

Zimmern, A. (1941). *From the British Empire to the British Commonwealth.* London: Longmans.

INDEX

Note: Page numbers followed by "*n*" refer to notes, "*t*" refer to tables.

Acts of Union (1707), 111–12,
  120–1, 124, 126, 131, 299
  "Article 5", 121
  Ireland, 114–21, 156, 281–2,
    301
  Scotland, 107–14, 134, 146,
    281
  Wales, 100–6, 281
Adrian IV (Pope), 49
Adrian V (Pope), 58
Áedán mac Gabráin (King of Dál
  Riata), 27
Ælfgar (Earl of Mercia), 23, 52, 53
Æthelflæd (Queen of western
  Mercia), 33–4
Æthelred the Unready (King of
  England), 35, 46
Æthelstan (King of Mercia and
  Wessex), 9–10, 29, 34, 60,
  292–3

Agricola (Roman general), 25
Alexander II (King of Scotland),
  63, 64, 83–4
Alexander III (King of Scotland),
  63, 64, 83–4
Alfred the Great (King of Wessex),
  33, 292
Alien Act (1705), 111
Alliance Party, 205, 263, 264
Amsterdam Treaty (1997),
  213–14
ANC (African National Congress),
  318
Angevin Empire, 39–42
Angles, 9, 32, 291
Anglican Church, 273, 274
Anglo-Dutch Wars, 109
Anglo-French Treaty of Paris
  (1259), 93, 94

369

INDEX

Anglo-Irish Treaty (1921), 158, 162, 168–9, 170, 171, 175, 176, 179, 255, 282

Anglo-Saxon Chronicle, 293

Anglo-Saxons, 9–10, 30, 32, 34, 39, 292, 301

Anglo-Scottish Treaty, 60

Anne (Queen), 108, 111, 116, 134

Anselm (Archbishop of Canterbury), 48

anti-Catholicism, 129, 156

Apartheid policy, 182, 184–5

Aquitaine, 93, 94

Archbishops of Canterbury, 47, 55

Argentina, 143

'Argument on Behalf of the Catholics in Ireland' (Tone), 118

Armagh monastery, 46

Arthur (King), 21

Arthur Wellesley (Duke of Wellington), 155

Asiatic Society of Bengal, 143

Association of Commonwealth Universities, 181

Atlantic slavery, 133, 135

Attlee government, 259

Attlee, Clement, 177, 180–1

Augustine, St., 32

Auld Alliance, 64–5, 87, 111

Australia, 136, 150, 166, 167, 184, 251

Bacon, Anthony, 142

Bagehot, Walter, 3

Bahamas, 136

Baldwin, Stanley, 174–5

Balfour Declaration, 173–4

Balfour, Arthur, 173

Balliol, John Balliol (King of Scotland), 84, 85, 87, 88

Bance Island, 148

Battle(s)
of Bosworth Field (1483), 77
of Bouvines (1214), 42
of Brunanburh (937), 9, 29, 34, 293
of Carham (1018), 10, 30, 59
of Castillon (1453), 96
of Clontarf (1014), 19, 46
of Culblean (1335), 88
of Culloden (1746), 114
of Dyrham (577), 32
of Edington (878), 33, 292
of Glenmama (999), 18, 45
of Hastings (1066), 23, 39, 294
of Mons Badonicus (c. 500), 32
of Mons Graupius (83 CE), 25
of Mynydd Carn (1081), 54
of Nechtansmere (685), 26, 28
of Neville's Cross (1346), 88
of Pinkie (1547), 91
of Solway Moss (1542), 90
of Stirling Bridge (1297), 86
of Sucoilt (967), 17–18
of the Boyne (1690), 82
of the Standard (1138), 61

Bede, Venerable, 26, 27, 47, 289, 291–2, 293, 300

370

INDEX

beef, salted, 153

Belfast Agreement. *See* Good Friday Agreement (GFA)

Benedictines of Dunfermline, 97

Beyond Oil and Gas Alliance, 280

Biden, Joe, 252–3

Black Death pandemic, 73, 76, 88, 95

Black, Asian and Minority Ethnic (BAME), 309

Blair government, 277–8, 283

Blair, Tony, 213–14, 269

Boer War (South Africa, 1899–1902), 157, 167

Bogdanor, Vernon, 314

Book of Armagh (manuscript), 18

Bordeaux, 94, 96

Bourbon, 134

brass, 141

'Brexit', 5–6, 223–54, 263, 285, 287
  Article 50 of the Treaty on European Union, 232–3
  Britain Stronger in Europe, 227
  England excluding London (EexL), 230, 231*t*
  English views on migration, 233
  English voters opposition to EC membership, 214–22
  EU–UK Trade and Cooperation Agreement, 238, 263–4, 316
  exports and imports after, 250

implications of, 246–54
  joint report (Dec 2017), 234–5
  May's draft agreement (Jan 2019), 236
  Northern Ireland Protocol, 240–6, 263–4
  Northern Ireland, London, Scotland and Wales (NILSW), 230–1, 231t
  referendum (Jun 2016), 222, 223, 225–32, 231t, 313
  Scotland Stronger in Europe, 228
  trade agreements negotiations with rest of the world (ROW), 249–54
  trading privileges, loss of, 249–51
  transition period, 238
  UK's withdrawal, 224
  withdrawal agreement (Oct 2019), 237

Brian Boru (High King of Ireland), 13, 17, 18, 19, 45–6, 51

Bristol, 135, 146

British armed forces, 154–5

British Army, 127

British Board of Ordnance, 142

British Commonwealth of Nations. *See* Commonwealth of Nations

British Empire
  African slave labour in the colonies, 152

371

INDEX

emergence of, 2
exhibitions hosted by Glasgow, 145
lifetime of, 1–2
naval supremacy, 135–6, 137, 138
as official name, 140
protectorates, acquisition of, 137
rise of, 134
slavery, abolition of, 137
territorial acquisitions, 134, 135–7
British Guiana, 137
British mandates, 161–2
British Nationality Act (1948), 304–5, 308
British North America Act (1867), 165
British Social Attitudes Survey, 209
British Union of Fascists, 308–9
Britishness, 2, 4
in Caribbean, 300
in the colonies, 161
decline of, 4–5
definition of, 300–1
England and sense of, 131–8
EU membership and meaning of, 199, 202, 203, 205, 255
Ireland and sense of, 2, 151–9
meaning of, 304–5, 308
post-Imperial Britishness, 222
preserving, 162
Scotland and sense of, 145–51

and volunteer army recruitment, 161
See also 'English questions'
Britons, 21
newcomers' culture, adoption of, 32
in post-Roman Britain, 31
Brown, Gordon, 270, 312
Brussels, 203, 238, 314
Burma (Myanmar), 1, 179–80, 304

Cabot, John, 96–7
Caesar, Julius, 30
Calman Commission, 271
Cameron, David, 220, 221, 222, 225, 226–7, 232, 233, 270, 284, 313
Canada, 135, 136,150, 163–5, 167, 180, 304
British emigration to, 164
budget (1859), 165
Constitutional Act (1791), 163
dominion status, 165–6
Durham Report, 163–4
Canterbury, 67
Capetian dynasty, 41
Caratacus, 30
Caribbean, 109, 131, 135, 136, 305
Britishness in, 300
Irish Protestant in, 152–3
salted provisions export, 153
slave plantations in, 144, 147–9
Catherine of Braganza, 109
Catholicism, 81, 82, 90, 105, 112
Cattle Acts (1665 and 1667), 153

INDEX

Catuvellauni, 30–1

Celtic culture, 10, 14–15, 24

Celtic language, 14, 15, 19, 27

Celts, 14

Cennétig mac Lorcáin, 17

census

    1790 (US), 154

    1801, 120–1

    1921, 258, 274

    1991, 308

    2011, 229, 261

    2021, 282, 322n12

Central African Federation, 182

Ceylon (Sri Lanka), 1, 178, 304

Chamberlain, Joseph, 174, 333n15

Channel Islands, 42, 123

Charles ('the Young Pretender'), 114

Charles I, 91–2, 131

Charles II, 82, 192, 07, 109, 131, 133

Charles III, 273

Charles the Simple, 41

China, 250, 251, 252, 253, 254

China's Belt & Road Initiative, 252

Christianity, 11, 14, 21

    acceptance of, 32

    arrival of, 15

    converted to, 26, 292

Church of England, 102, 105–6, 145

Church of Ireland, 117, 127, 154

Churchill, Winston, 1, 176–7

Claudius (Emperor), 30

Clinton administration, 242

Cnut (King of England), 35, 59, 294

coal, 142

Cockfield, Lord, 212

Cold War, 194, 196

Colley, Linda, 126, 129–30

Colonial Office, 164

Columba, St., 26, 27

Columbus, Bartholomew, 96

Columbus, Christopher, 96

Common Agricultural Policy, 198

Commonwealth Day (1966), 181

Commonwealth Heads of Government Meetings, 184

Commonwealth Immigrants Act (1962), 186, 306

Commonwealth Immigrants Act (1968), 187, 306

Commonwealth immigration, 185–7

Commonwealth Institute, 181

Commonwealth of England (1649–60), 115

Commonwealth of Nations, 4, 169–83, 193

    Commonwealth, word usage, 177–8, 180, 184

    dominions, 162, 163–9

    EC membership and, 202–3

    establishment of, 162

    meeting (1948), 304

    non-white immigration, hostility to, 184–7

INDEX

privileges of membership,
178–9
sense of Britishness,
preservation of, 162
Commonwealth War Graves
Commission, 181
Commonwealth Games, 181
Company of Scotland Trading to
Africa and the Indies, 109–10,
112, 113
Congress of Vienna (1814–15),
136–7
Conservative government, 200,
276–7
Conservative Party, 187, 191, 192,
195, 196, 198, 200, 204, 205,
206–7, 213, 233–4, 236, 260,
284, 318, 340n9
election (2014), 220–1, 221t
general election (2015), 284–5
growing unpopularity in
Wales, 277
manifesto, 212
non-white voters, attempt to
gain, 309–10
and referendum (Jun 2016),
223, 225, 232
Constantine II, 60
copper, 141, 142
Cornwall, 105
Council of Wales, 103
COVID-19 pandemic, 224, 239,
247–8, 313
Craig, James, 258
Cripps, Stafford, 177

Cromwell, Oliver, 81–2, 92, 105
Cromwell, Thomas, 101
Cronica Walliae (Llwyd), 139–40
Cumbria, 59, 60, 61, 62, 63
Cyfarthfa iron foundry, 142

D'Hondt system, 345n31
Dafydd (eldest son of Llywelyn ap
Iorwerth), 58, 70, 71
Dál Riata Kingdom, 25–6, 26–7,
28
Dalyell, Tam, 283
Danes, 29, 32–3, 294
Darién, 110, 145
David I, 61, 62
David II, 87, 88, 89
David, St. (Archbishop of Wales),
21
Davies, John, 24
Davies, Rees, 68
de Brus, Robert, 84, 85
de Gaulle, Charles, 197, 198
de Valera, Éamon, 175–6, 179,
334n18
Declaration of Arbroath (1320),
86–7
Declaratory Act (1720), 116–17
decolonisation, 181–2
Dee, John, 140
Defoe, Daniel, 113
Deheubarth, 54, 55
Democratic Unionist Party
(DUP), 205, 228, 234, 237,
242, 243, 244, 245, 246,
262–3, 264

374

INDEX

Denmark, 59, 188, 199

Despard, Marcus Edward, 155

Diarmait Mac Murchada (King of Leinster), 47, 49–50

Disraeli, Benjamin, 137

dominions, 162, 163–9, 172, 178, 181

citizenships, 305

Domnall (King of Dál Riata), 28

Domnall Brecc (Áedán's grandson), 27

Donaldson, Arthur, 189

Douglas, Sylvester, 156

Duchy, 41

Duke of Hamilton, 111–12

Dundas, Henry, 156

Durham, Lord: Durham Report, 163–4

Eadred (Æthelstan's brother), 10

Earl of Cromartie, 125

East India Company, 109, 110, 132–3, 135, 143–4

Easter Uprising (Dublin, 1916), 130, 158

Ecgferth (son of Offa), 32

Economic and Monetary Union (EMU), 208–9, 212

Eden, Anthony, 195

Edgar (King of England), 30

Edgar (King of Scotland), 48

Edith (sister of David I), 61

Edmund (King of Wessex), 29

Edward Bruce, 51

Edward Colston of Bristol, 133

Edward I, 69, 70, 71–3, 83–4, 89, 297

Edward II, 86

Edward III, 52, 72, 87, 88, 95

Edward the Confessor (King of England), 13, 23, 35, 38, 52–3, 294

Edward the Elder, 33–4, 60

Edward VI, 79, 80, 90

Edward VIII, 176

Egypt, 194

Eisenhower, Dwight D., 194

Eleanor (daughter of Simon de Montfort), 69, 70

Eleanor of Aquitaine, 93

election (2014), 220–1, 221t

election (2017), 234

Electoral Commission, 227, 229

Elizabeth I, 2, 80, 83, 91, 97, 131, 184, 273

slave trade under, 133

Emma (Æthelred's widow), 35, 38

empire, definition, 3

England

annexation of Wales, 280–1, 298

anti-imperialism, 138

anti-Welsh feeling, 296, 297–8

arrival of Roman troops, 30–1

birth of, 30–5

British Empire and sense of Britishness, 131–8, 300

civil war (Anarchy), 61, 62

colonisation, 37–8

Danish invasion of, 294

375

INDEX

decentralisation of, 283–4
dominance of, 100
EC budget, 211
EC participation issue, 200,
206–7
English control over
institutions, 129
EU membership, public
against, 219–20
general election (2015), 284–5
'Great Britain' or 'UK', coexist
with the label, 122–3
hegemonic position inside
Great Britain and UK,
129–31, 257, 206, 280–7
national flag, 102, 120, 125,
299, 309, 310
national football team, 138
non-white population, 305,
308
as Norman colony, 37
Norman conquest, 38–9
Norman invasion of, 294
Norman rule, 38–41, 43
Normans' colonising attempt,
294–5
population, 282, 296, 297,
324n6, 339n44
and referendum (Jun 2016),
230–2, 231t
Roman conquest, 30
slave trade participation, 133
statehood, 122–8
state-to-state relations, 38–45
territorial consolidation, 30

in thirteenth century, 296
transatlantic slavery, 135
English Civil War, 81, 91
English Constitution, The, 3
English exceptionalism, 3, 4, 5,
290, 296, 301–3
English imperialism
beginning of, 68
Ireland, 75–83
Scotland, 83–92
Wales, 68–75
English language, 40, 103, 298
English-language schools,
introduction of, 123, 124
English overseas empire
into British Empire, 134
colonies of, 131–2
labour shortage, 132, 133
See also dominions
English parliament, 298–9, 313–14
English people: name origin, 9–10
English Privy Council, 90
'English questions', 283–4,
289–319
associated with whiteness,
308–9
Britishness, definition of,
300–1
changing nature of
Englishness, 289–90
defining Englishness, 303–4
dimension of Englishness,
290–1
in England & Wales (E&W),
316–18

376

INDEX

Englishness, racial definition, 290

as federalism, 313–14

ideology of Englishness, 302

imperial Englishness, 297–304

meaning of Britishness, 304–5, 308

post-Imperial Englishness, 311–19

postwar Englishness, 304–11

pre-Imperial Englishness, 291–7

See also Britishness

English Votes for English Laws (EVEL), 313, 284–5

'English' identity, 4, 126, 127

Englishness. *See* 'English questions'

Enquiry into the State of Education in Wales. See Treachery of the Blue Books, The

Eóganán (nephew of Constantine), 28

Eric 'Bloodaxe' Haraldsson, 29

Euratom (energy agency), 197

European Coal and Steel Community (ECSC), 193, 197

European Commission, 205, 208, 211, 228, 238, 242, 245

European Communities (EC), 197–8

EC budget, 210–12

English voters opposition to EC membership, 214–22

first post-referendum surveys (1975), 209

Labour manifesto (1983), 215–16

referendum (Jun 1975), 191–2, 200–7, 223

regional policies, 204

renegotiation of the terms, 211

share of UK goods exports, 210

UK membership and meaning of Britishness, 199, 202, 203, 205, 255

UK membership, 4, 188, 190, 208–14, 197–8, 208

UK membership approval, 198–200

UK's regional trade statistics, 210

See also European Union (EU)

European Communities Act (1972), 203

European Communities Bill, 199

European Council, 226–7

European Court of Justice, 208, 235, 245

European Customs Union, 195, 208, 234–5, 237–8, 240–1, 242, 243, 245, 246–7

European Economic Community (EEC), 183, 191, 193, 195

British application for membership, 1, 195–8

De Gaulle's veto, 197

377

INDEX

UK's negotiations to join the, 195–200, 201

European Free Trade Association, 187

European Parliament, 213, 214, 218, 220, 226

European parliamentary elections (2014), 229

European Research Group (ERG), 235, 236

European Structural and Investment Funds, 285

European Union (EU), 4, 209
    Britain's relationship with, 209–10
    Common Travel Area', 241–2
    EC into, 4
    nature of EU immigration, 218–19, 219*t*
    net EU migration, 248–9
    new members of, 214
    referendum (Jun 2016), 222, 223, 225–32, 231*t*, 313
    single currency, launch of, 213, 214
    single market, 213, 224, 234, 235, 238, 240–1, 243, 246–7, 253
    UK membership, opposition to, 191–3
    UK's friction with EC partners, 210–12
    See also 'Brexit'; European Communities (EC)

European Union Referendum Act (2015), 227

euroscepticism, 4, 5, 216, 217, 220

Evans, Gwynfor, 188

Ewing, Winnie, 189, 256

fertility rate, 247–8

FIFA World Cup final (1966), 310

First Crusade (1095), 48

Flanders, Michael, 215

Foster, Arlene, 228

Frame, Robin, 76–7

France, 41, 64, 92, 122, 129, 153, 193, 194, 196
    English military campaigns in, 68
    French settlers in Canada, 163, 164
    Gascony disputes, 93–6
    Great Britain war with (1793), 119
    Normandy, capture of, 37, 43
    state-building, 99
    treaty between Wales and, 74
    Vikings in, 41–2

French Revolution (1789), 118

Gaelic language, 28, 124

Gaitskell, Hugh, 183, 184, 187, 306

Gascony, 43, 93–6, 280

GDP, 253–4

General and Rare Memorials pertayning to the Perfect Arte of Navigation (Dee), 140

INDEX

general elections
    1918, 171
    1964, 184
    1970, 198
    2001, 218
    2005, 220
    2010, 220
Geoffrey of Monmouth, 88, 126
George III, 120
George IV, 265
George, David Lloyd, 106, 172
Gerald FitzGerald (eighth Earl of Kildare), 77
Gerald FitzGerald (ninth Earl of Kildare), 78
Gerald of Wales, 69, 325n18
Germanic invaders, 31–2, 291, 292, 294
    Britons against, 21
    raids, 31
Germany, 1, 99
Gibb, Andrew, 150–1
Gibraltar, 134
Gildas, 291
Gilmour, John, 267
Gladstone, William, 157, 266, 283
Glasgow Courier (newspaper), 149
Glasgow West India Association, 149
Glasgow, 145, 148–9
Goidelic language, 10
Gold Coast (Ghana), 182
Goldsmith, James, 217

Good Friday Agreement (GFA), 5, 224, 234–5, 240–6, 256, 257, 261, 263, 283
Goschen formula, 267, 344n23
Government of Ireland Act (1920), 170, 240
Government of Wales Act (1998), 278
Grattan, Henry, 120
Great Britain
    armed forces development, 126
    creation of, 2, 99, 111–12, 281
    political parties, 126
    thirteen colonies, independence of, 136
Great Depression, 174
Great War. *See* World War I
Greece, 214
Gregory VII (Pope), 47
Gruffydd ap Llywelyn (King of Wales), 13, 23, 46, 47, 52–3
Guthrum (leader of Danes), 33
Gwenwynwyn, 56
Gwynedd, 54–5, 56, 58

Haakon IV (King of Norway), 63
Hadrian (Roman Emperor), 25
Hannibal (slave ship), 141
Harold Godwinson (Earl of Wessex), 23, 38–9, 47, 53
Harthacnut (Cnut and Emma's son), 35
Hawkins, John, 133
Heath, Edward, 198, 260, 261
Heffer, Simon, 316–17

379

INDEX

Henry I, 48, 61

Henry II, 40, 49–50, 55–6, 62, 93, 94, 324*n*2

Henry III, 43–4, 57–8, 63–4, 69, 94, 295, 296, 326*n*33

Henry IV, 89

Henry of Huntingdon, 68

Henry V, 74

Henry VII, 77, 78, 89–90, 91, 96–7

Henry VIII, 78–9, 89, 90, 91, 102, 104, 106, 131, 273, 290, 298
Ecclesiastical Appeals Act, 97

Heseltine, Michael, 3

Hiberno-British Isles, 2, 67, 96, 290, 293

Historia Ecclesiastica Gentis Anglorum (Bede), 291–2

Historia Regum Britanniae (Geoffrey), 88–9

Hogg, Quintin, 199

Holy Roman Empire, 13

Home Rule Party, 127–8

Hong Kong, 1

House of Commons, 103, 106, 113, 115, 120, 127, 157, 171, 201, 208–9, 236–7, 242, 259, 282, 286

House of Lords, 106, 113, 116, 157,177, 199

House of Stewart, 89, 90

Huawei, 252

Hugh Capet, 41

Hugh de Champfleury (Chancellor), 55

Hugh O'Neill (Earl of Tyrone), 81

Humber, 293

Hume, David, 124, 265

Hundred Years' War (1337–1453), 50, 89, 95–6

Hywel Dda (Hywel the Good), 22

Immigration Act (1971), 307–8

Imperial Conference (1926), 173

Imperial Conference (1937), 176

imperial economic conference (Ottawa, 1932), 174–5

Imperial War Conference (1917), 168

India, 1, 135, 137–8, 174, 177, 250, 254, 304
Commonwealth membership, 180, 181
decolonisation, 181–2
dominion status, 168–9, 178
Indian discrimination in South Africa, 185
UK's trade negotiations with, 251–2
Welsh migrants to, 143–4

Indian National Congress, 177

Indian subcontinent, 135, 143, 305

Indian Union, 177

industrial revolution, 135, 138

Innocent III (Pope), 56

Institute of Commonwealth Studies, 181

Internal Market Act, 239

Ionian Islands, 137

INDEX

IRA (Irish Republican Army), 158, 190, 260

Ireland, 68
    Act of Settlement (1652), 82
    Acts of Union, 114–21, 156, 281–2, 301
    Anglo-Irish society, 76–7
    anti-imperialists march (Dublin, 1897), 157
    Brehon laws, 15
    under Brian Boru, 18, 19
    British Empire and sense of Britishness, 2, 151–9
    Celtic culture, 10, 14–15, 24
    Christianity, arrival of, 15
    Commonwealth, secession from, 179
    Declaration of Independence (1776), 117
    EEC membership, 188, 199
    emigration from, 156–7
    England-Ireland relationship, 46–7
    English imperialism in, 75–83
    fear of French invasion, 155
    general election (1874), 157
    high kings, 15–16
    Home Rule debate, 4–5
    Irish Catholics, 114–15, 118–20, 121, 127, 130, 152–3, 154–5, 156
    Irish elections (1932), 175
    Irish kings and Pope relationship, 47–8
    Irish unification, 19
    Lordship of Ireland, 43, 76–9, 296
    marriage alliances, 45–6
    nation-state, birth of, 14–19
    partition of, 161
    population, 19, 297, 329–30n26
    Presbyterian's experience of discrimination, 121
    state-to-state relations, 38, 45–52
    'surrender and regrant' policy and rebellions, 79–80
    unified Irish state, 83
    Vikings, arrival of, 16–17

Irish Church Act (1869), 127

Irish Confederacy, 81

Irish famine (1845–6), 156

Irish Free State, 2, 3, 161, 168–9, 170–1, 172, 173, 175–6, 178, 258, 282

Irish parliament (Dublin), 77–8, 114–15, 116–20, 157–8
    autonomy, 151–2
    dominated by Catholics, 158
    Penal Laws, 114–15

Irish Parliamentary Party, 158

Irish rebellion, 100

Isle of Man, 2, 63, 123

Italy, 99, 248

Jacobite rebellions, 114, 145, 264, 265

Jamaica, 144, 147–8, 182

INDEX

James I (King of England), 81, 125, 131, 298–9

James II, 82–3, 131, 133

James IV, 89, 90

James V, 90

James VI. *See* James I (King of England)

James VII, 107

James VIII, 113–14

Japan, 248

Jeffreys family, 140–1

Jeffreys, John, 140–1

Jews, 73

John (King of England), 42

John (son of Henry II) (Lord of Ireland), 50, 56, 57, 93

John Maitland (Duke of Lauderdale), 107

John of Salisbury, 64

John XXII (Pope), 51, 86

Johnson administration, 239, 245–6

Johnson, Boris, 236–7, 241, 42

Jones, Harford, 144

Jones, Robert Tudur, 105

Jones, William, 143

Jutes, 291

Kenneth mac Alpin (King of Alba), 28–9

Kent, William, 281

Kilbrandon Report (1973), 189–90, 203

Kildare family, 76, 78

Kingdom of Alba, 10, 29, 60

Kingdom of Kent, 31–2

Kingdom of Northumbria, 9 conquest of, 10, 32, 33–4

Kingdom of Scotland, 10–11, 61–2

Kingdom of Wessex, 32–3

Kissinger, Henry, 196

Knight v. Wedderburn case, 300–1

Kynniver Llith a Ban, 104–5

Labour government, 188–9, 198

Labour Party and Political Change in Scotland 1918–1929, The (Brown), 312

Labour Party Conference (1962), 183

Labour Party, 171, 184, 187, 188–9, 191, 192, 196–7, 200, 201, 204–5, 206, 213–14, 268–9, 309

election (2014), 220–1, 221*t*

general election (1922), 275

general elections (2010),220

manifesto (1983), 215–16

Lanfranc (Archbishop of Canterbury), 47–8

Laudabiliter, 49

Law, Andrew Bonar, 3–4

Lawson, Nigel, 226

League of Nations, 161–2, 169–70

Leger, Anthony St., 78–9

Leinster, 18

Levelling Up the United Kingdom (white paper), 314

Lewis, Saunders, 274–5, 346*n*41

Liberal Democrats, 225

382

INDEX

Liberal Party, 127, 172, 174, 195, 206, 207, 277

linen industry/trade, 148, 149–50, 153–4

Liverpool, 135, 146, 185

Llwyd, Humphrey, 139, 140

Llywelyn ap Gruffydd (Prince of Wales), 58–9, 69, 70, 71, 296

Llywelyn ap Iorwerth (Llywelyn the Great), 56–8

Lockhart, John Gibson, 265

London Declaration (1949), 180

London Rotary Club, 307

London University, 181

Londonderry city, 81

Lothian, 59, 60, 88

Louis VII, 55, 64

Louis IX, 43–4

Louis XIV, 114

Louis, Prince (son of Philippe II), 42, 296

Maastricht Treaty (1992), 213

mac Alpin dynasty, 10, 28–9, 30

Macaulay, Thomas Babington, 303

MacBeth, 60–2

Macdonald, John, 166

Macmillan, Harold, 186, 195, 196, 198

Macpherson, James, 264

Madoc (Prince of Wales), 139–40

Madox, Ford, 302–3

Máel Sechnaill mac Máele Ruanaid, 17

Magna Carta, 42, 43, 44, 57, 72

Magnus Barelegs (King of Norway), 48

Magnus VI (King of Norway), 63

Major, John, 213, 268

Malawi, 182

Malcolm Canmore (the Great). *See* MacBeth (Malcolm III)

Malcolm I, 29–30

Malcolm II, 10, 13, 29, 30, 46, 59

Malcolm III, 60-1

Malcolm IV, 62

Manx language, 123

Marchia Wallia, 53, 54

Maredudd ap Owain, 22–3

Margaret ('Maid of Norway'), 84

Margaret (daughter of Henry VII), 89, 90

Mary (Queen of Scotland), 90–1, 108

Mary I (Queen of England), 79, 80

Maryland, 132

Mathgamain (King of Munster), 17–18

Maxwell, Henry, 115–16

May, Theresa, 232, 233–4, 236, 241, 242

mercantilism, 109

Merger Treaty (1967), 197

Mesopotamia, 162

Messina conference (1955), 193, 194

Methodism, 106

Mitchell, George, 242

Mons Badonicus, 21

Montserrat island, 152

383

INDEX

Morgan, Henry, 140

Morgannwg (today Glamorgan), 23

Muirchertach mac Lochlainn, 48, 49

Munster rebellion, 79–80

Munster, 153

Naismith, John, 149

nation, definition, 7

National Covenant (1638), 91–2

National Party (South Africa), 182, 184–5

National Party of Scotland, 172–3

National Party of Wales. *See* Plaid Cymru

nation-states, 7–8, 14

Nelson, Horatio, 155

net inward migration, 247–9

New Zealand, 136, 150, 166, 167, 184, 251

Newfoundland, 97, 109, 131, 165, 167, 333*n*7

Niall Noígíallach (high king), 16

Ninian, St., 26

Nonconformism, 105, 106

Norman imperialism, 67–8

Normandy, 37, 41

    Danelaw in, 34–5

    loss of, 93, 296

    Viking stronghold in, 38–42

Normanitas, 295

Norse people, 16–17

North America, 117, 118, 131

    British colonies in, 163

English emigration to, 136

French presence in, 135

Presbyterian settlers, 154

slave plantations in, 147–9

Northern Ireland Act (1974), 261

Northern Ireland Assembly, 190, 205, 244, 246, 256, 263, 315

Northern Ireland Constitution Act (1973), 190, 260

Northern Ireland Protocol Bill, 245–6

Northern Ireland

    Catholic minority, 258, 261–2, 264

    devolution, experiencing, 255–6, 282

    EC budget, 211

    EC membership issue, 205, 217

    elections (May 2022), 263–4

    Good Friday Agreement (GFA), 5, 224, 234–5, 240–6, 256, 257, 261, 263, 283

    IRA split, 190

    Irish nationalists, 173

    low-skilled immigration, 249

    maritime border, 237, 242

    nation concept, 7

    nationalism, rise of, 188, 190

    Northern Ireland questions, 315–16

    parliament, 5, 170, 190, 255, 258, 260

    population, 261–2

    Protestant hegemony, 258–60

384

INDEX

and referendum (Jun 2016), 223, 224, 228–9

reunification, 4–5, 6, 195, 257–64

self-identification, 261–2

Sunningdale Agreement, 261

US support for post-Brexit arrangements, 242

Northumbria Kingdom, 26, 27–8, 29, 59, 61, 63, 293

Malcolm I's invasion of, 29–30

William I invaded, 62

Norway, 59, 63, 85

Nova Scotia, 109, 163, 164

O'Neill, Terence, 259–60

Óengus (King of the Picts), 27

Offa (King of Mercia), 21, 32

Offa's Dyke, 21–2

Office for Budget Responsibility (OBR), 253, 254

Old English (language), 32, 292

Olympics, 257–8

Orange Boys, 119

Orderic Vitalis (monk), 40

Ormonde, SS, 349n31

Orwell, George, 303–4

Oskytel (Archbishop of York), 34

'othering', 8

Owain ap Gruffydd, 54–5, 74

Owain Glyndŵr (Prince of Wales), 74, 273, 297

Oxford English Dictionary (OED), 7–8, 301

Pakistan, 1, 178, 304

Palestine, 162

Paris, Matthew, 296

Parnell, Charles, 157, 158

Paterson, William, 110

Patrick, St., 15, 16, 21, 45

Peace of Middle (1234), 57

Pennant, Gifford, 144

Pennant, Richard, 144

Perfeddwlad, 69, 70

Philippe II (King of France), 41–2

Pictland, 24, 26, 27

Picts, 24, 25–6, 28, 31, 291, 294

Pitt, William, 118, 120, 155–6, 163

Plaid Cymru, 172, 188–9, 200, 204, 205, 257, 274–5, 278–9, 314

general election (1922), 275

elections (1974), 276

Plaid Genedlaethol Cymru, 172

Poems of Ossian (Macpherson), 264

Poitou, 42, 43, 93, 95

Political Discourses (Hume), 124

postwar British economy, 185–6

Powell, Enoch, 186–7, 307–8, 349n33

Poynings, Edmund, 77–8

Poynings' Law, 77–8, 115

Presbyterians, 81, 105, 118–19, 121, 155, 156

Protestant Ascendancy, 82, 117–19, 120, 154

Protestant English, 131–2

Protestantism, 90, 105, 112, 129

385

INDEX

Ptolemy, 24

Pura Wallia, 53–4

Puritanism, 105

'race' riots, 186

Raleigh, Walter, 80

Redwood, John, 277

Referendum Party, 217–18

Report of the Committee on Scottish Administration (1936), 267

Representation of the People Act (1918), 171

Republic of Ireland Bill, 179

Rex Anglorum (Bede), 292

Rhodes, Cecil, 130

Rhodri Mawr (Rhodri the Great), 22

Rhys ap Gruffydd, 55–6

Rhys ap Maredudd, 73

Rhys ap Tewdwr, 54

Richard I, 56, 62

Richard II, 74

River Tweed, 30, 59

Robert Bruce (Robert I) (King of Scotland), 51, 86, 87, 89

Robert II, 88

Robert III, 89

Robinson Crusoe (Defoe), 113

Roman invasion (43 CE), 19, 20, 24

Roman rule, 20, 24

Royal Africa Company (RAC), 109, 133

Royal Africa Company of England, 133–4

Royal Commission on Scottish Affairs, 267

Royal Commission on the Constitution (1969), 189–90

Royal Commission on the Constitution (1973), 267–8, 276, 283

Ruaidrí (Rory) (High King of Ireland), 49, 50

Rule Britannia (poem), 125

Saint-Domingue, 153

salted provisions export, 153–4

Schengen agreement, 214

Scotland Act (1998), 270, 271

Scotland

    absorption of, 120

    Act anent Peace and War (1702), 110

    Act of Security (1704), 110

    Act of Settlement (1701), 108

    Act of Union, 107–14, 134, 146, 281

    Act of Union, resistance to, 113–14

    British Empire and sense of Britishness, 145–51

    Campaign for a Scottish Assembly, 268

    Claim of Right Act, 108

    Competitors, 84, 85

    cooperation agreement with England, 316

    devolution, experiencing, 256, 313

INDEX

EC budget, 211
EC membership, response to, 203–4
elections (1999), 269
electoral system, 269–70
English backlash, 217
English imperialism in, 83–92
English trade policy, 109–10
The Equivalent, 112
on European integration, 195
homage paying, 43
home rule for, 266
imperial administration and military affairs, 146
as an independent country, 37
industrialisation, 150
inhabited by, 24
low-skilled immigration, 249
monarchy, restoration of, 107
nationalism, rise of, 188, 189
nation-building, 24–30
Pictish kings, 26
population (end of the 1200s), 297
population of, 149
pre-Roman, 24
rebranding as 'North Britain' attempt, 125–6
referendum on independence, 5, 6
Romans' frontier establishment, 25
School Establishment Act, 124
Scots, name origin, 10

Scottish clothing industry, 148, 149–50
Scottish Conservatives, 266
Scottish independence, ambitions for, 270–3
Scottish Liberals, 266
Scottish nationalism, 264–73
Scottish parliament, 268–70
Scottish privy council, 109, 113, 124
Scottish Vote Leave campaign, 227–8
second referendum on Scottish independence, 315
Secretary of State for Scotland post, 267
share of the UK population, 267
state-to-state relations, 59–65
Stewart rule, 88, 89
Stuart rule, 91
UK budget and, 267
Wars of Independence, 85–6
Scotland's Future (white paper), 270–1
Scots Magazine, The, 124
Scott, Walter, 265–6
Scottish Green Party, 272
Scottish Home Rule Association (SHRA), 266–7, 268
Scottish Labour Party Conference, 201
Scottish National Party (SNP), 173, 189, 200, 204, 228, 256, 267, 269–70, 271, 272, 318

387

INDEX

Scottish Office, 267

Scottish Party, 173

Scottish Unionist Party, 195

Secretary of State for Commonwealth Affairs, 181

Seven Years' War (1756–63), 135, 136,154

Sewel convention, 239

Shared Prosperity Fund, 285, 287

Sigtrygg Silkbeard (Viking king of Dublin), 18–19, 45

Simon de Montfort, 44, 45, 70, 94

Single European Act (Feb 1986), 212–13

Sinn Féin, 158, 171, 190, 205, 246, 262, 263–4, 315

Slave trade, 109, 130, 133, 134–5, 141, 153, 300–1
abolition of, 137
Scottish merchants in, 146–7

slavery, 130, 137, 142–3, 146, 147, 153, 301

slaves, dress for, 142–3

Smith Commission, 271

Smith, Adam, 265

Social and Democratic Labour Party (SDLP), 190, 200, 205, 262

Society in Scotland for Promoting Christian Knowledge, 124

Society of United Irishmen, 119

Somerset v. Stewart dispute (1772), 300

Song of Patriotic Prejudice, A, 215

South Africa, 172, 184–5

colonies, 166–7

South Sea Company, 134–5

Southern Rhodesia, 174, 182

Spain, 82, 99, 214

Spenser, Edmund, 80

The Spirit of the People: An Analysis of the English Mind (Madox), 302–3

Standard Eurobarometer, 209

Statute of Westminster, 174

Statutes of Iona (1609), 124

Statutes of Kilkenny, 52

Strathclyde Kingdom, 26, 27, 28, 29, 59

Stuart, John (Prime Minister), 126

Suez Canal, Anglo-French invasion of, 194

sugar, slave-grown, 147, 152

Sun, The (newspaper), 215

Sunak, Rishi, 310

Sunningdale Agreement, 261

'surrender and regrant' policy, 79

Sutherland, John, 265–6

Swann, Donald, 215

Sweyn Forkbeard, 35, 39, 59

Tara hill, 16

Tariff Reform League, 174

Tender of Union, 92

Tewdwr family, 74, 75

Thatcher, Margaret, 207, 211,212–13, 216–17, 268, 276–7, 309–10

INDEX

Thewliss, Alison, 286

Thomas, Silken, 78

tobacco plantations, slave-grown, 147, 148

tobacco trade, 152

Togodumnus (king), 30

Toirdelbach (High King of Ireland), 47, 48

Toirdelbach Ua Conchobair (High King of Ireland), 49

Tone, Theobald Wolfe, 118, 119, 122, 329n23

Tonga, 182

Trade with Africa Act (1697), 133

Traditional Unionist Voice, 263

Treachery of the Blue Books, The, 103–4, 124, 274

Treaty(ies)
   of Aberconwy (1277), 70
   of Abernethy (1072), 60–1
   of Alfred and Guthrum (c.880), 33
   of Berwick (1357), 88
   of Birgham (1290), 84
   of Brétigny (1360), 95
   of Chinon (1214), 42
   of Corbeil (1326), 64
   of Falaise (1174), 62, 63
   of Greenwich (1543), 90–1
   of Lambeth (1217), 42, 43
   of Le Goulet (1200), 41–2
   of Limerick (1691), 82–3, 153
   of Montgomery (1267), 58–9, 69, 70

of Paris (1295), 43–4, 64–5, 85

of Paris (1783), 135, 136

of Perpetual Peace (1502), 89

of Perth (1266), 63

of Rome (1957), 187, 195, 336n8

of Troyes (1420), 328n33

of Utrecht (1713), 134

of Versailles (1919), 161, 169–70

of Windsor (1175), 50, 75–6, 83

of Woodstock (1246), 58, 69

of Worcester (1218), 57

of York (1237), 63

triangular trade, 140, 141

Trinidad, 137

Troubles, 190, 224, 255–6, 260

Trump administration, 252

Truss, Liz, 245, 272, 310

Tudors, 2, 89, 256, 281, 297, 298

Tusk, Donald, 226

Ua Conchobair, 48–9

Uí Néill dynasty, 16, 17, 18, 51

Ulster Special Constabulary ('B-Specials' or 'B-Men'), 259, 260

Ulster Unionist Party (UUP), 173, 195, 205, 258, 259, 260, 263, 336n6

Ulster Volunteers, 259

Ulster, 80–1, 154, 158, 170, 258, 283

Union of South Africa, 167

INDEX

United Kingdom Independence
Party (UKIP), 217–18, 220–2,
227, 229, 230
United Kingdom Internal Market
Act, 285, 287
United Kingdom of Great Britain
and Northern Ireland (UK)
emigration from, 167
English responses on survival
of the union (2020), 286–7,
286t
European integration,
enthusiasm for, 195
formation of, 99, 100, 120
free trade, shift to, 137
frictionless trade, 240–1
internal market, 239
internal markets bill, 286, 287
Irish response to, 127
as nation-states, 7–8
referendum (Jun 1975), 191–2,
200–7, 223
and sense of nationhood,
122–3
statehood, 122–8
Support for European
membership, 192
United Nations Security Council,
316–17
United States Information
Agency, 194
United States of America (US),
136, 162, 196, 198, 250, 251
anti-imperialist organisations,
138

Scottish emigration to, 150
tariffs, 174
trade policy, 252–3
trade with Great Britain, 136
UK–US relations, 242
War of Independence, 117,
148, 149, 154, 163
University College London, 313
US–UK free trade agreement, 251,
252–3

Vanguard Unionist Progressive
Party, 205
Victoria (Queen), 137
Diamond Jubilee, 138, 157
Vietnam War, 198
View of the State of Ireland
(Spenser), 80
Vikings, 9, 10, 17–19, 29, 292,
293, 294
raids, 22, 32–3
Vortigern, 31

Wales Act (1978), 276
Wales and Berwick Act (1746),
281
Wales, 37, 46, 217
Acts of Union, 100–6, 281
autonomy, 6, 23–4, 277–80
birth of nation-state, 19–24
British Empire and sense of
Britishness, 138–45
campaign for Welsh home
rule, 274
Christianity, spread of, 21

390

INDEX

conquered by England, 38, 273, 280, 290, 311

Court of Great Sessions, 102–3

cultural nationalism, 256–7, 273–4

Cyfraith Hywel (Laws of Hywel), 22

devolution, 278–9

EC budget, 211

EC membership issue, 204–5

Edward I's military campaign, 70–1

eisteddfodau celebration, 273, 274

emigration from, 143

English imperialism in, 68–75

on European integration, 195

general election (1922), 275

Independence Commission, 279–80

Independent Commission on the Constitutional Future of Wales, 280

inhabited by, 20

Last War of Independence, 74

low-skilled immigration, 249

Marcher lords, 53, 54–5, 57, 72, 100

miners' strike (1984), 277

nation-building, 21–3

New Testament (Welsh version), 105

population, 297

rebellions of (1316–17), 73

and referendum (Jun 2016), 223, 229

Roman Catholicism, rejection of, 105

rulers' homage paying, 43

self-identification, 277

state-to-state relations, 52–9

Statute of Wales, 71–3

Swansea–Neath area, 141–2

uprisings (1294–5), 73

Wales Acts of 1535 and 1542, 138–9, 276

Welsh assembly, 276, 277–9

Welsh courts, 298

Welsh nationalism, 7, 188, 257, 273–80

Welsh nobility, decline of, 273–4

Welsh Parliament, 257, 278–9

War of the Spanish Succession, 134, 135

Wars of the Roses (1455–87), 89

Washington, George, 136

Waverley (Walter Scott), 265

Welsh Court of Great Sessions, 298

Welsh gentry, 102, 103, 125, 139, 140

Welsh Language Act (1967), 275–6, 277–8

Welsh language, 103–4, 106, 124–5, 273, 274–6, 328n4

Welsh Office, 275, 277

Wesley, John, 106

Wessex, 23, 32–3

INDEX

West Germany, 193

West Indies Federation, 182

West Indies, 149, 182, 305

West Lothian question, 283, 284–5, 313

Westminster parliament, 258, 259, 267, 270, 277, 313

'white Australia' policy, 167

William I (William the Lion), 62, 64

William II of Scotland (William III of England), 108, 110, 133

William of Malmesbury, 296

William the Conqueror (William I), 39, 40, 47, 53, 54, 60–1, 295

William Wallace, 86

Williams, Gwyn, 145

Wilson government, 184, 226, 275–6

Wilson, Harold, 189, 197,198, 200, 201, 208–9, 212, 220, 226, 259–60, 276, 283

Wilson, Woodrow, 169

Wool Act (1699), 153

World Trade Organization, 238

World War I, 106, 157, 161, 167–8, 172

World War II, 162, 169, 176–7, 179, 184, 193, 198, 290, 302, 304, 305–6, 317

Yny lhyvyr hwnn ('In this book'), 104

York, 9, 29, 67

Zambia, 182